Maureen
Happy Birthday

Love
Mom & Dad

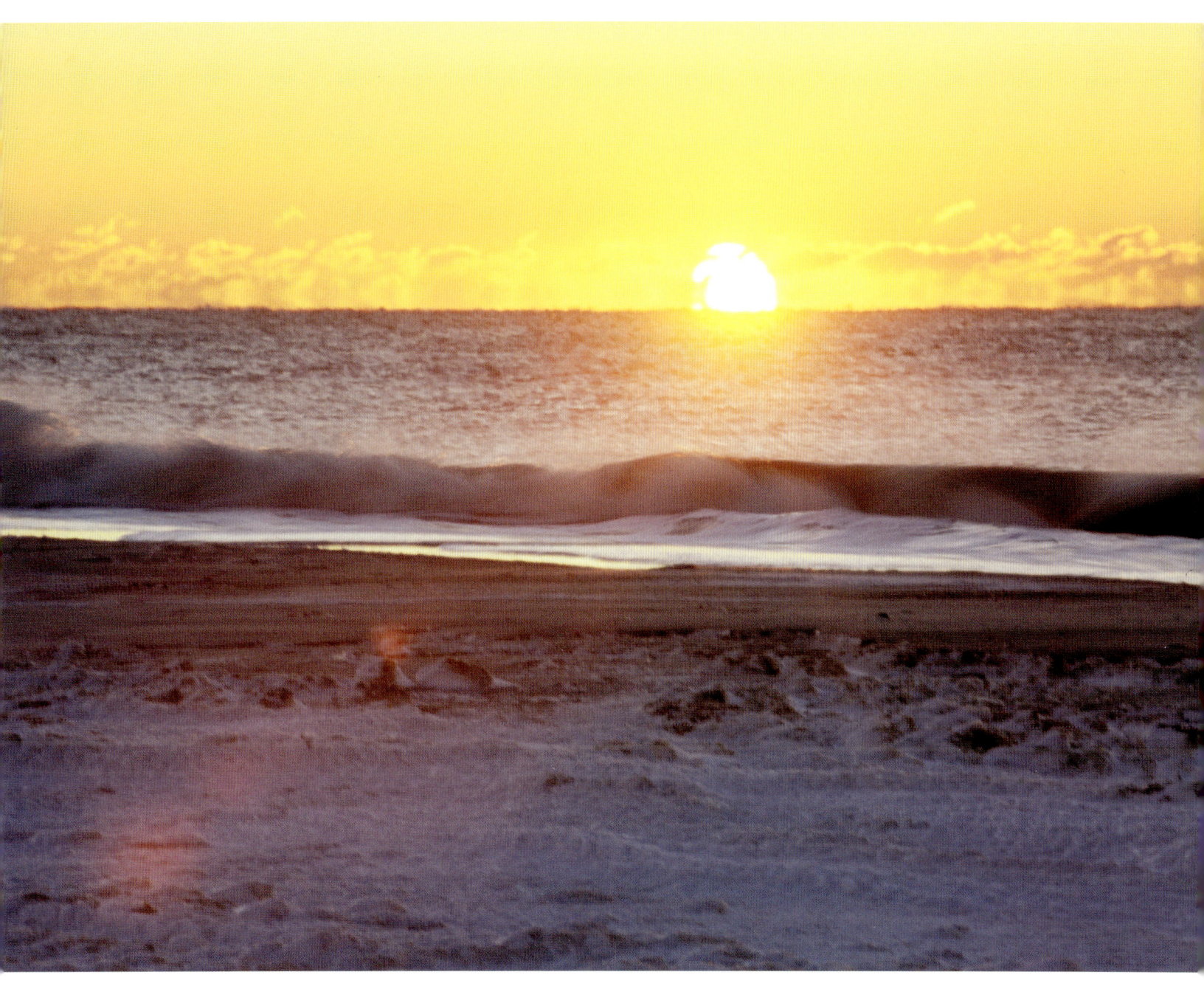

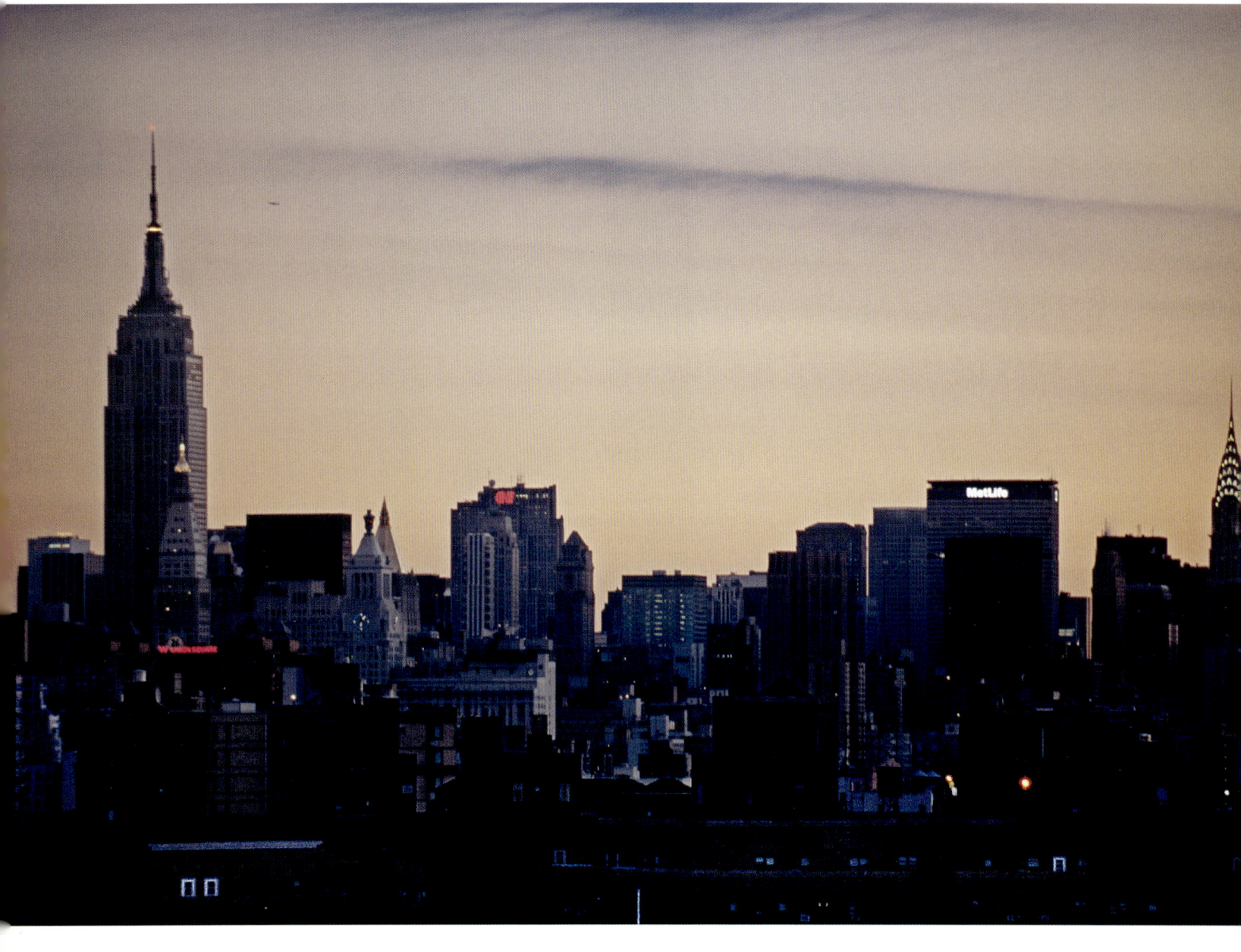

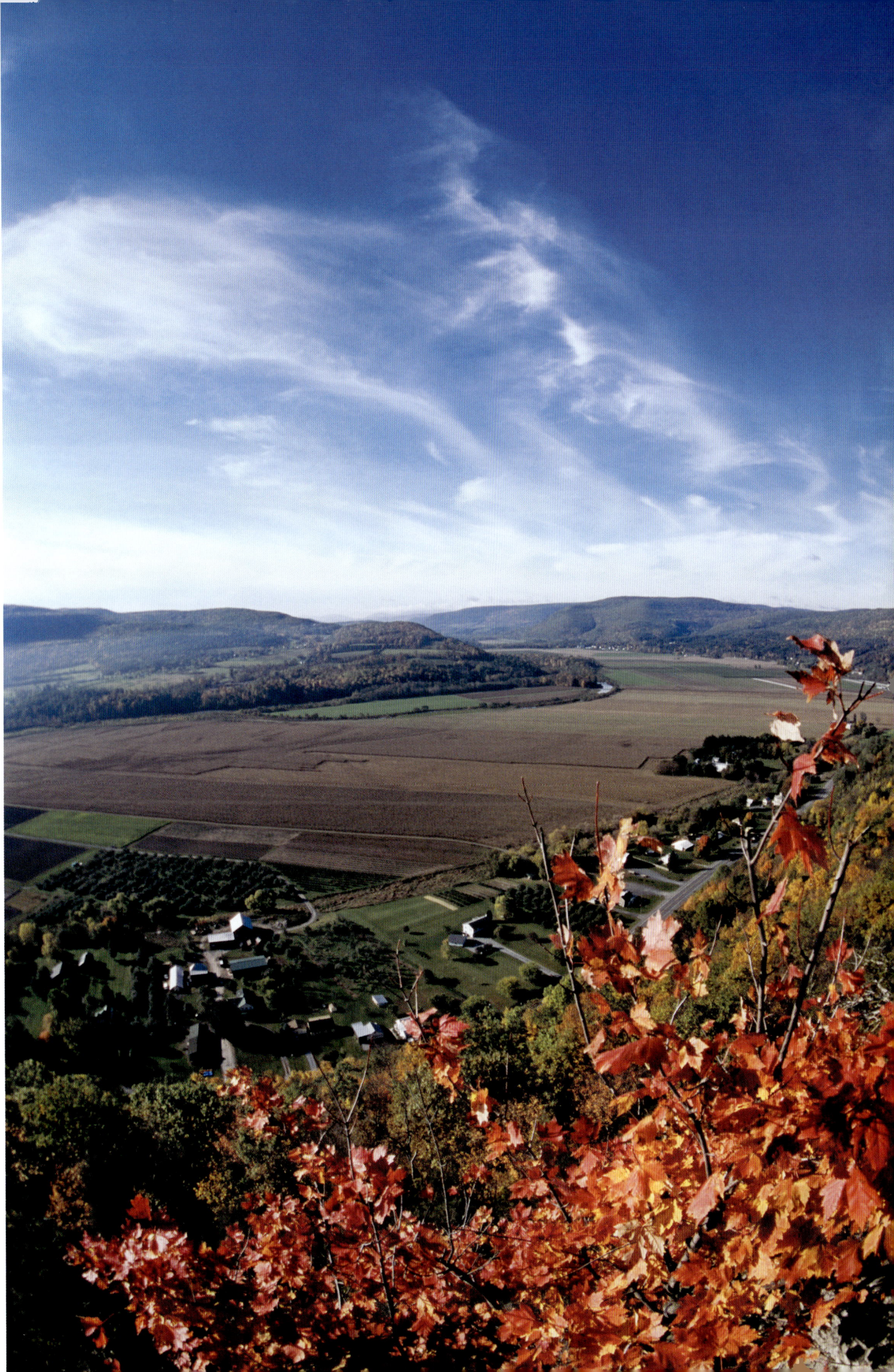

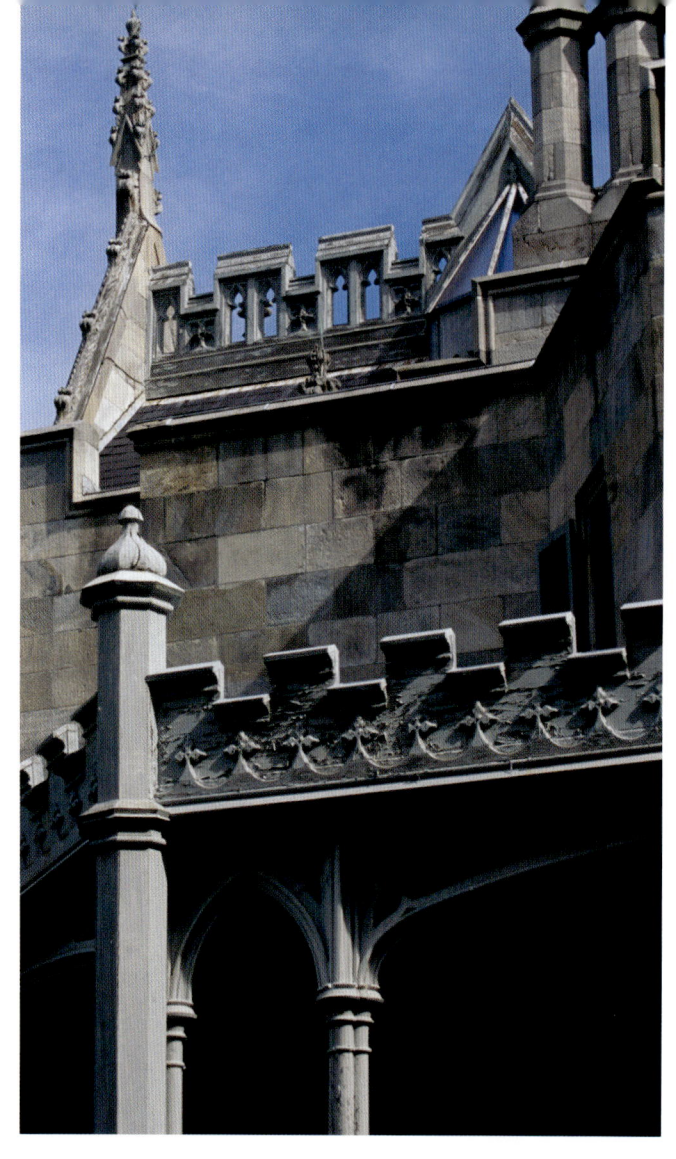

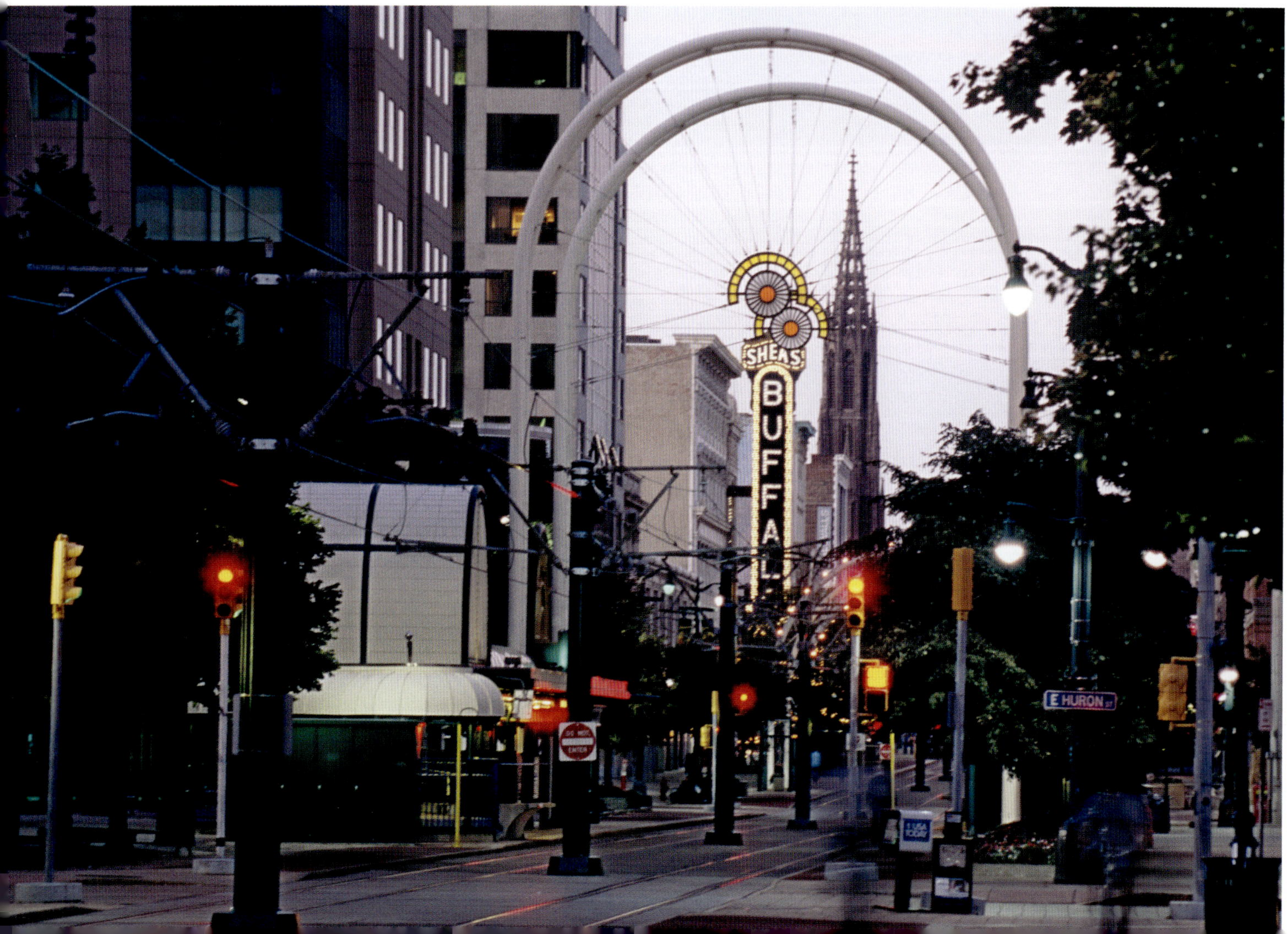

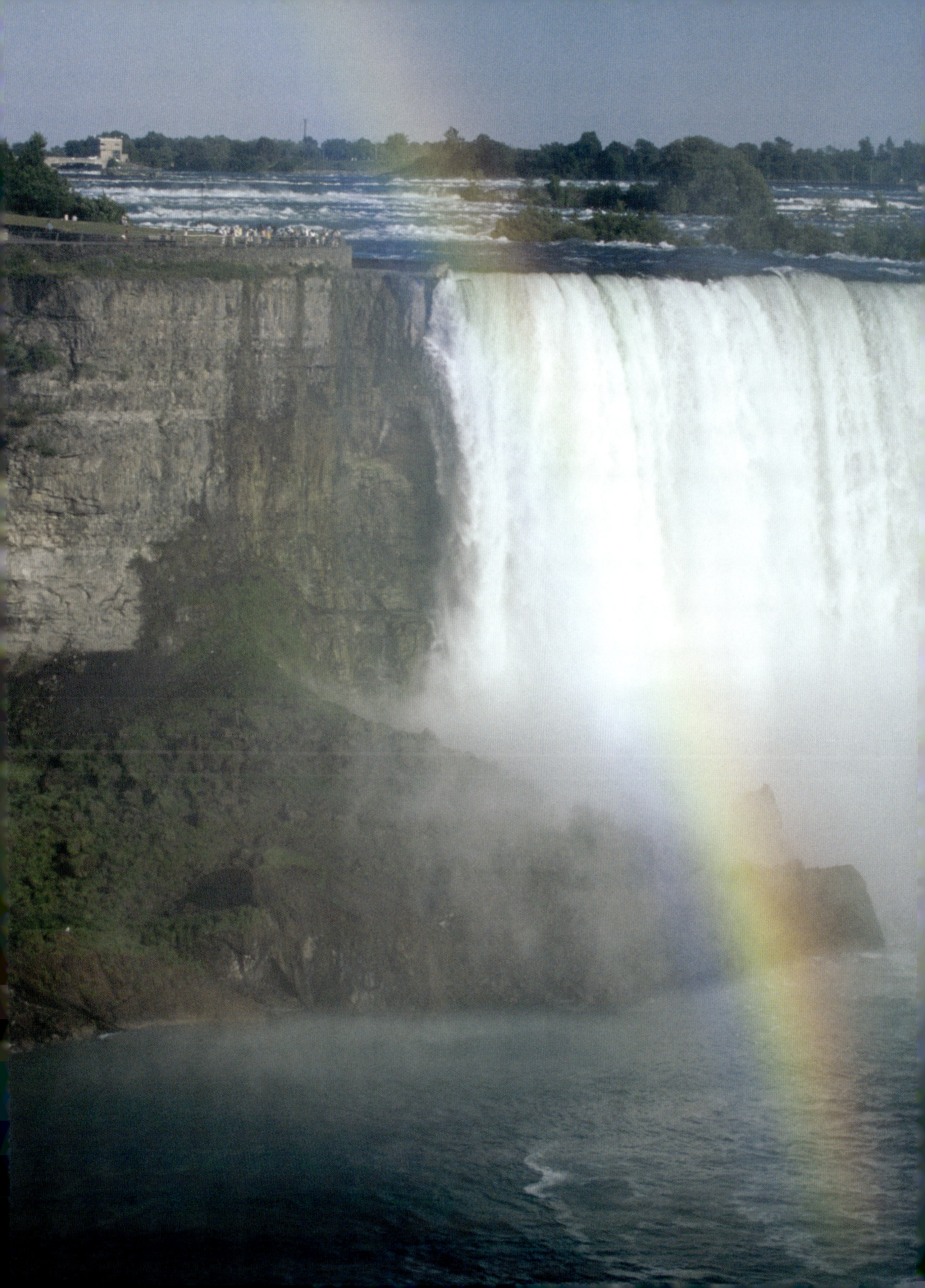

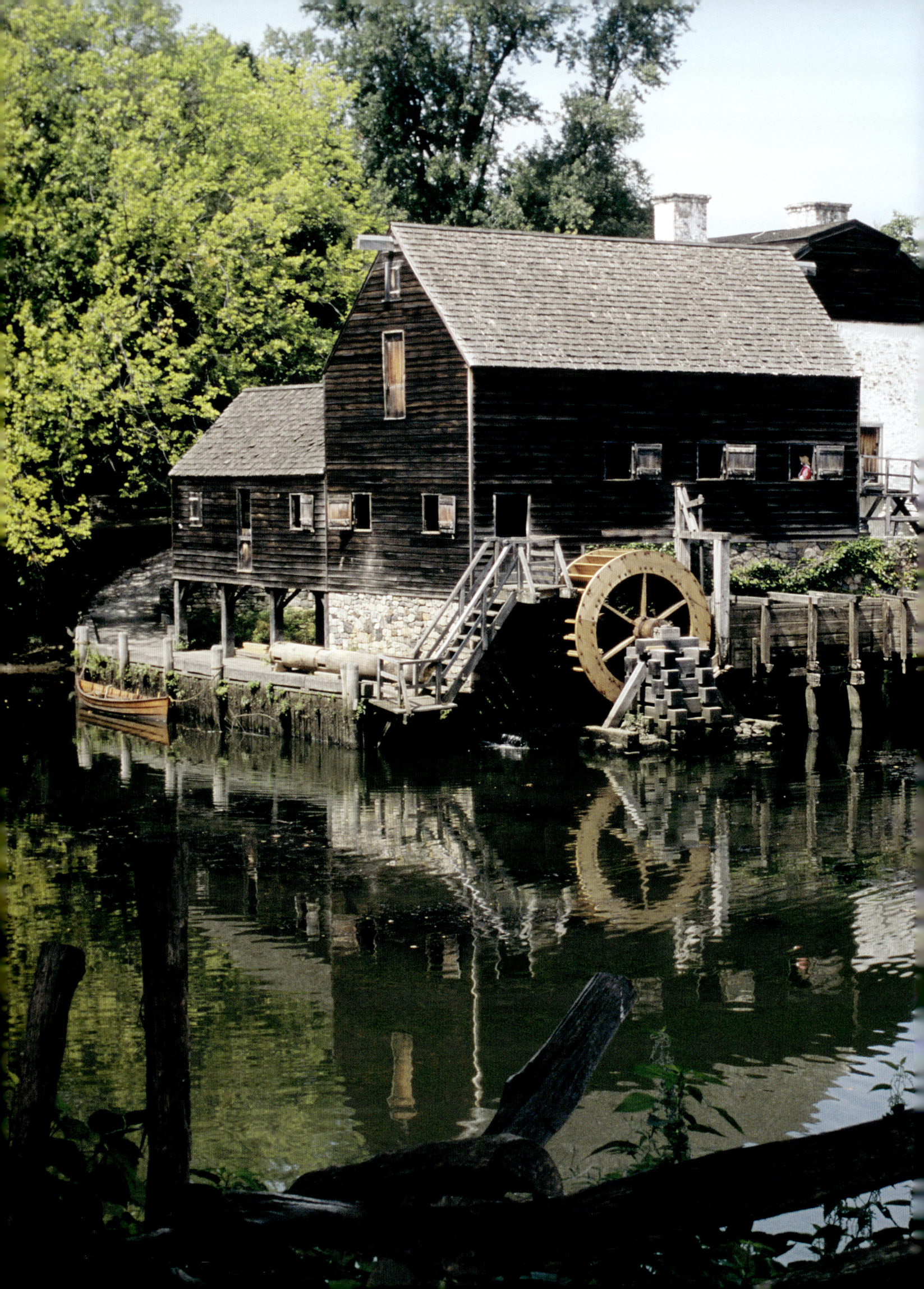

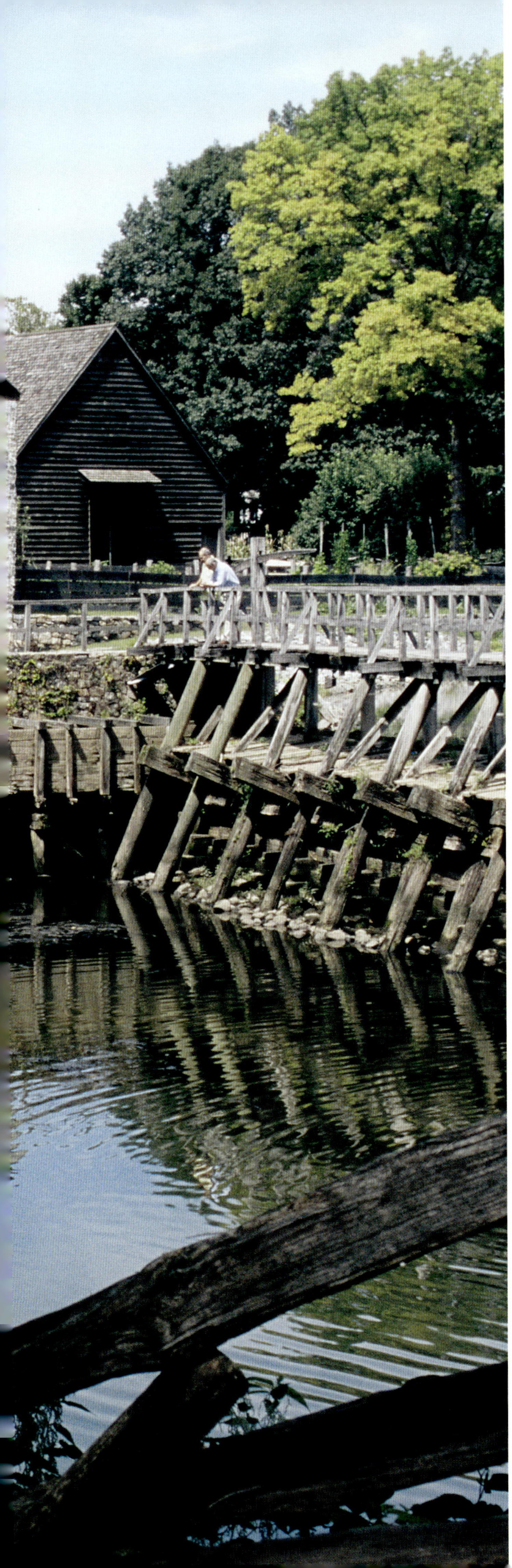

Our New York

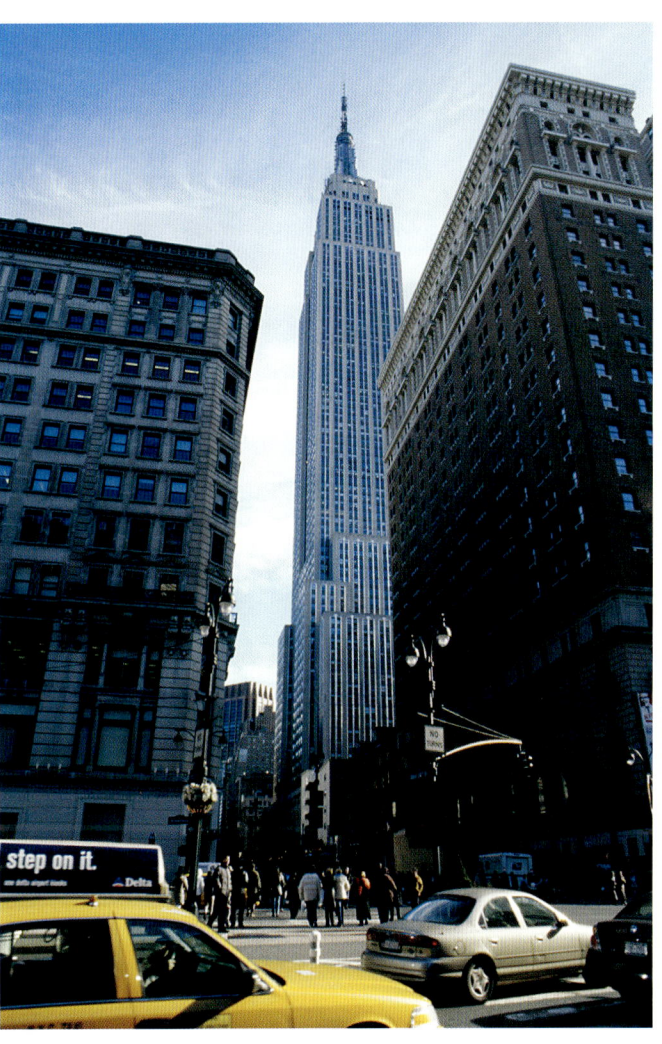

Carl E. Heilman II

Voyageur Press

First published in 2006 by Voyageur Press, an imprint of MBI Publishing Company, Galtier Plaza, Suite 200, 380 Jackson Street, St. Paul, MN 55101-3885 USA

Copyright © 2006 by Carl E. Heilman II

All rights reserved. With the exception of quoting brief passages for the purposes of review, no part of this publication may be reproduced without prior written permission from the Publisher.

The information in this book is true and complete to the best of our knowledge. All recommendations are made without any guarantee on the part of the author or Publisher, who also disclaim any liability incurred in connection with the use of this data or specific details.

We recognize, further, that some words, model names, and designations mentioned herein are the property of the trademark holder. We use them for identification purposes only. This is not an official publication.

MBI Publishing Company titles are also available at discounts in bulk quantity for industrial or sales-promotional use. For details write to Special Sales Manager at MBI Publishing Company, Galtier Plaza, Suite 200, 380 Jackson Street, St. Paul, MN 55101-3885 USA

Editor: Josh Leventhal
Designer: LeAnn Kuhlmann

Printed in China

Library of Congress Cataloging-in-Publication Data

Heilman, Carl
   Our New York / by Carl E. Heilman II.
      p. cm.
   ISBN-13: 978-0-7603-2580-3 (hardcover)
   ISBN-10: 0-7603-2580-4 (hardcover)
   1. New York (State)—Pictorial works. I. Title.
F120.H45 2006
974.7—dc22

ON THE FRONT COVER
The subtle hues of evening twilight combine spectacularly with the colored lights at Niagara Falls.

PAGE 1
A clear dawn highlights the shoreline at Jones Beach after a winter snowstorm.

PAGE 2
The mid-Manhattan skyline is illuminated in the early morning light, as viewed from the Brooklyn Bridge.

PAGE 3
Vroman's Nose, just west of the Catskills, overlooks the farmlands of the Schoharie Valley.

PAGE 4, TOP
Architectural detail of Lyndhurst, one of several historic mansions situated along the Hudson River.

PAGE 4, BOTTOM
The historic Shea's Performing Arts Center marquee shines on Main Street in Buffalo.

PAGE 5
A rainbow illuminates the mist from Horseshoe Falls, one of the three waterfalls that make up Niagara Falls.

TITLE PAGE, MAIN
Philipsburg Manor in the town of Sleepy Hollow features a water-powered grist mill and other restored historic buildings.

TITLE PAGE, INSET
The Empire State Building towers above the busy streets of Manhattan.

ON THE BACK COVER
TOP The Farmers' Museum in Cooperstown celebrates the agricultural and community life of nineteenth-century New York.
MIDDLE Lounging on the beach at Southampton is a lovely way to spend a summer's day.
BOTTOM The Brooklyn Bridge glows in the morning sunlight as it frames the Manhattan skyline.

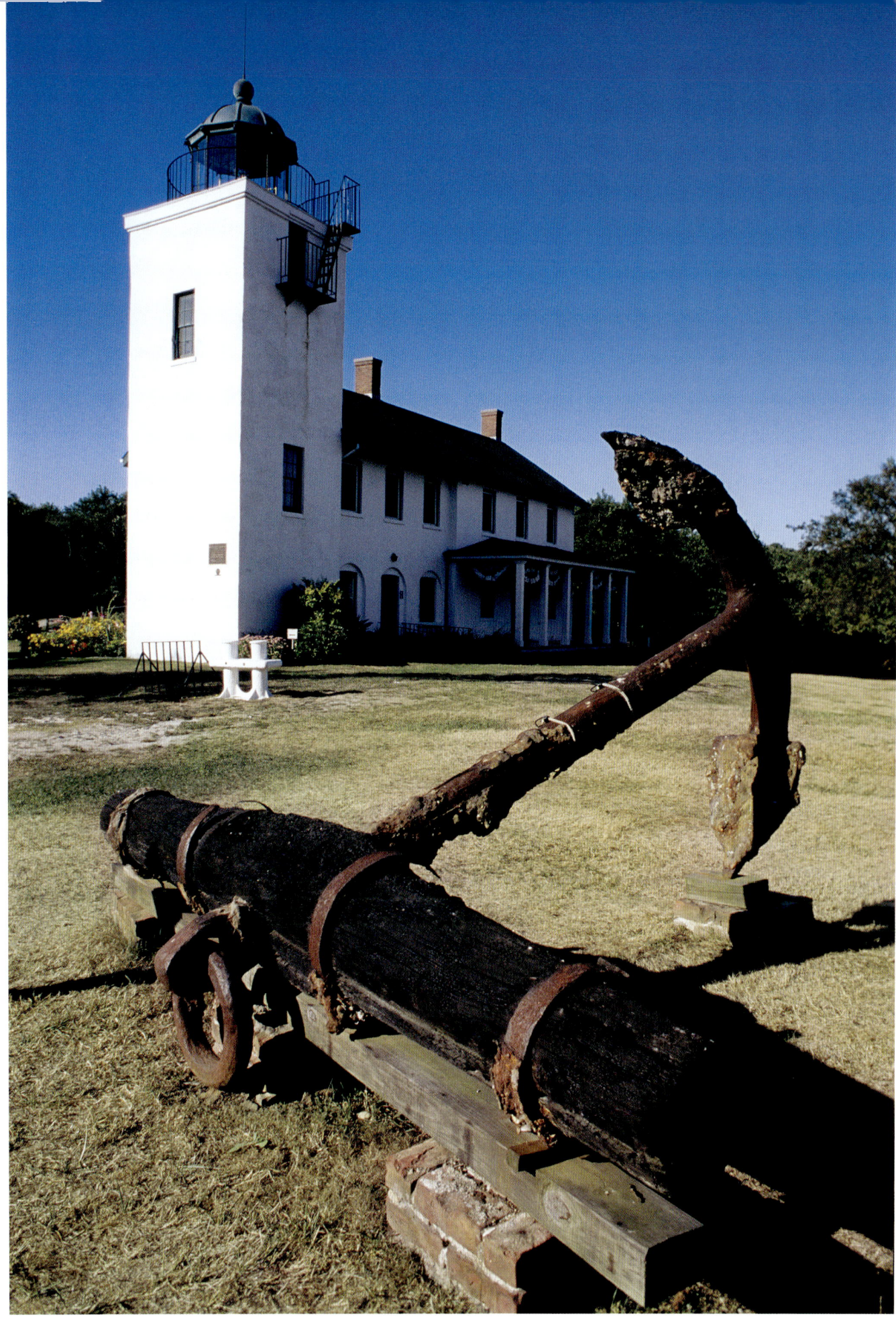

ABOVE

Horton Point Lighthouse, on the North Fork of Long Island, was first commissioned by President George Washington in 1790 but wasn't completed until 1857.

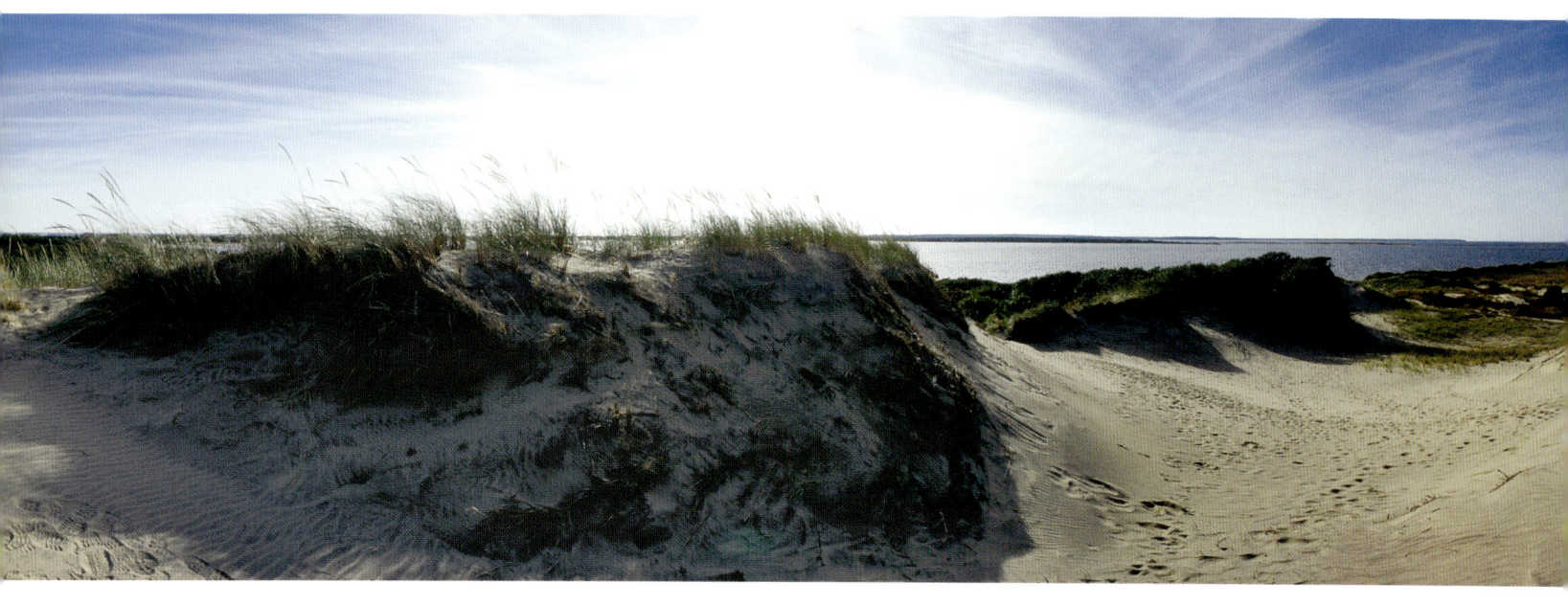

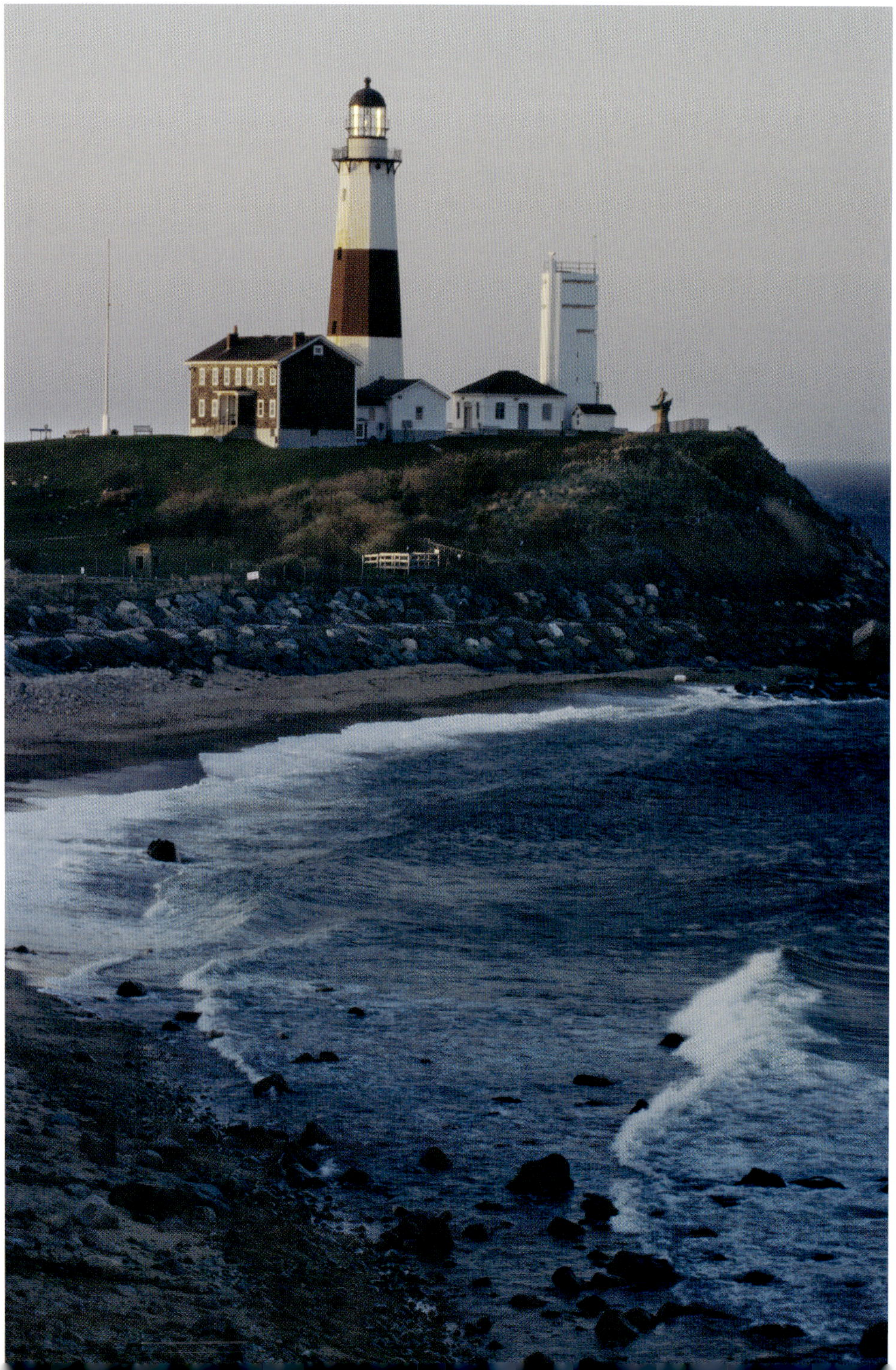

ABOVE

The Walking Dunes of Hither Hills State Park, at the eastern end of Long Island, are migrating over the shrub oak trees at a rate of about three to ten feet per year.

LEFT

Montauk Point Lighthouse, built in 1796, was the first lighthouse in New York and the fourth oldest in the United States.

RIGHT

Seals bask in the sun on a rock in Block Island Sound at the end of the Seal Haulout Trail in Montauk Point State Park.

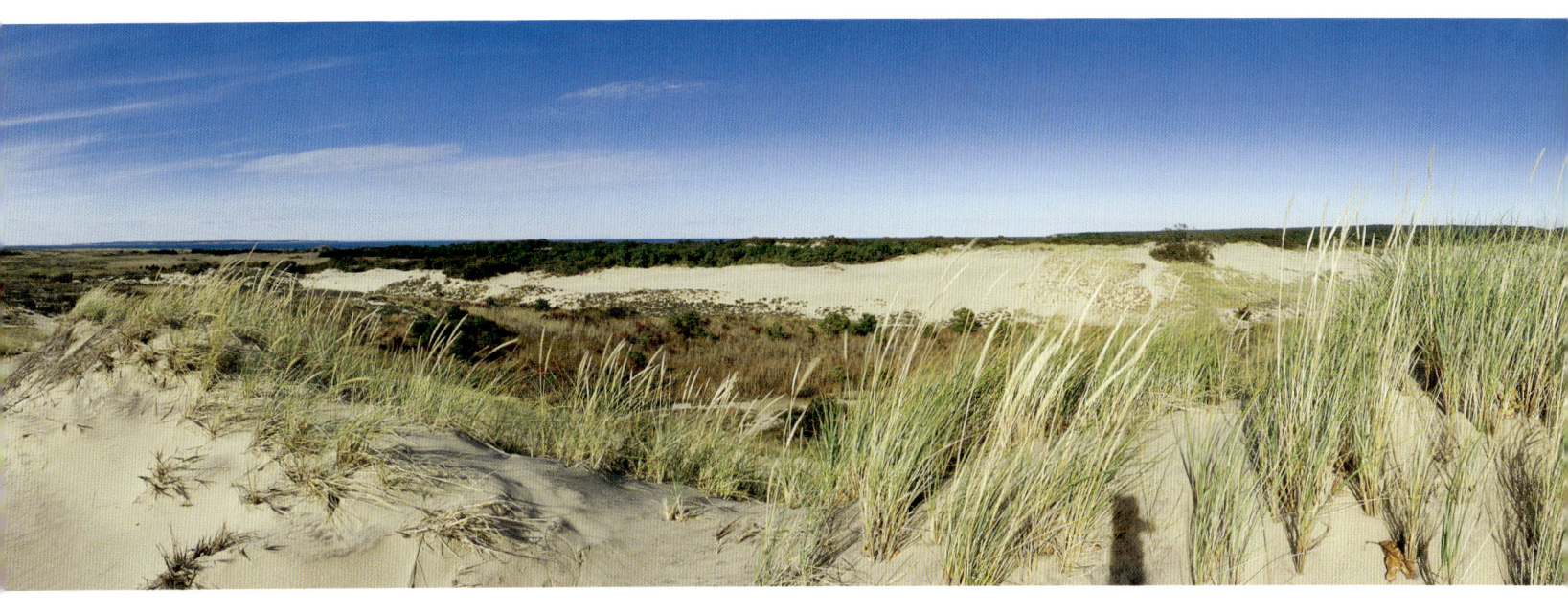

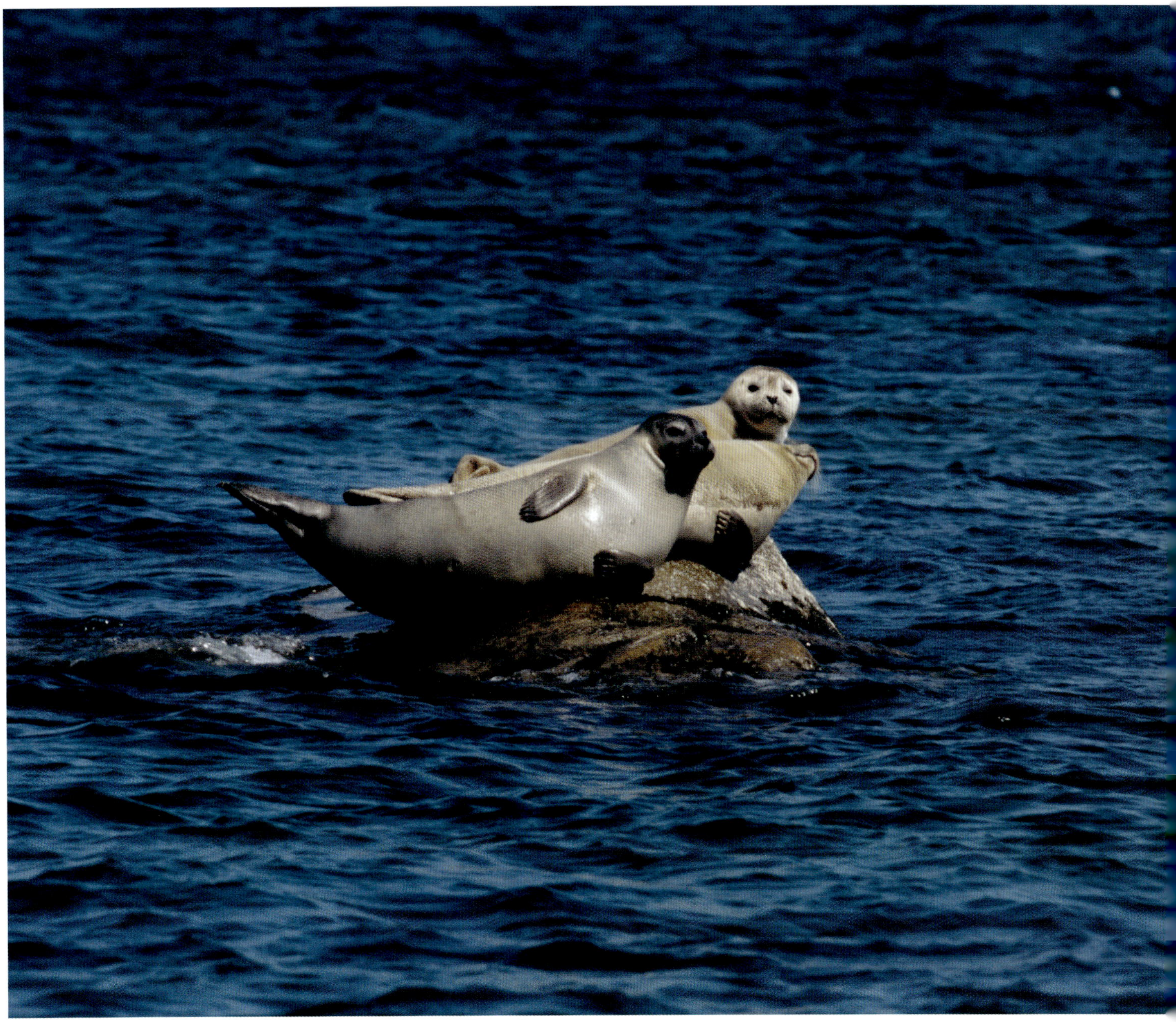

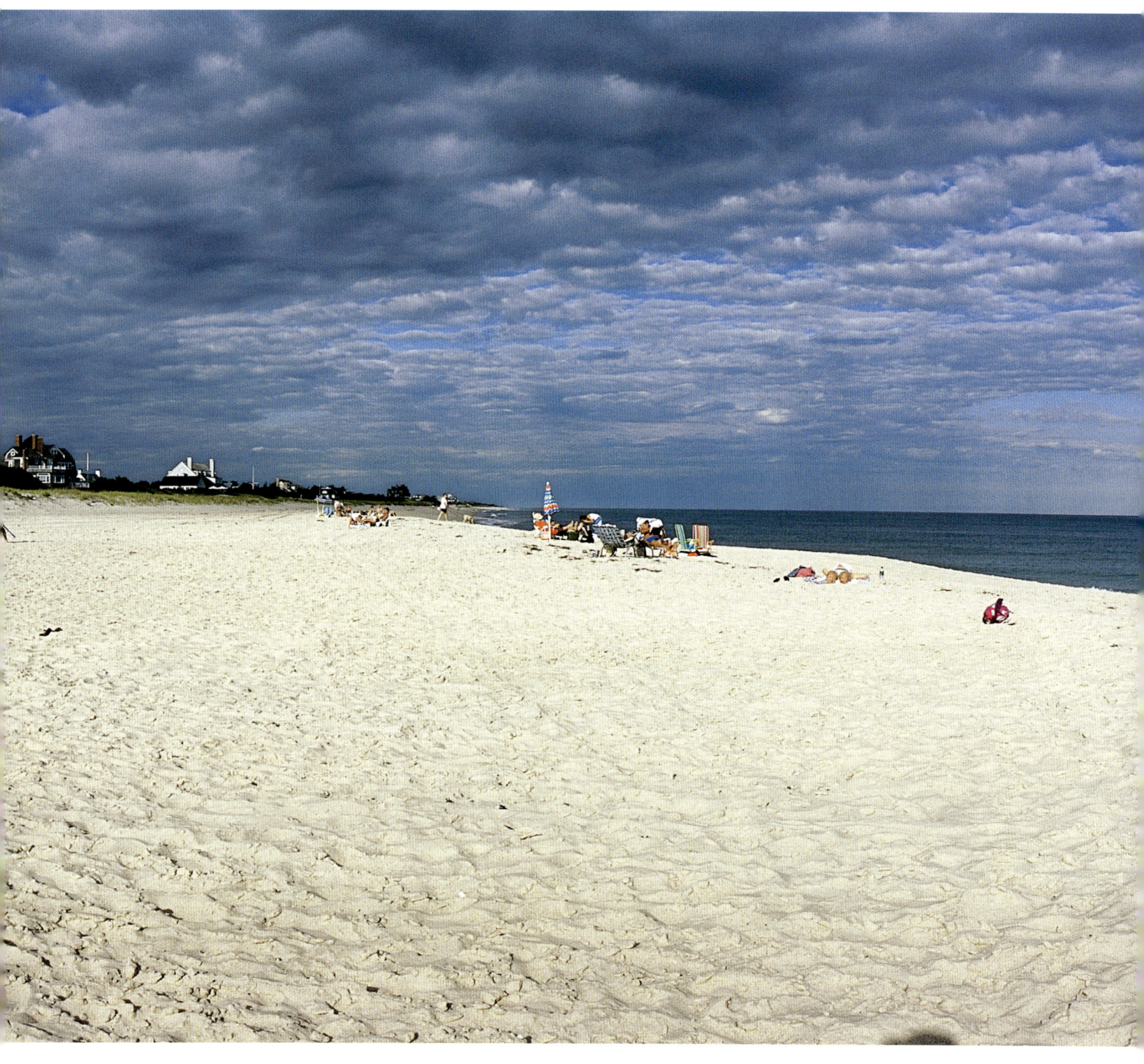

ABOVE

The wide sandy beaches of the Hamptons are considered some of the finest in the world. This panorama was taken on a balmy summer day at Southampton.

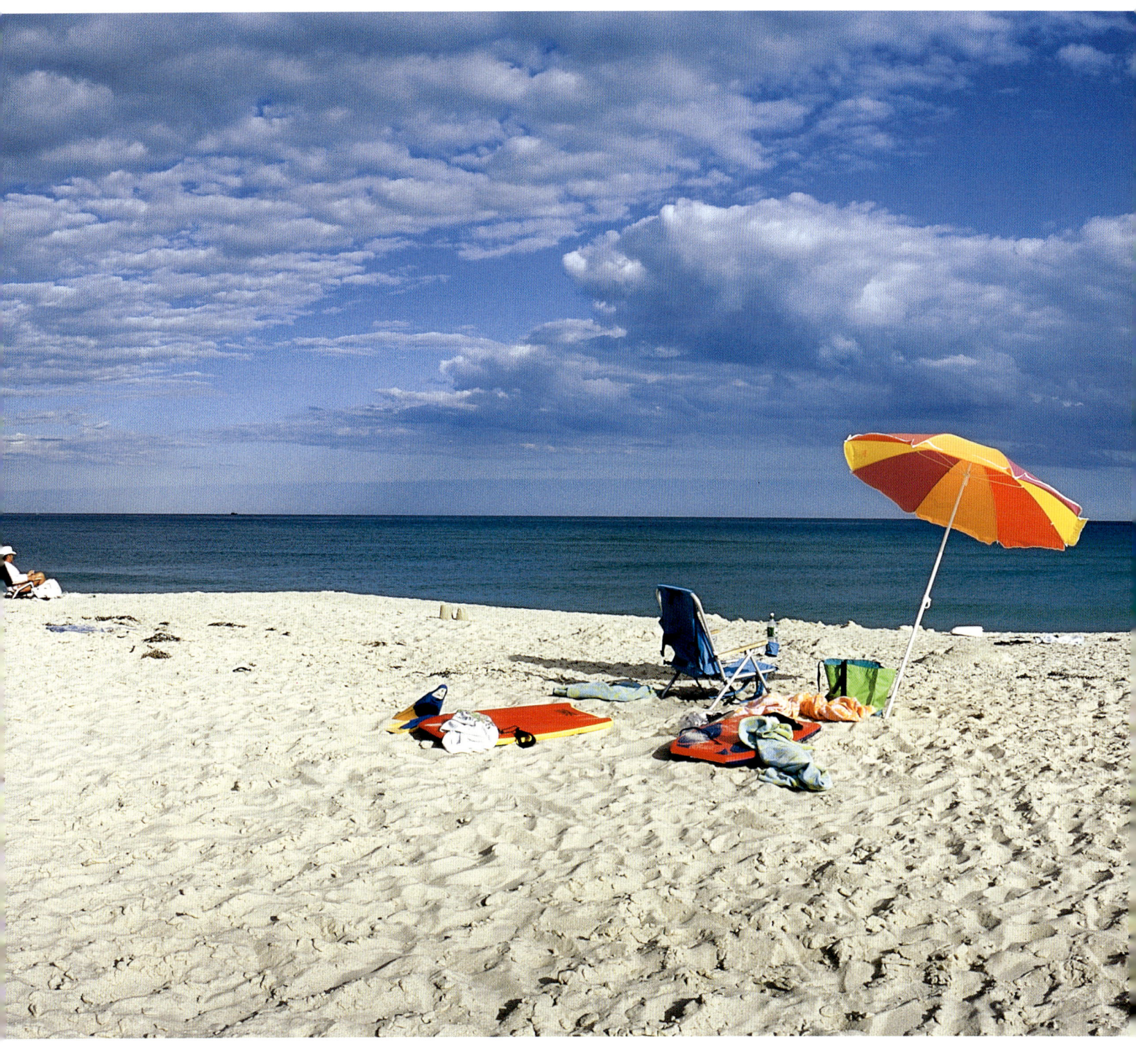

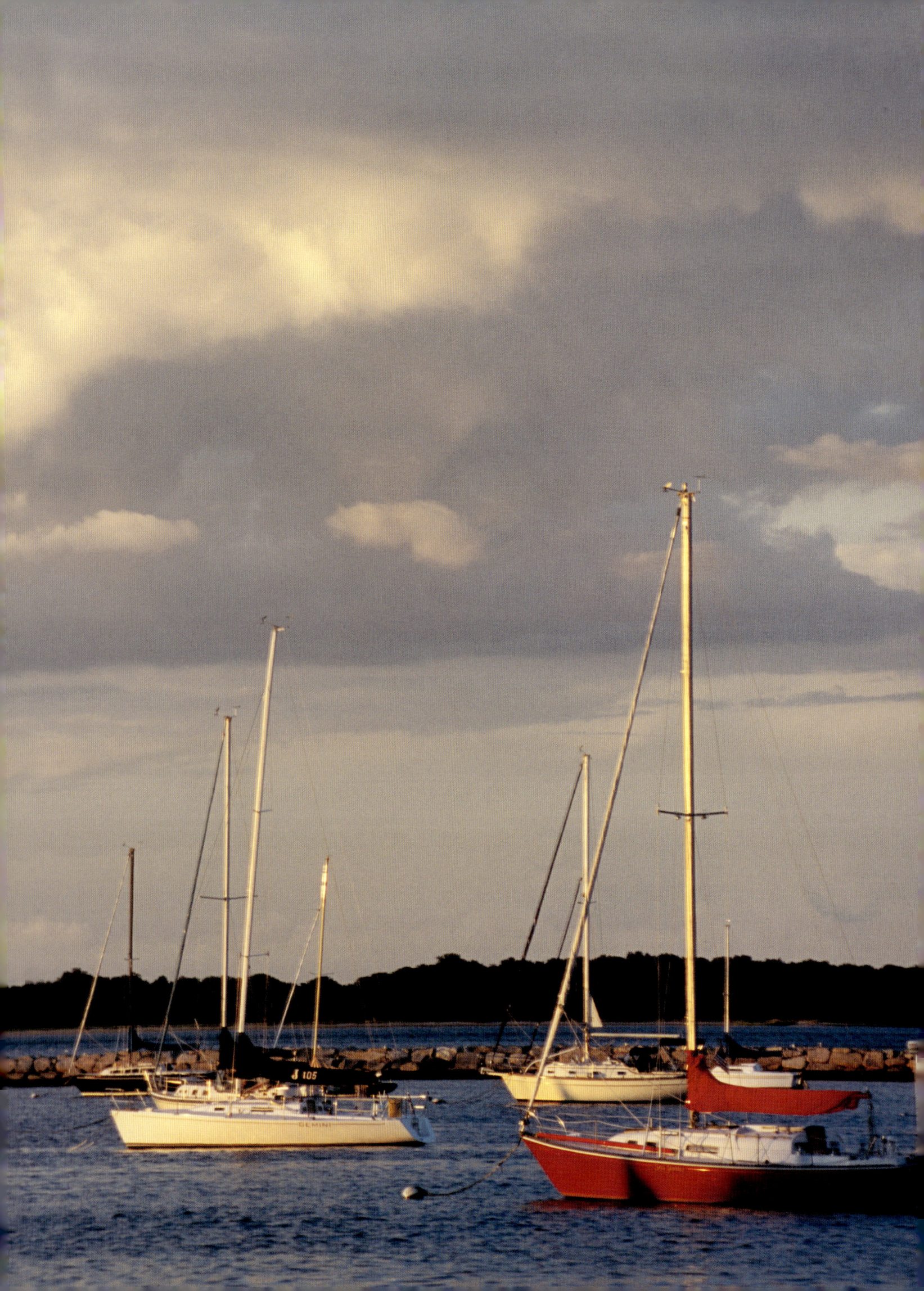

LEFT

Once a bustling whaling port, Sag Harbor maintains its strong maritime tradition. Here, evening sunlight highlights the anchored sailboats at Waterfront Marina.

RIGHT

This sculpture of an osprey stands on a perch that was made from a steel beam recovered from the World Trade Center. It is located in the harbor town of Greenport on Long Island's North Fork.

BELOW

The last twilight of the day illuminates the horizon at a North Ferry dock of the Shelter Island Ferry. This ferry system is both the fastest and most enjoyable way to travel between the North and South Fork of eastern Long Island.

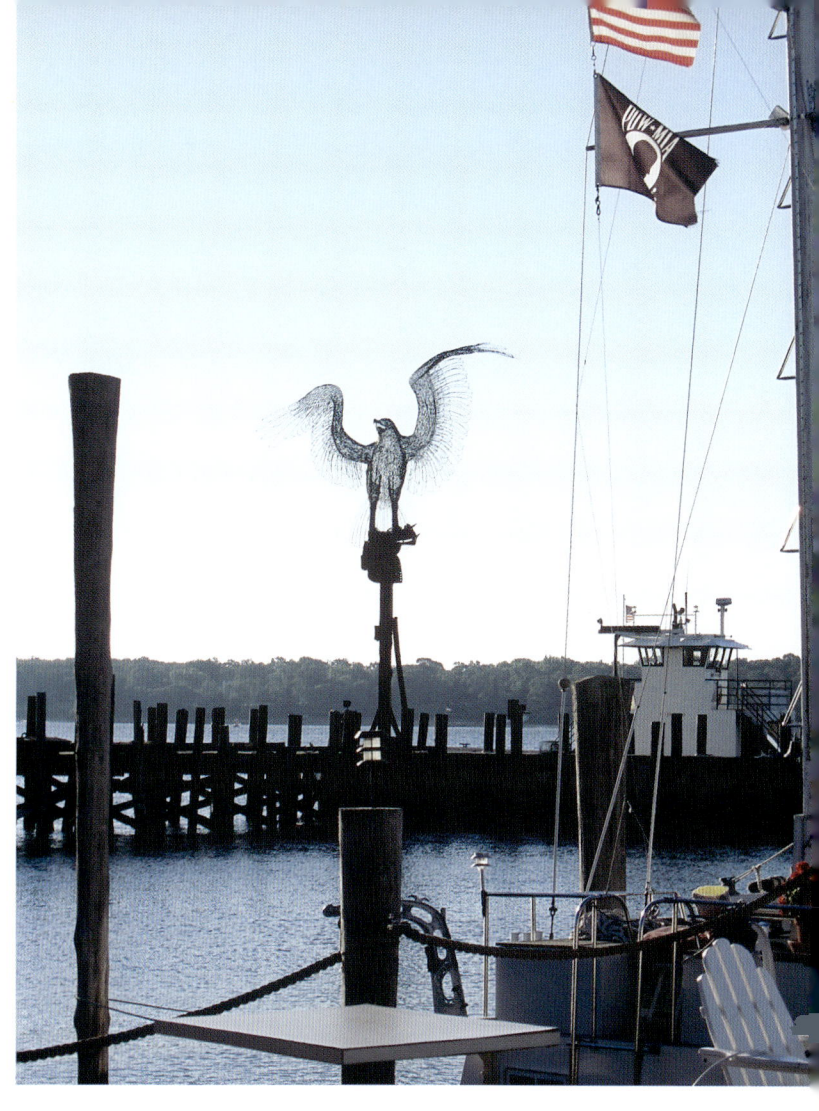

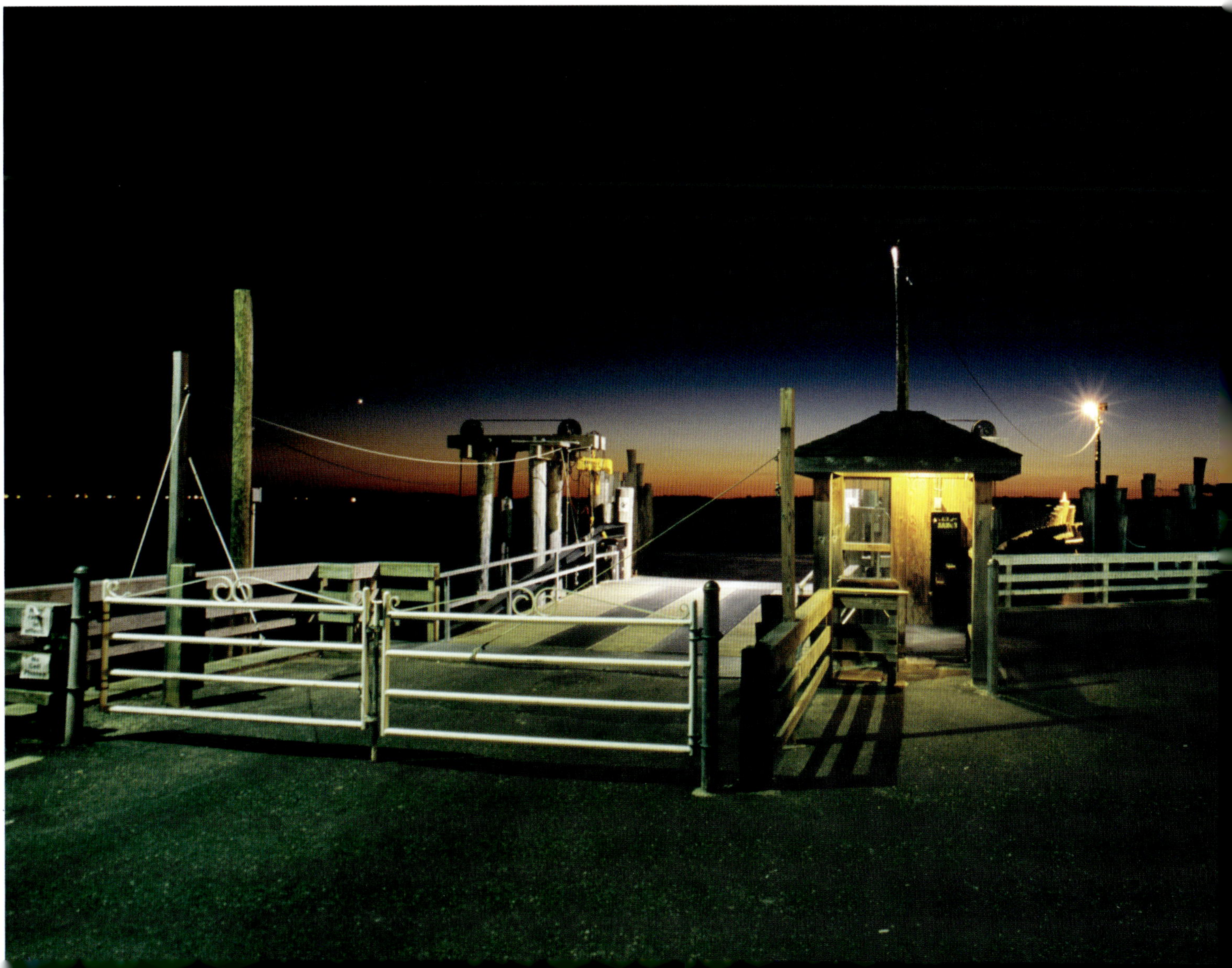

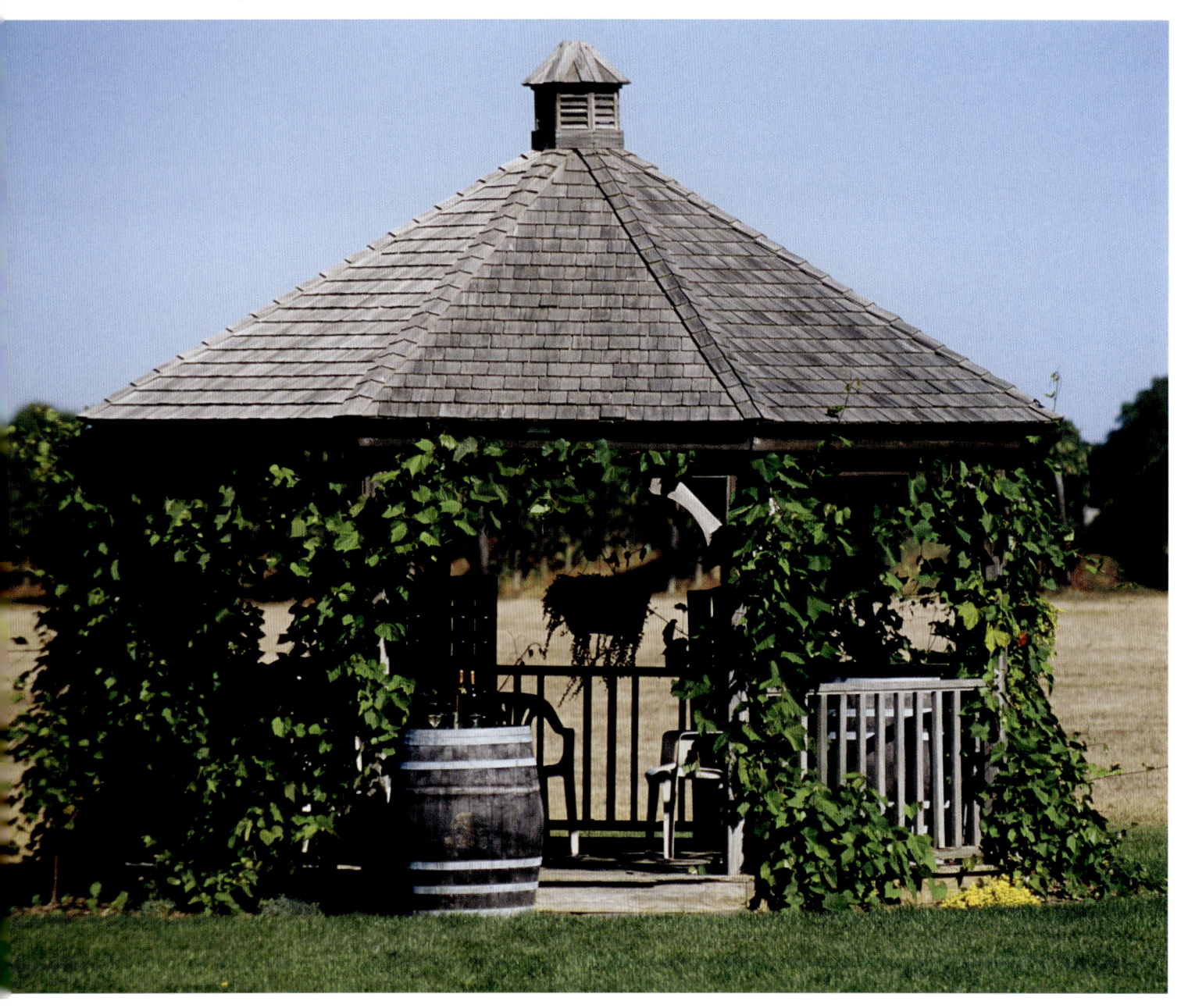

ABOVE

Eastern Long Island is becoming well known for its wines. The grape vines growing on this gazebo at the award-winning Osprey's Dominion Vineyards are the root stock for all the vines at the vineyard.

RIGHT

The village of Bay Shore dates back to 1708. The United Methodist Church was built in the late 1800s.

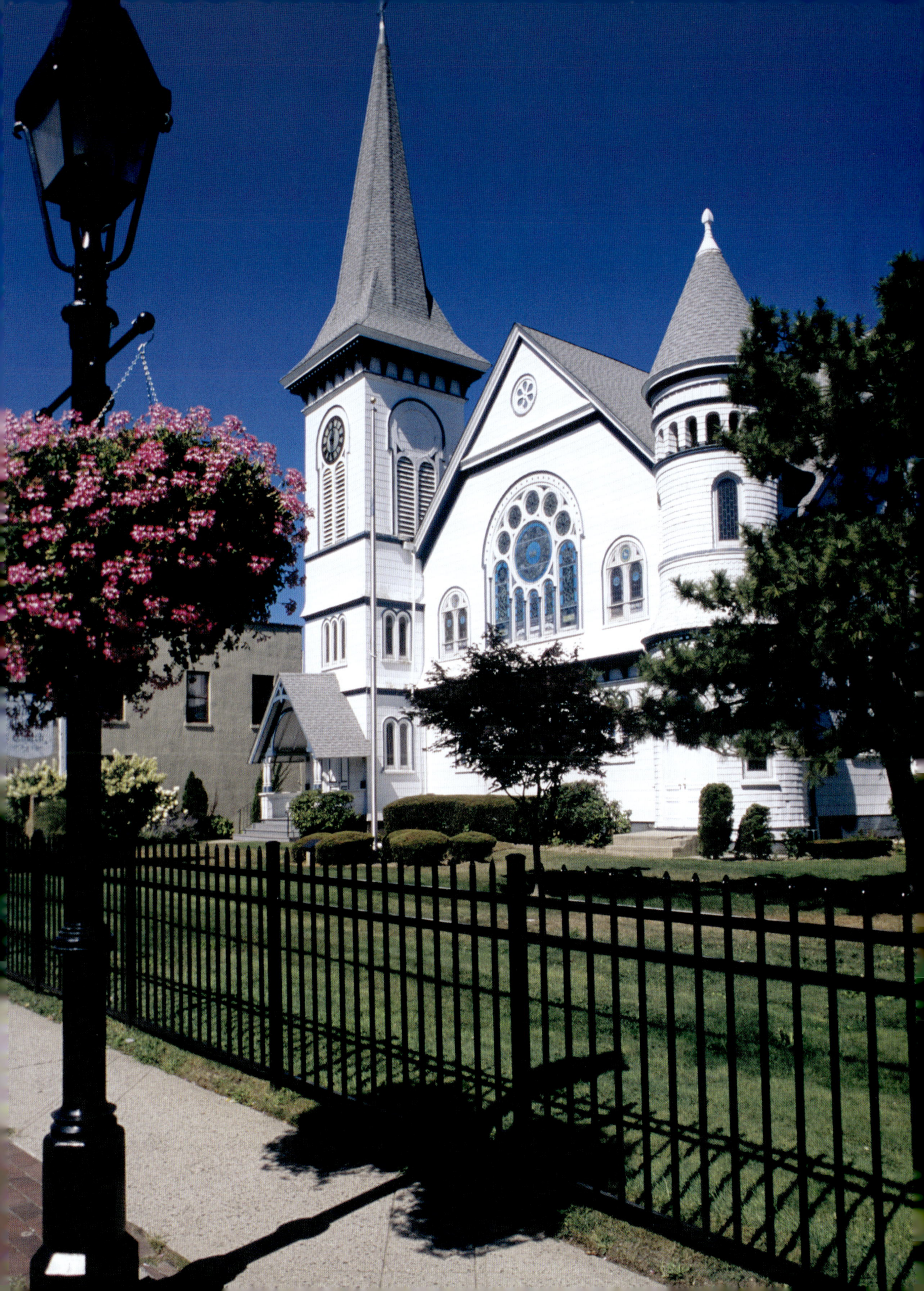

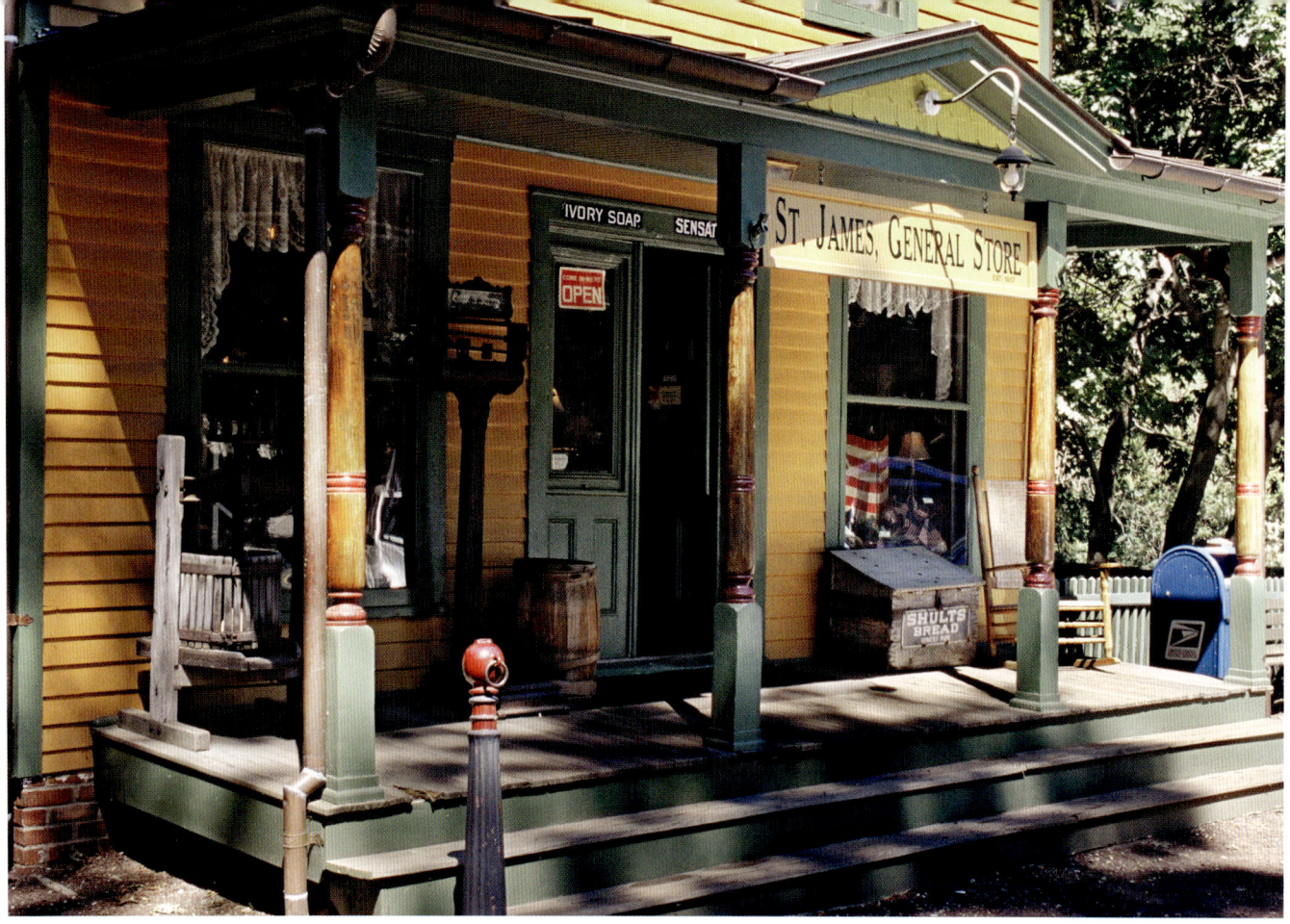

ABOVE

In operation since 1857, the fully restored St. James Store is the oldest continuously operating general store in the United States.

BELOW

The Islip Grange is a small community of restored buildings in Sayville. The Robinson House was built in 1840 and the American Farm Windmill in 1895.

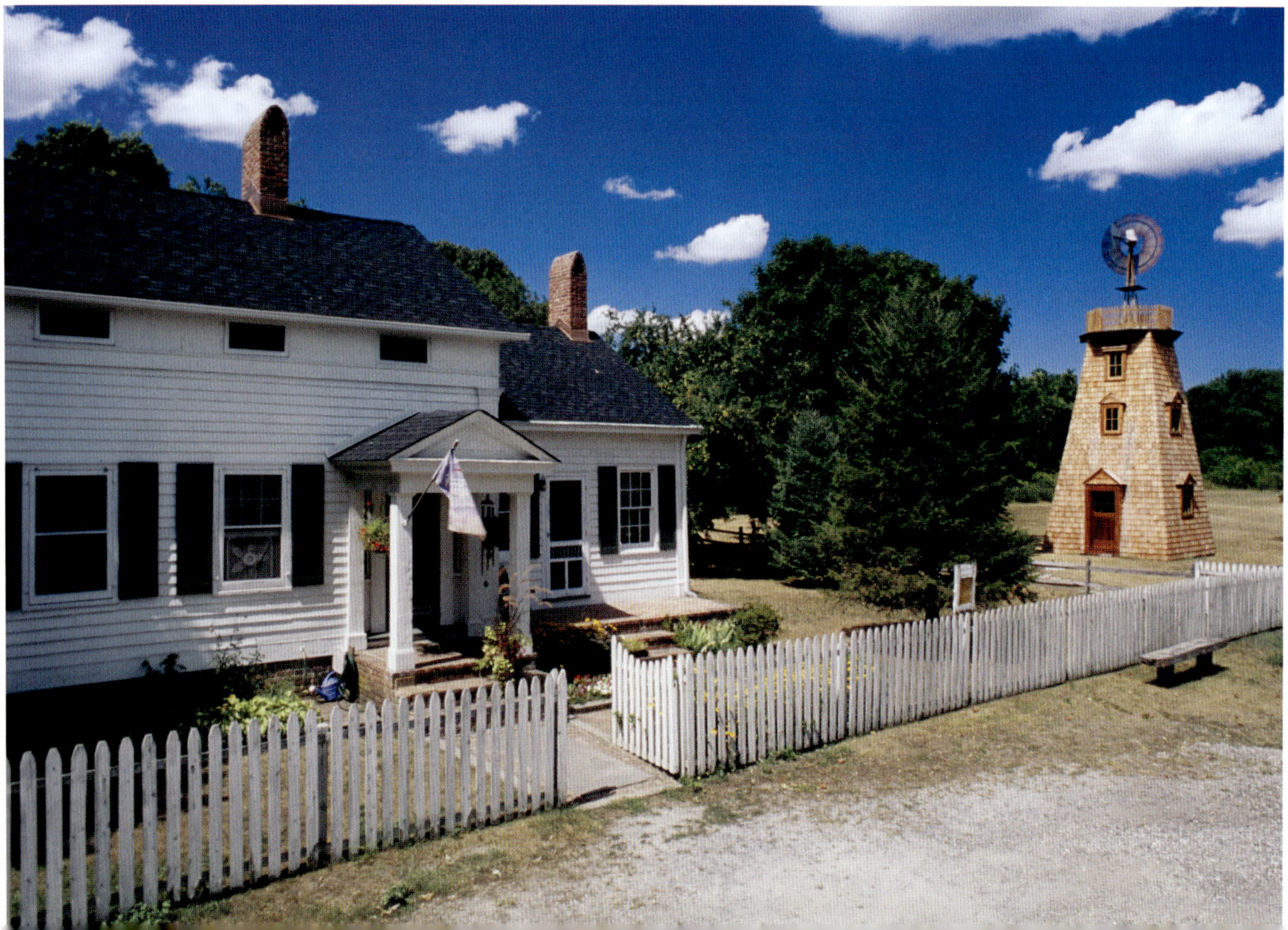

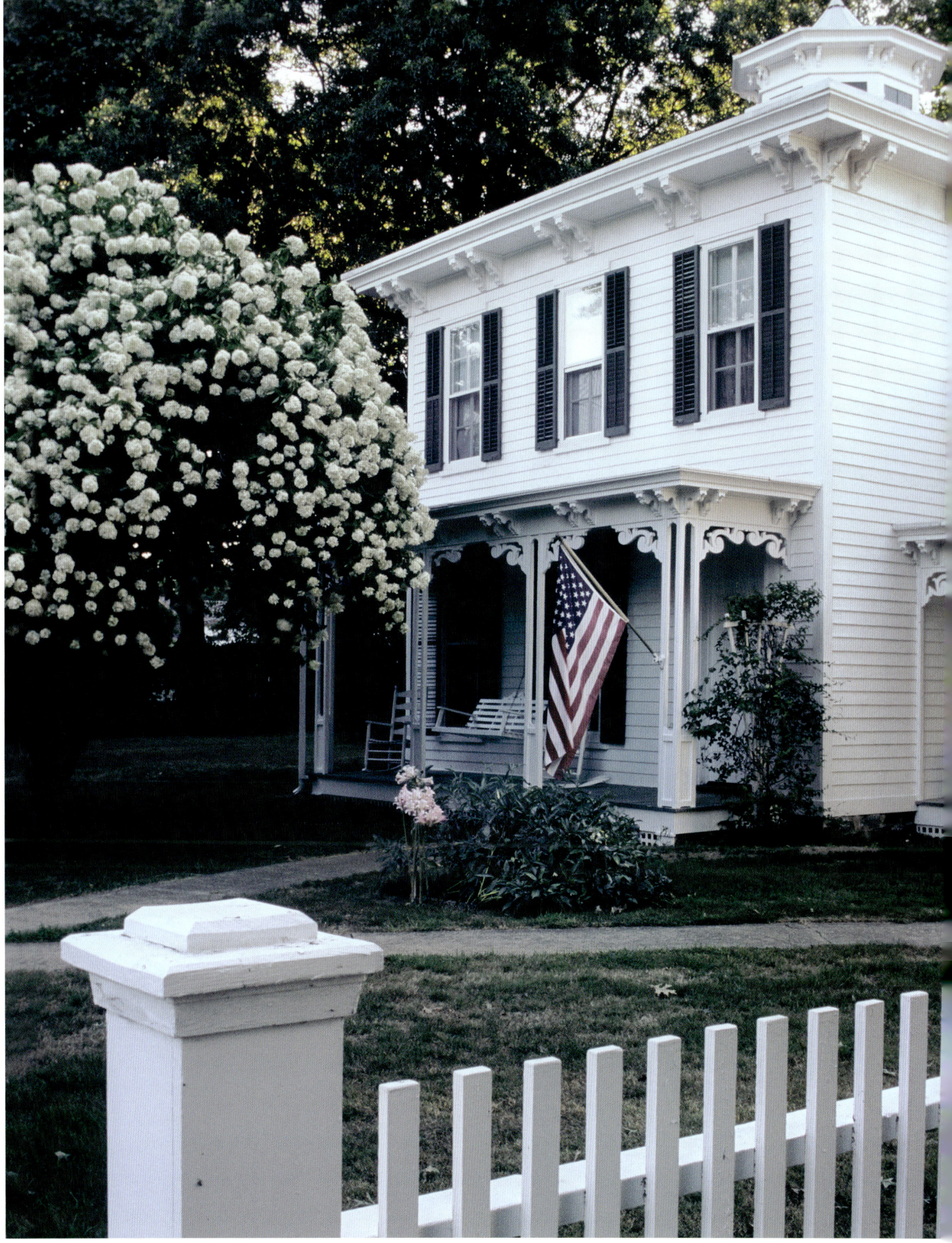

ABOVE

This home in Orient, at the east end of the North Fork, reflects the quaint character still evident in the many fishing villages of eastern Long Island.

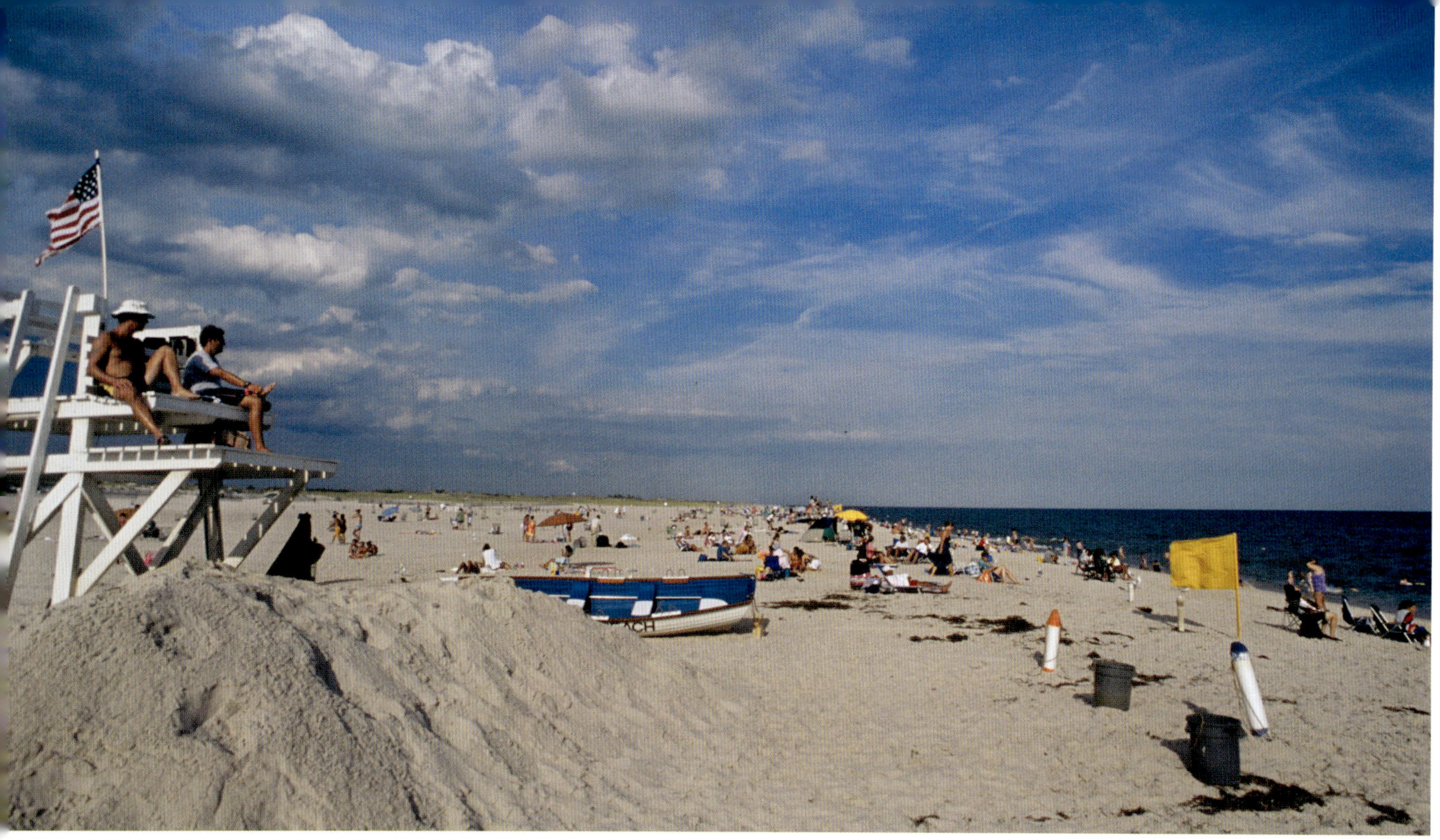

ABOVE

The boardwalk, theater, and wide sandy beaches make Jones Beach State Park a popular summertime destination that's located less than an hour from midtown Manhattan.

BELOW

From the 1870s until the opening of Disneyland in 1955, Coney Island was America's premier amusement park destination. Nathan's hot dog stand has been a Coney Island institution since 1916, and it has hosted its annual hot dog eating contest ever since.

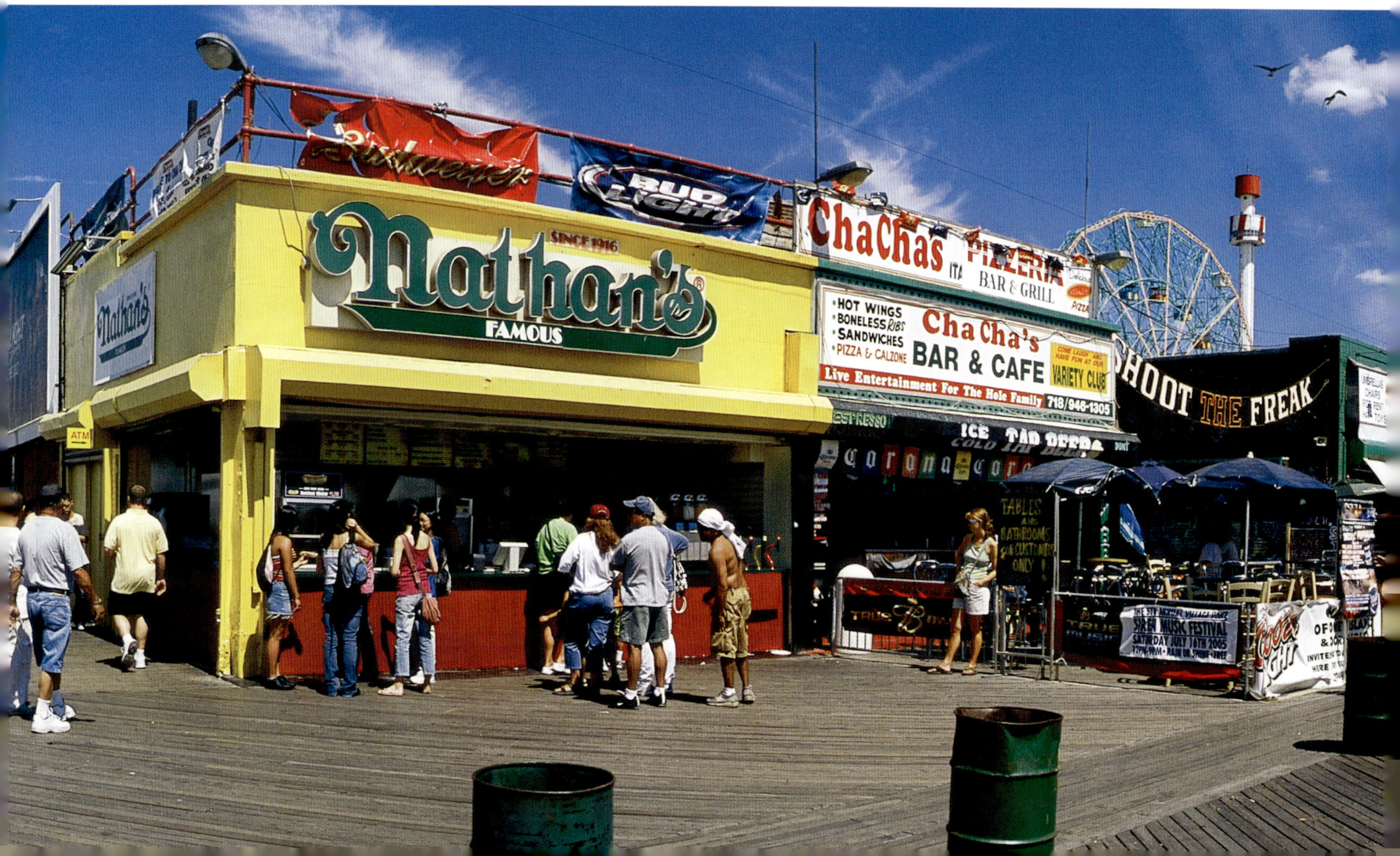

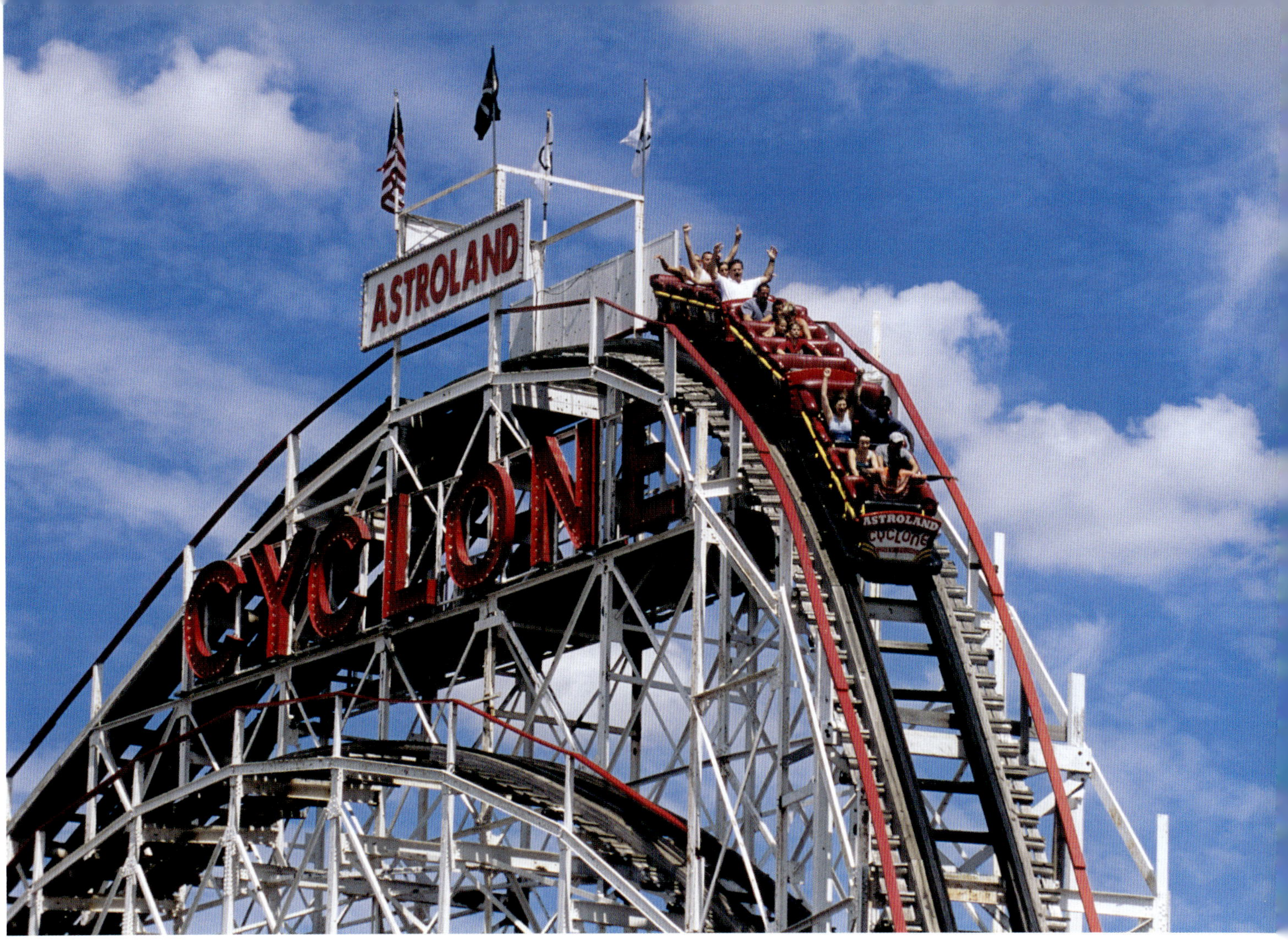

ABOVE

You can feel the wind in your hair and hear the passengers' screams as the historic coaster begins its free fall. The Cyclone has been a highlight of Coney Island's Astroland Park since 1927, and it is often ranked as the top roller coaster ride in the world.

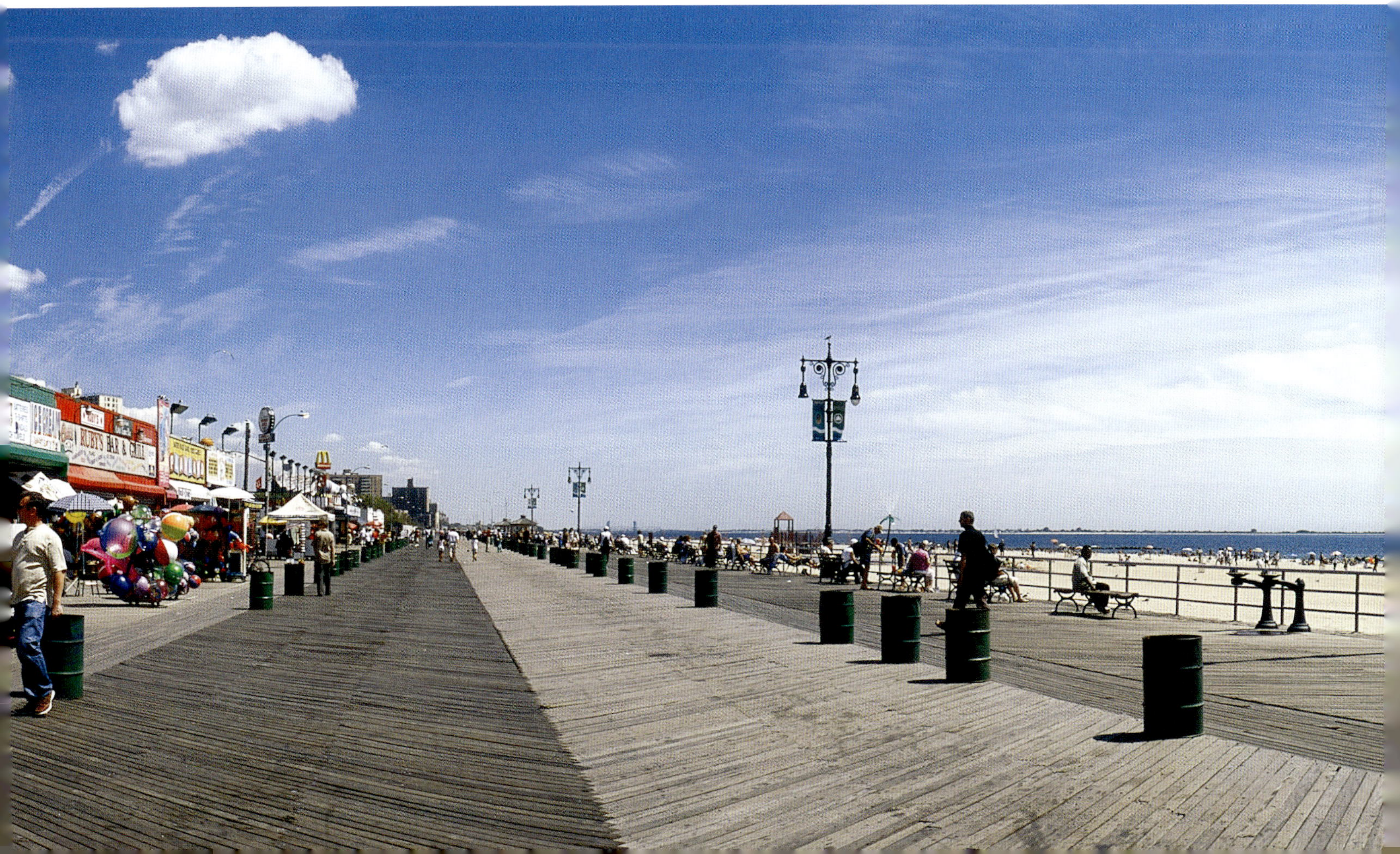

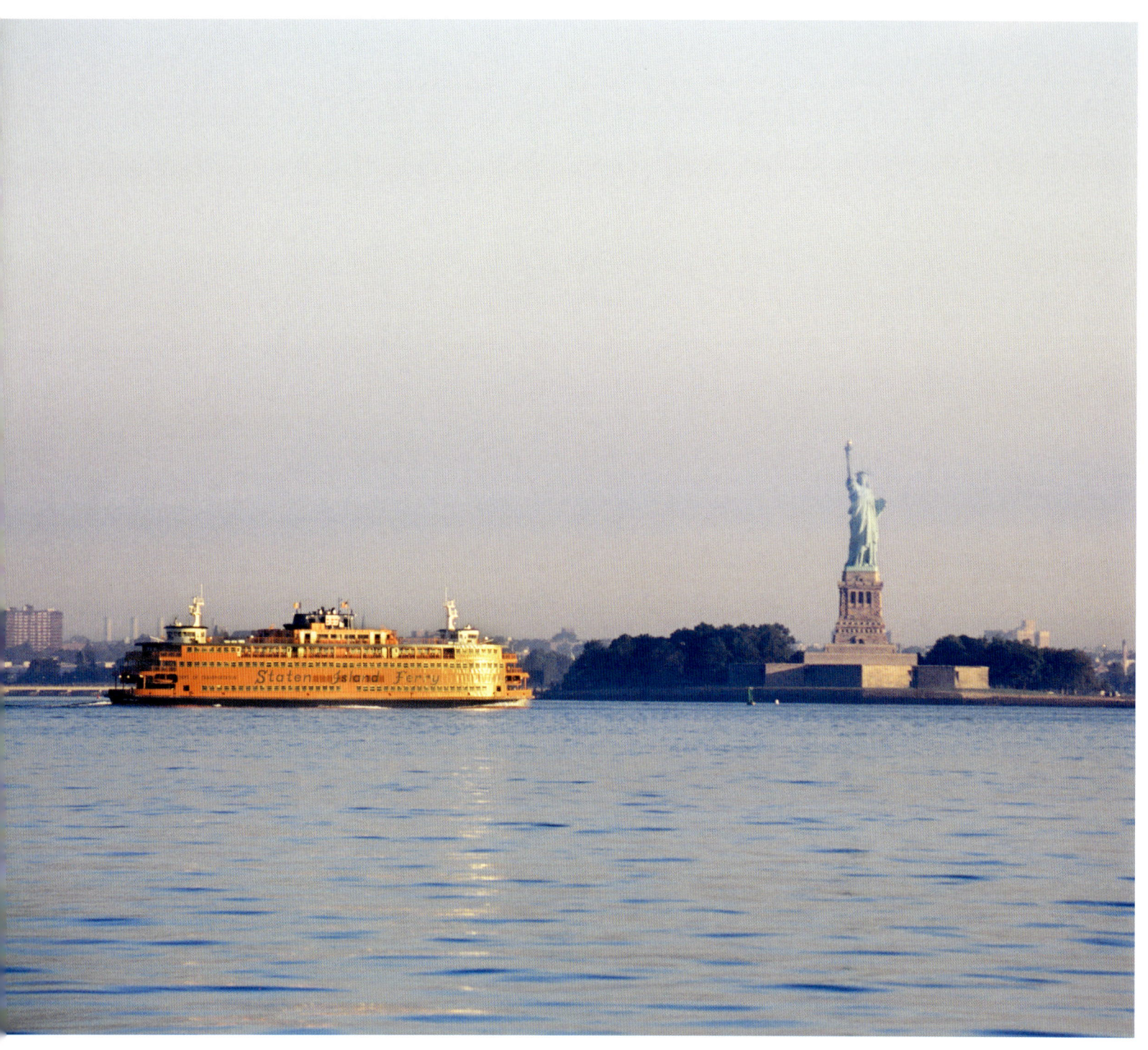

ABOVE

The Staten Island Ferry and the Statue of Liberty *are* New York City. A ride on the ferry offers one of the best views of Lower Manhattan and New York Harbor, as well as of the Statue of Liberty, which has stood as a symbol of freedom and democracy since 1886.

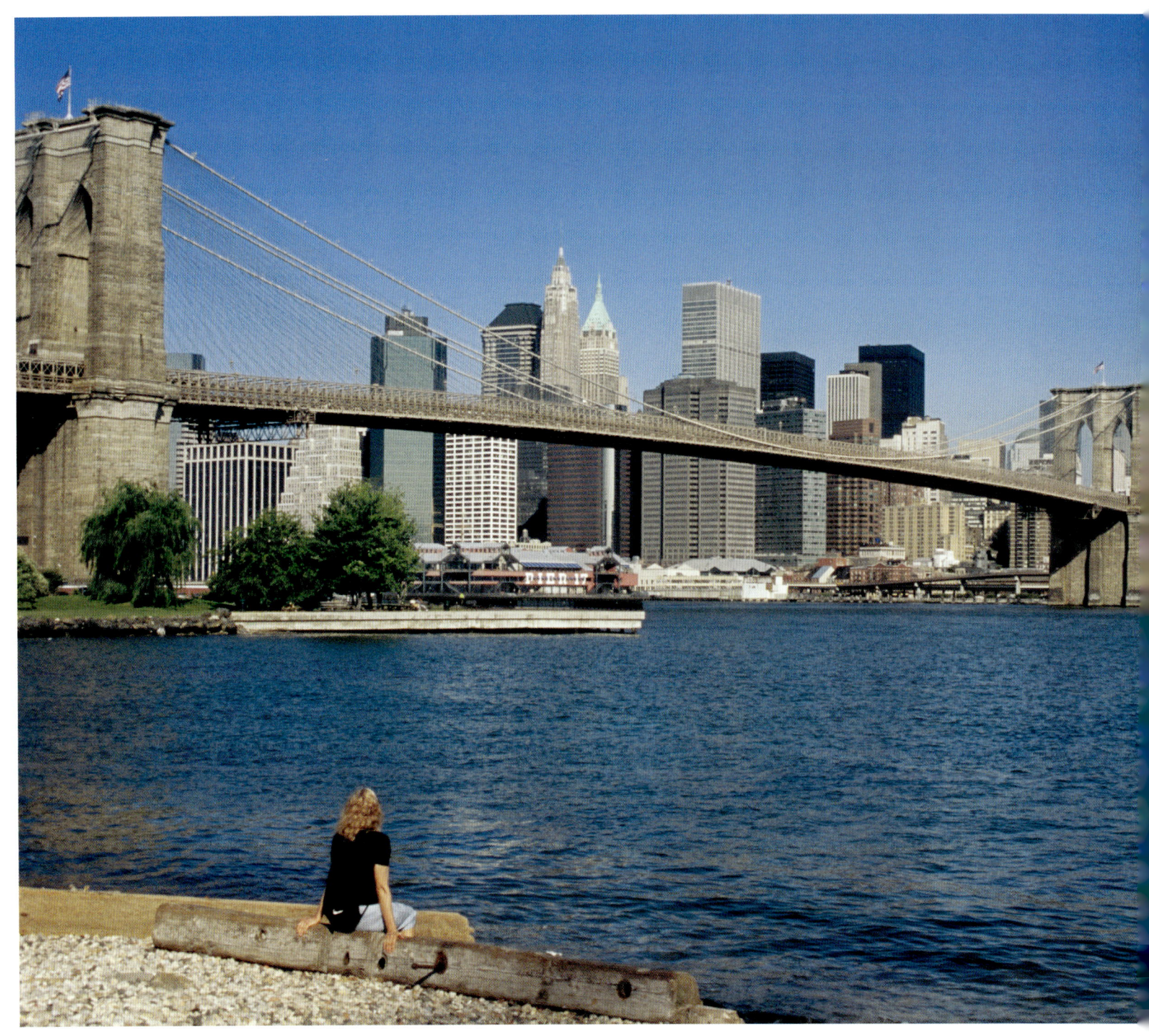

ABOVE

Brooklyn Bridge Park is another prime spot from which to take in the Manhattan skyline. Completed in 1883, after fourteen years of construction, the Brooklyn Bridge spans more than a mile over the East River. It was the largest suspension bridge in the world for twenty years.

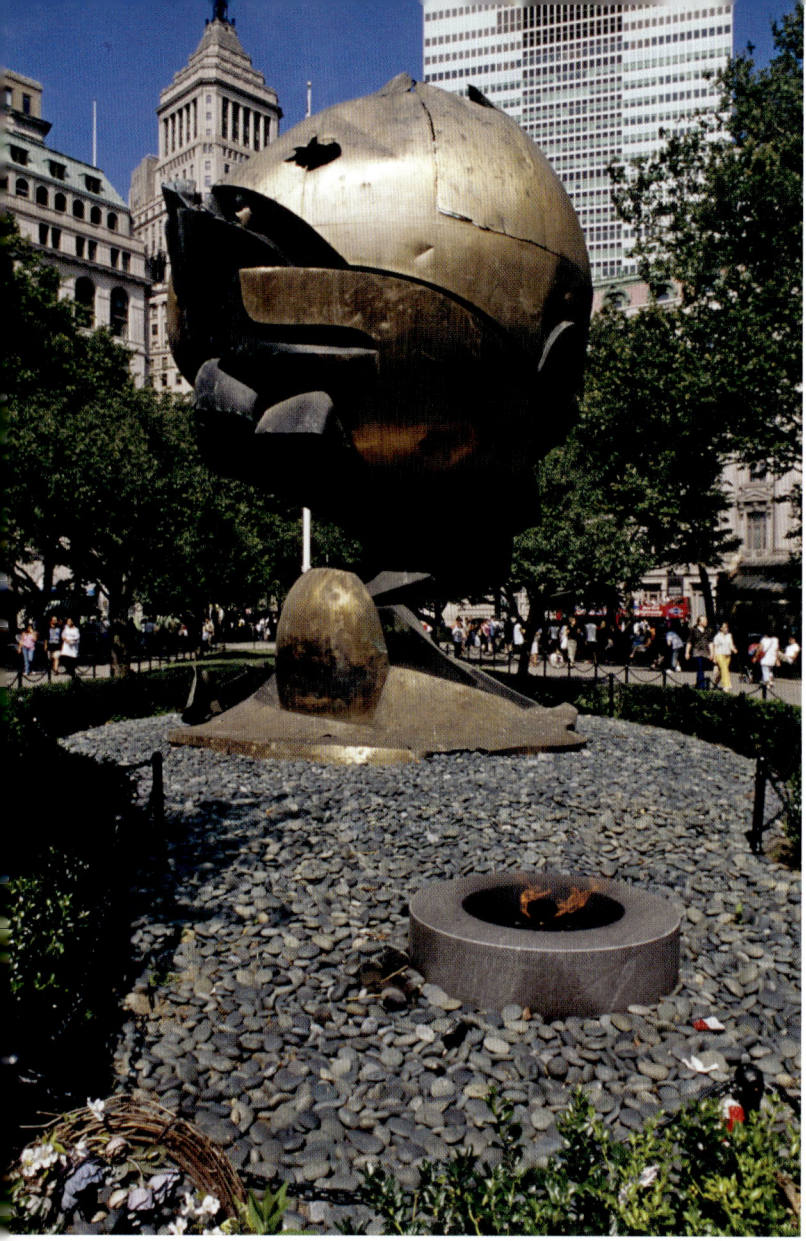

LEFT

The Sphere is a sculpture symbolizing world peace that originally stood in a courtyard of the World Trade Center. It was recovered from the debris of the towers and moved to Battery Park, where it now stands, along with an eternal flame, "in memory of all who lost their lives to terrorist attacks at the World Trade Center."

RIGHT

Greenwich Village, once a hamlet of Manhattan, retained its original street layout when the rest of the city went to a grid layout in 1811. It has long been a mecca for avant-garde and alternative cultural movements, and many prominent authors, actors, comedians, and musicians got their start in Greenwich Village coffeehouses and clubs.

BELOW

With its numerous restaurants, shops, and open-air markets, Chinatown is the best known of the city's many ethnic neighborhoods. Chinatown celebrates the Chinese New Year every year with firecrackers, dances, music, and dragon parades.

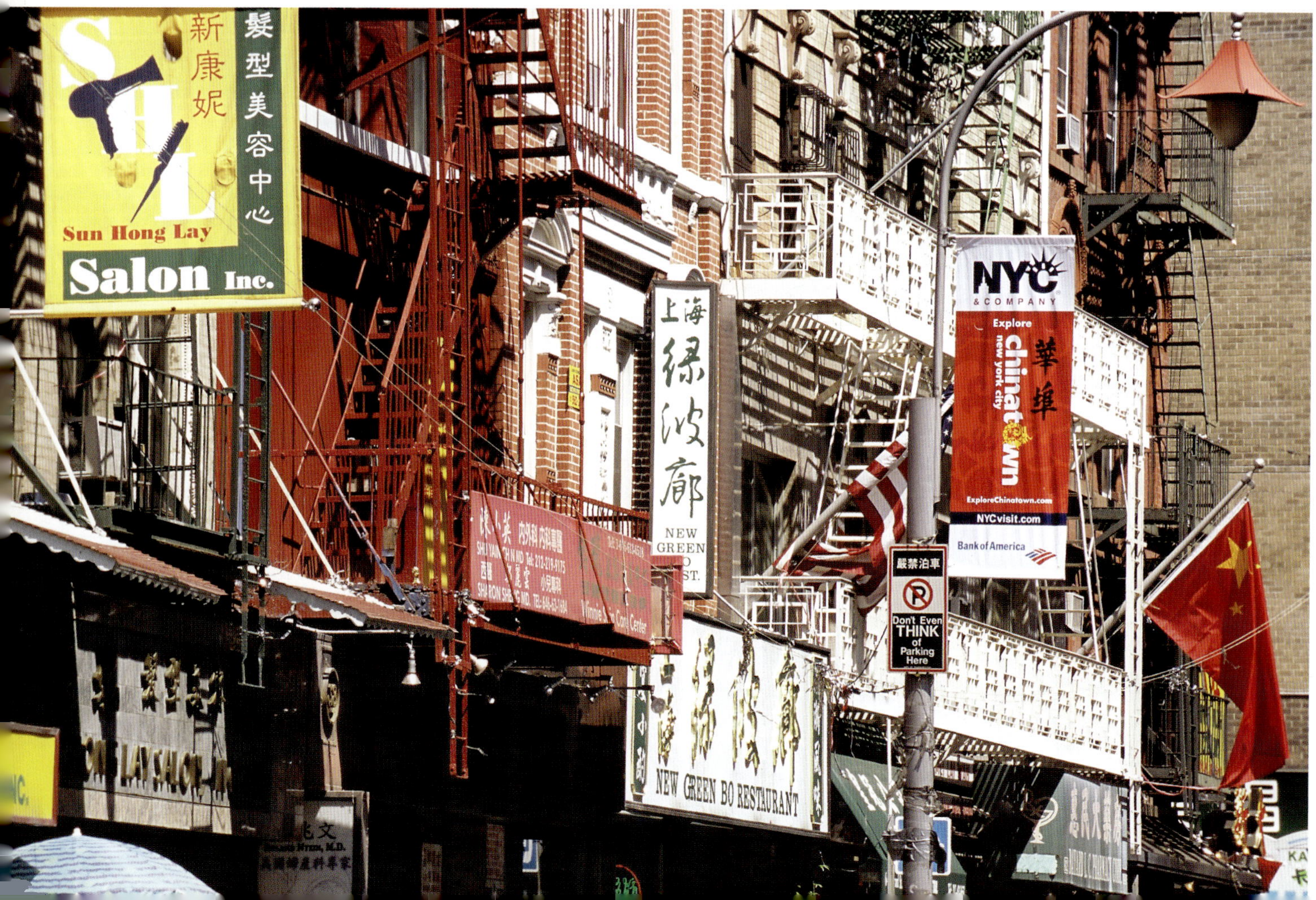

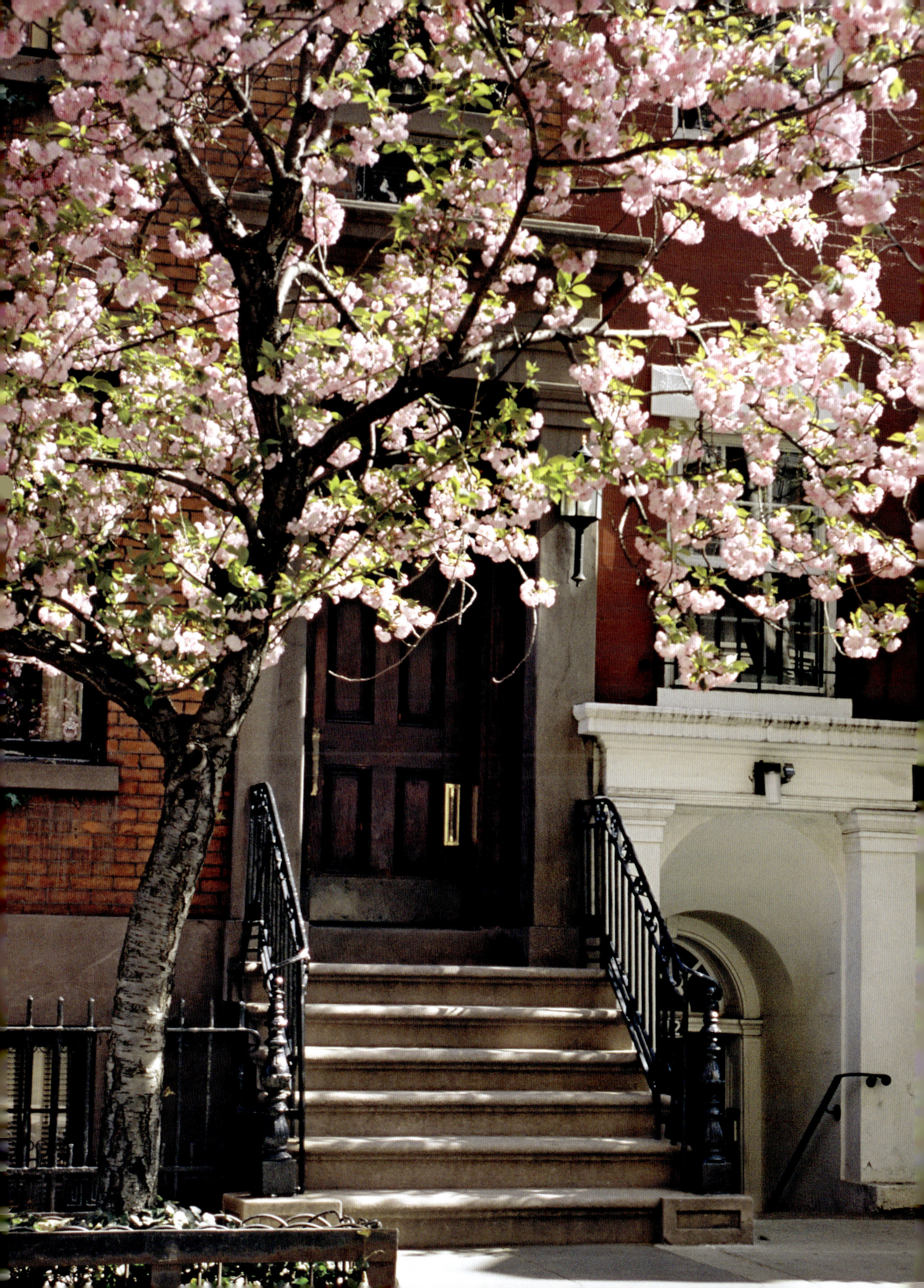

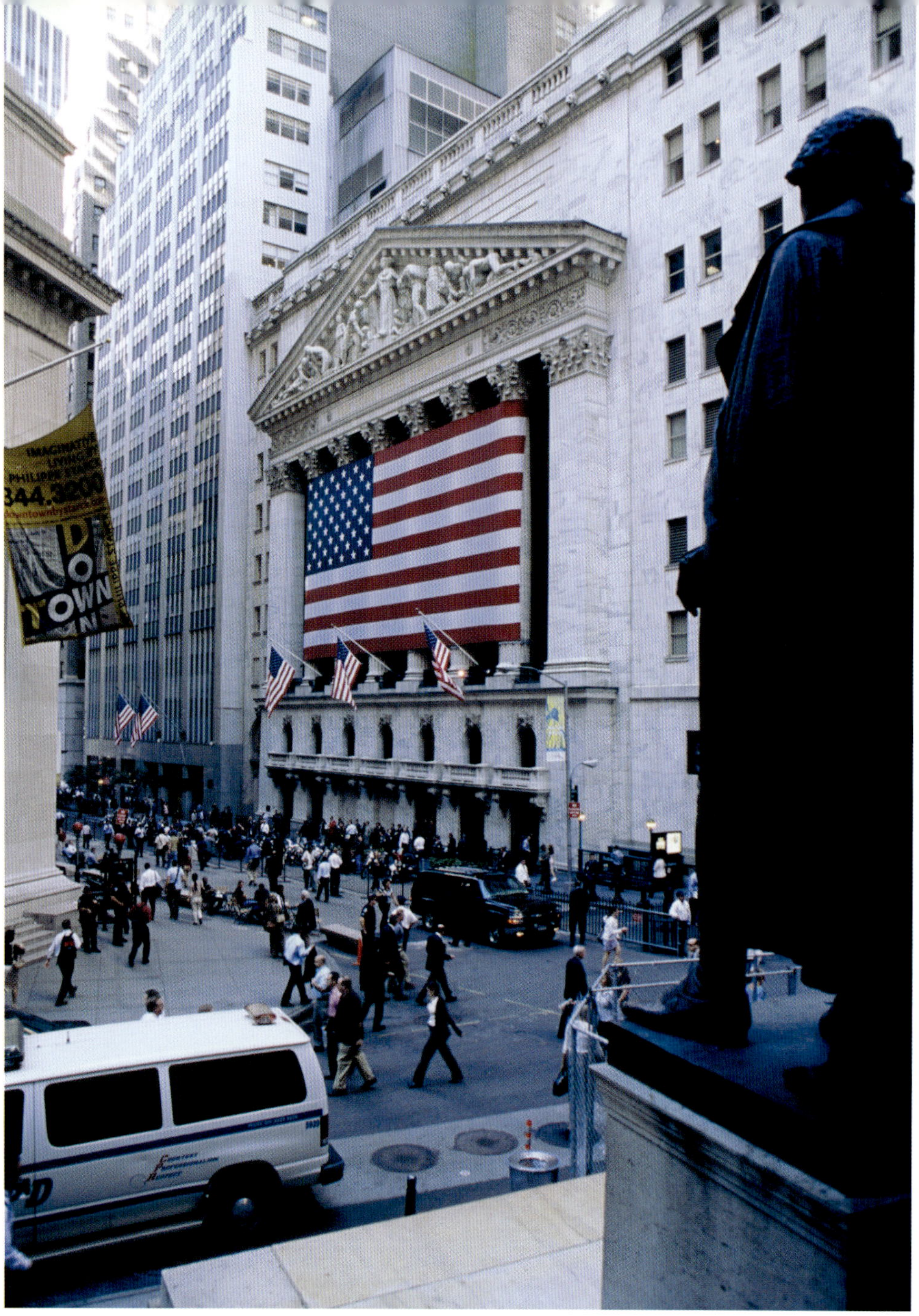

RIGHT

A statue of George Washington overlooks Wall Street and the New York Stock Exchange, the largest stock exchange company in the world.

BELOW

This seven-thousand-pound bronze bull sculpture was created two years after the 1987 stock market collapse as a symbol of the "strength and power of the American people." It is located at Bowling Green Park in Lower Manhattan, the oldest green park in the city.

OPPOSITE

Although the current Grand Central Terminal dates to 1913, the site at 42nd Street and Park Avenue has been a transportation hub for New York City since the late 1800s. When the old steam locomotives were replaced by electric trains in the early 1900s, trains were able to travel underground through the city. The landmark terminal was restored to its original glory in the 1990s.

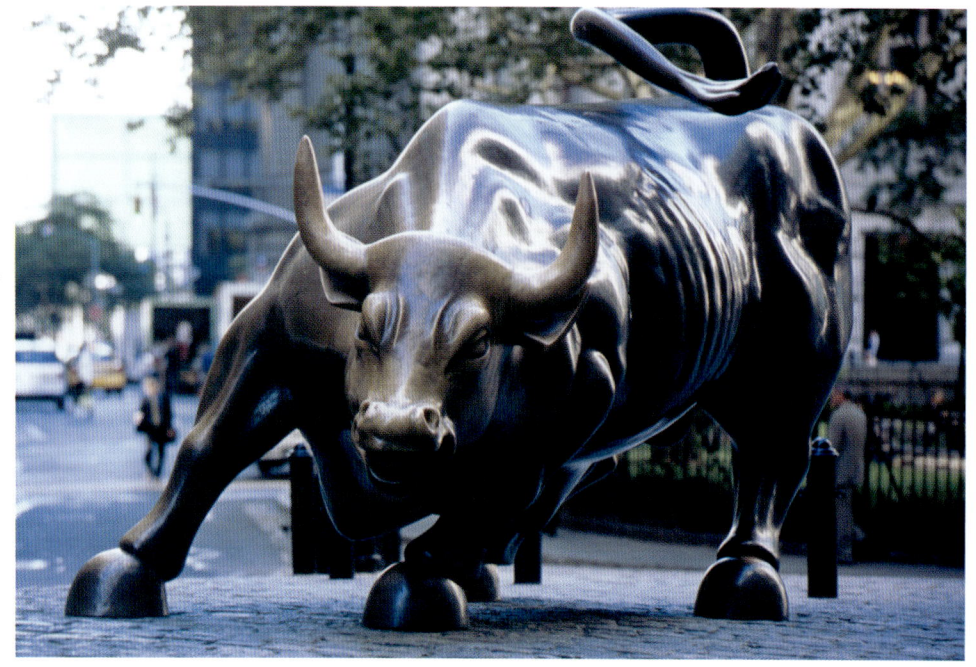

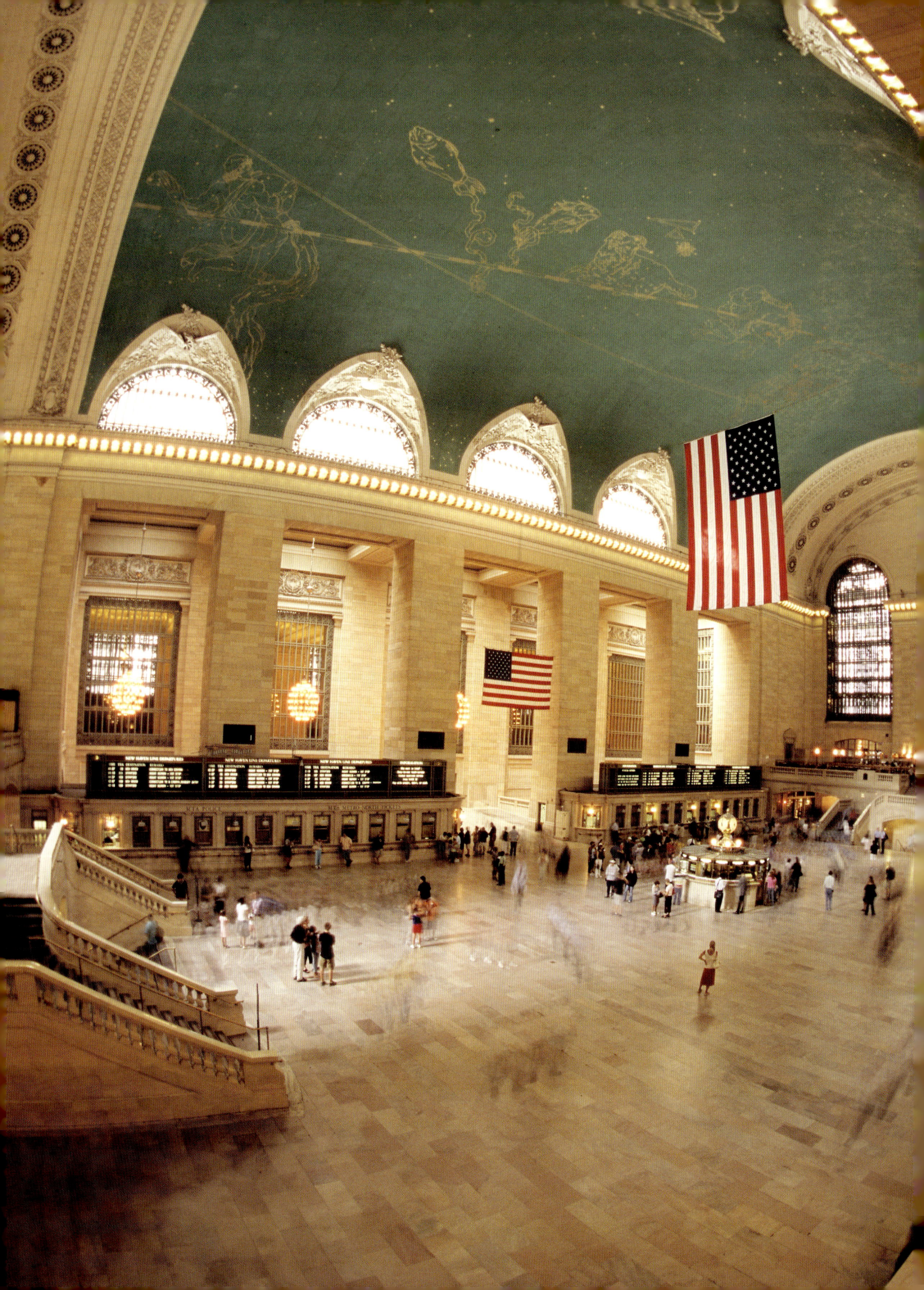

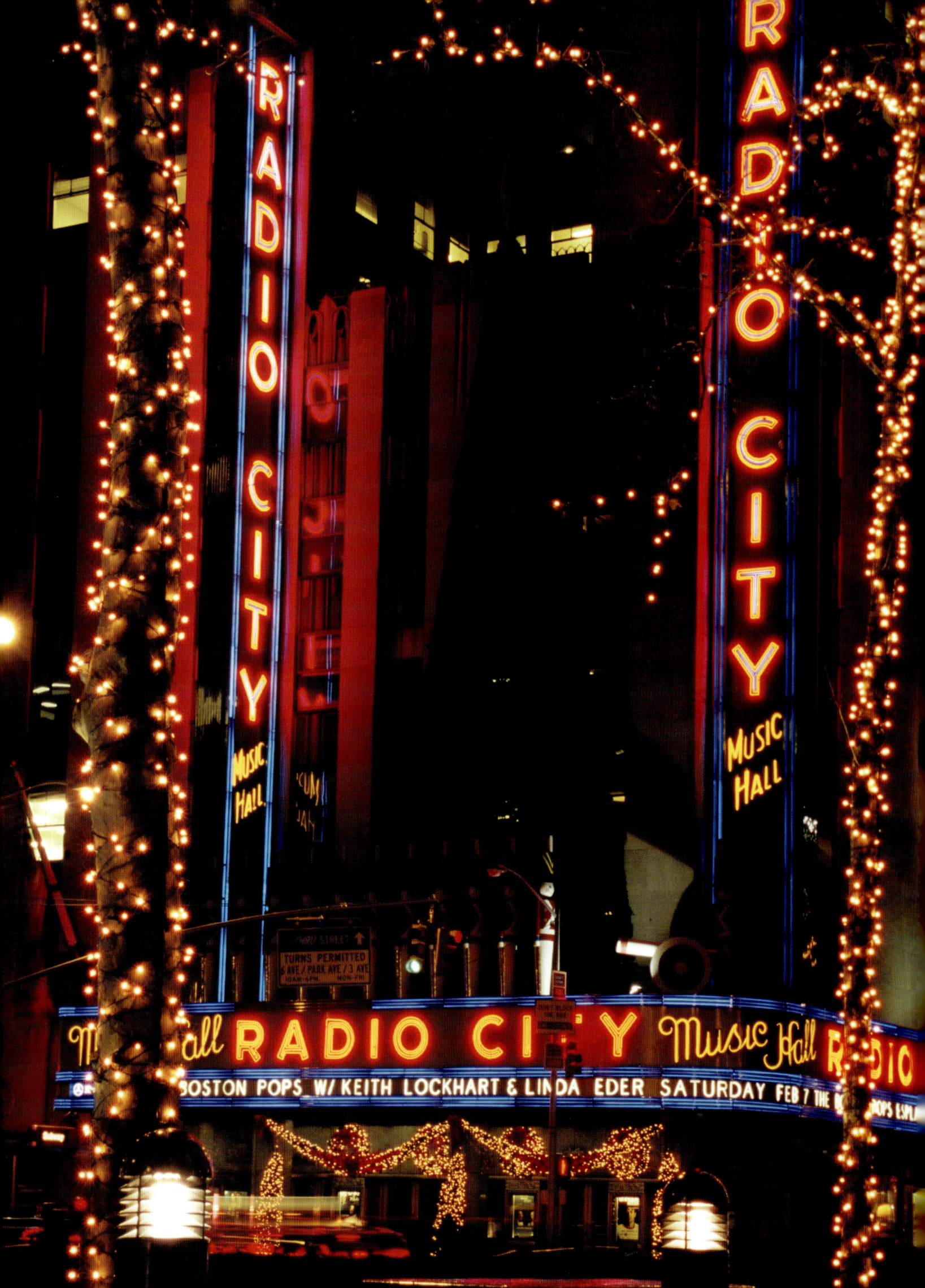

OPPOSITE

New York, New York . . . Broadway shows, movies, concerts, and of course, Radio City Music Hall and the Rockettes. Since 1932, Radio City has dazzled spectators with its "larger than life" presentations in the largest indoor theater in the world.

RIGHT AND BELOW

Fifth Avenue, from about Rockefeller Center to Central Park, is known as one of the world's richest shopping districts. People come from all over to check out the latest fashions in shops ranging from H&M to Saks Fifth Avenue.

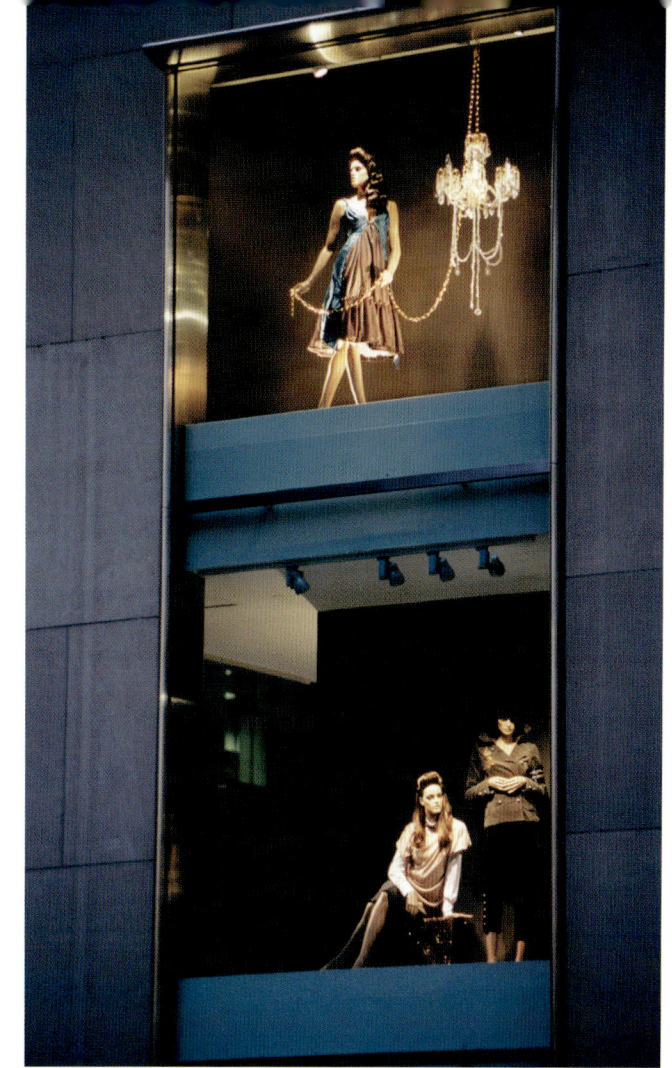

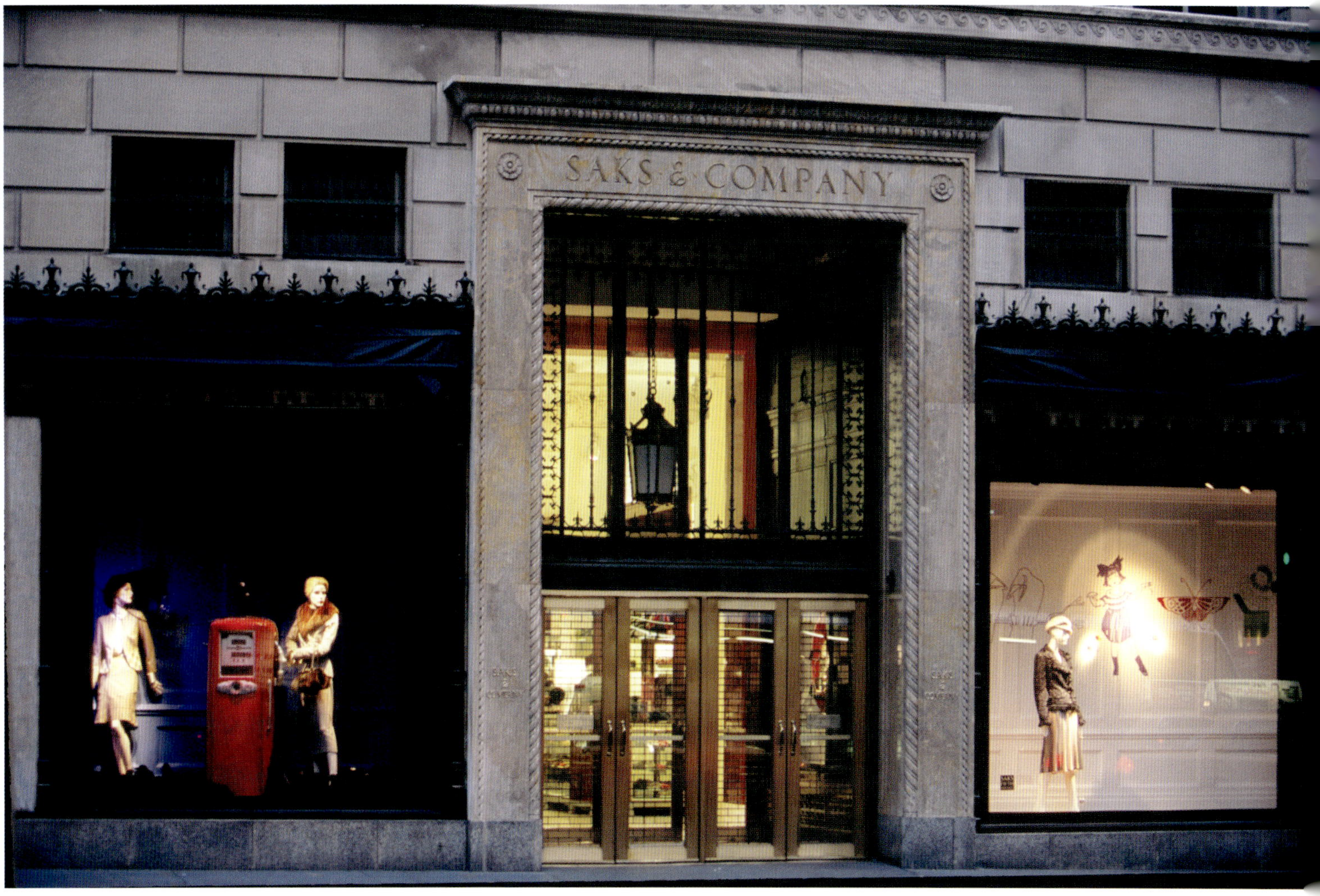

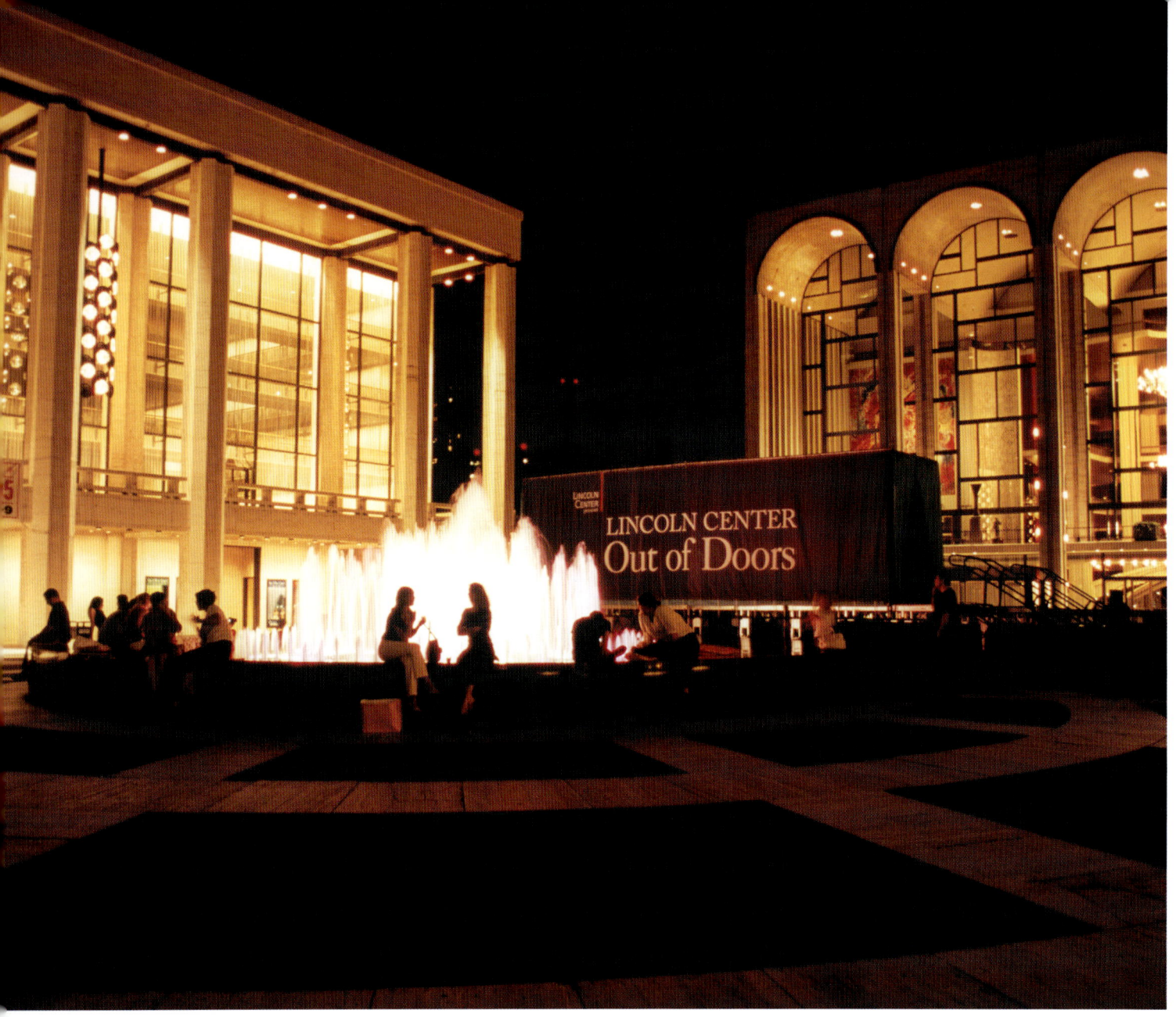

ABOVE

The Lincoln Center complex is home to many of the city's top performing arts, including ballet, theater, film, opera, jazz, and symphony and chamber orchestras. In summertime the center hosts outdoor performances as well.

OPPOSITE, CLOCKWISE FROM UPPER LEFT

New York's Municipal Building, an early skyscraper from 1914, was the first building to have a subway station built into its foundation.

The Chrysler Building is one of the finest examples of art deco skyscrapers. More than seventy-five years after its completion, it is still the tallest brick building in the world.

The modern glass-façade Bloomberg Tower, completed in 2005, measures in at 806 feet. The fifty-four-story building includes offices as well as luxury condominiums above the thirty-first floor.

Viewed from Park Avenue, the eighty-story MetLife Building, of 1963, contrasts sharply with the 1929 art deco Helmsley Building in front of it.

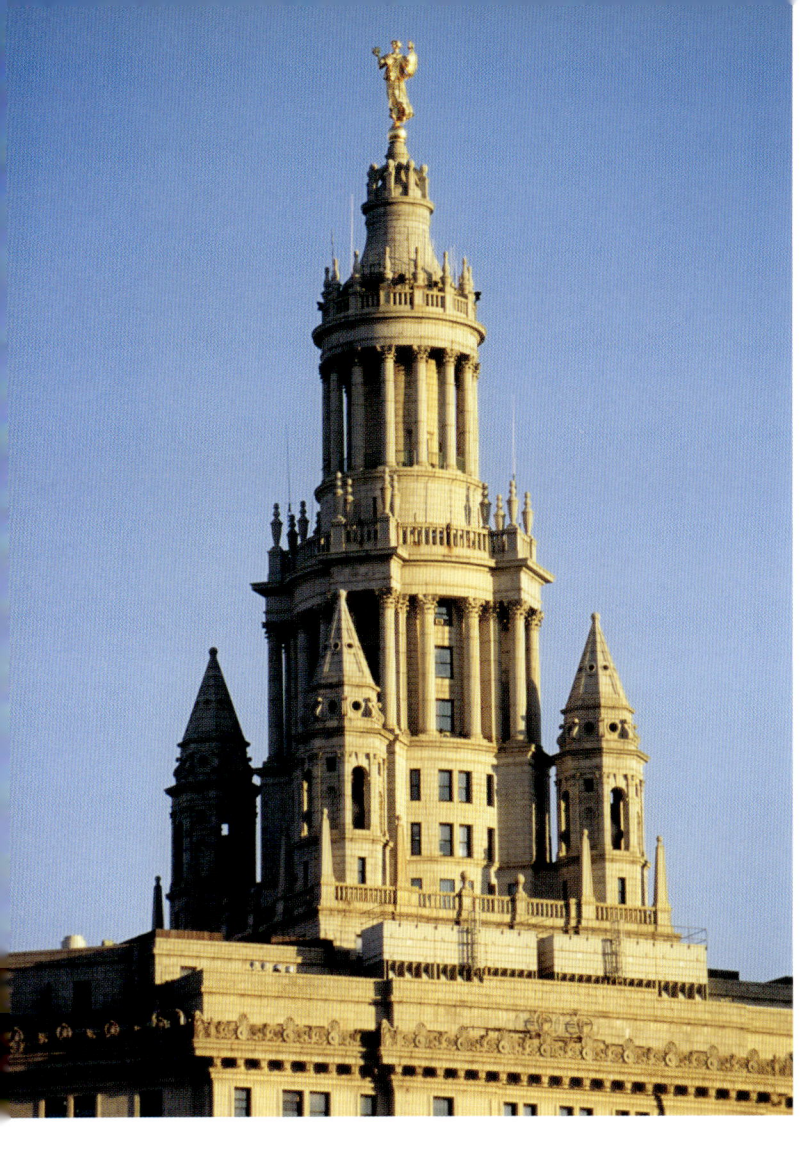
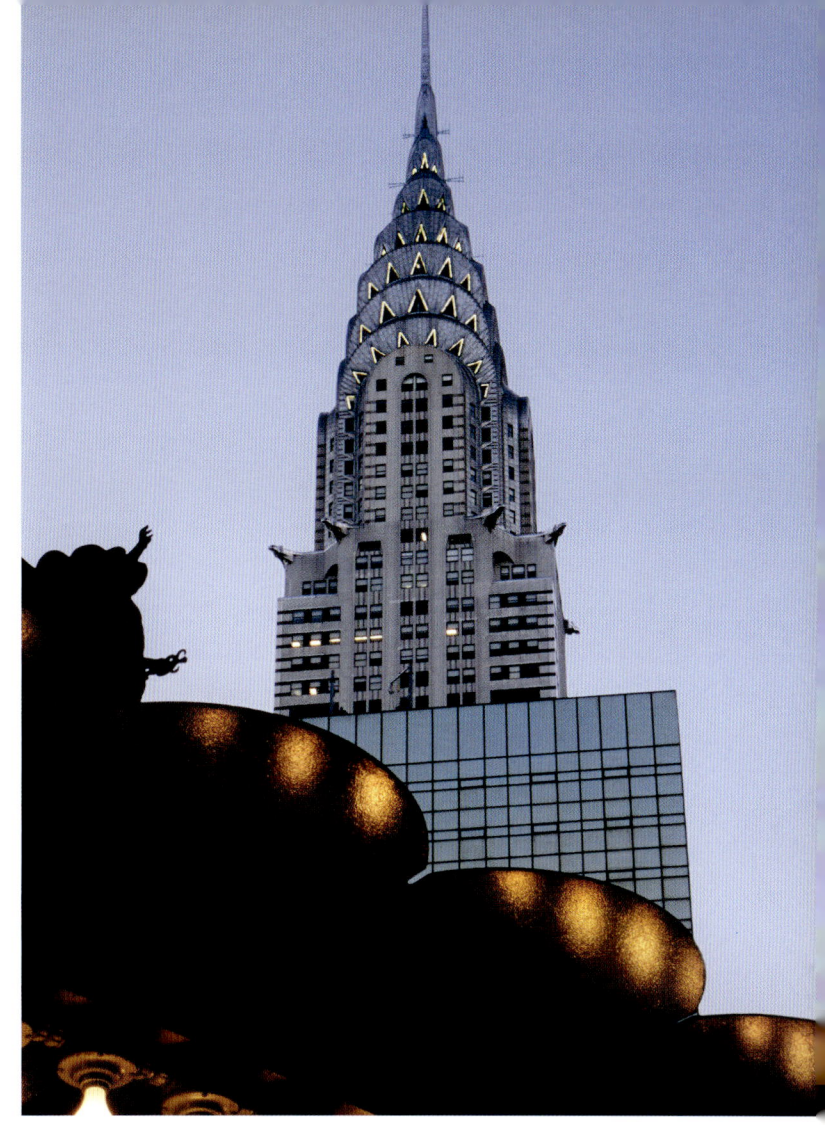
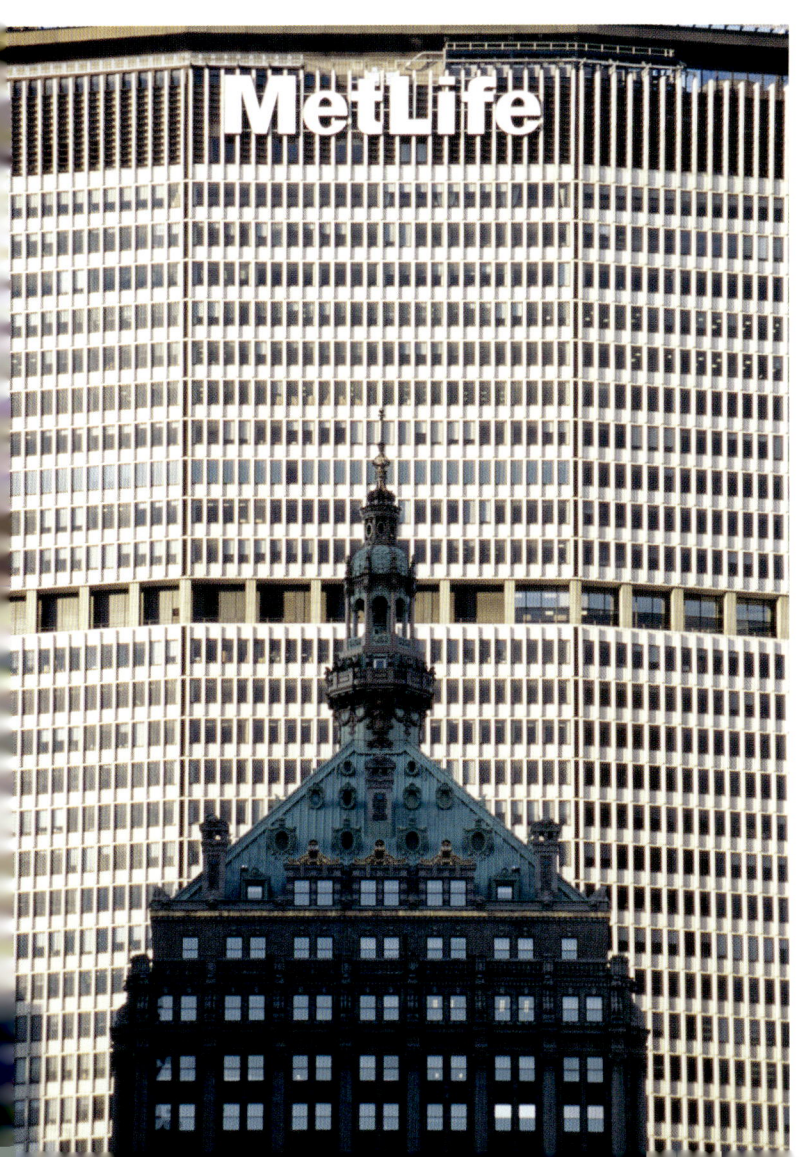
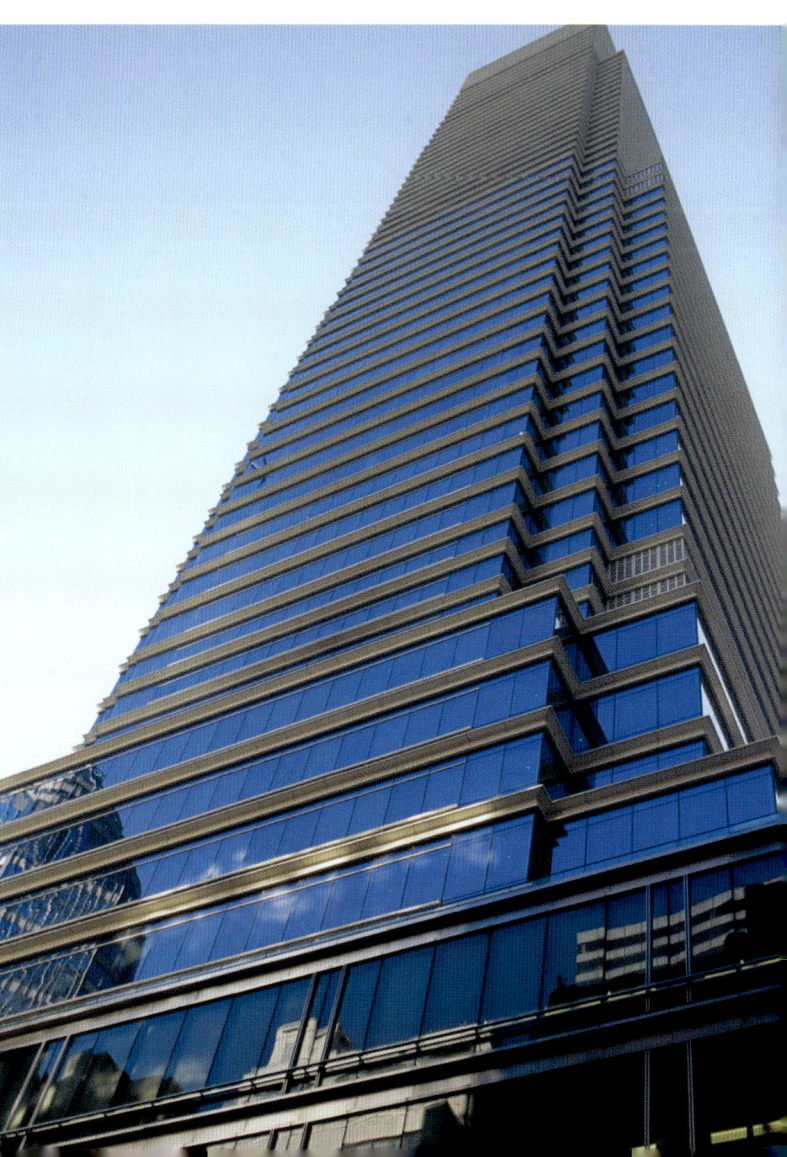

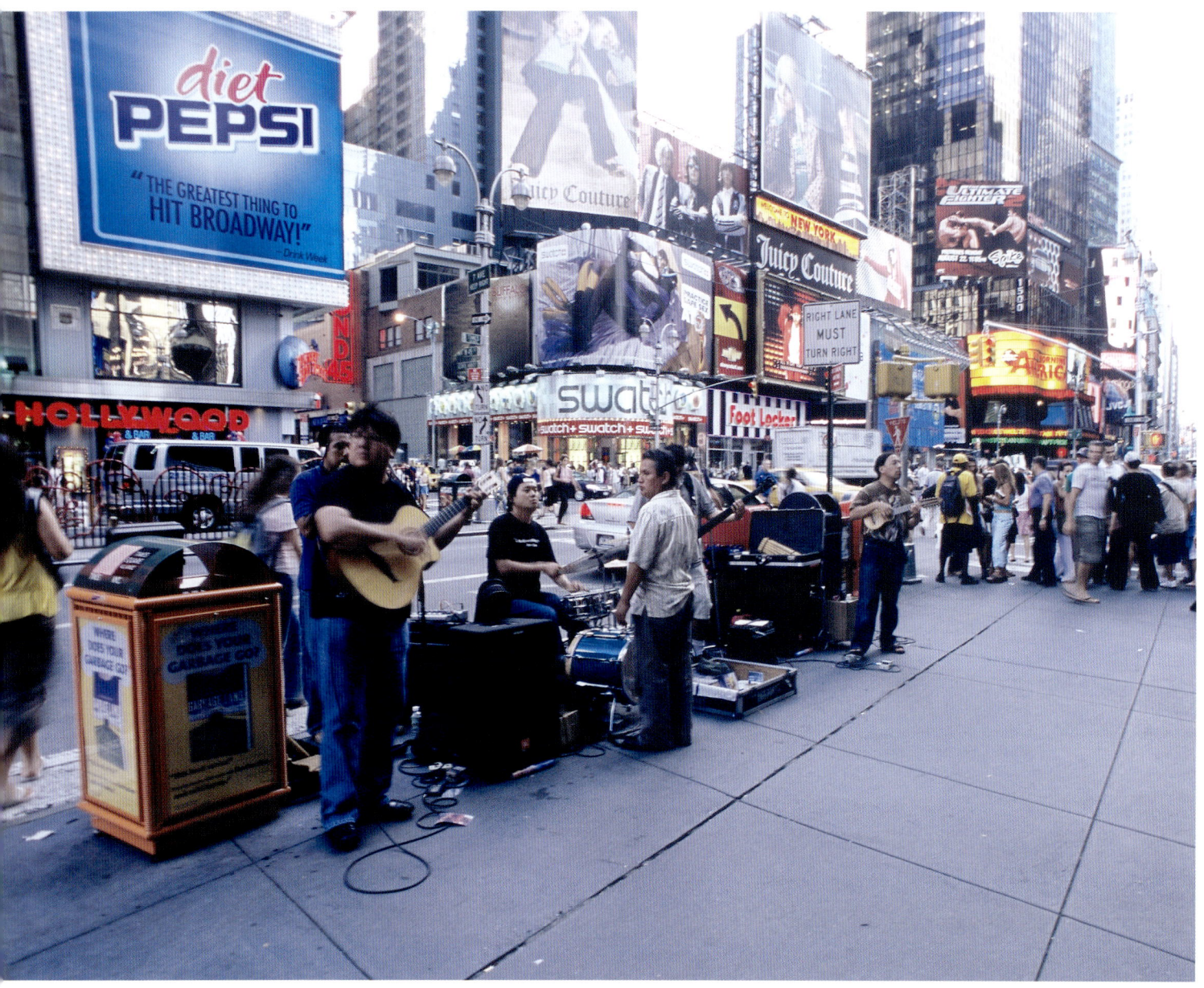

ABOVE

Originally known as Longacre Square, the "Crossroads of the World" was renamed Times Square in 1904, when the *New York Times* opened its headquarters there, which the paper celebrated with the square's first New Year's Eve celebration. Through its recent gentrification, Times Square remains a crossroads for performers, shoppers, theater-goers, tourists, and people from all walks of life.

RIGHT

An oasis in the middle of a bustling metropolis, the ponds and landscapes of Central Park are explored by millions from all over the world. Frederick Law Olmsted and Calvert Vaux drew up the original plans for the half-mile by two-and-a-half-mile park in 1858, and it was completed twenty years later.

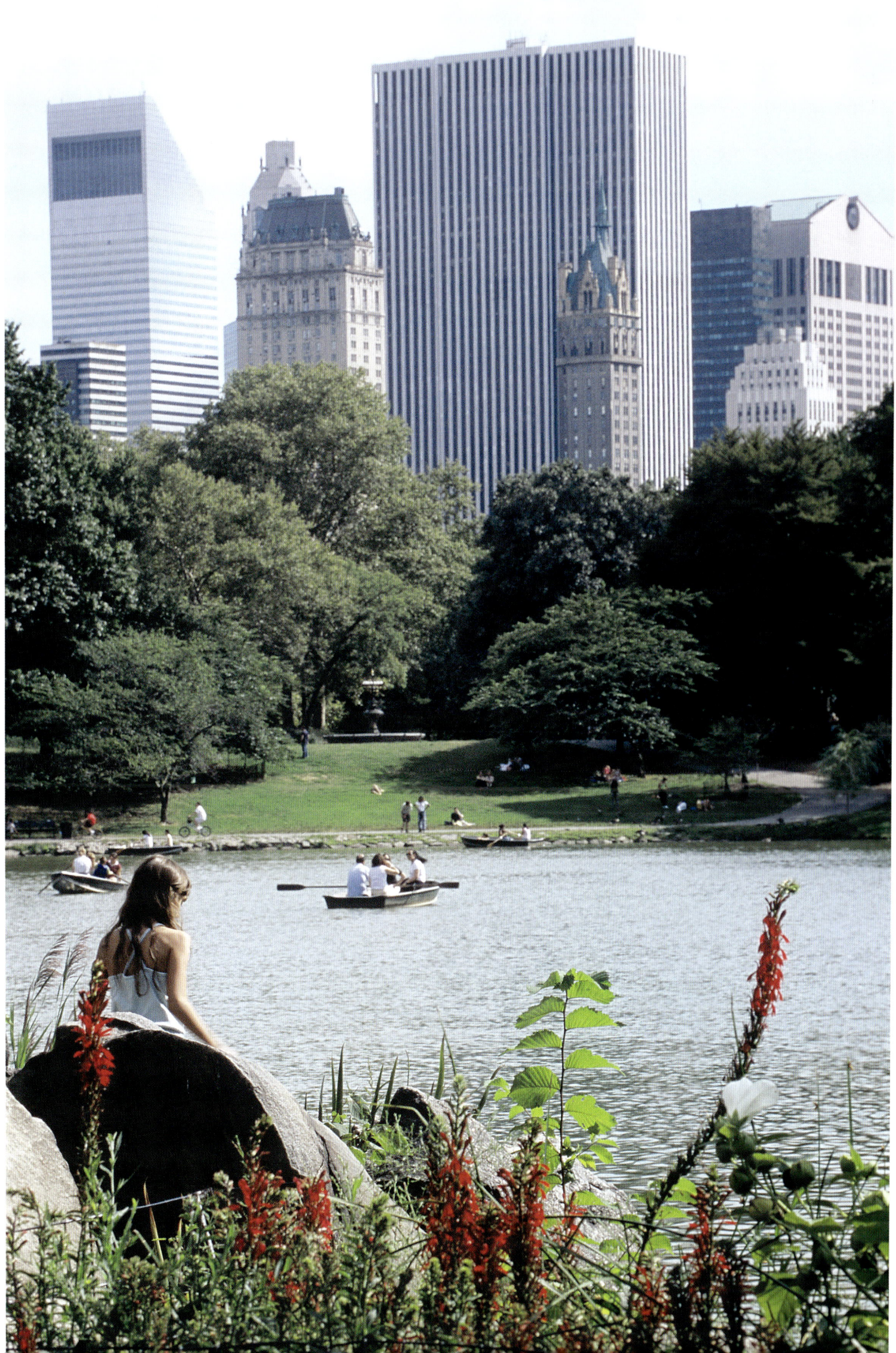

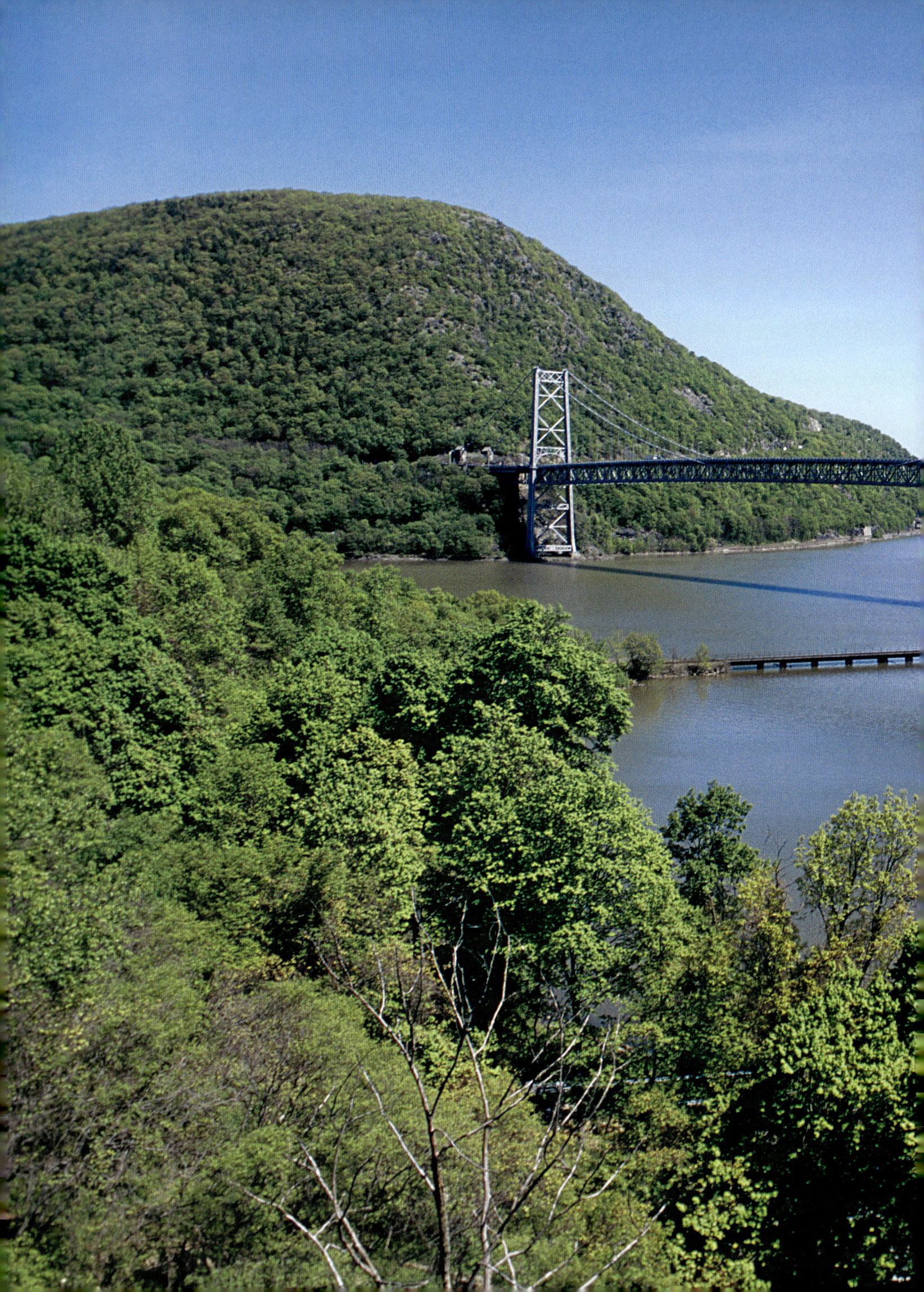

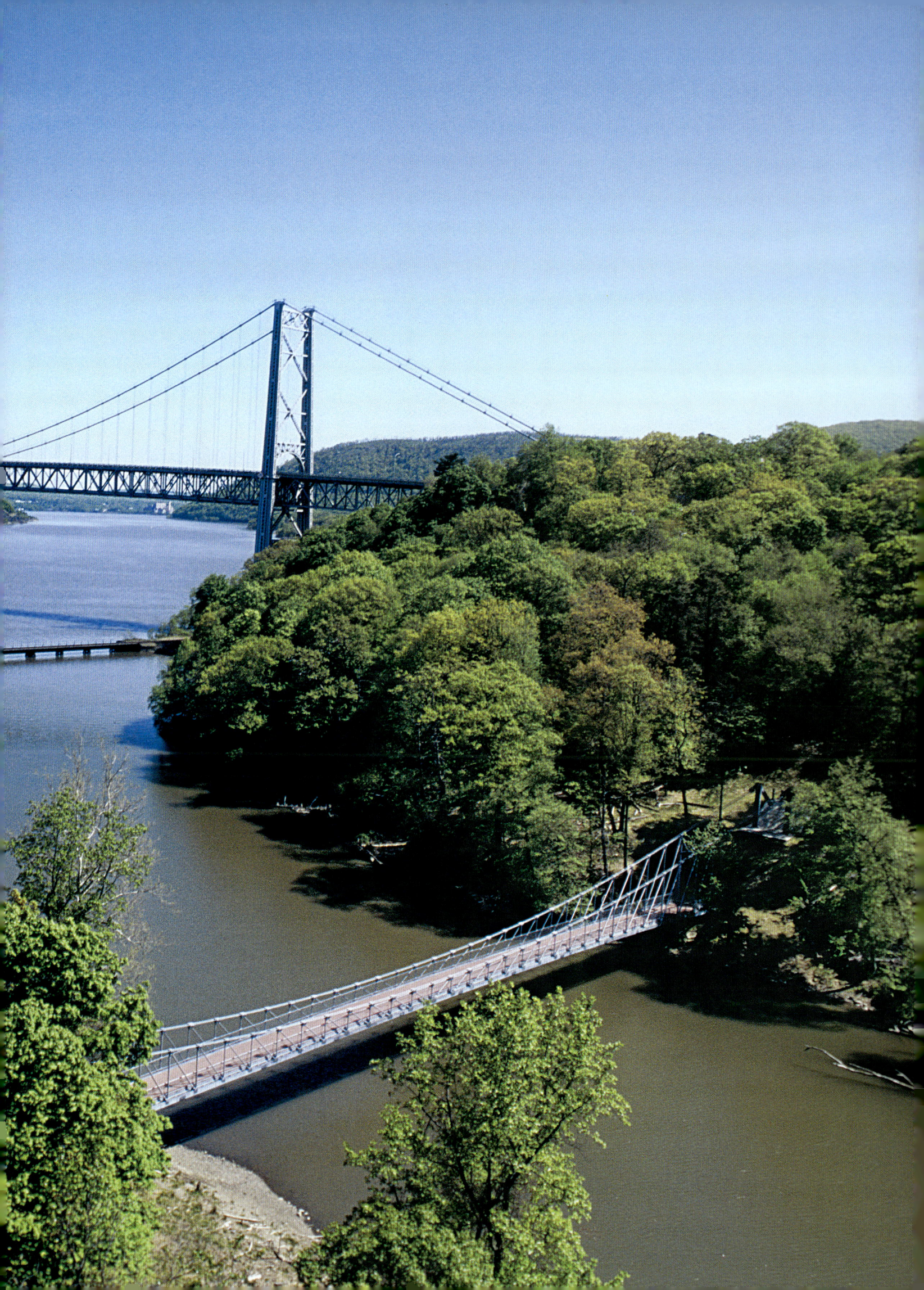

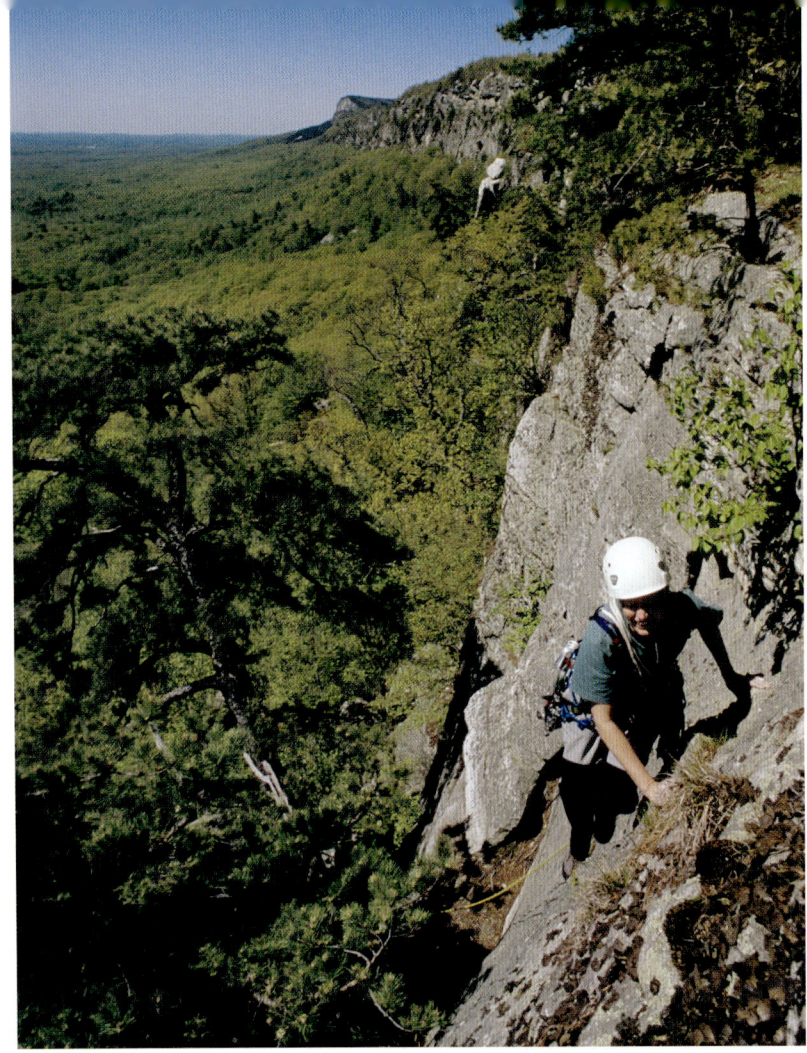

PREVIOUS SPREAD
Near Fort Montgomery, with the Bear Mountain Bridge in the background and the Popolopen Creek footbridge in the foreground, this view overlooks where colonists placed a chain across the Hudson River, attempting to hold back British forces during the American Revolution.

LEFT
The extensive cliffs on the east face of the Shawangunk Mountains near New Paltz are a world-renowned rock climbing location.

BELOW
The Riverfront Green Park in Peekskill overlooks Bear Mountain and the Hudson Highlands. It is part of a revitalization project to celebrate and protect the historic river.

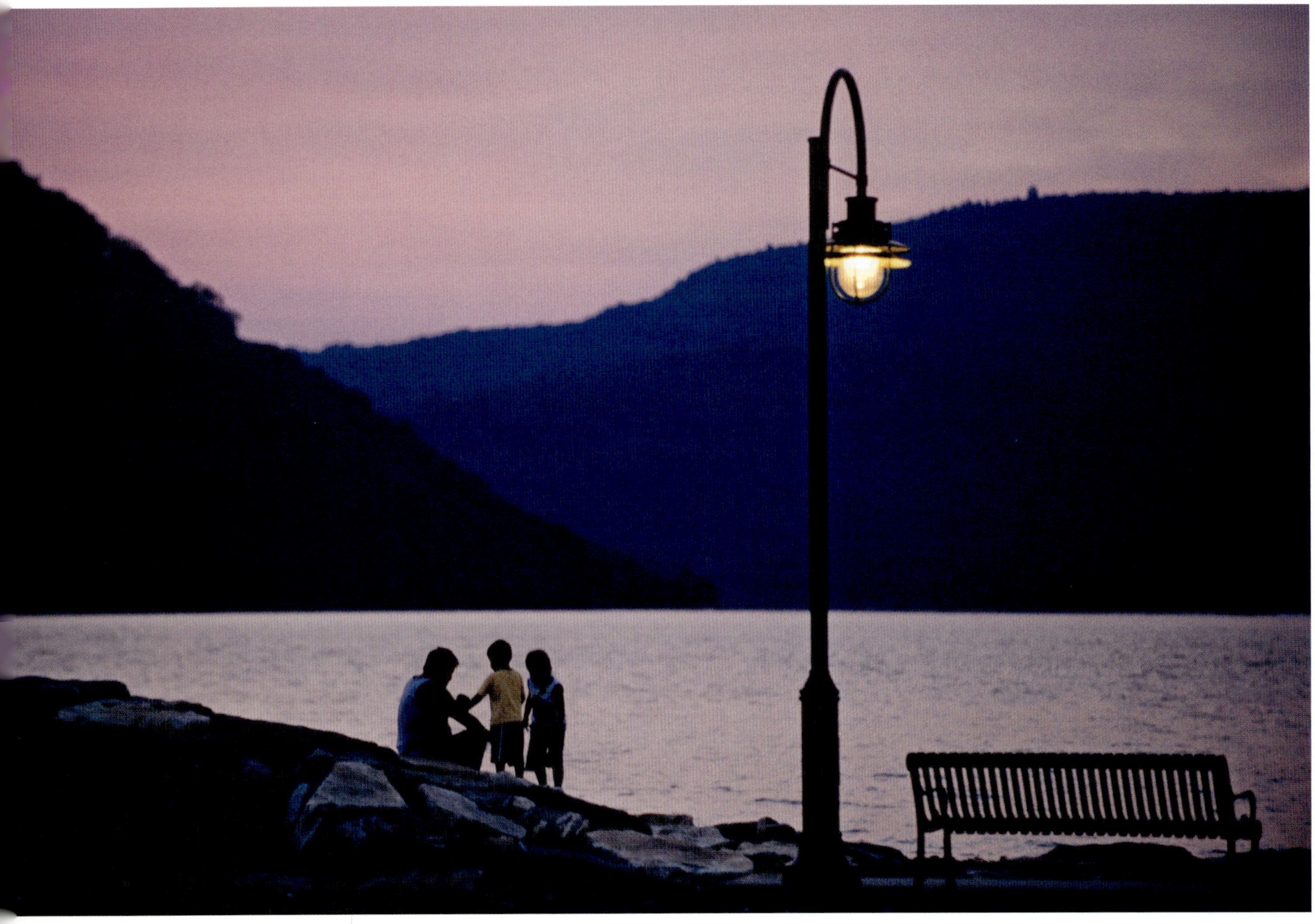

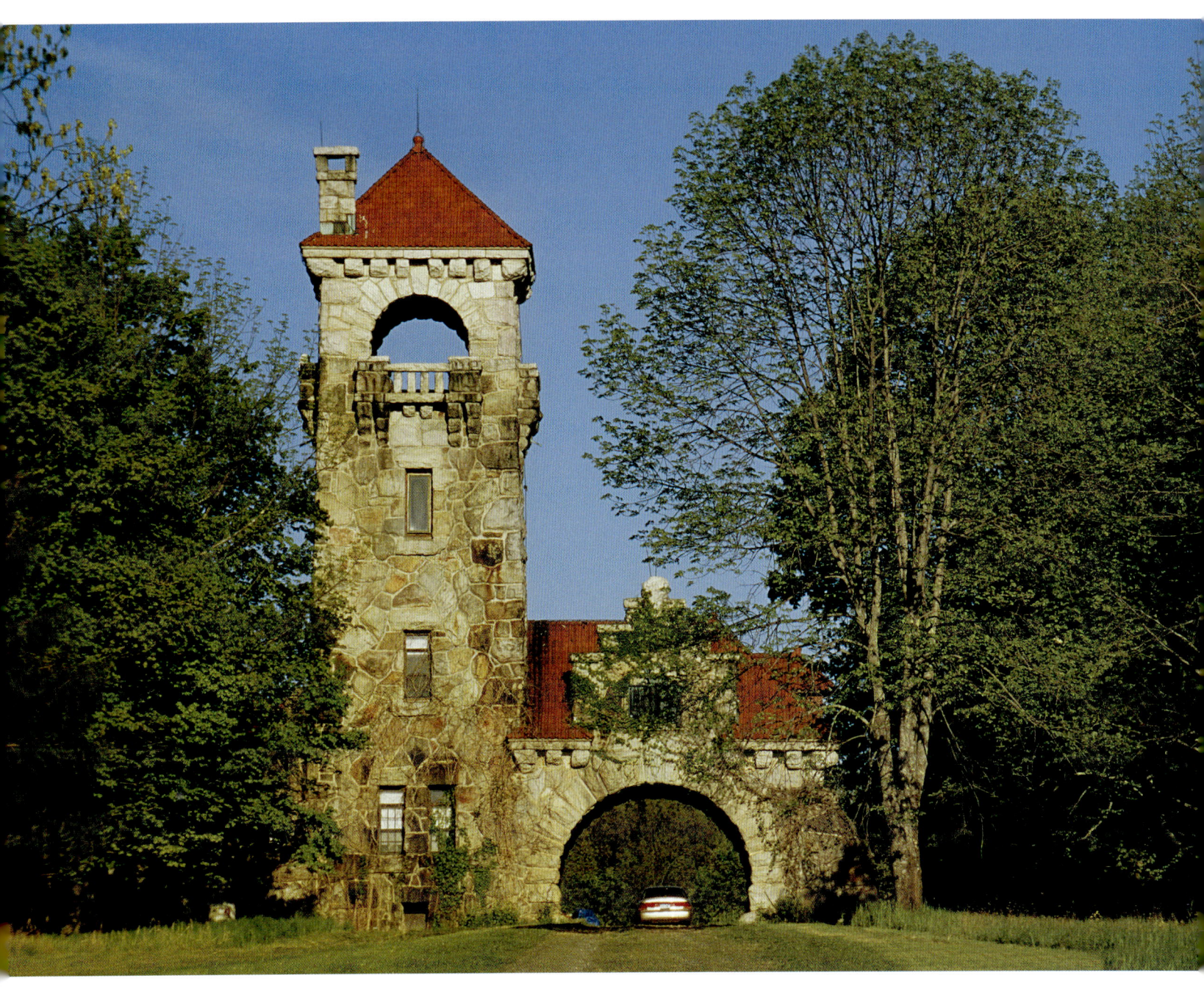

ABOVE

This stone gatehouse originally served as the main entrance for the Mohonk Mountain House resort, west of New Paltz. The resort is located within the Mohonk Preserve, which protects more than 6,500 acres of unique Shawangunk forests and cliffs.

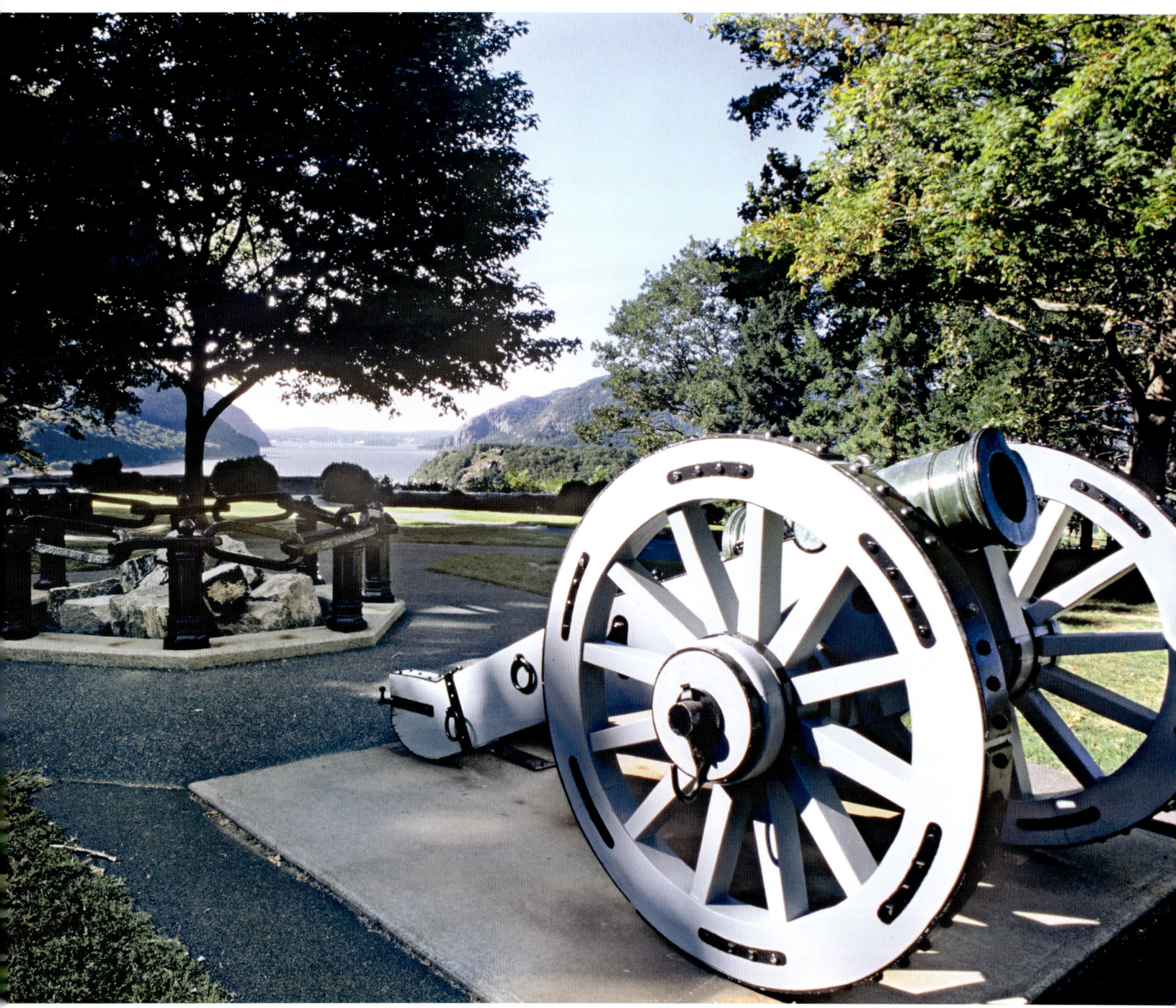

ABOVE

Trophy Point at the United States Military Academy at West Point offers a commanding view of the Hudson River. The chain is a section from the 1,500-foot-long, 186-ton chain that was stretched across the river to block the British advance during the Revolutionary War.

OPPOSITE, TOP AND BOTTOM

Built for oil tycoon John D. Rockefeller, the Kykuit estate is one of the most majestic of the grand estates in the beautiful Hudson River Highlands. Extensive terraced gardens, sculptures, and other works of art are perfectly situated around the estate. Four generations of Rockefellers lived at Kykuit, including Nelson A. Rockefeller, a four-term governor of New York and vice president of the United States under President Gerald Ford.

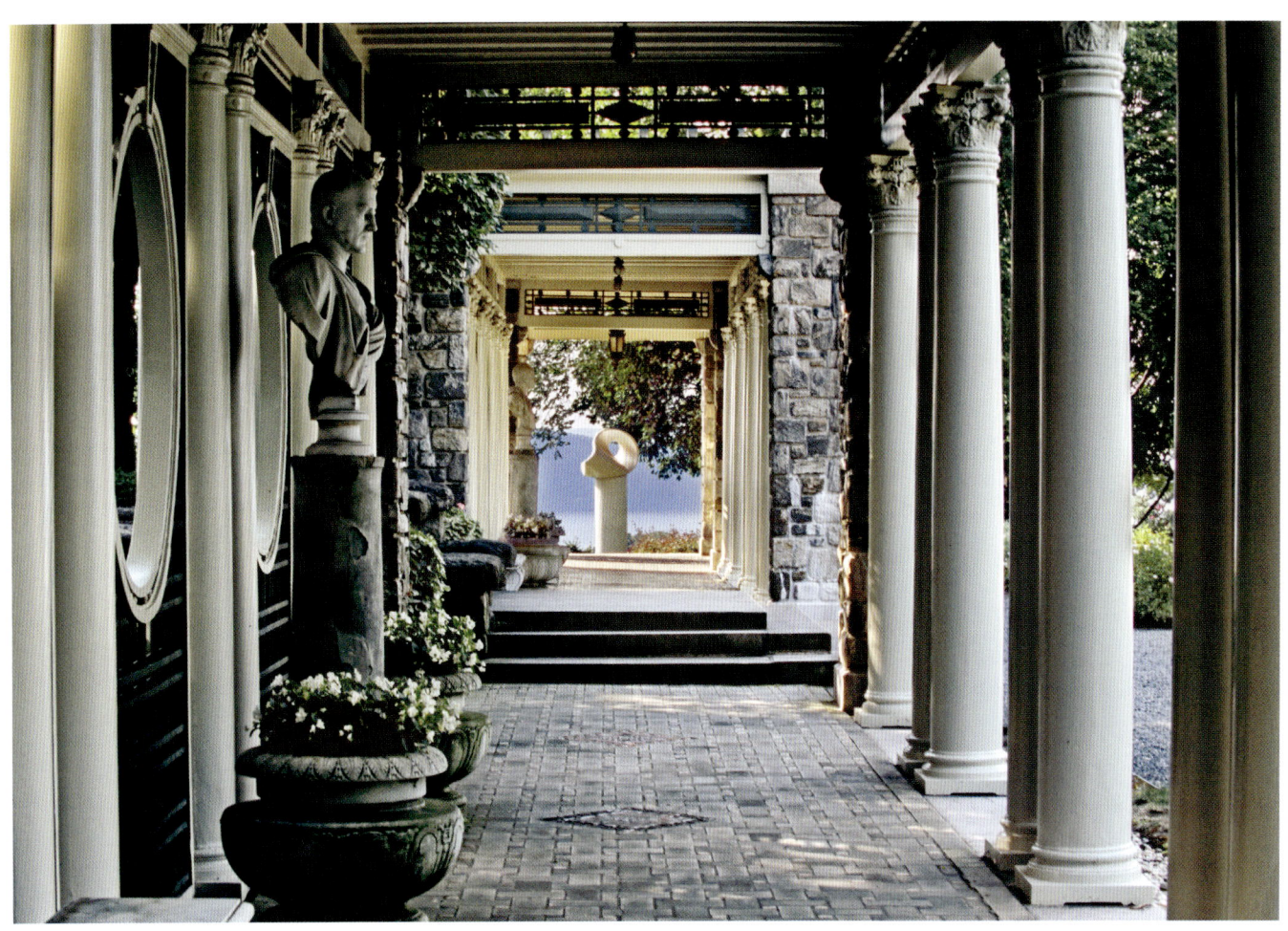

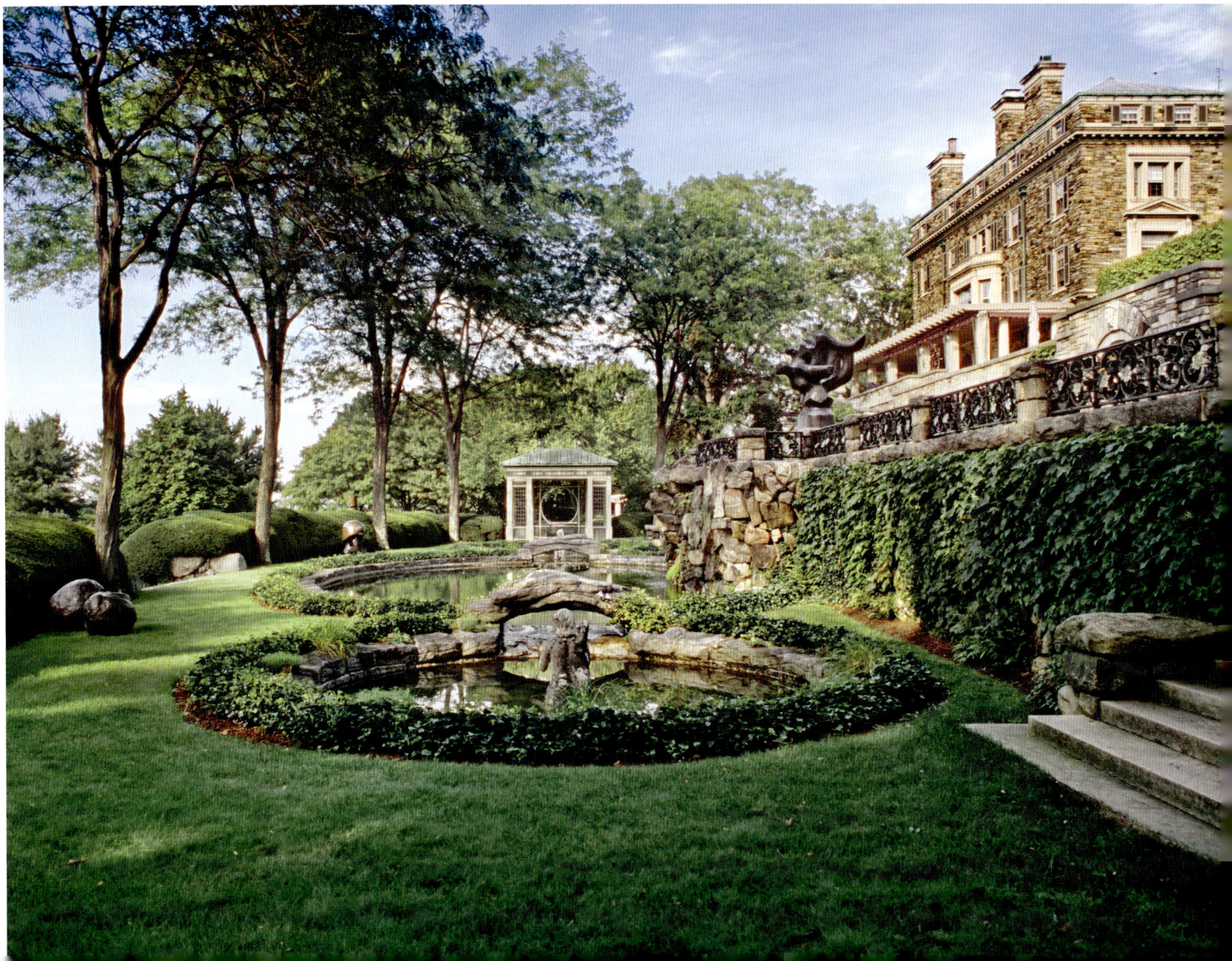

RIGHT

Sunnyside, another Hudson Valley classic home, is the restored residence of author Washington Irving, best known for his works *Rip Van Winkle* and *The Legend of Sleepy Hollow*.

BELOW

Lyndhurst, situated on a scenic Hudson overlook in Tarrytown, is an exquisite example of a Gothic Revival mansion. It was designed by renowned architect Alexander Jackson Davis in 1838.

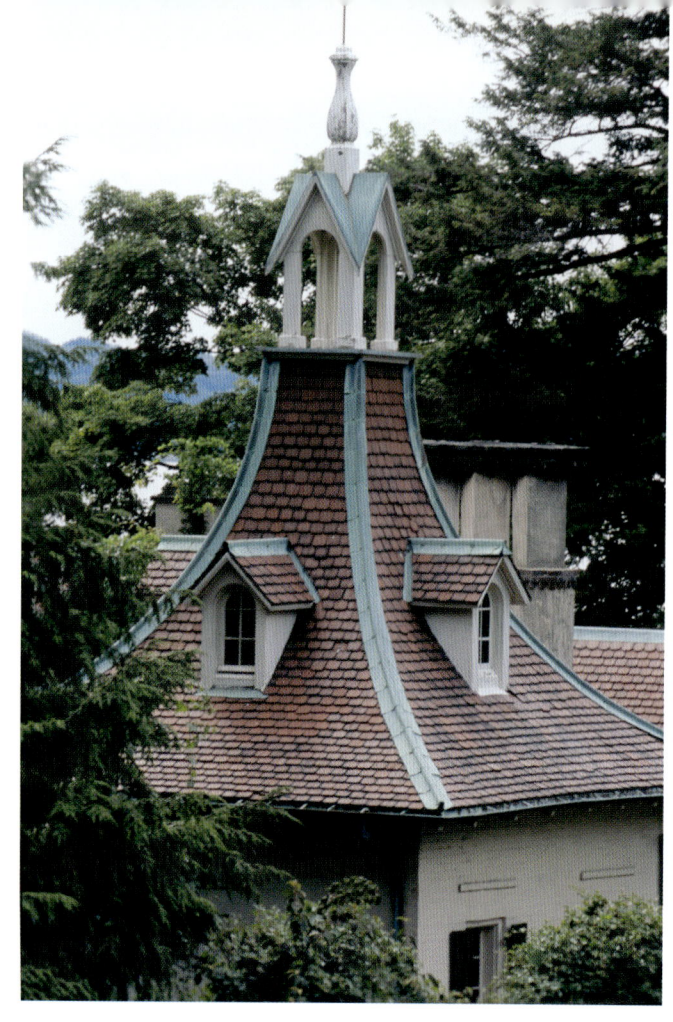

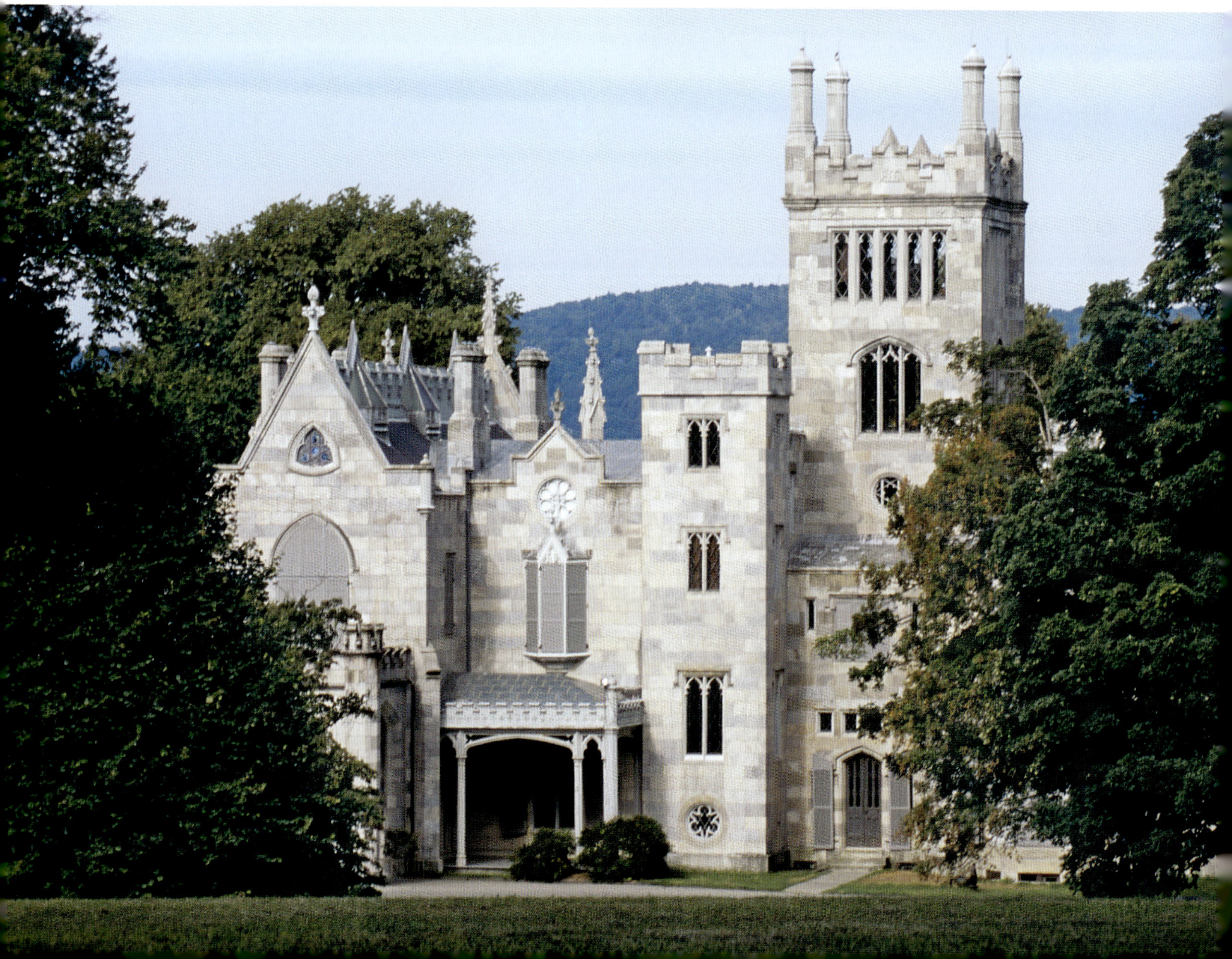

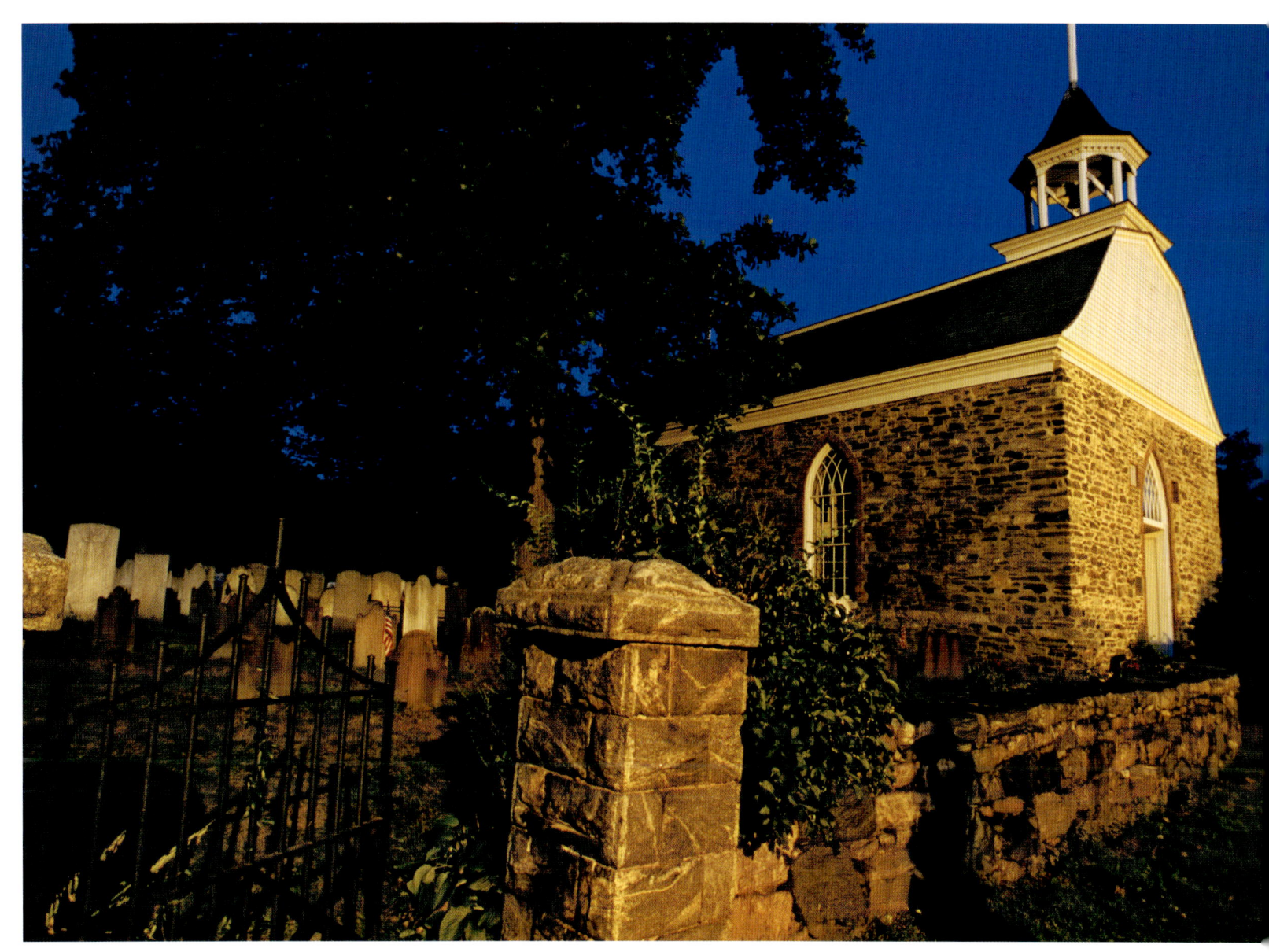

ABOVE

In the town of Sleepy Hollow is the Old Dutch Church and cemetery, which is surrounded by the Sleepy Hollow Cemetery—the setting for Washington Irving's legendary tale.

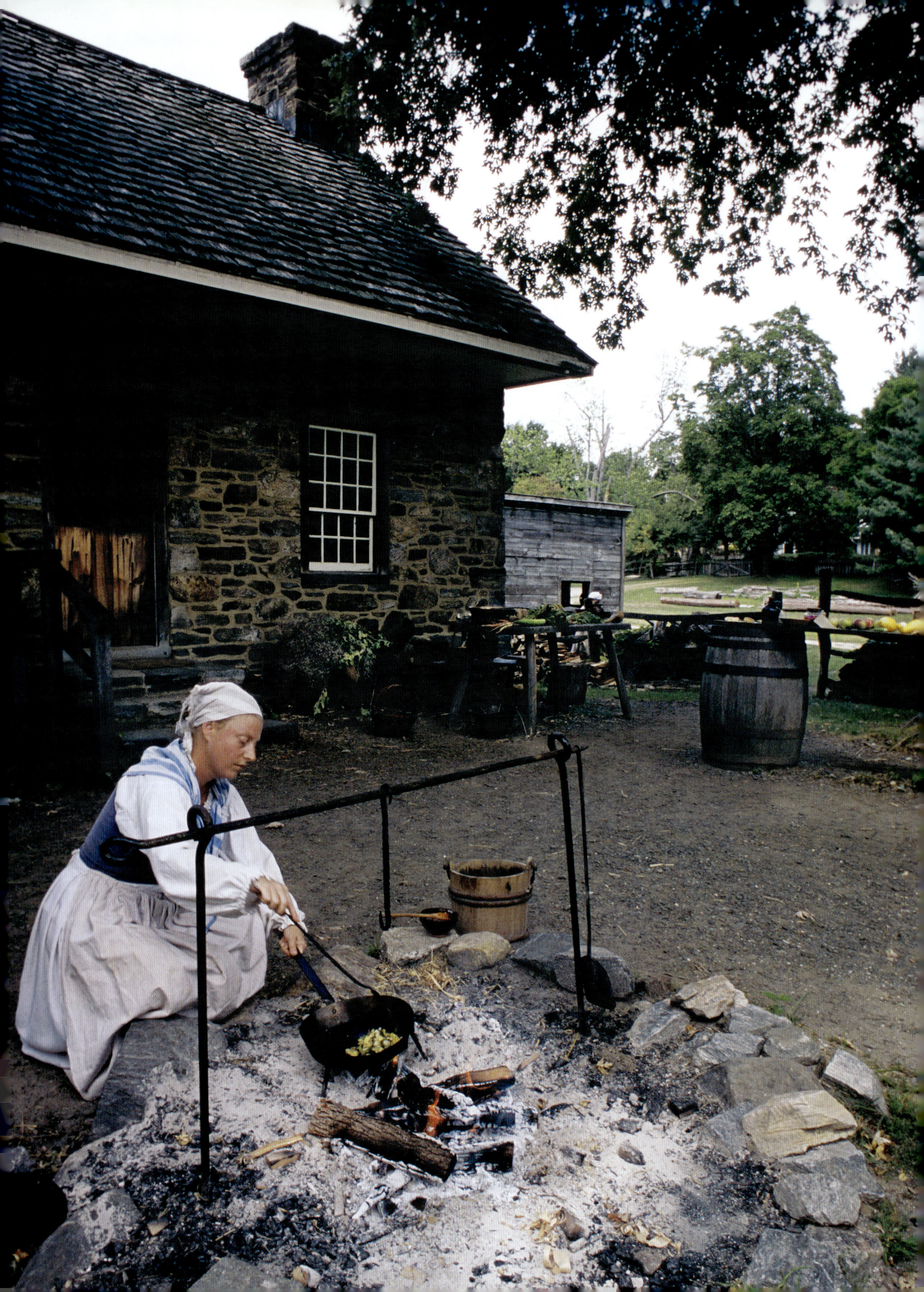

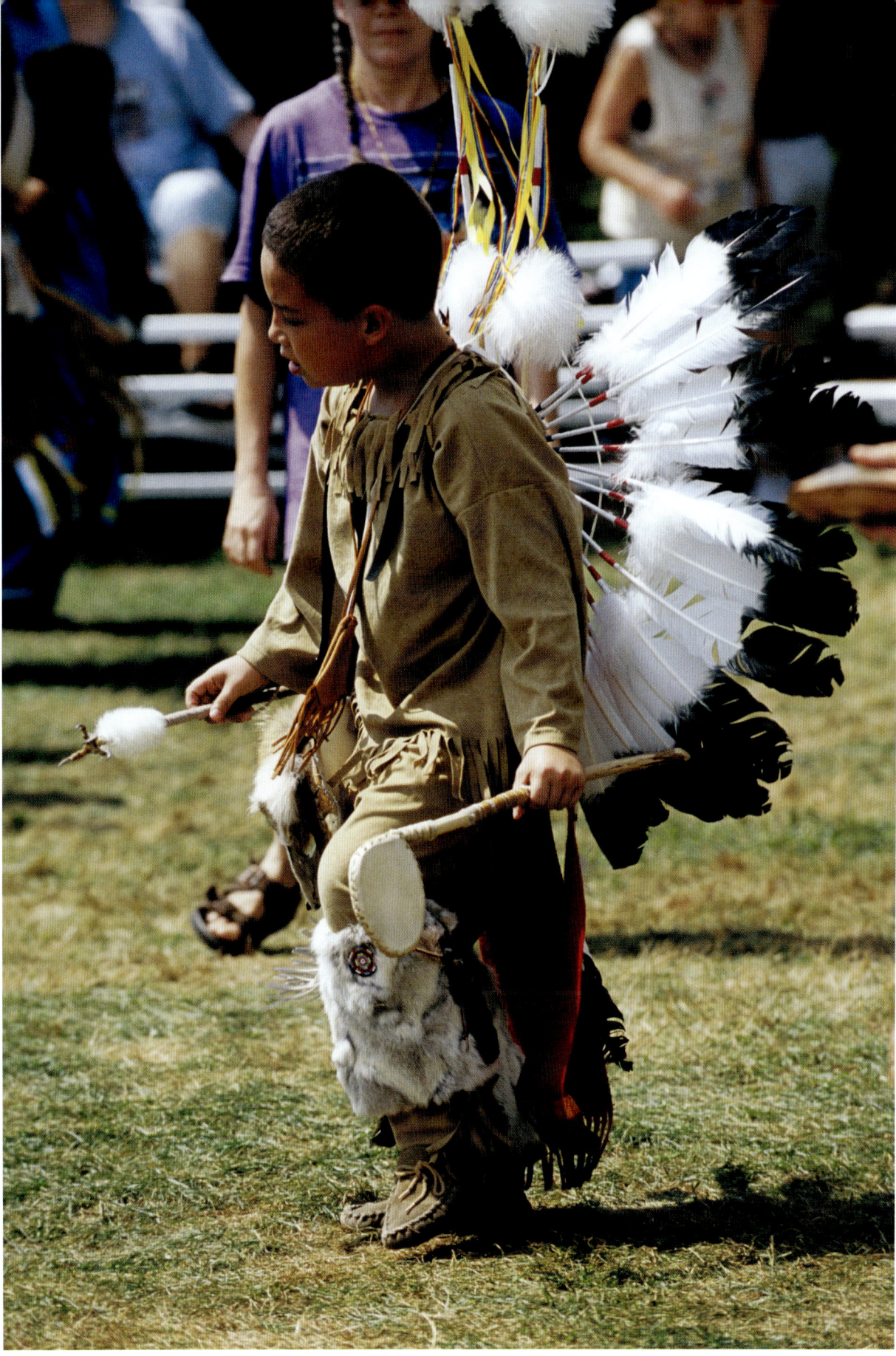

LEFT

Philipsburg Manor is an authentically restored trading complex of the early 1700s that was once a sizeable Hudson Valley manor. The grounds include the manor house, a tenant house, a grist mill, a slave garden, a working barn, and traditional livestock.

ABOVE

Native Americans have lived in New York since the retreat of the last glaciers thousands of years ago. Their history and culture continue to be celebrated in regional pow wows, such as the Daniel Nimham Intertribal Pow Wow in Putnam County.

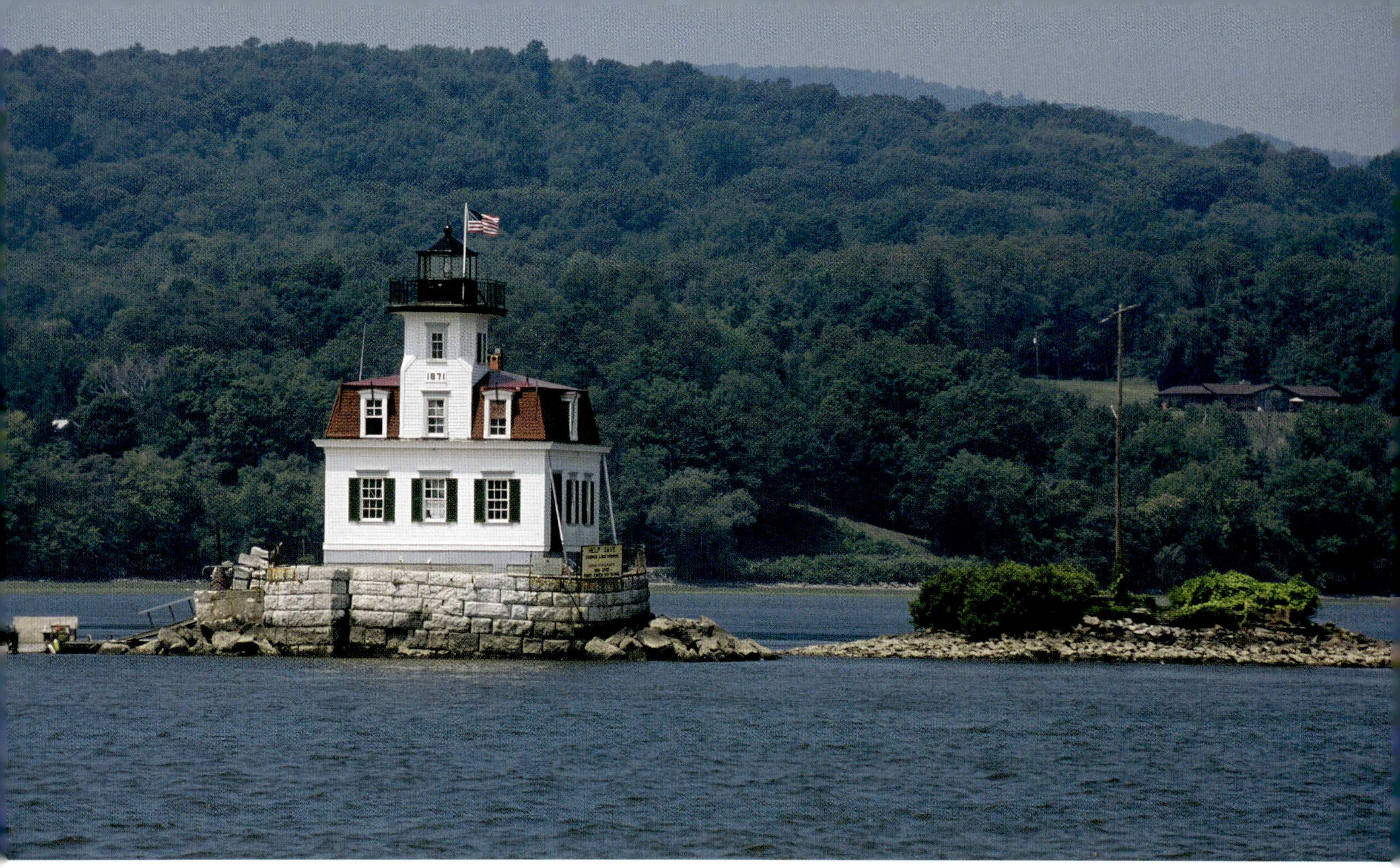

ABOVE

Four of the Hudson River's seven active lighthouses are found between Hyde Park and the city of Hudson. Esopus Lighthouse is the last of the wood-frame lighthouses on the river and has been recently restored for active use.

BELOW

Rondout Lighthouse, located in Kingston, was built in 1913–1915 and restored in the 1980s.

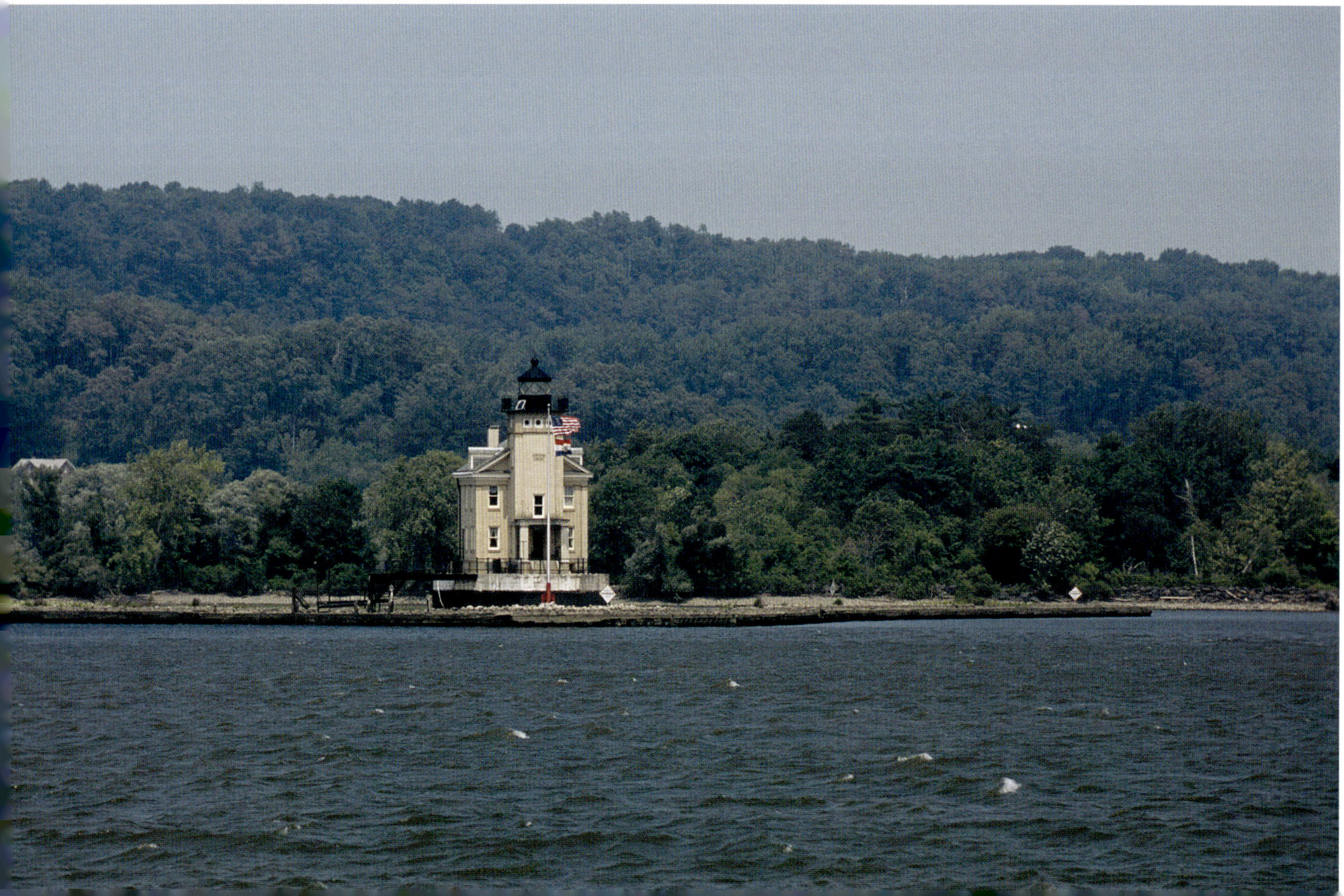

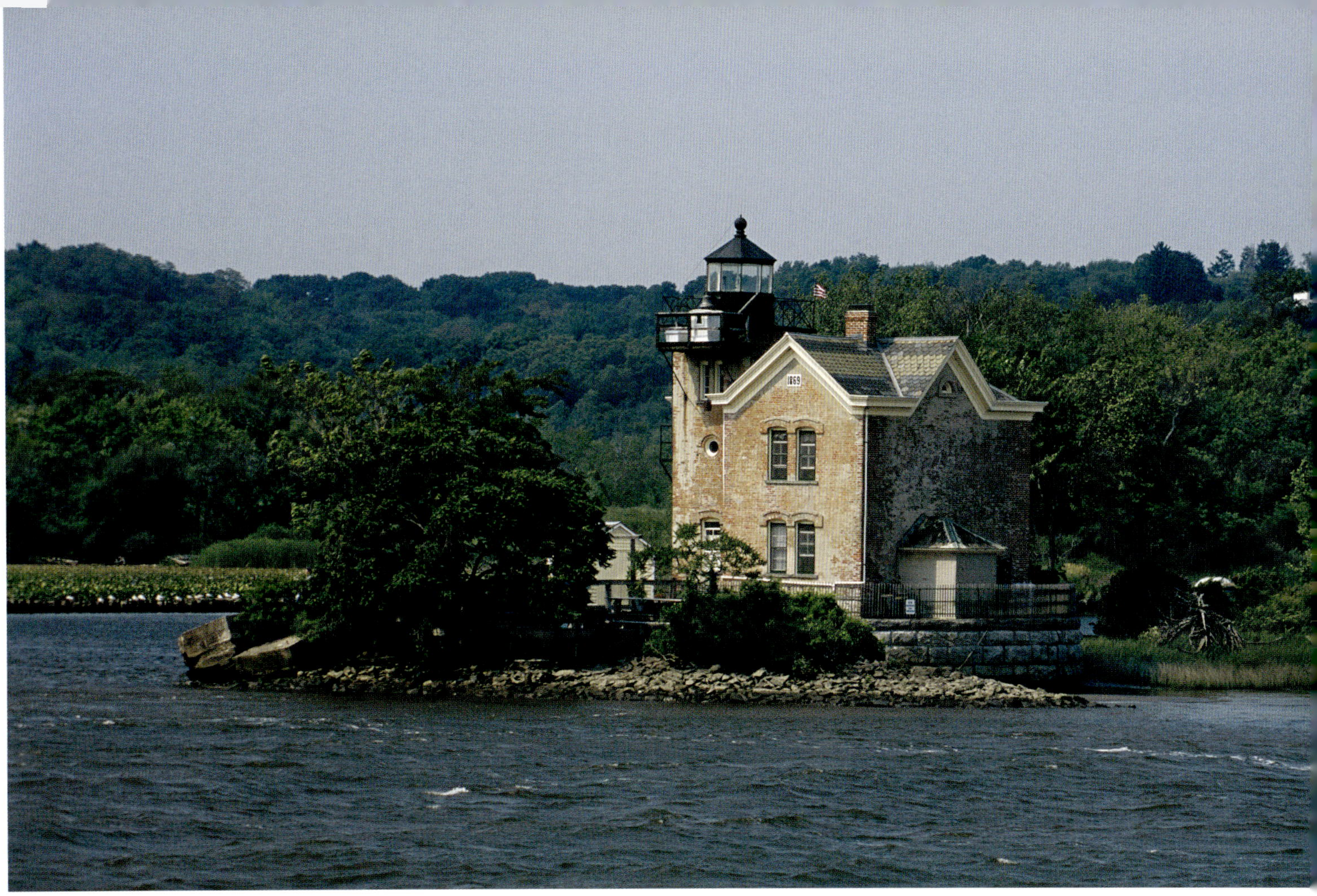

ABOVE
The 1869 Saugerties Lighthouse was fully restored in the late 1980s and is currently operated as a bed and breakfast.

BELOW
The beautifully restored Hudson-Athens Lighthouse has one of the few remaining fog bells in the United States.

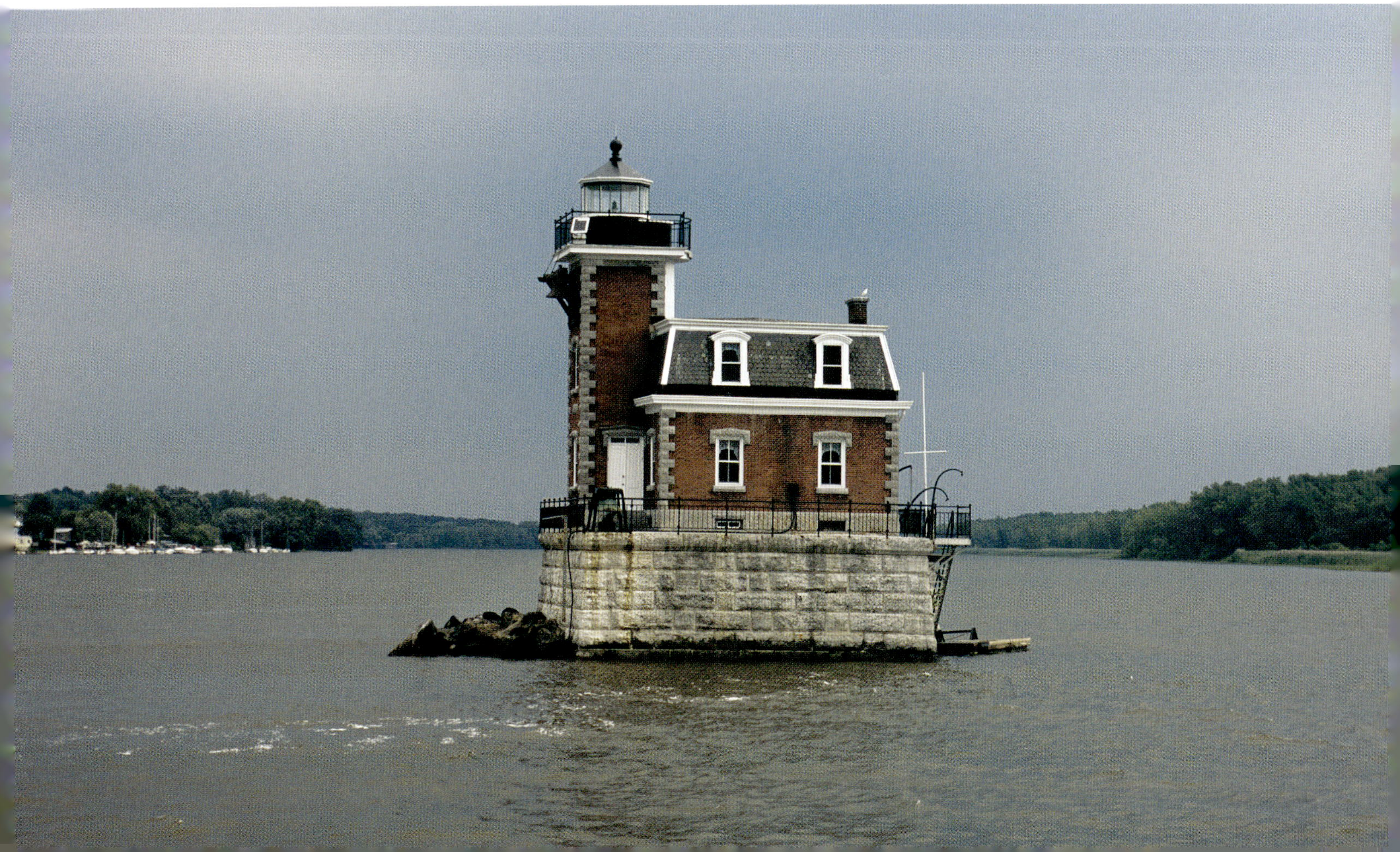

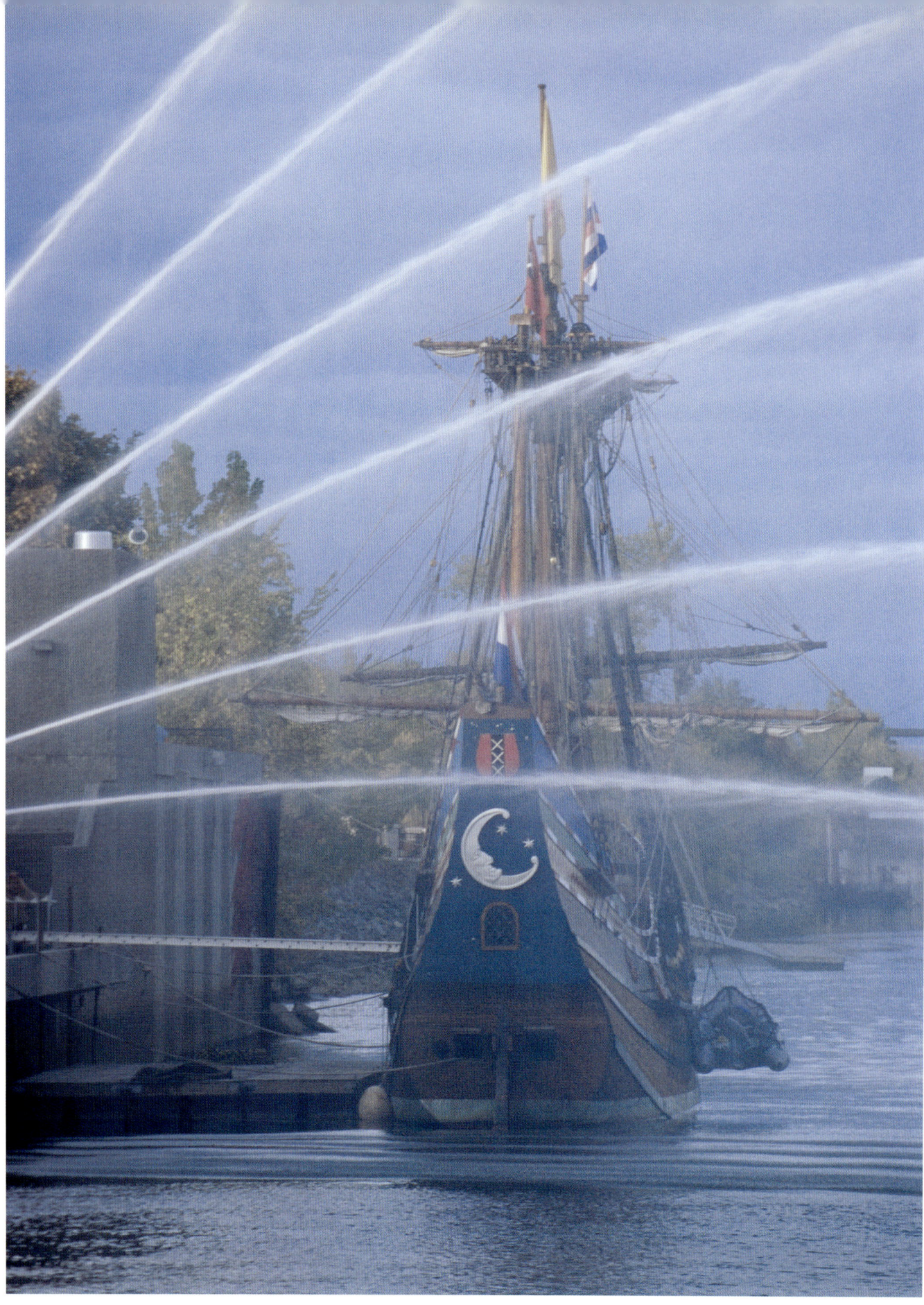

ABOVE

A replica of the *Half Moon*—the 85-foot-long ship on which Henry Hudson sailed up the Hudson River in 1609—prepares to leave Albany's Corning Preserve waterfront, with water cannons blasting.

RIGHT

A combination of Italian Renaissance and Romanesque architecture, the capitol building in Albany is among the most interestingly designed government buildings in the United States.

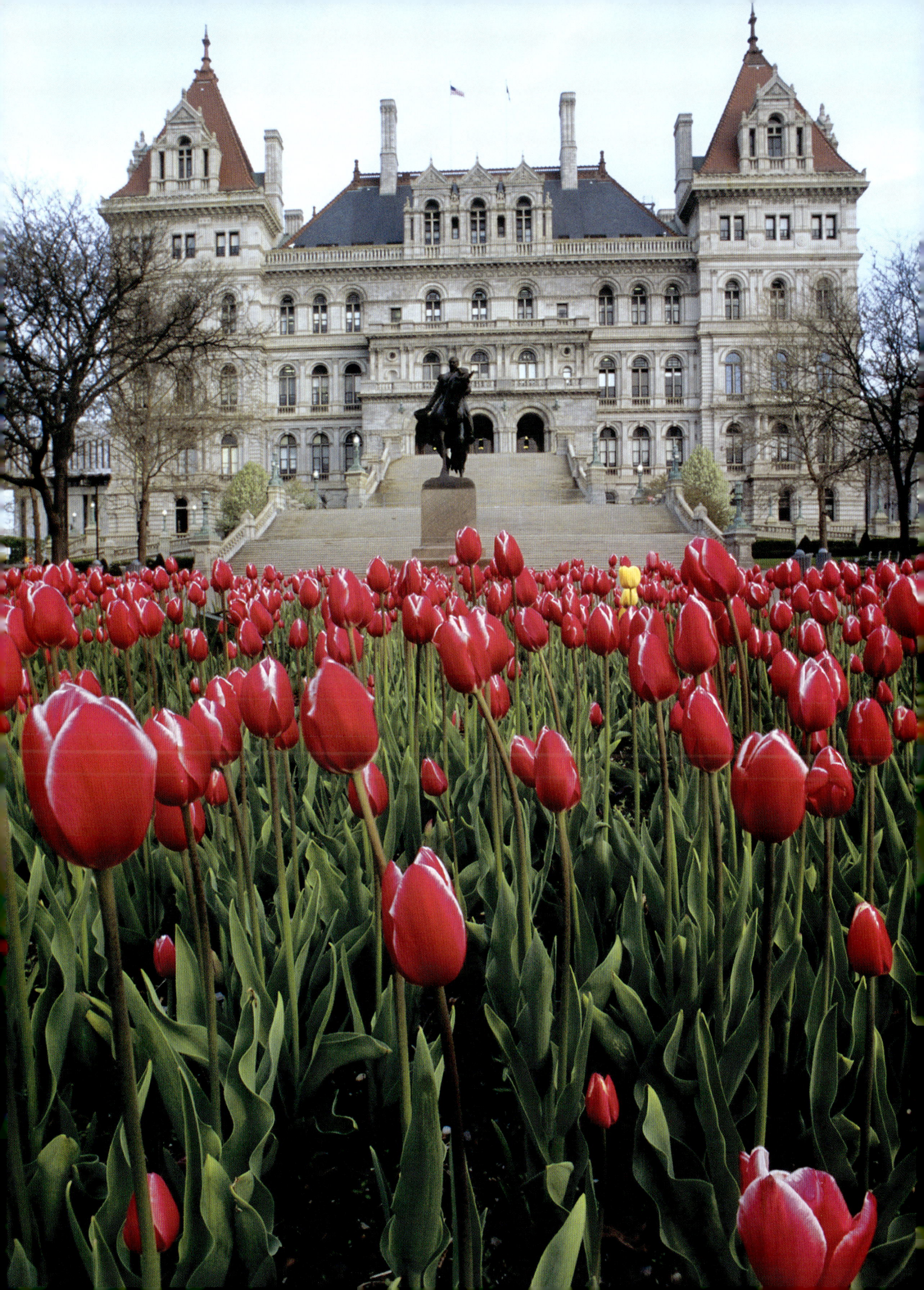

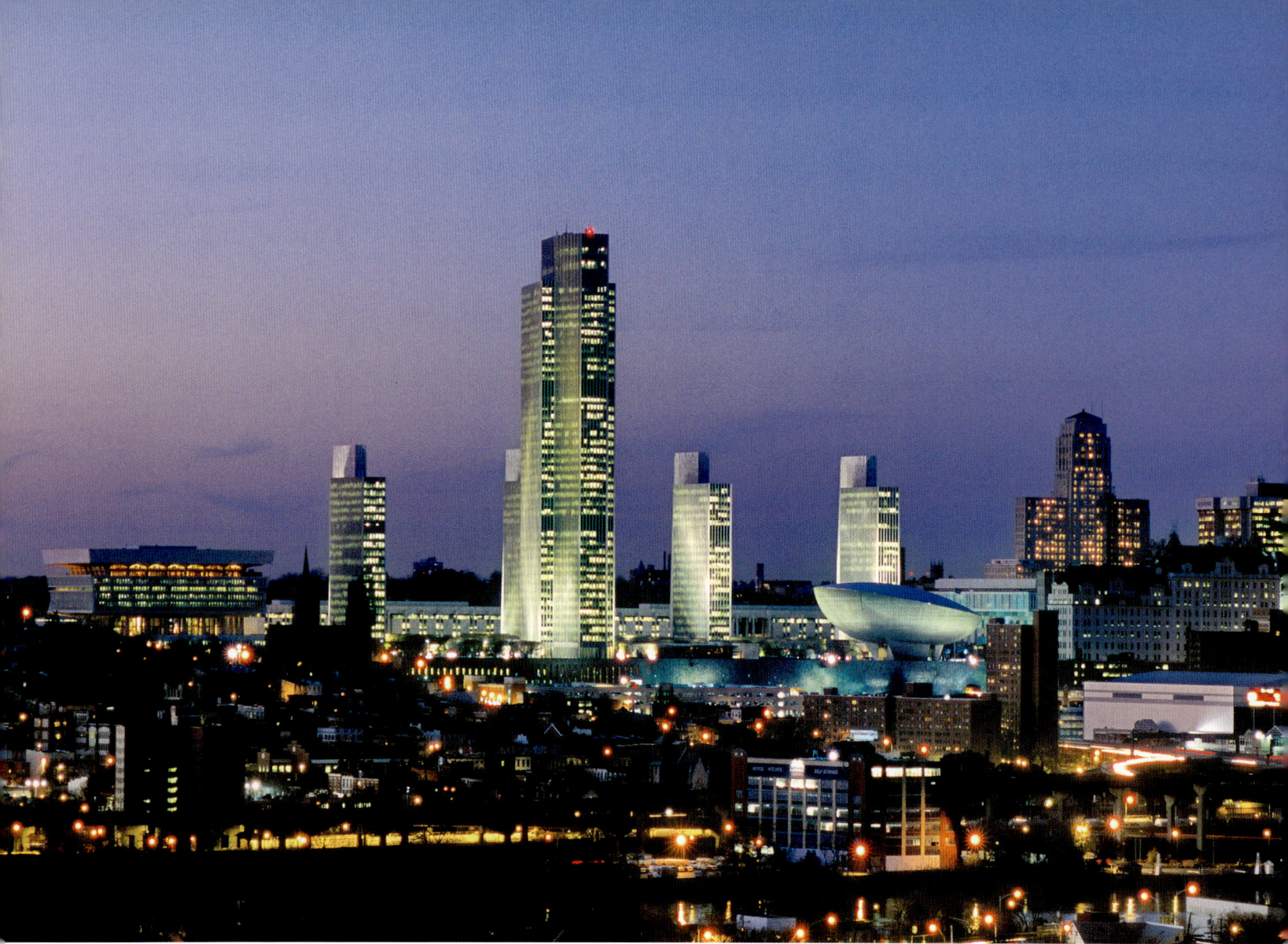

ABOVE

Albany, the capital of New York, is a glorious site in evening twilight. The centerpiece of downtown Albany is the Empire State Plaza. Nearby are the state capitol and office buildings.

RIGHT

Among Albany's many annual events is the Tulip Festival, held each year in Washington Park.

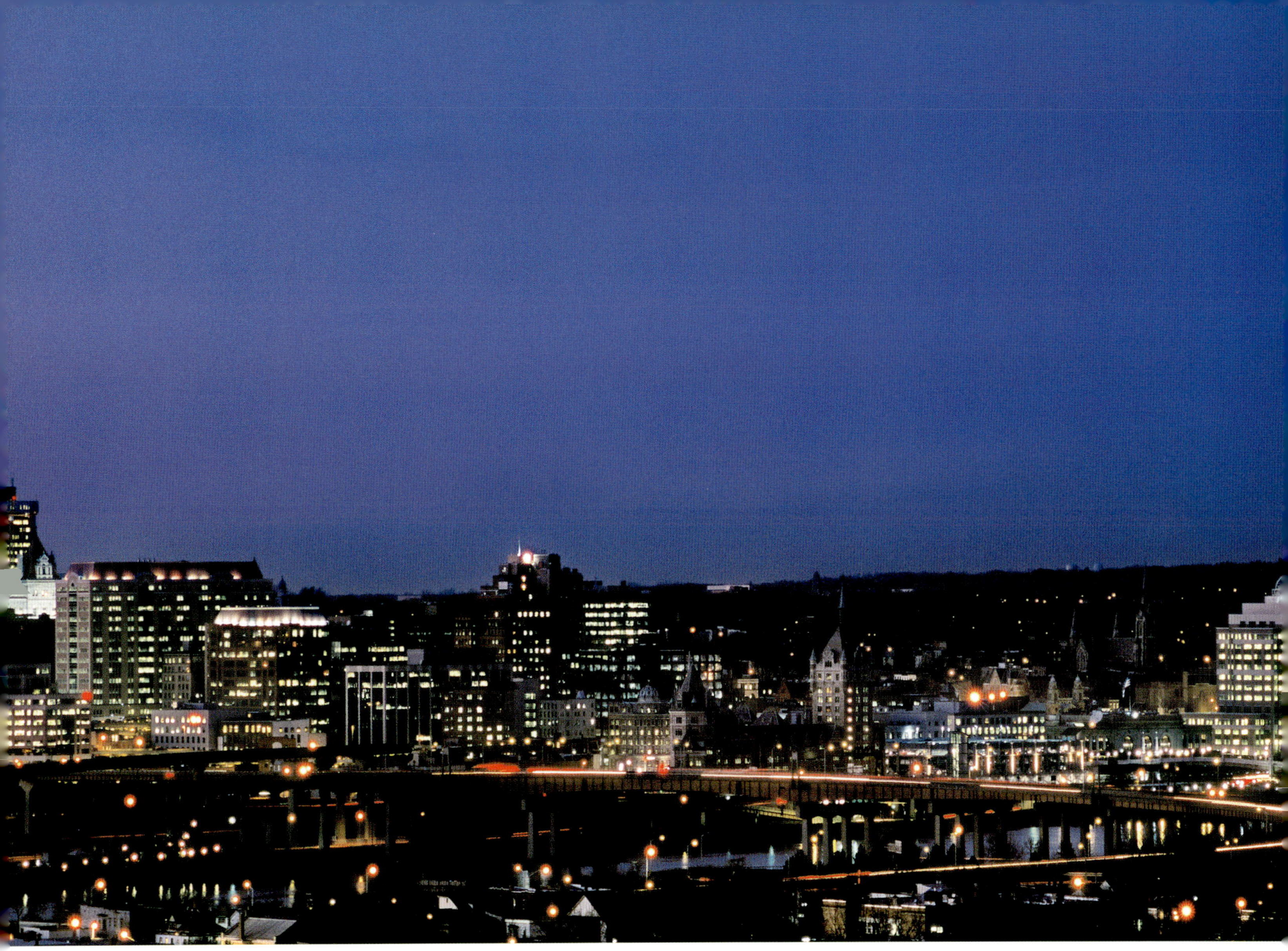

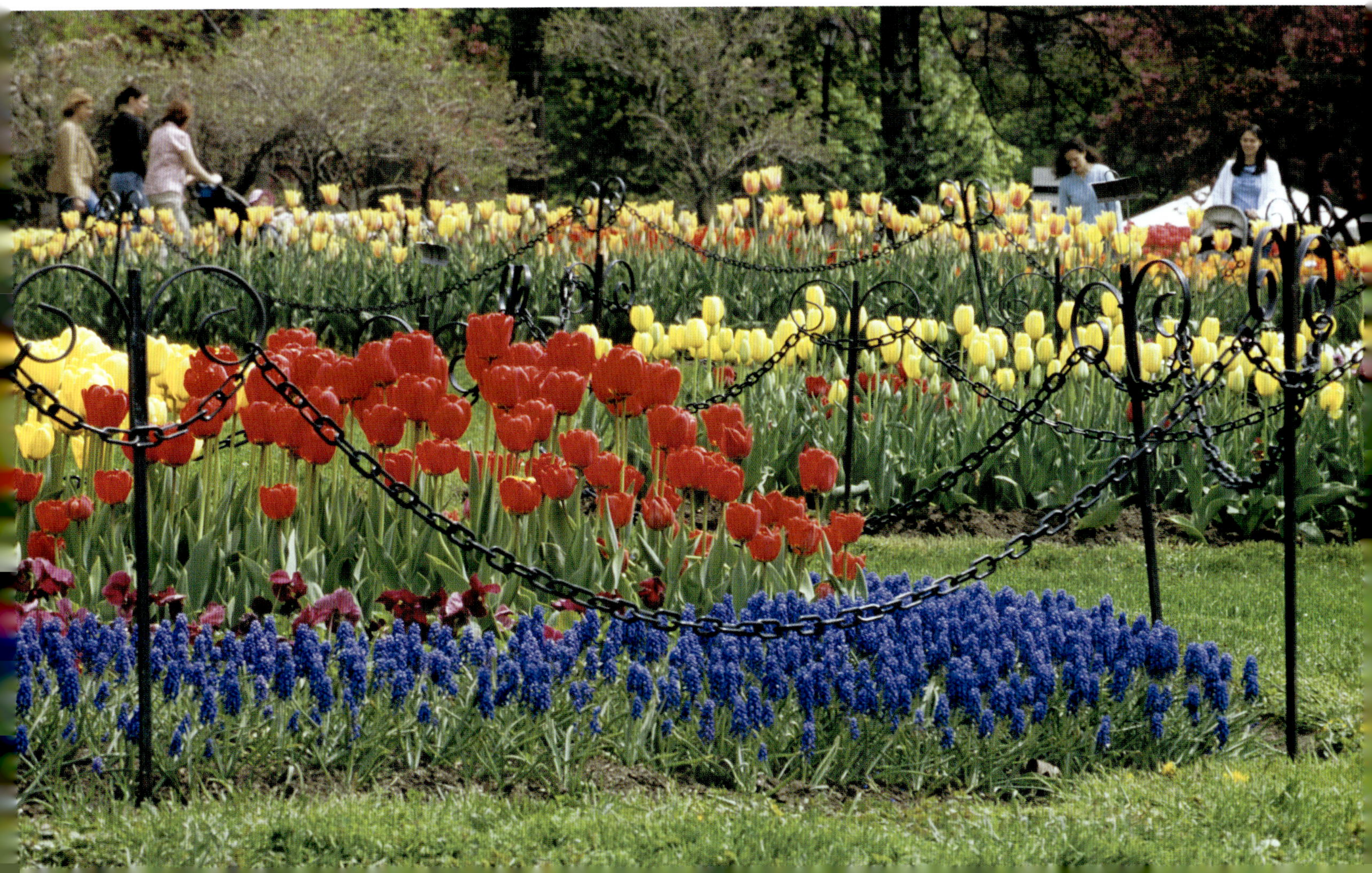

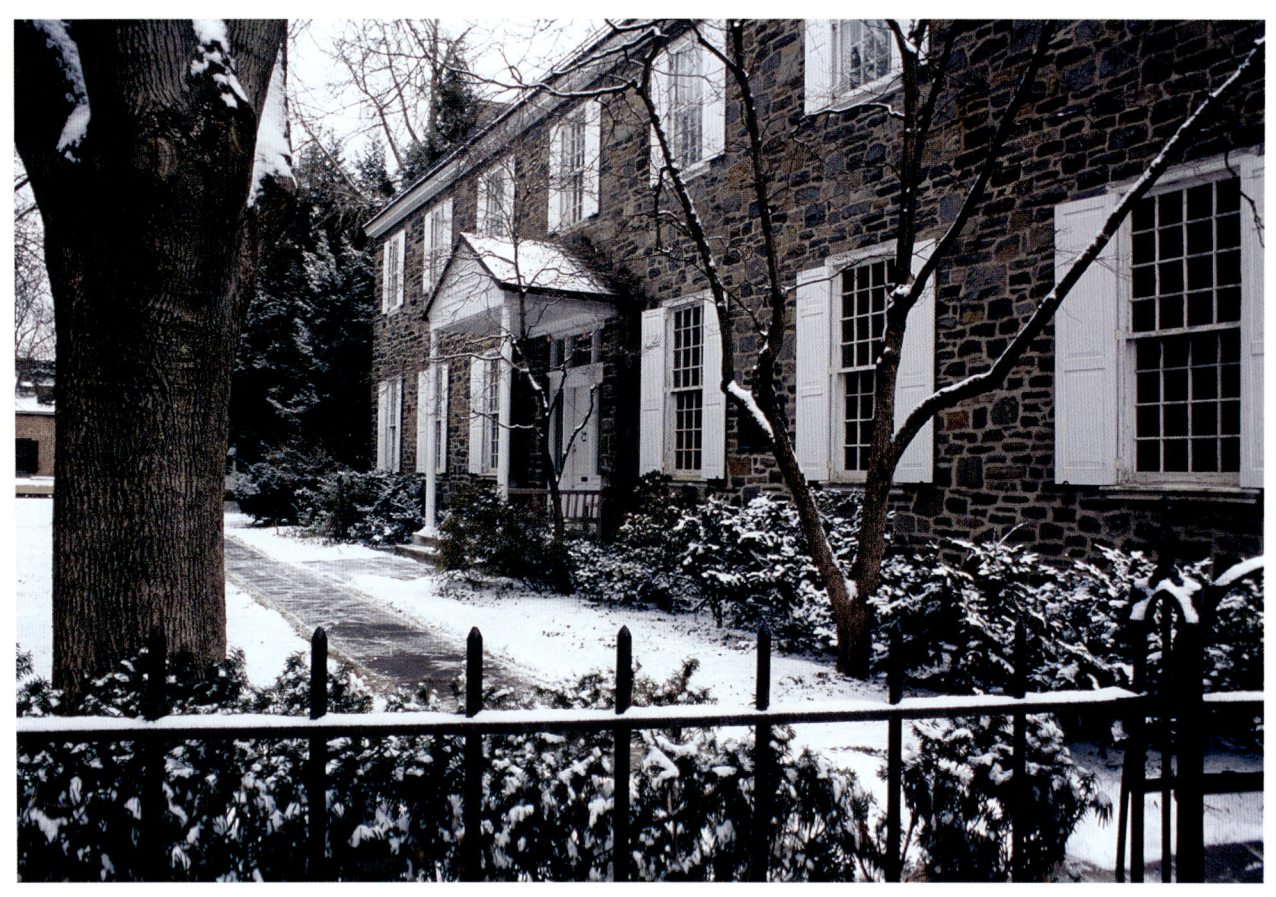

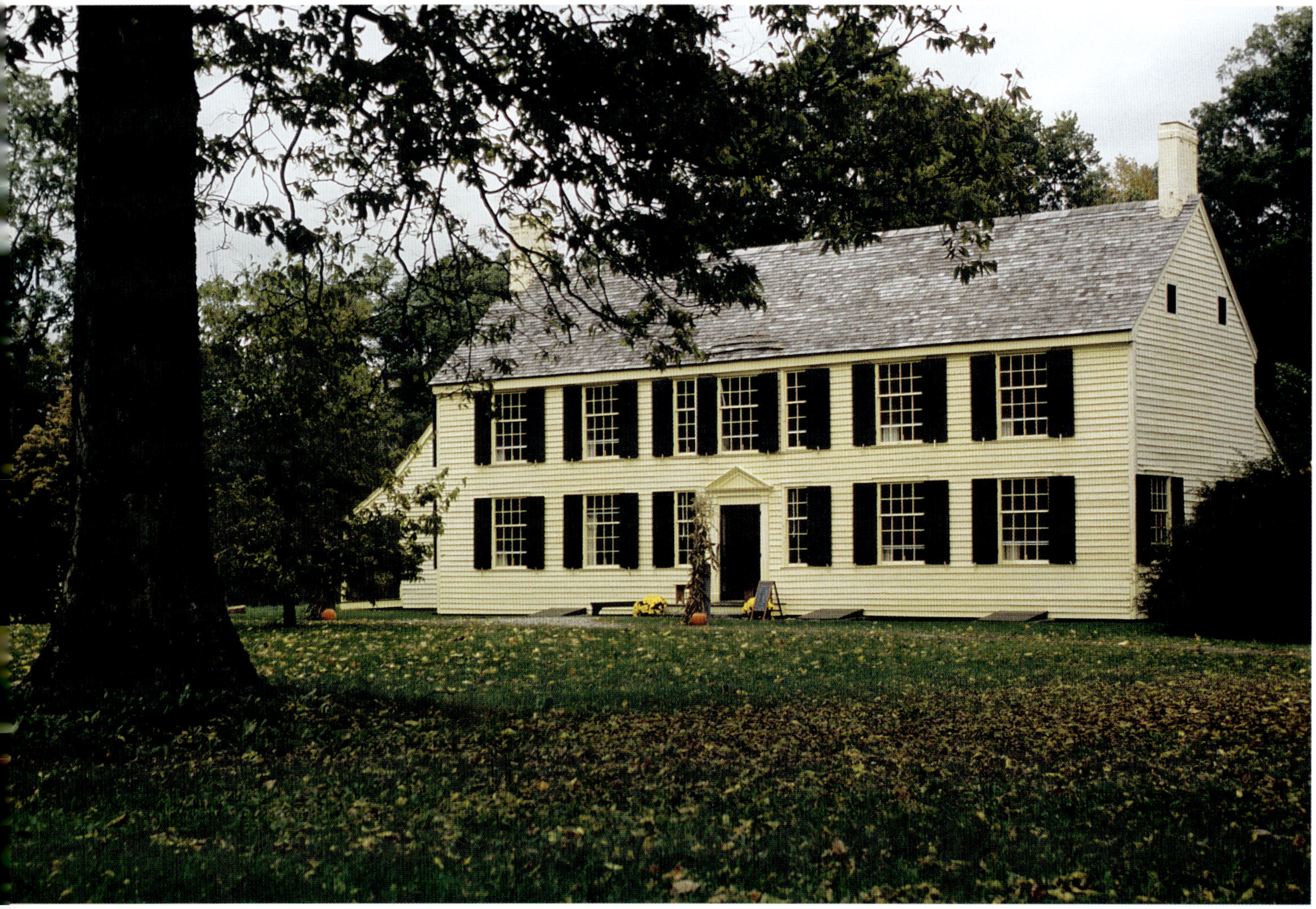

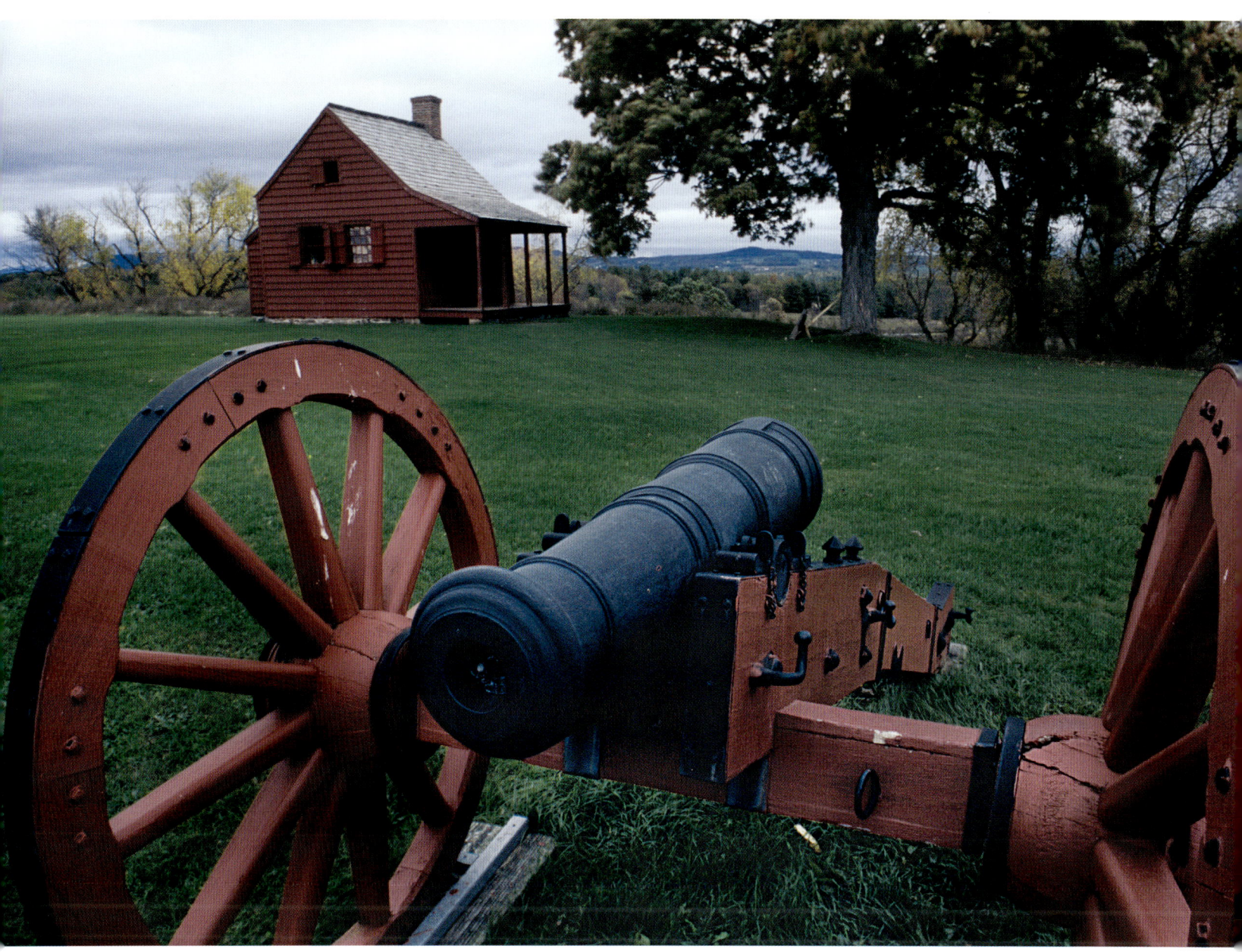

ABOVE

The Battles of Saratoga played a pivotal role in our nation's fight for independence. The Neilson Farm, located on Bemis Heights above the Hudson River, served as quarters for American staff officers in September 1777. From entrenched positions on Bemis Heights, the Americans, under General Horatio Gates, held off two advances by British troops under General John Burgoyne. On October 17, 1777, Burgoyne surrendered to Gates, in what is considered the turning point of the Revolutionary War.

OPPOSITE, TOP

In September 1777, the New York legislature met for the first time in Kingston, making it the first capital of New York State.

OPPOSITE, BOTTOM

The Schuyler House was the summer retreat of General Philip Schuyler. It was burned by General Burgoyne in September 1777 and later rebuilt on the same spot. The home hosted many notable visitors, including George Washington, Benjamin Franklin, Alexander Hamilton, and the Marquis de Lafayette.

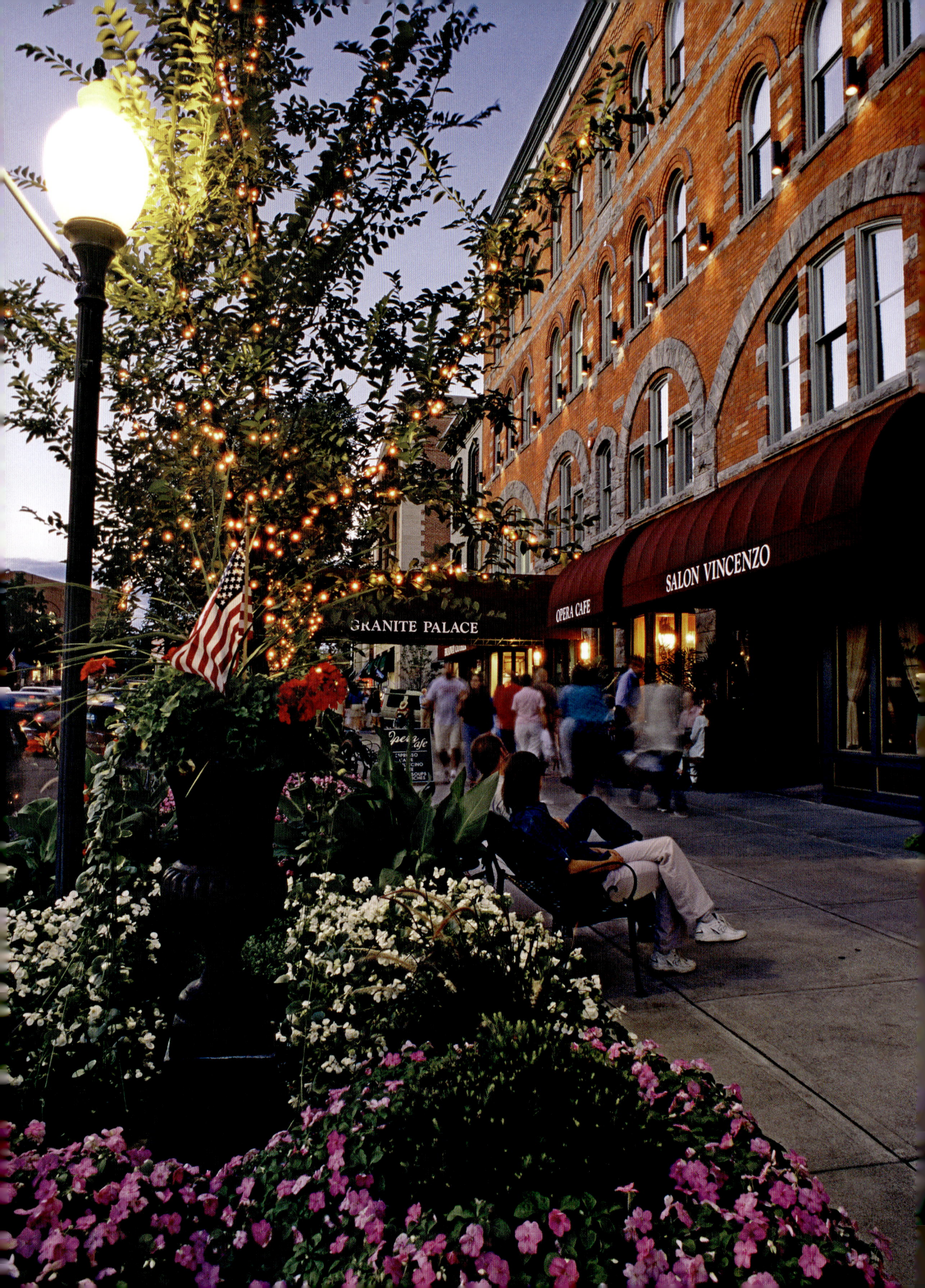

RIGHT

In operation since 1863, Saratoga Race Course is the oldest horse racing track in the country. The Travers Stakes has been a highlight of each summer since 1864.

BELOW

Horses and jockeys prepare for the day's races at Saratoga Race Course with an early morning workout.

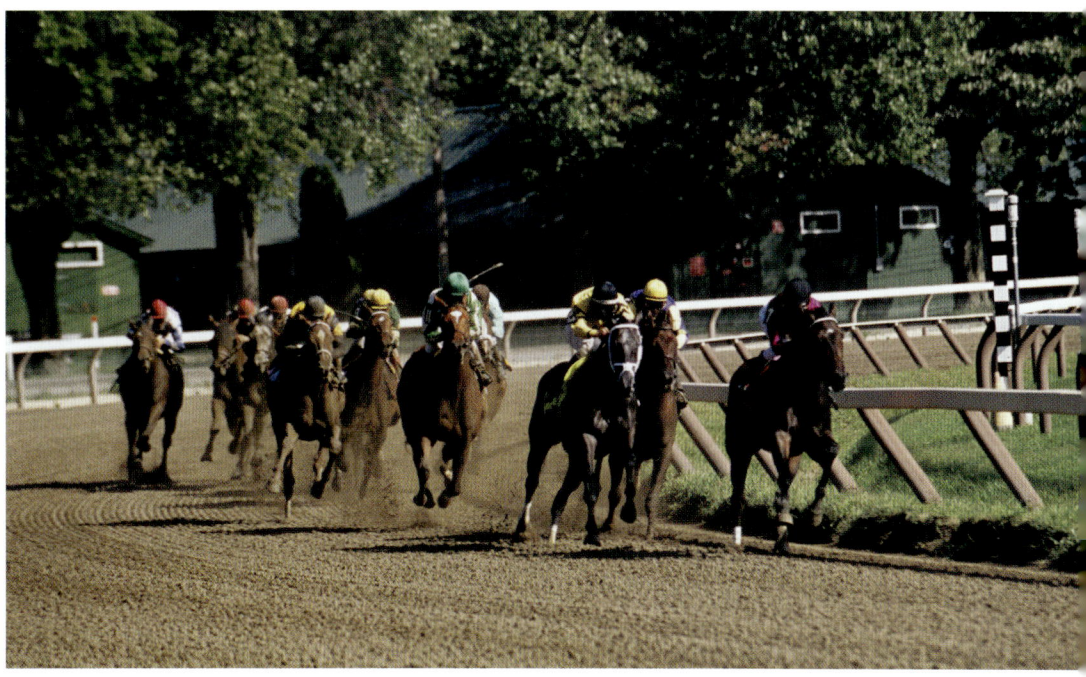

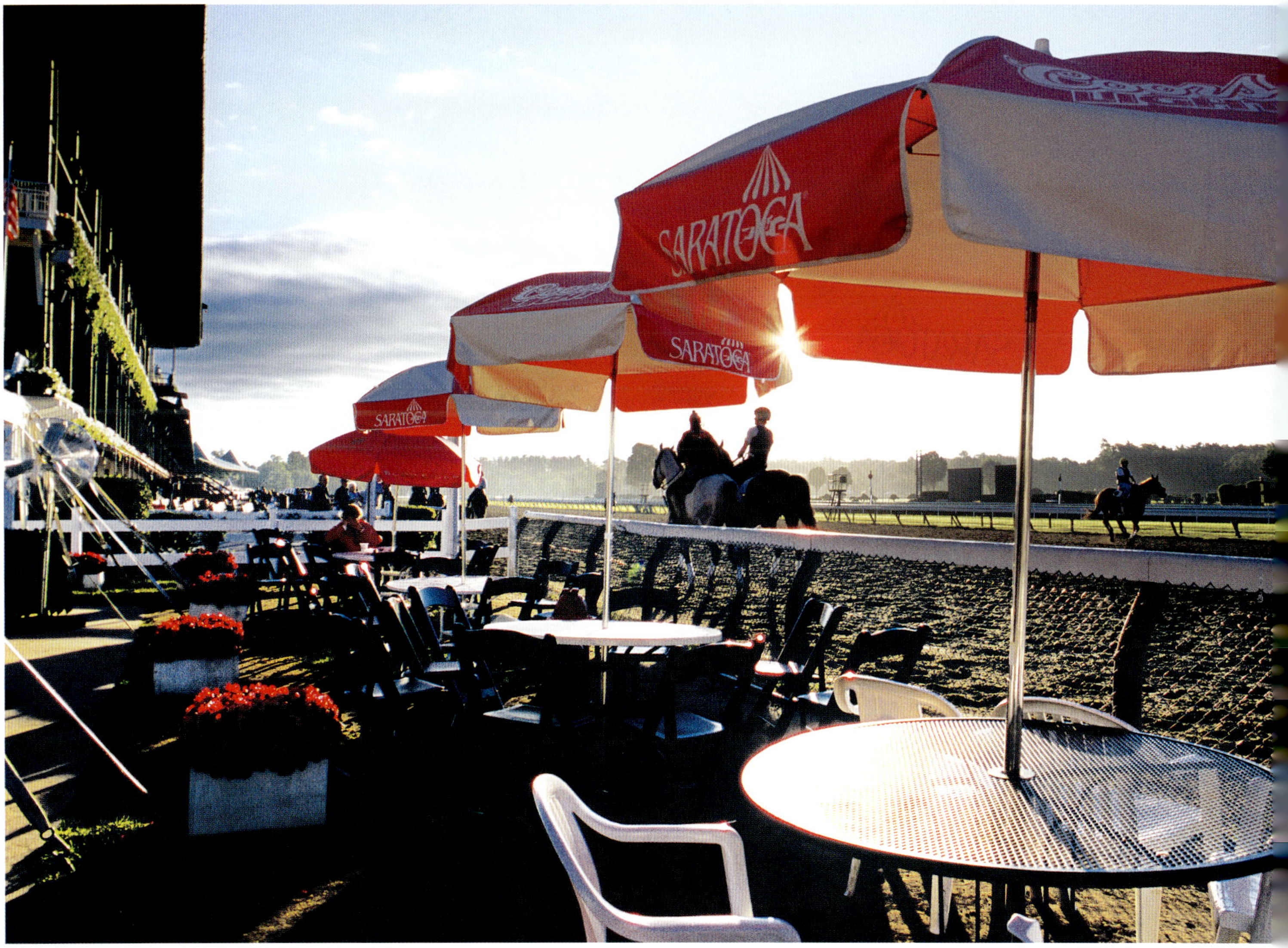

OPPOSITE

Saratoga Springs is the place to be in summer for dining, shopping, relaxing, and touring. The city has a Performing Arts Center and, with mineral springs throughout the city, is well known for its spas.

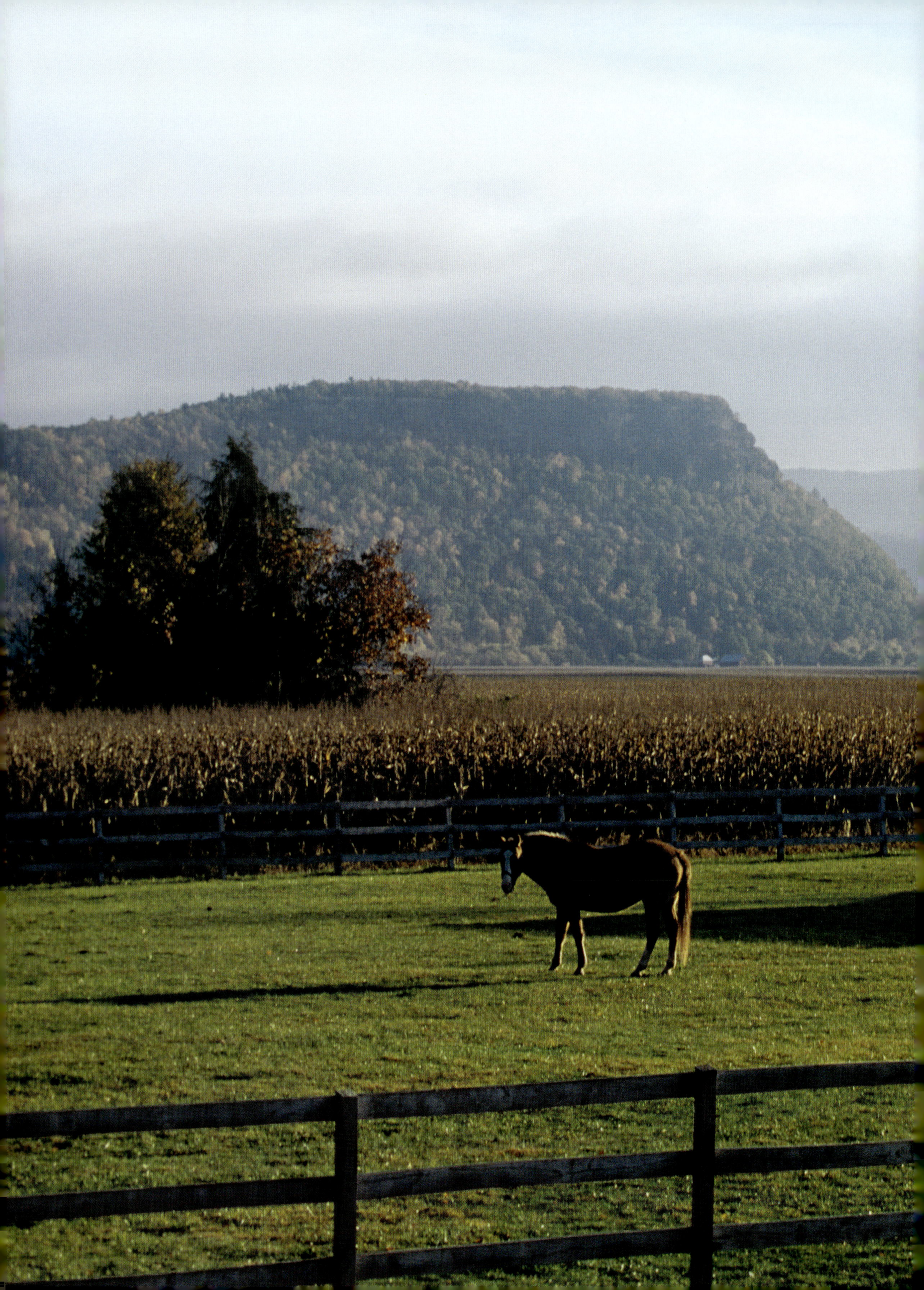

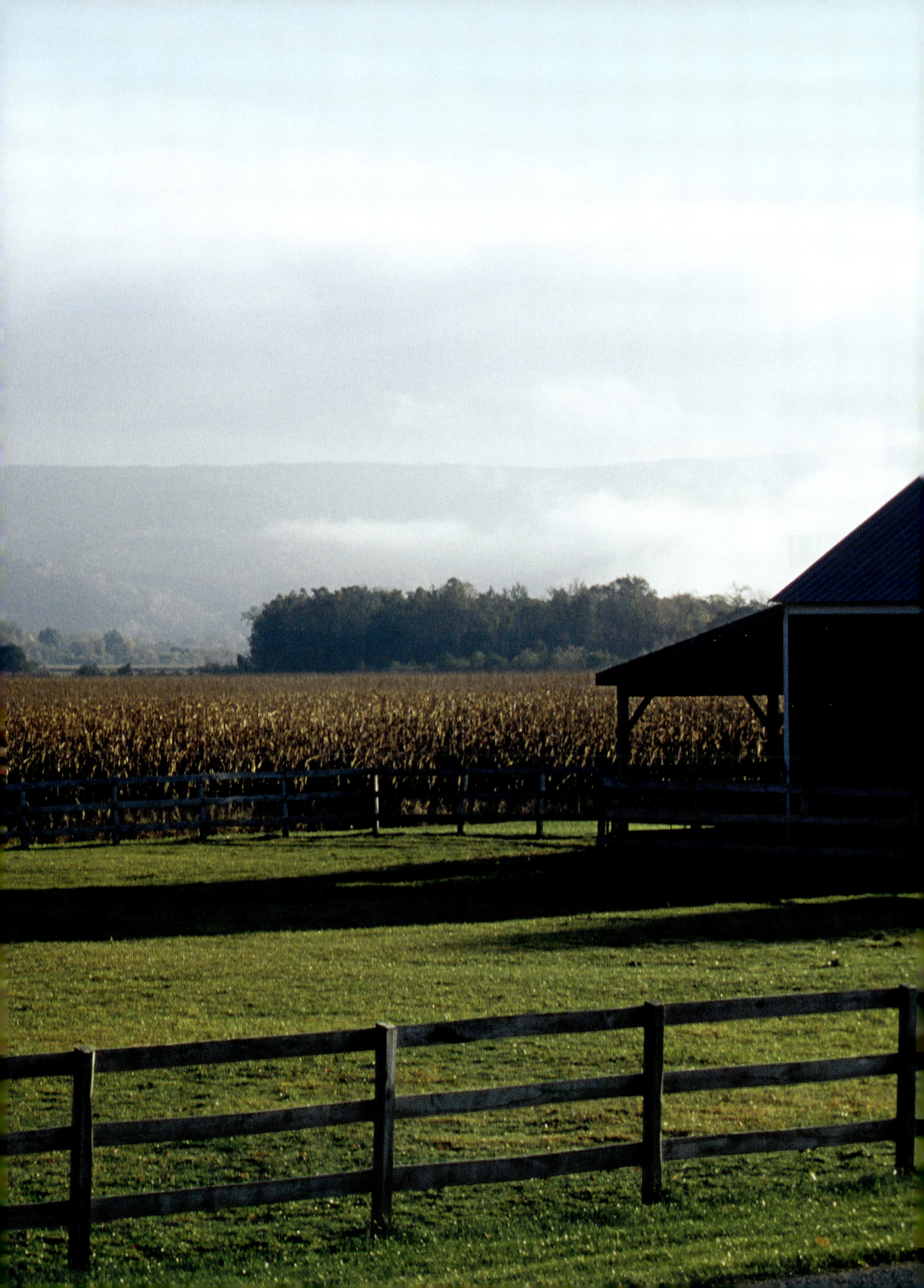

PREVIOUS PAGE
Settled in the early 1700s, the Schoharie Valley, northwest of the Catskill Mountains, has rich farmlands amidst beautiful wilderness.

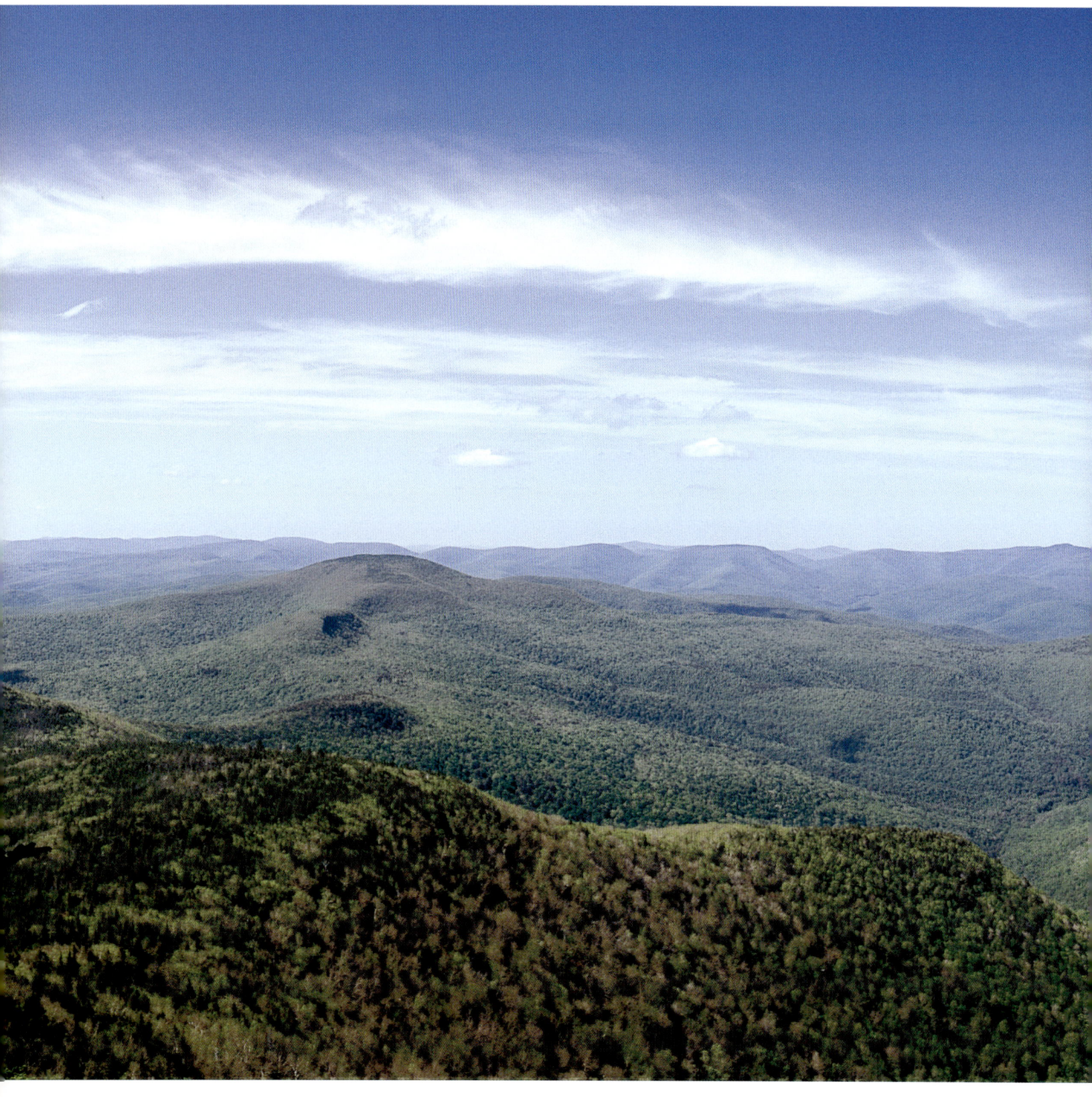

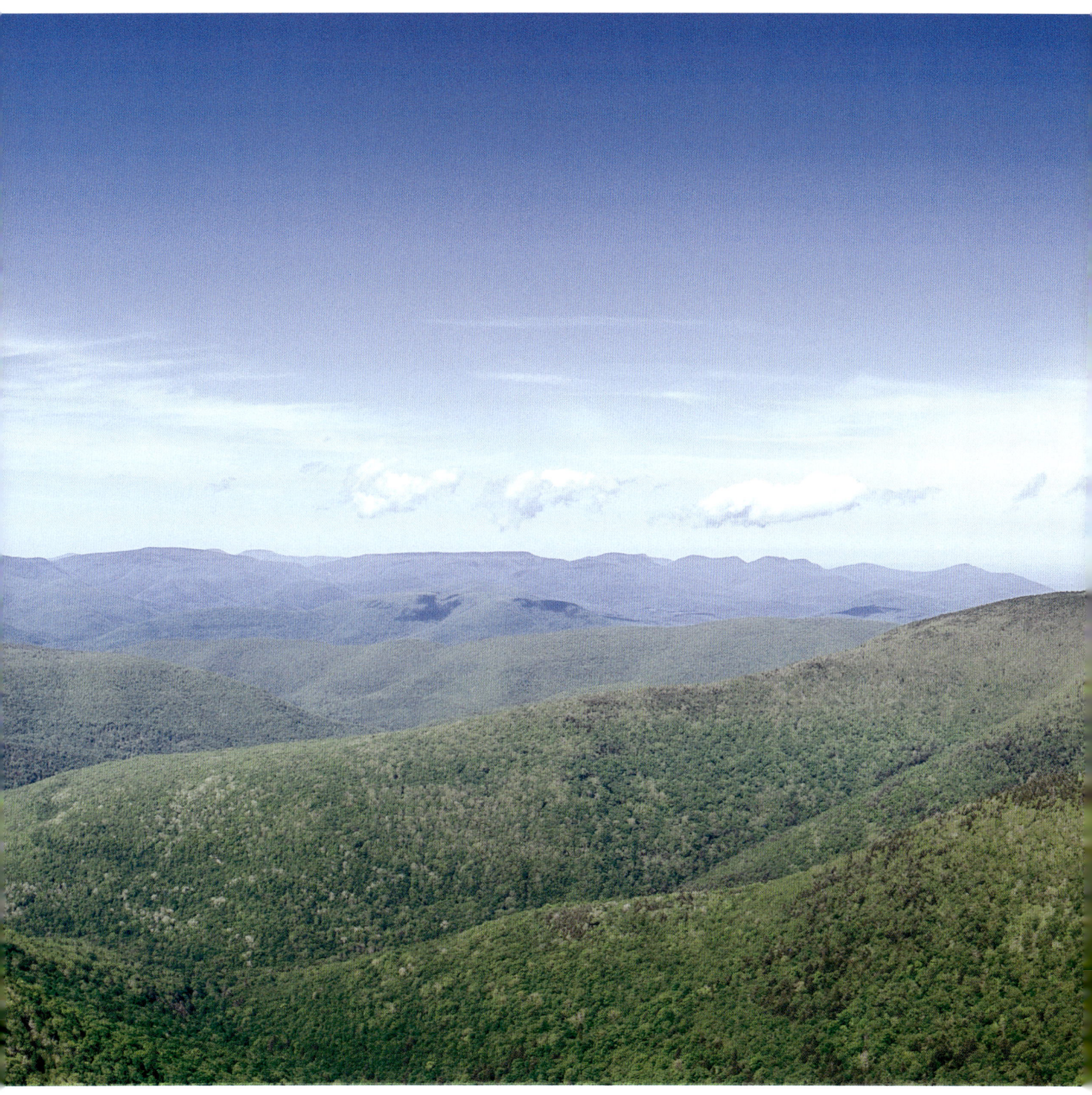

ABOVE

The Catskill Park was created in 1904 and today encompasses about seven hundred thousand acres of public and private land. Slide Mountain is the highest summit in the Catskills, offering a panoramic view of the surrounding mountains.

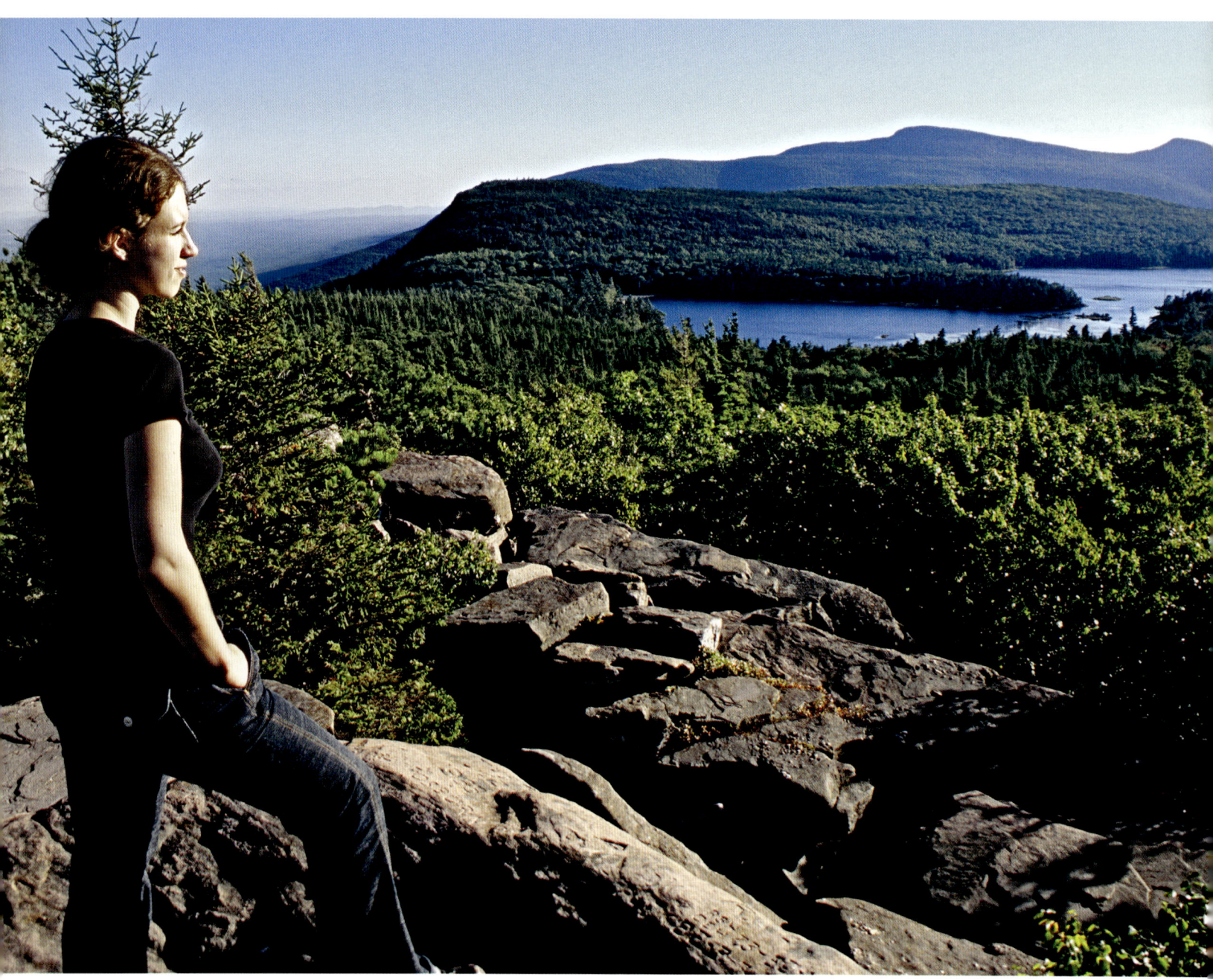

ABOVE

Numerous trails lead through the rugged beauty of the Catskills. One trail from the North-South Lakes Campground traverses the eastern escarpment and leads to this wonderful view from Sunset Rock.

RIGHT

The Catskills are considered the "birthplace of American fly fishing." The Catskill Fly Fishing Center and Museum in Livingston Manor documents the history of the sport, helps protect the environment, and also teaches others about fly fishing.

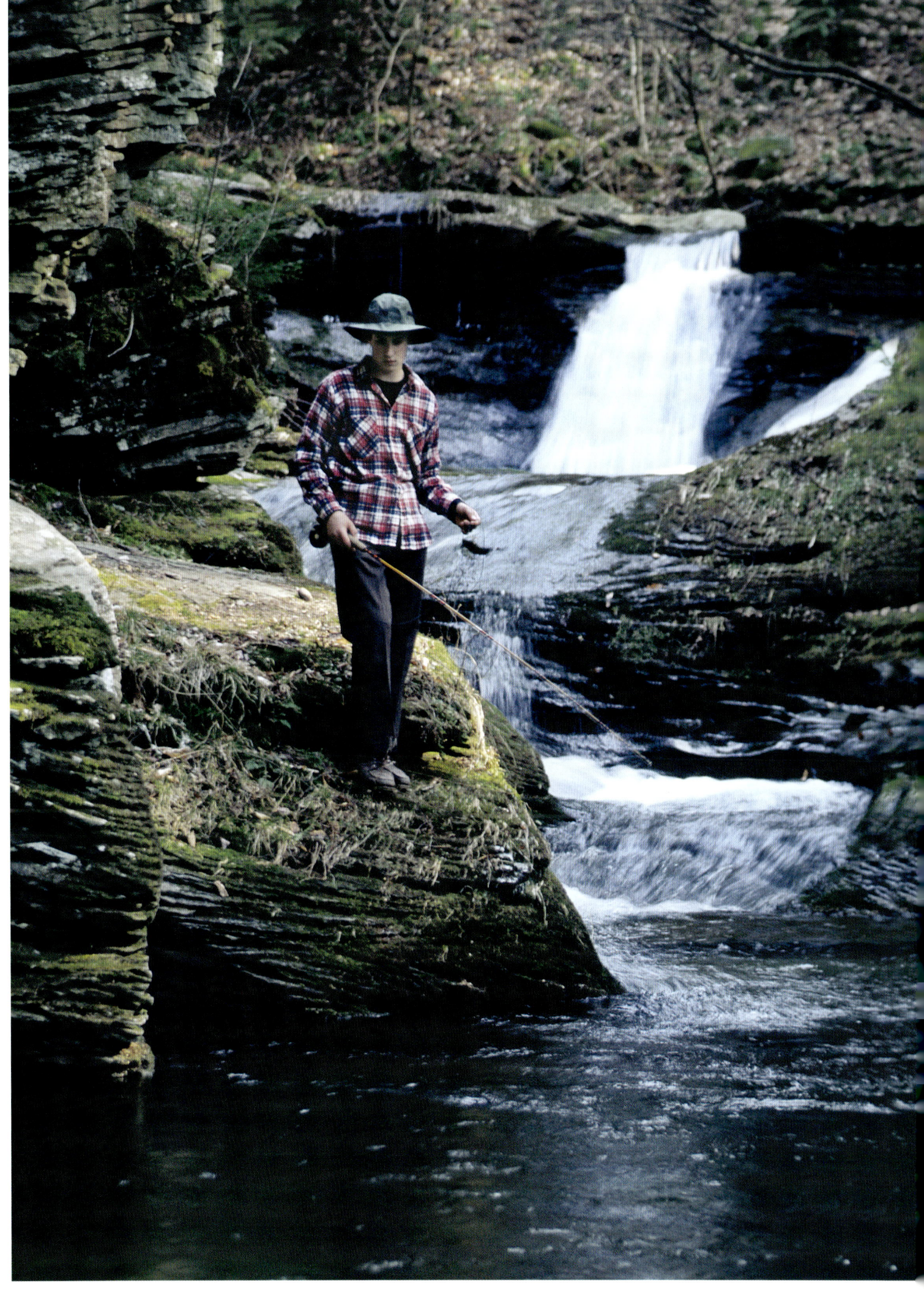

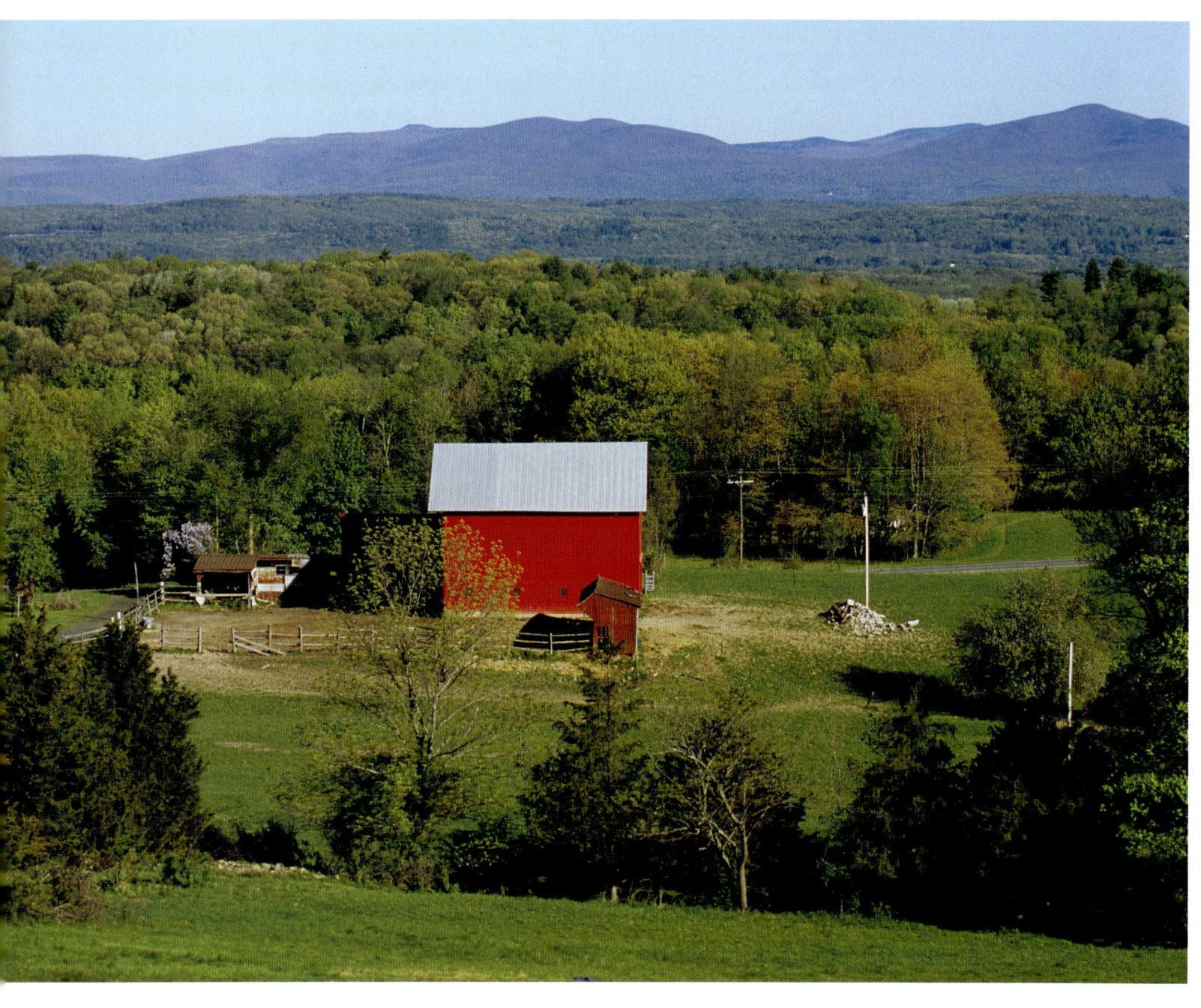

ABOVE

Spring greenery and lilacs set off the red barn in this view of the valley between the western Shawangunks and the Catskills.

RIGHT

Stone Arch Bridge Park, in the hamlet of Kenoza Lake, features one of only a few remaining triple-arch bridges in the country. It was built in about 1880 and is known for its unique design as well as the "hex murder" that took place on the bridge in 1882, when Adam Heidt's son Joseph killed George Markert to end the hex the Heidts believed Markert had placed on Adam.

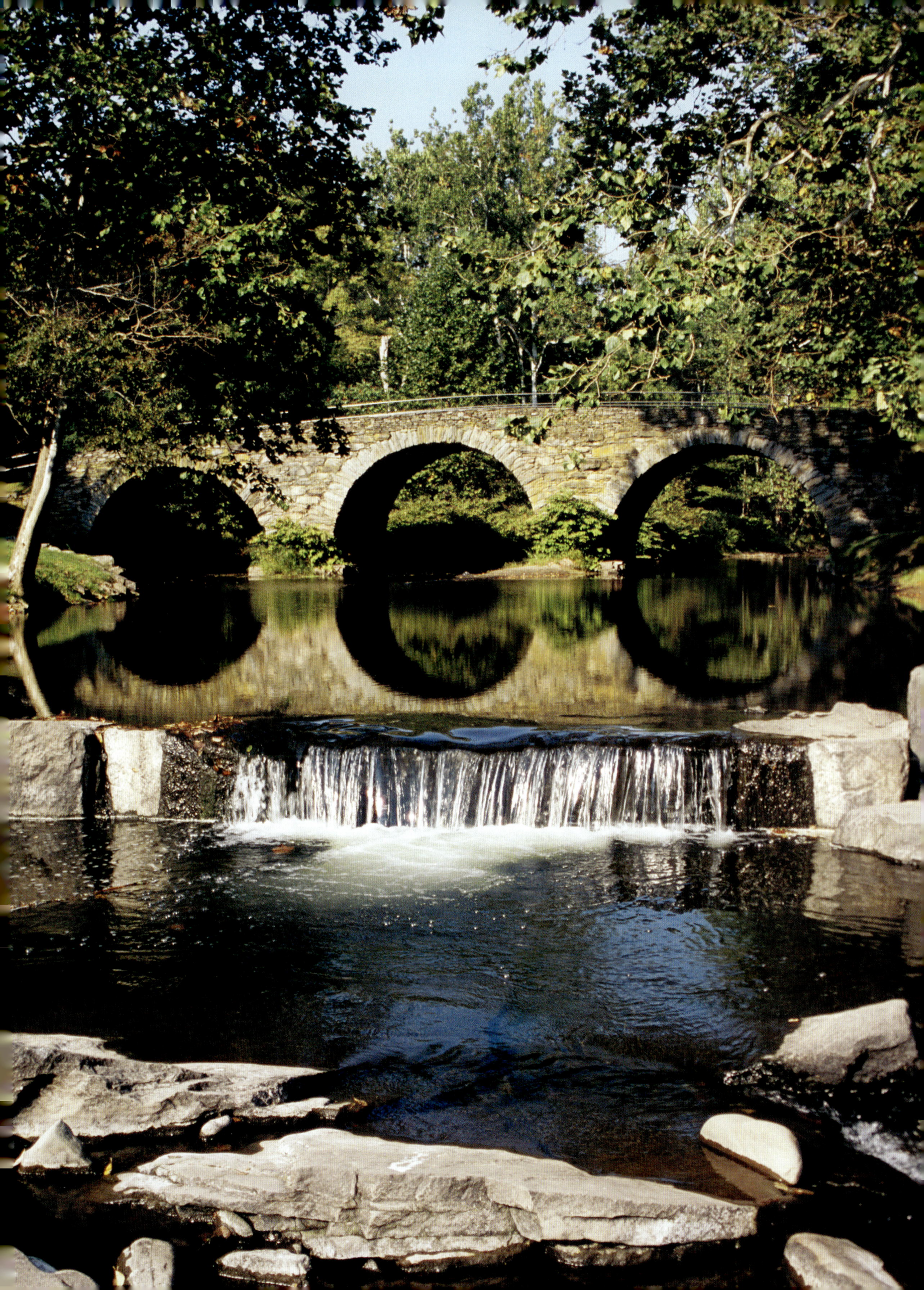

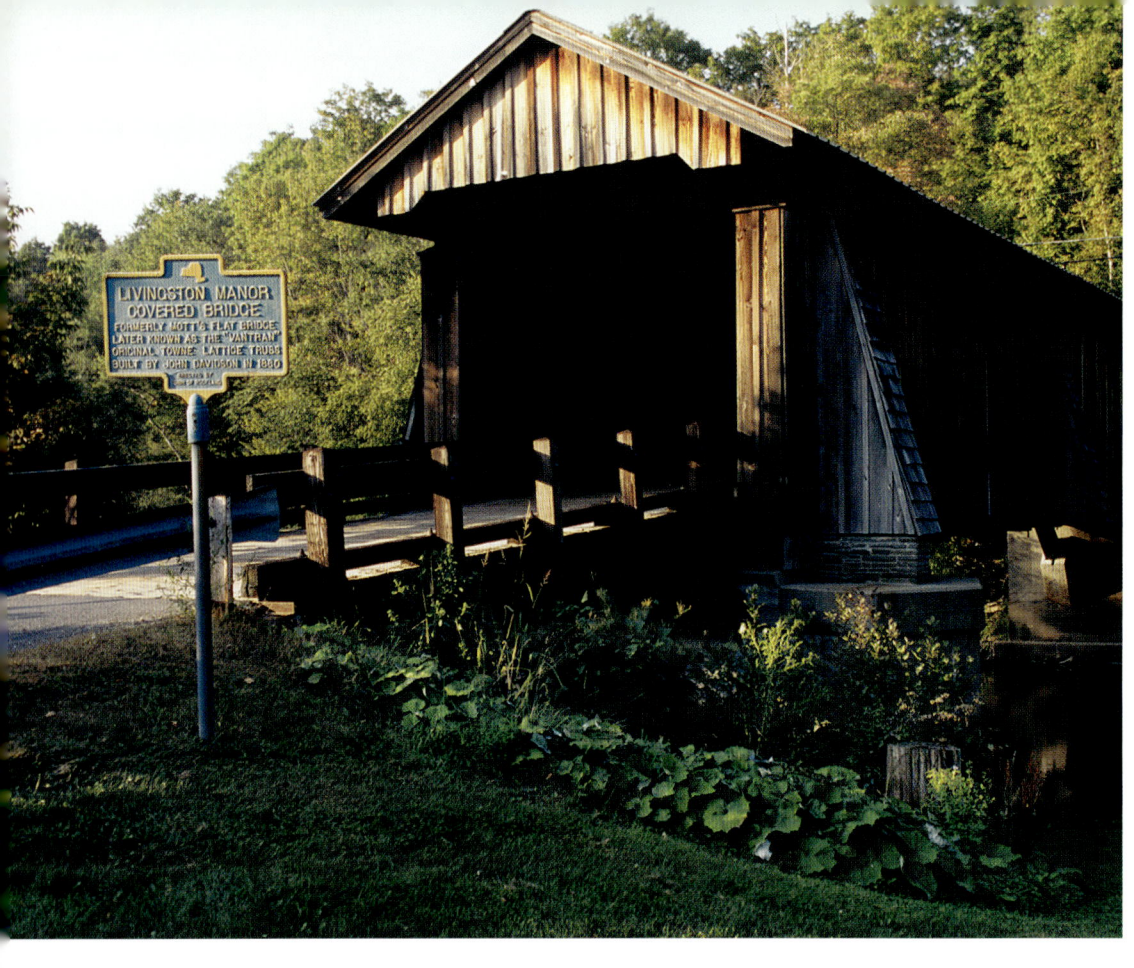

LEFT

Five covered bridges still stand in New York's Sullivan County, including this one at Livingston Manor. Spanning the Willowemoc Creek, the bridge was built in 1860 and refurbished in 1985.

BELOW

The Hanford Mills Museum recaptures the feel of a small, nineteenth-century industrial complex. Featured are a working water-powered saw mill, a grist mill, a woodworking shop, and a hardware store.

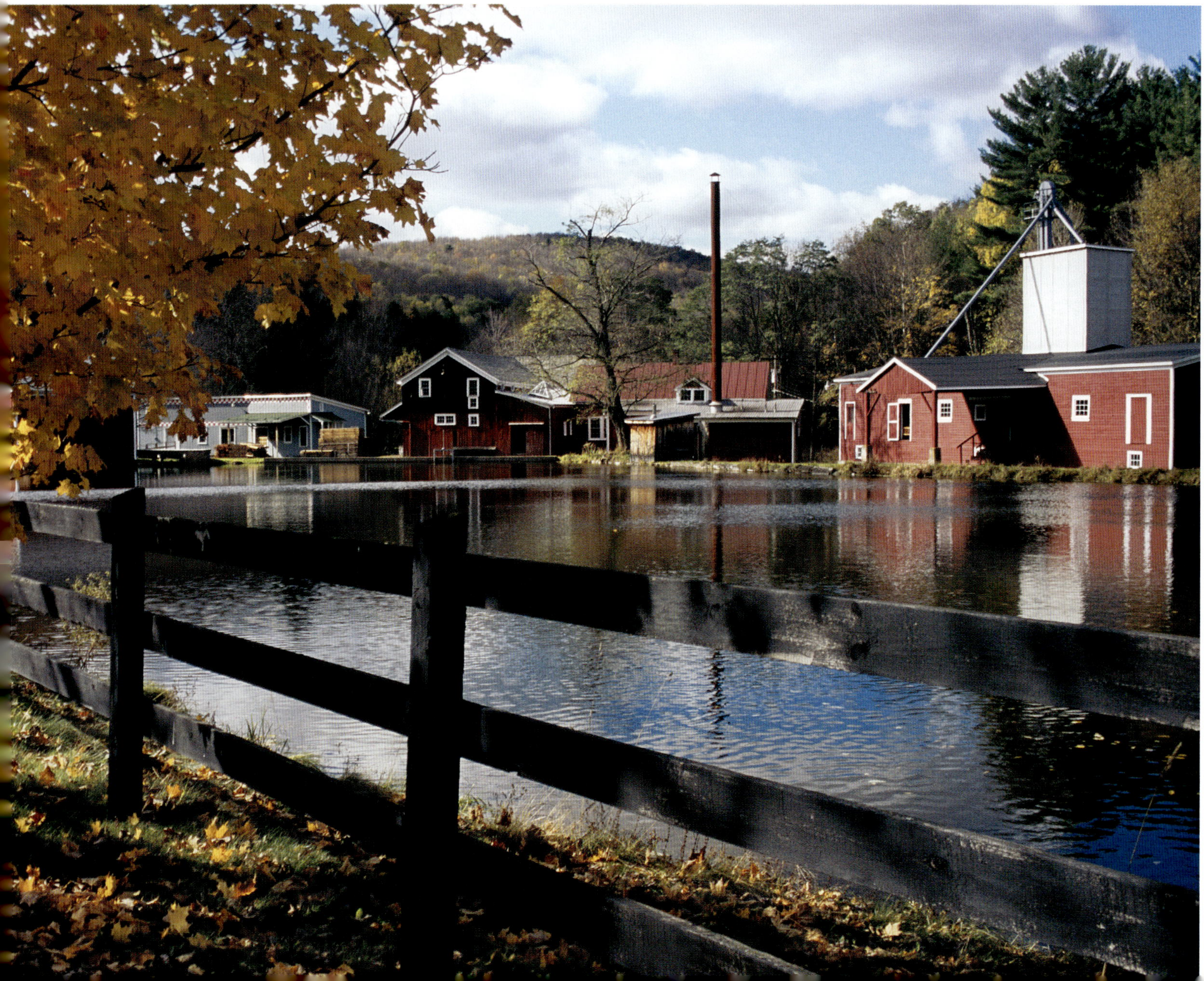

RIGHT

Overlooking Otsego Lake, Hyde Hall is one of the finest examples of a neoclassical country mansion in the country. The fifty-room house encloses a huge stone courtyard. Originally built beginning in 1817, the mansion is currently undergoing a complete restoration.

BELOW

Whitetail deer enjoy the tranquil beauty of a quiet fall day on the shores of Otsego Lake in Glimmerglass State Park. The Susquehanna River begins here at the outflow of the lake near Cooperstown.

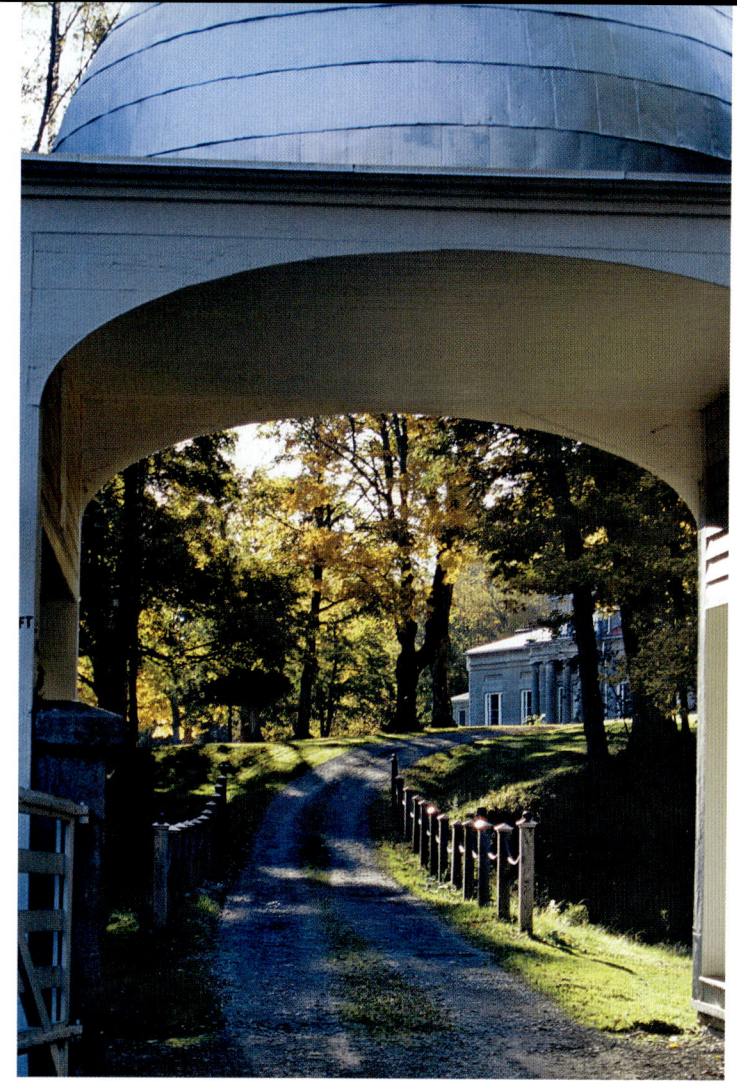

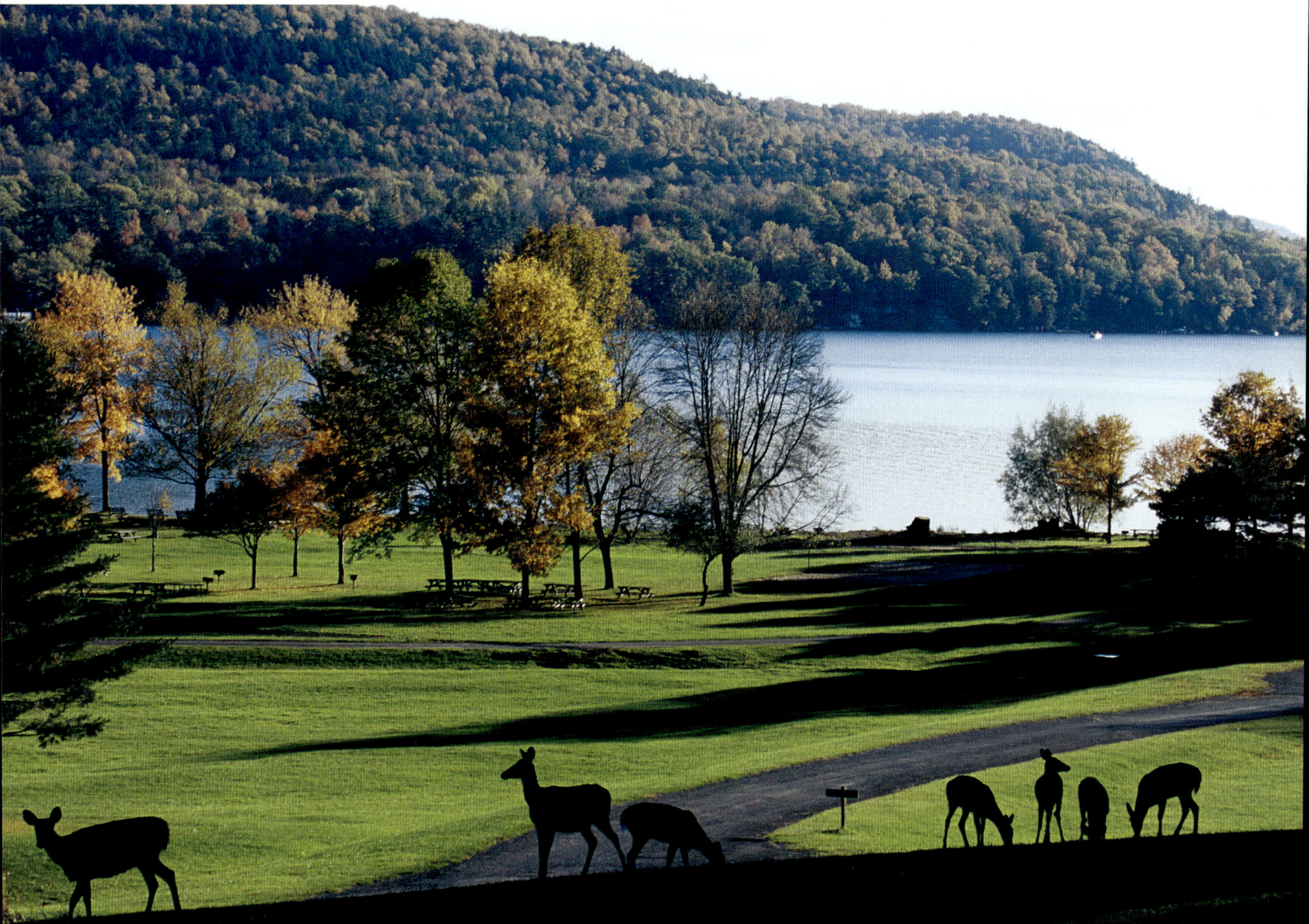

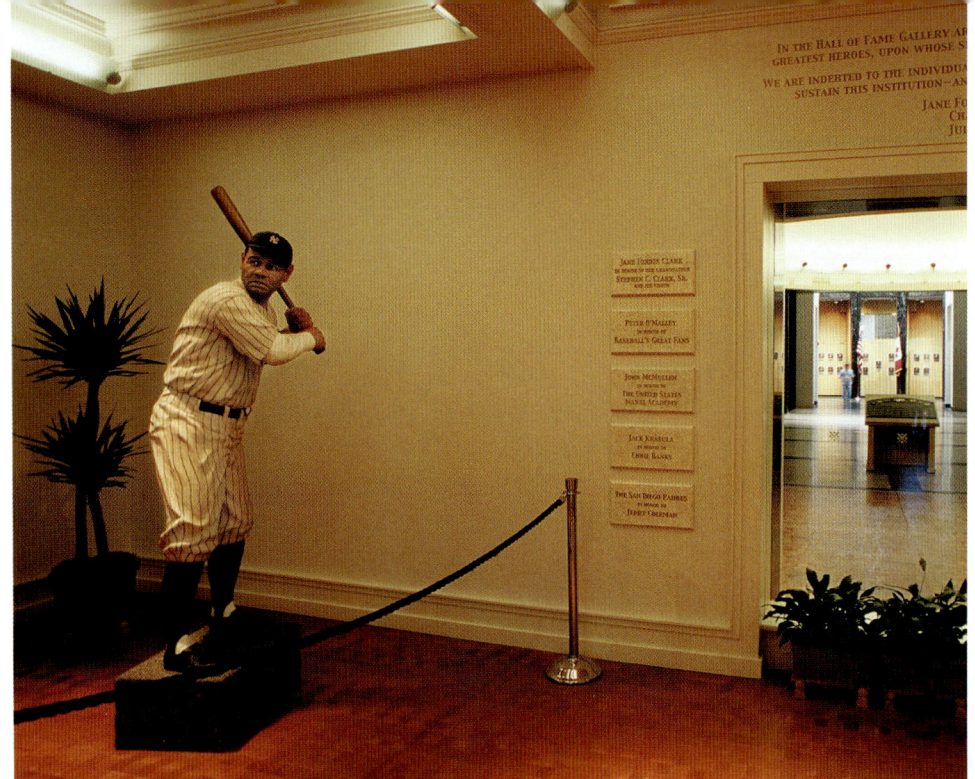

LEFT

The National Baseball Hall of Fame and Museum in Cooperstown features extensive collections of baseball memorabilia as well as the Hall of Fame itself. This statue of Babe Ruth stands at the entrance to the hall.

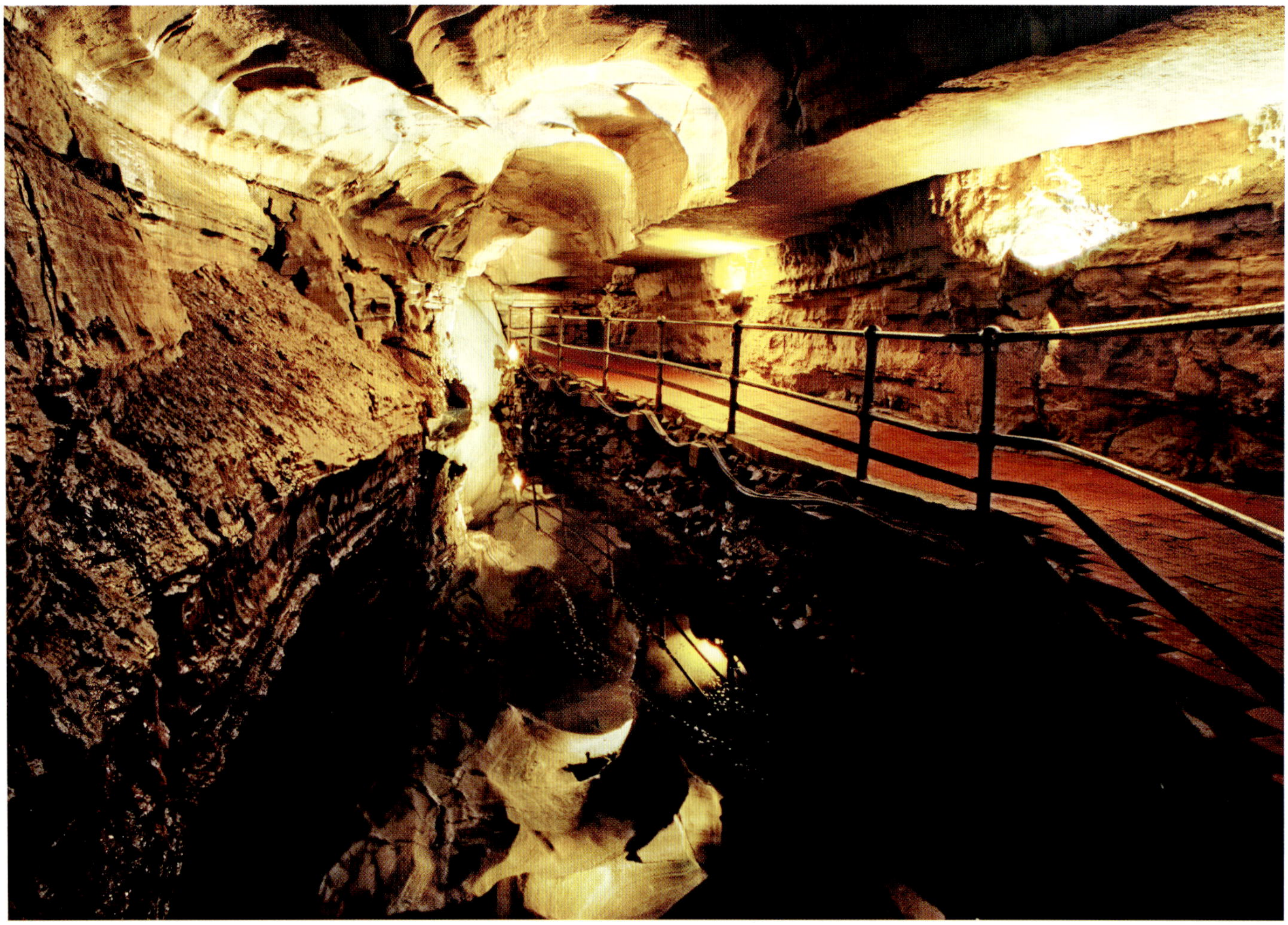

ABOVE

The eroded features and mineral formations found in Howe Caverns have been evolving for as long as six million years. These are among the top five show caves in the United States and the second most visited natural attraction in New York.

RIGHT

The Farmers' Museum in Cooperstown is an authentic farming village on land that once belonged to author James Fenimore Cooper. Buildings, gardens, and artifacts provide a look at farming and town life in the nineteenth century. It is jointly run with the neighboring Fenimore Art Museum, which houses one of the finest collections of American folk art.

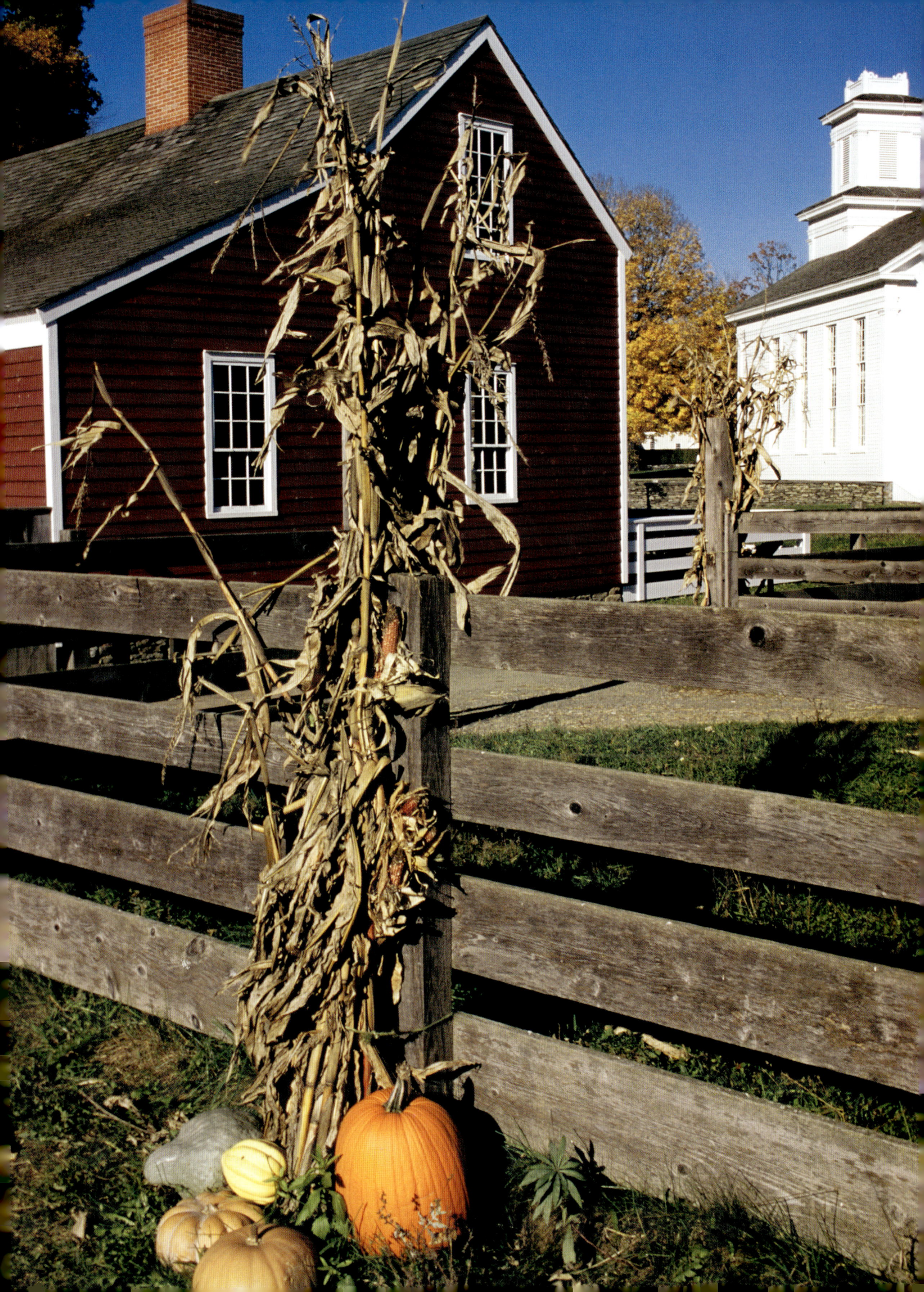

RIGHT
This twilight view of downtown Utica shows the 1900-vintage "Gold Dome" Bank and the Westminster Presbyterian Church steeple.

BELOW
Erie Canal Village, located at the spot where the first shovel of dirt was dug for the canal in 1817, is a living history museum that portrays village life in the 1800s. It also includes special events, such as a Civil War encampment and re-enactment.

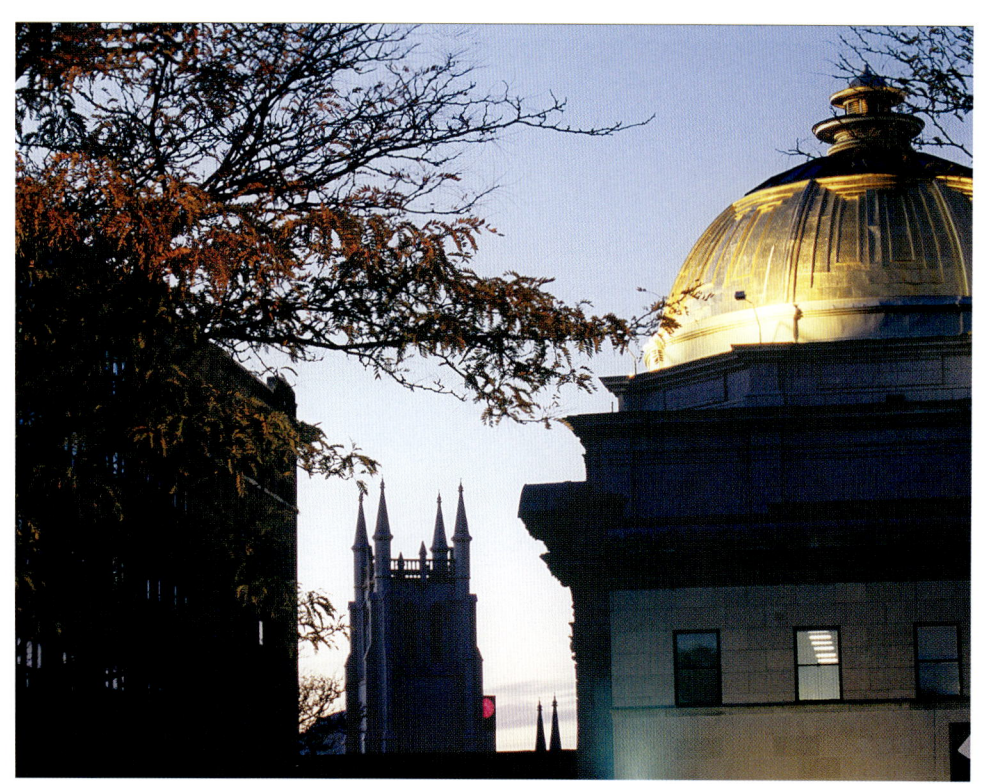

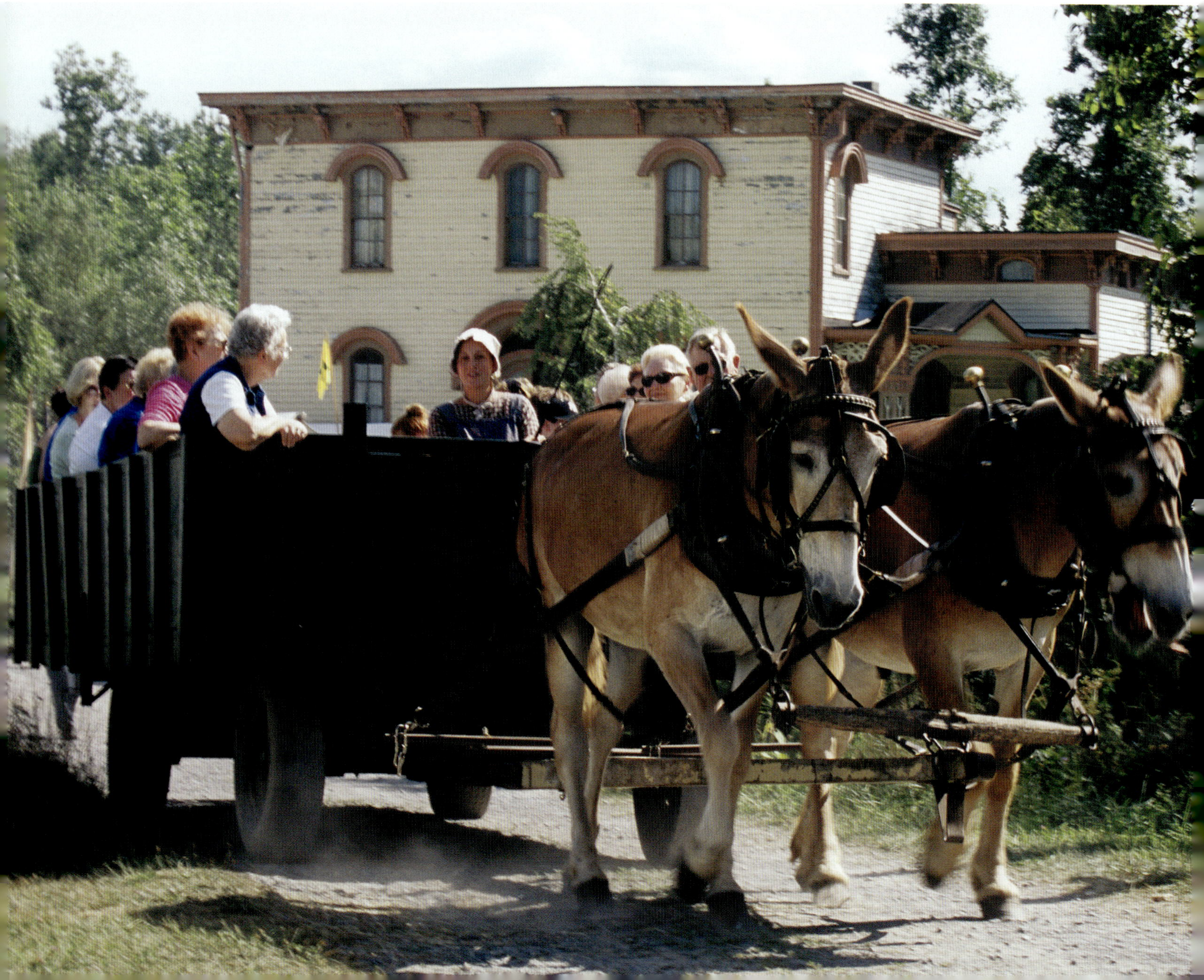

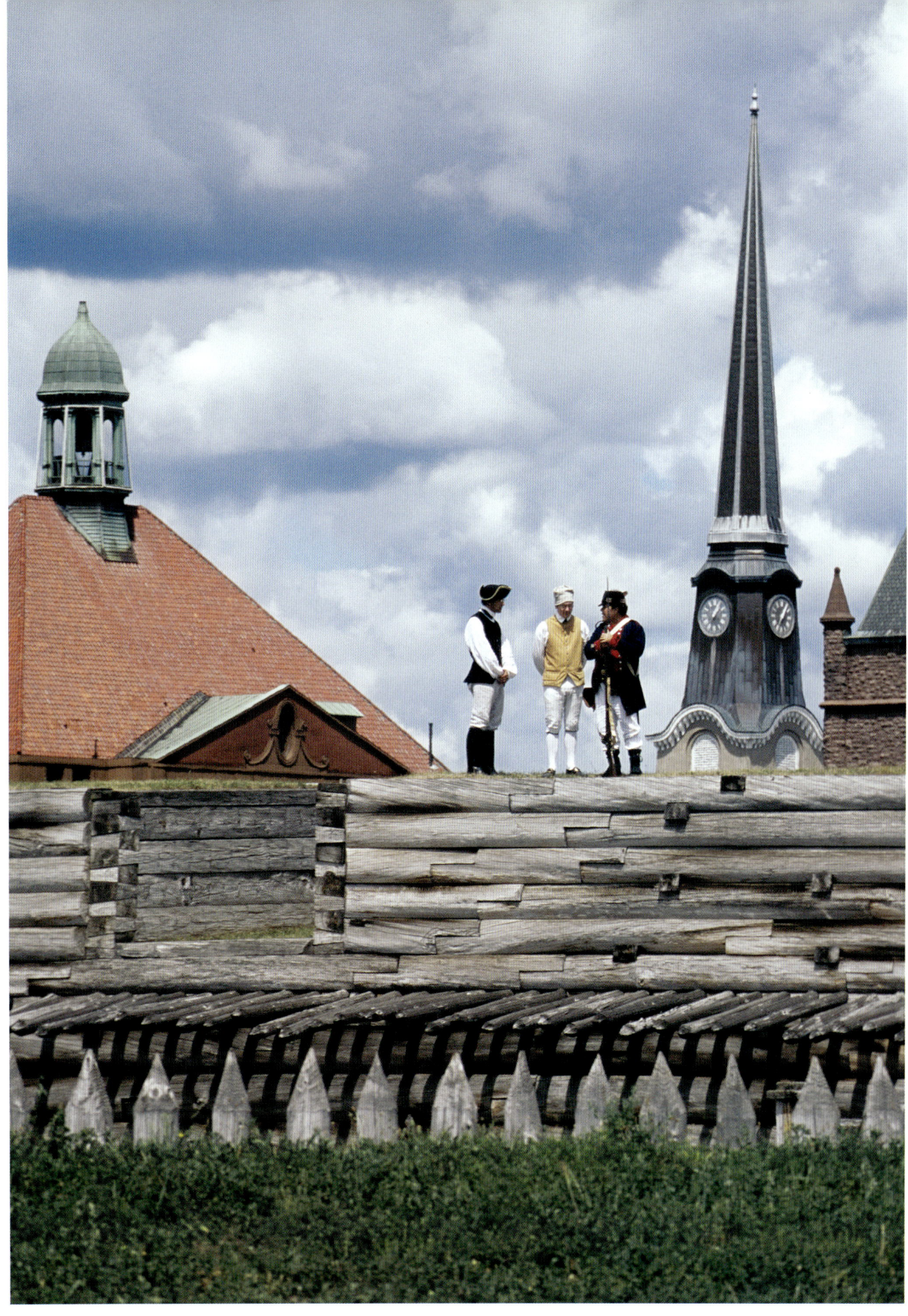

ABOVE

Fort Stanwix National Monument in downtown Rome celebrates the "fort that never surrendered." A combination of Revolutionary War battles in August 1777 at and nearby the fort helped lead to General Burgoyne's surrender at Saratoga that October.

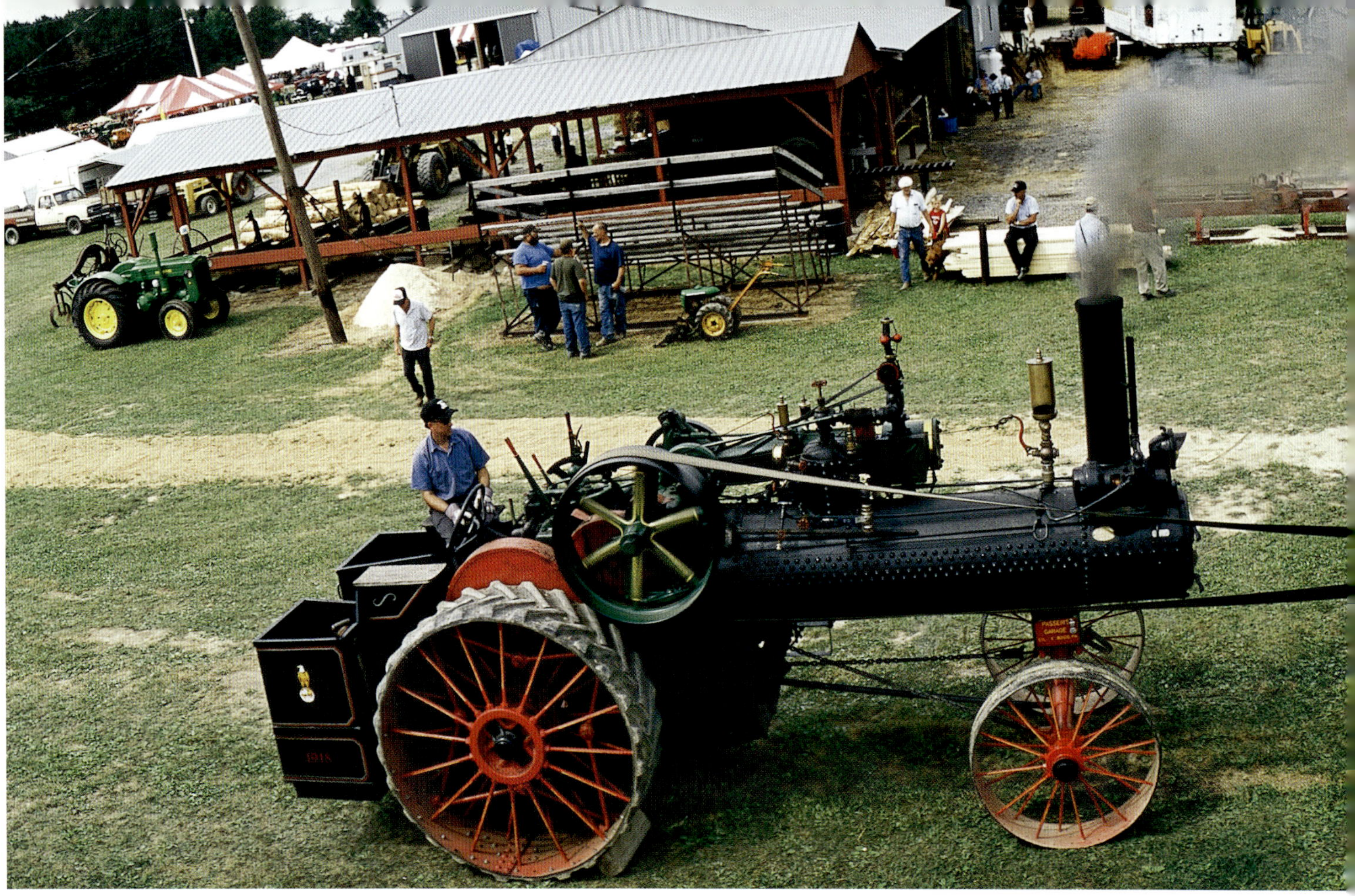

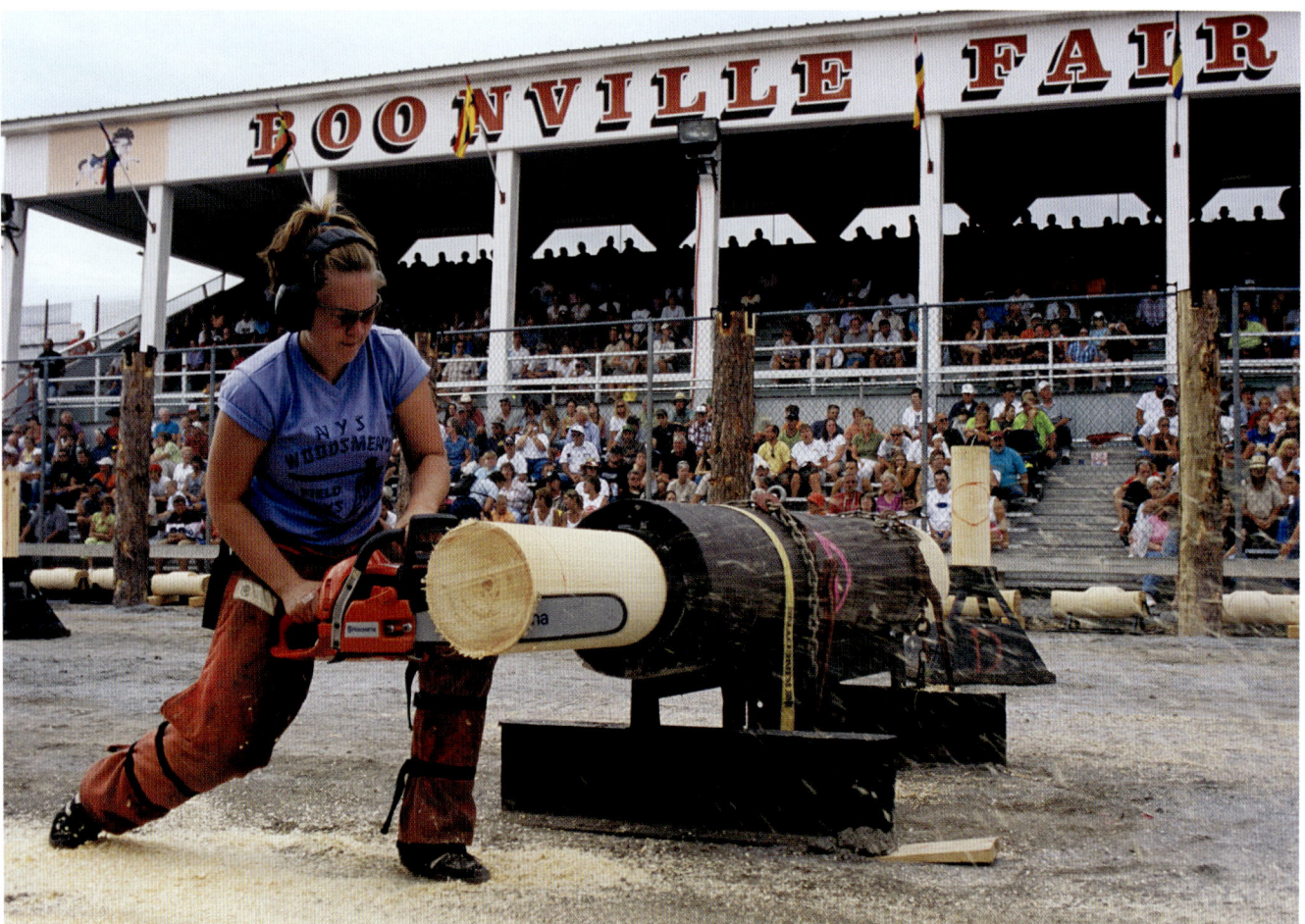

ABOVE

The New York State Woodsmen's Field Days, held every August in Boonville, is one of the nation's biggest lumberjack and lumberjill competitions. Participants come from as far away as Australia.

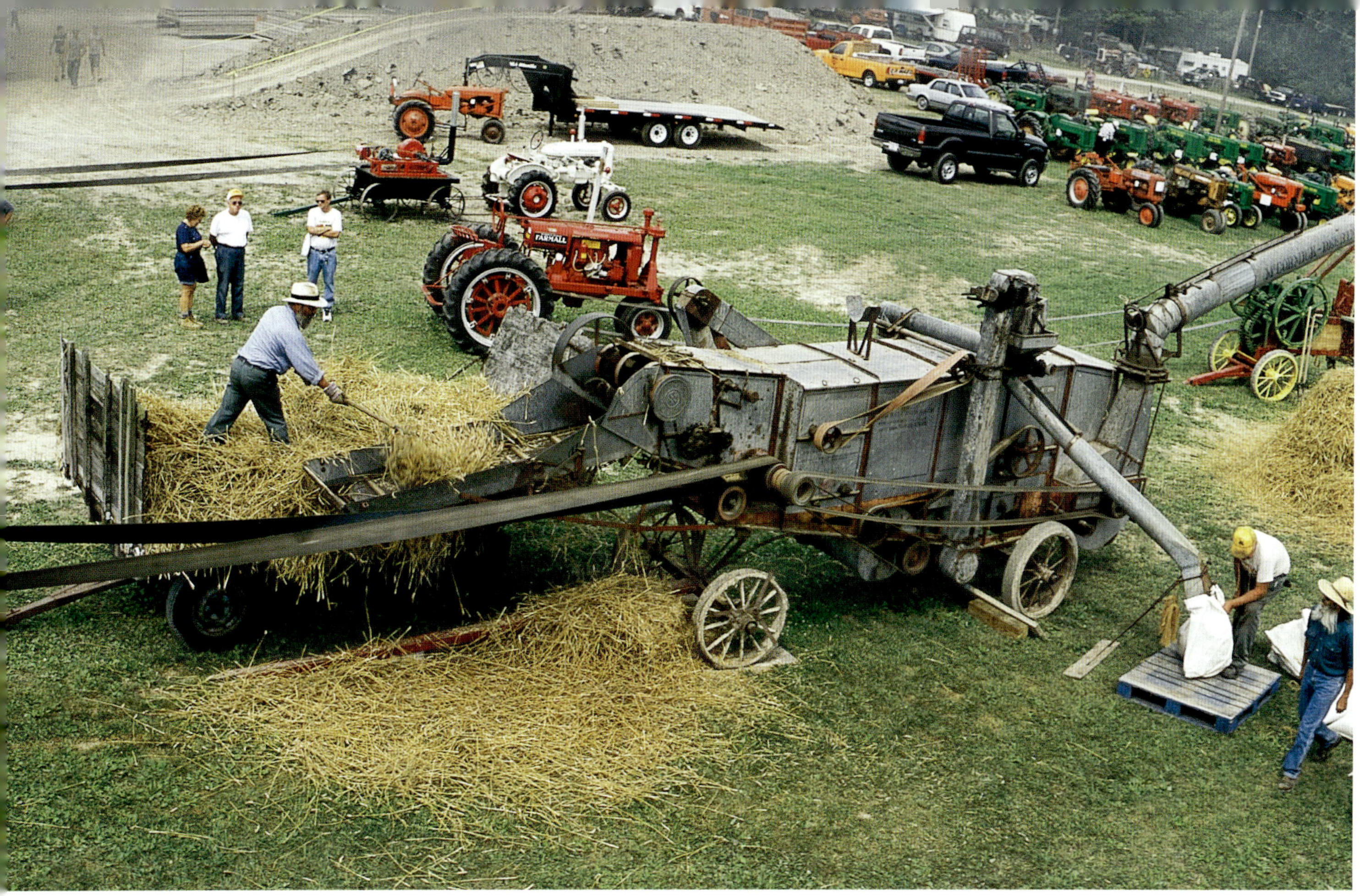

ABOVE

The New York Steam Engine Association has held an annual Pageant of Steam in Canandaigua since 1960. The festival showcases all kinds of antique tractors and farming implements. Here, visitors watch a threshing demonstration in front of the tractor-powered sawmill.

RIGHT

Thousands of jack-o'-lanterns fill Norwich's downtown square at the annual Pumpkin Festival in Chenango County.

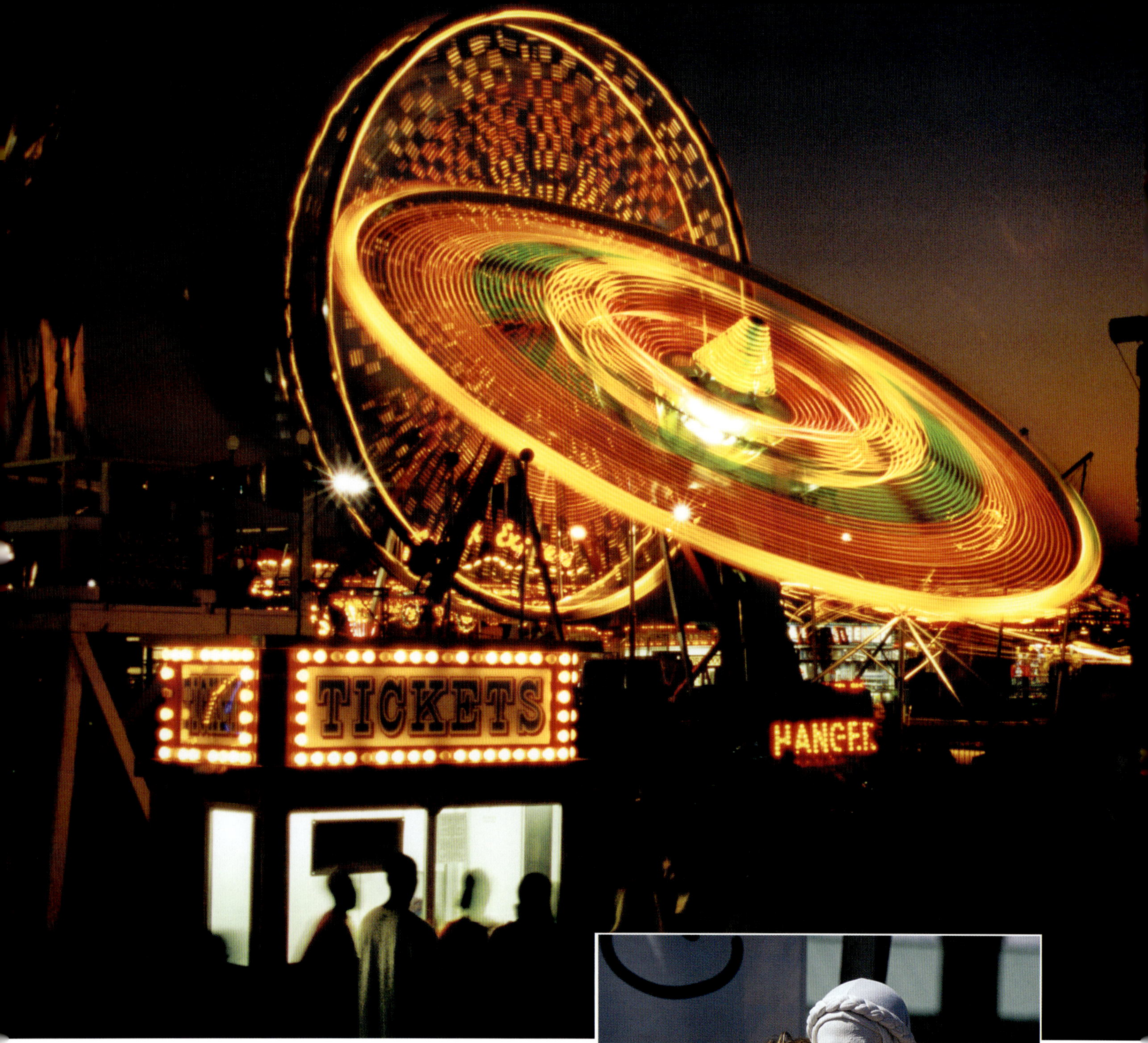

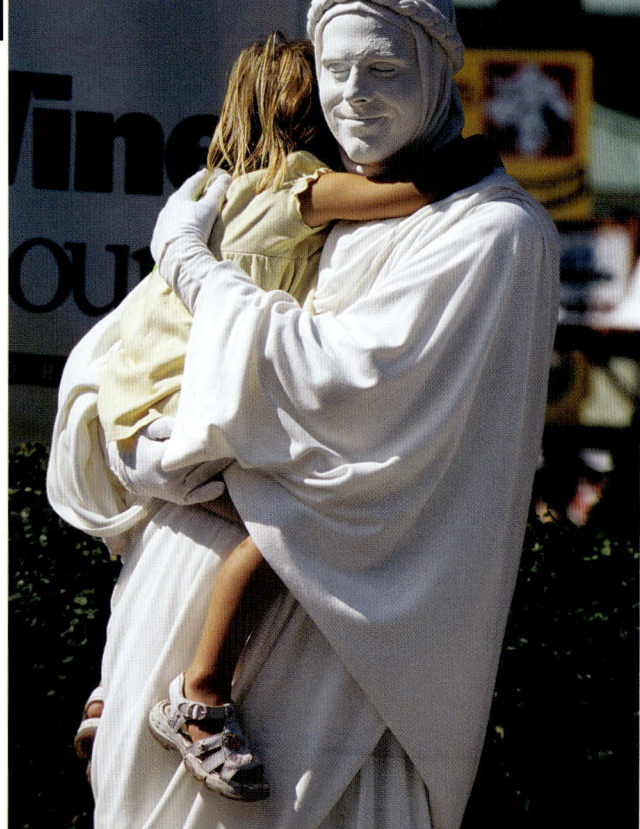

ABOVE

The annual Great New York State Fair, held at the Empire Expo Center in Syracuse, has something for everyone. Since 1841 the fair has promoted state agriculture and household manufacturers. A fifty-foot-tall, hand-powered wheel amusement ride was introduced at the Syracuse fair in 1849—predating the Ferris wheel by more than forty years.

RIGHT

A variety of performers appear daily at the state fair, including acrobats, street performers, and living statues (pictured here), to entertain the nearly one million attendees during the twelve-day event.

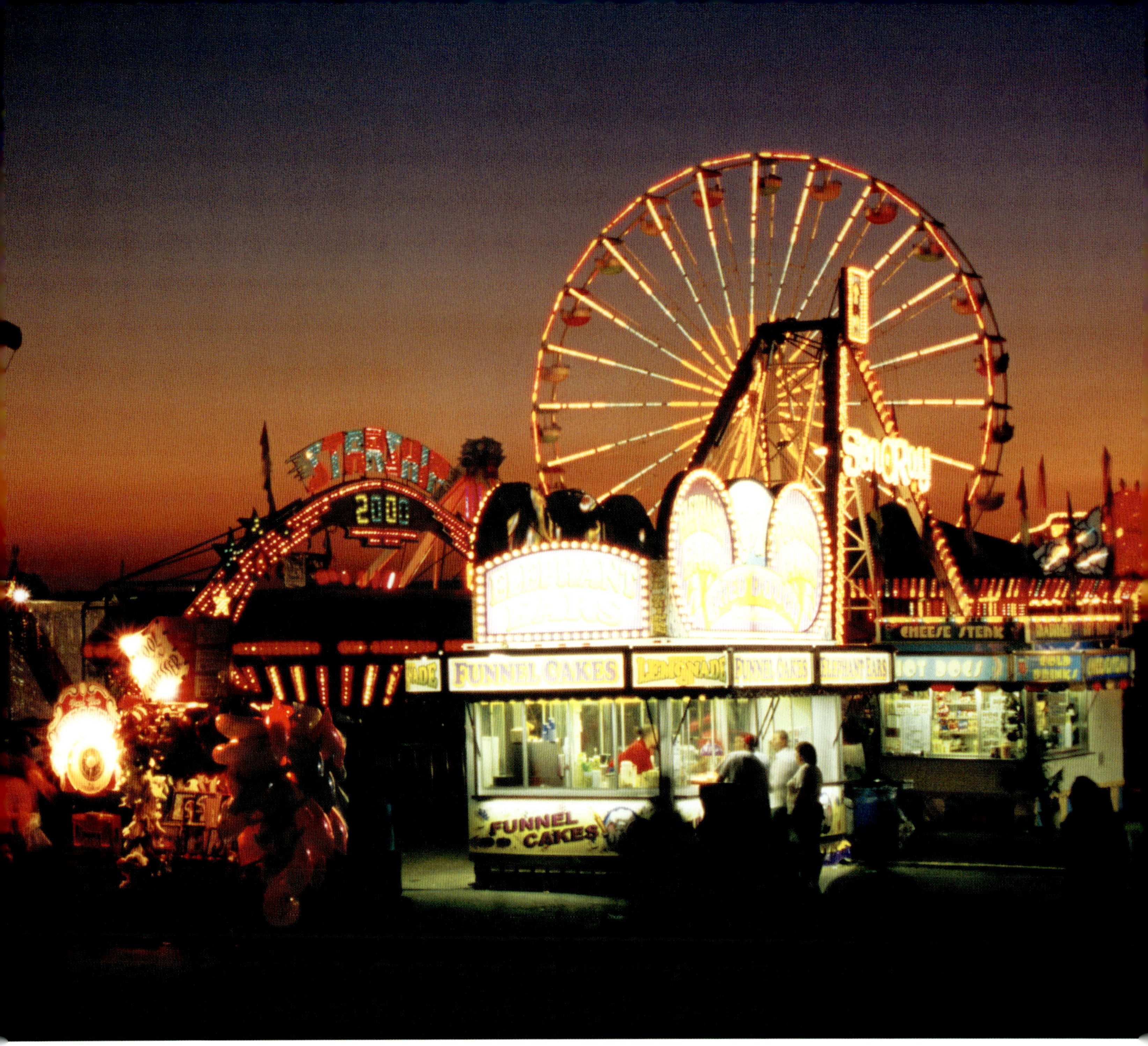

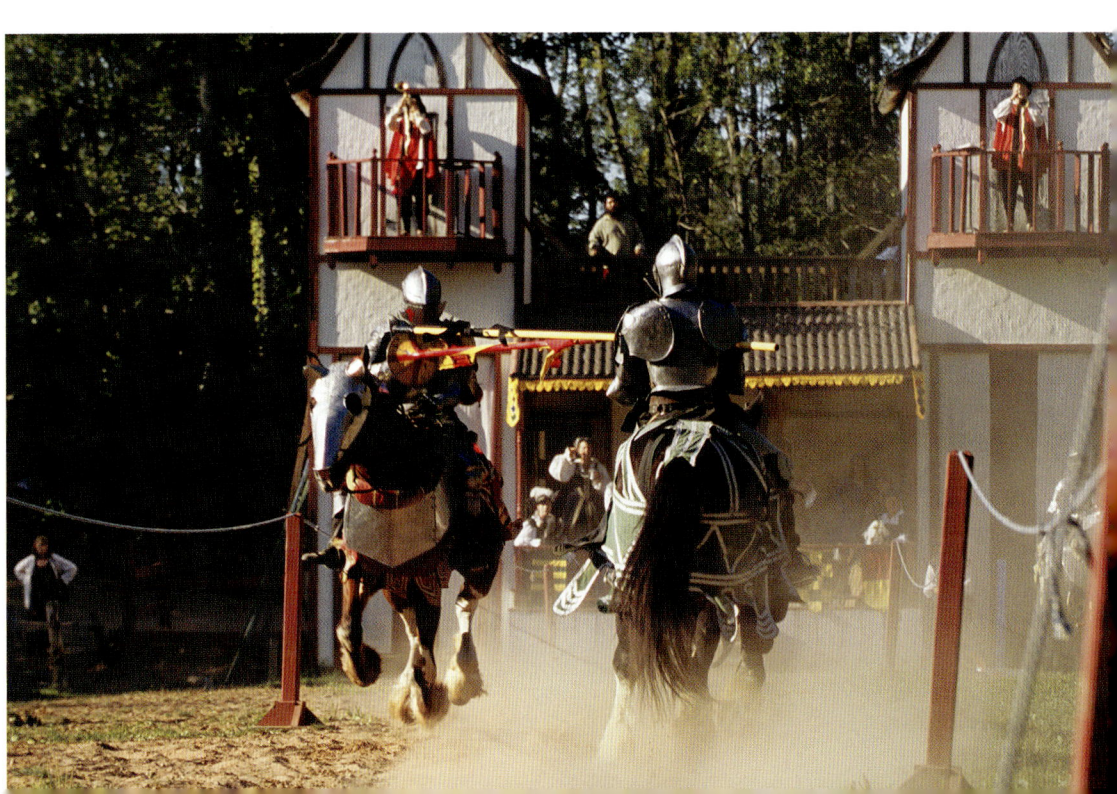

RIGHT
Go back to sixteenth-century England at the Sterling Renaissance Festival, south of Lake Ontario. Jesters, acrobats, and Shakespeare are all on hand to entertain Queen Elizabeth and guests. A highlight is always the thundering joust held for the queen and her court.

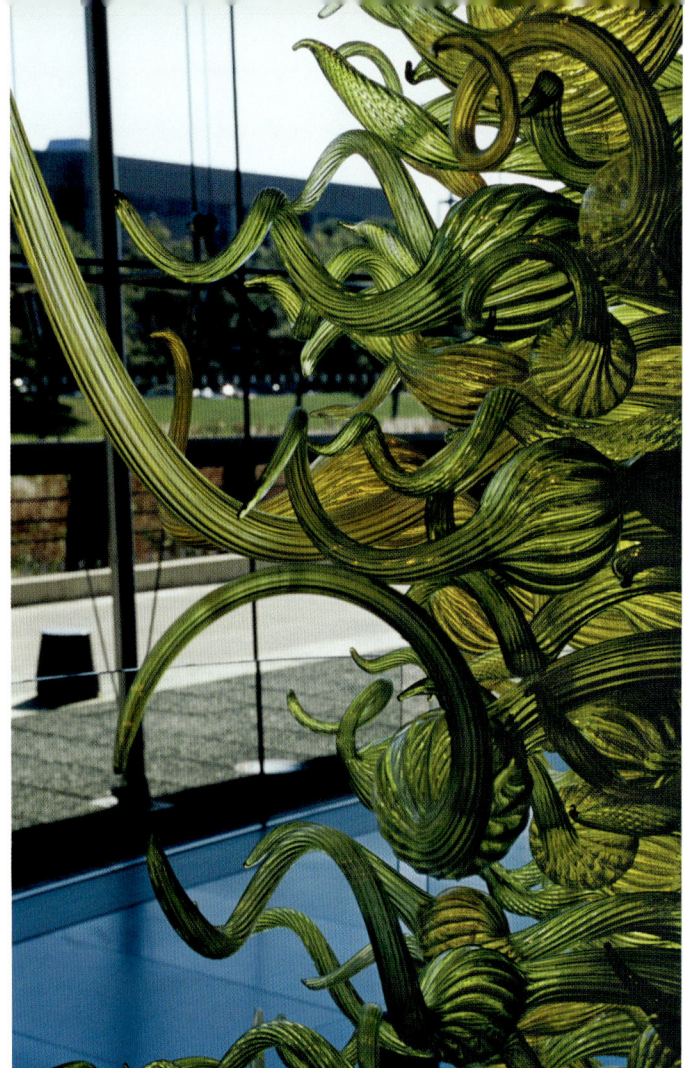

LEFT

This unique glass sculpture is just a taste of what's to be seen at the Corning Museum of Glass. Exploring the exhibit halls will give you a full appreciation of all that can be done with such a common medium.

RIGHT

Among the notable buildings in downtown Syracuse is the 1932 art deco Niagara Mohawk Building, viewed here from Clinton Square.

BELOW

The Seneca Falls Convention of 1848 is considered the birth of the women's rights movement. A statue portrays the meeting of early suffragists Elizabeth Cady Stanton, Susan B. Anthony, and Amelia Bloomer—the latter wearing the garment that now bears her name.

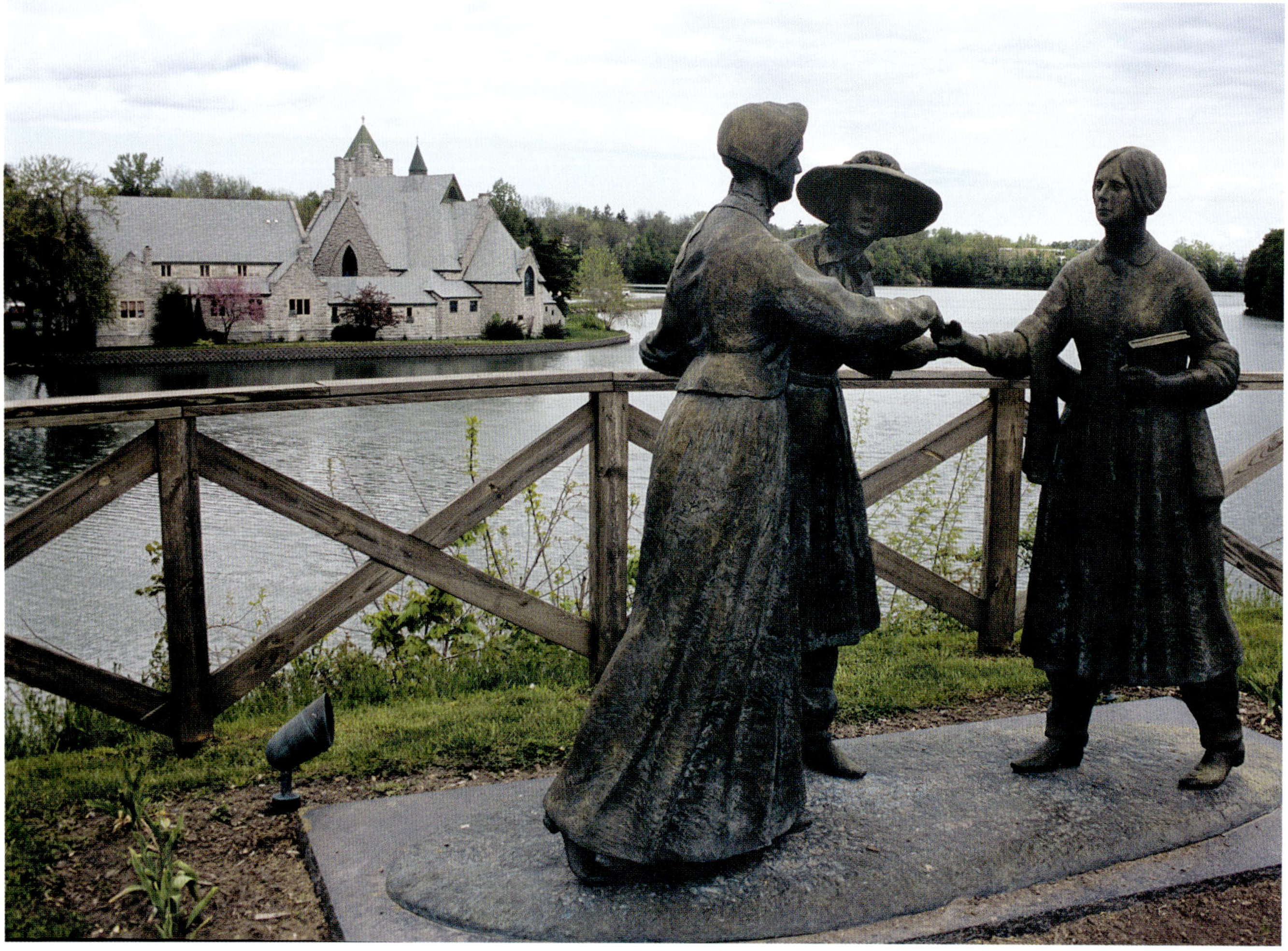

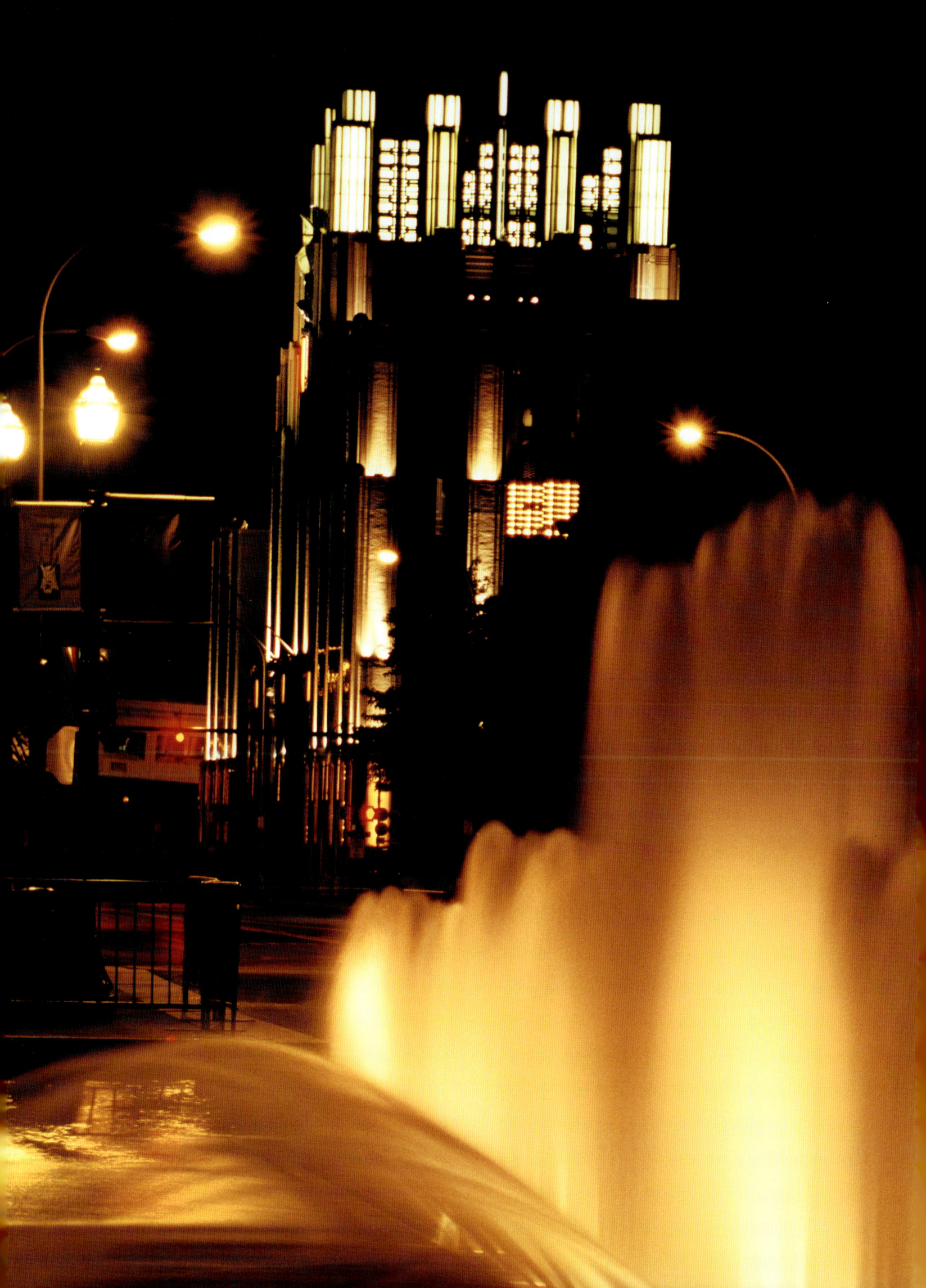

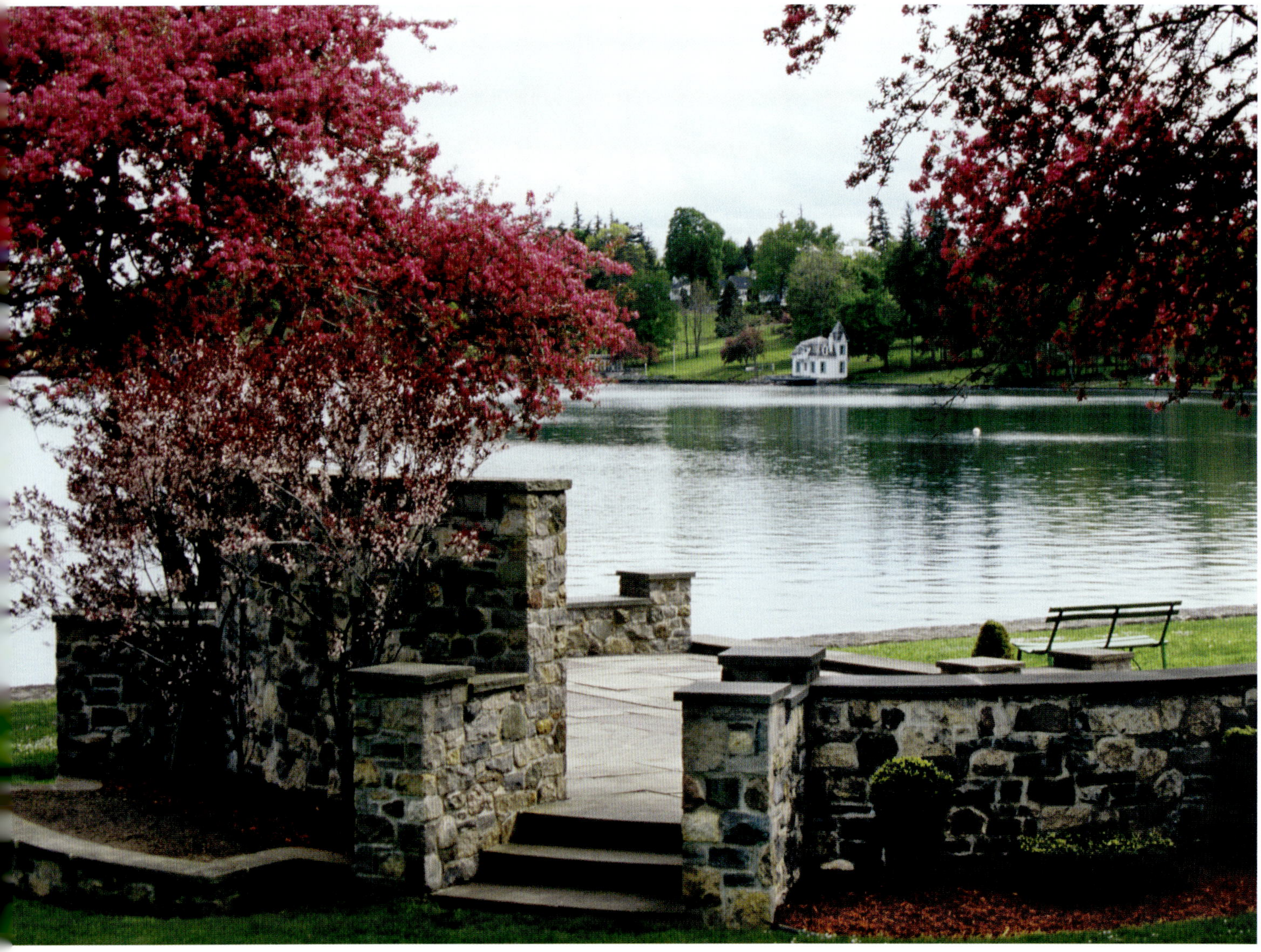

ABOVE

Skaneateles, settled in the late 1700s, is known as the eastern gateway to the Finger Lakes. There are a number of beautiful historic buildings in town and along the shoreline of the lake. Clift Park hosts a wide variety of activities through the year.

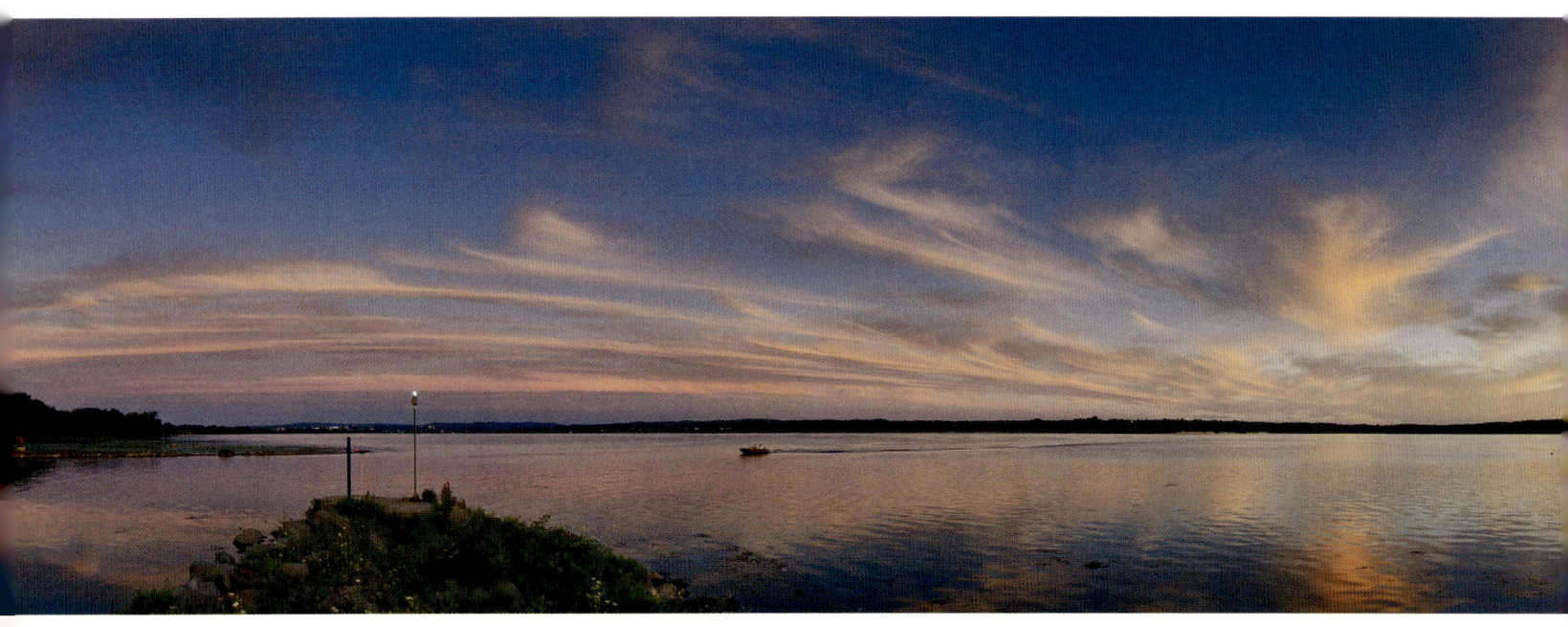

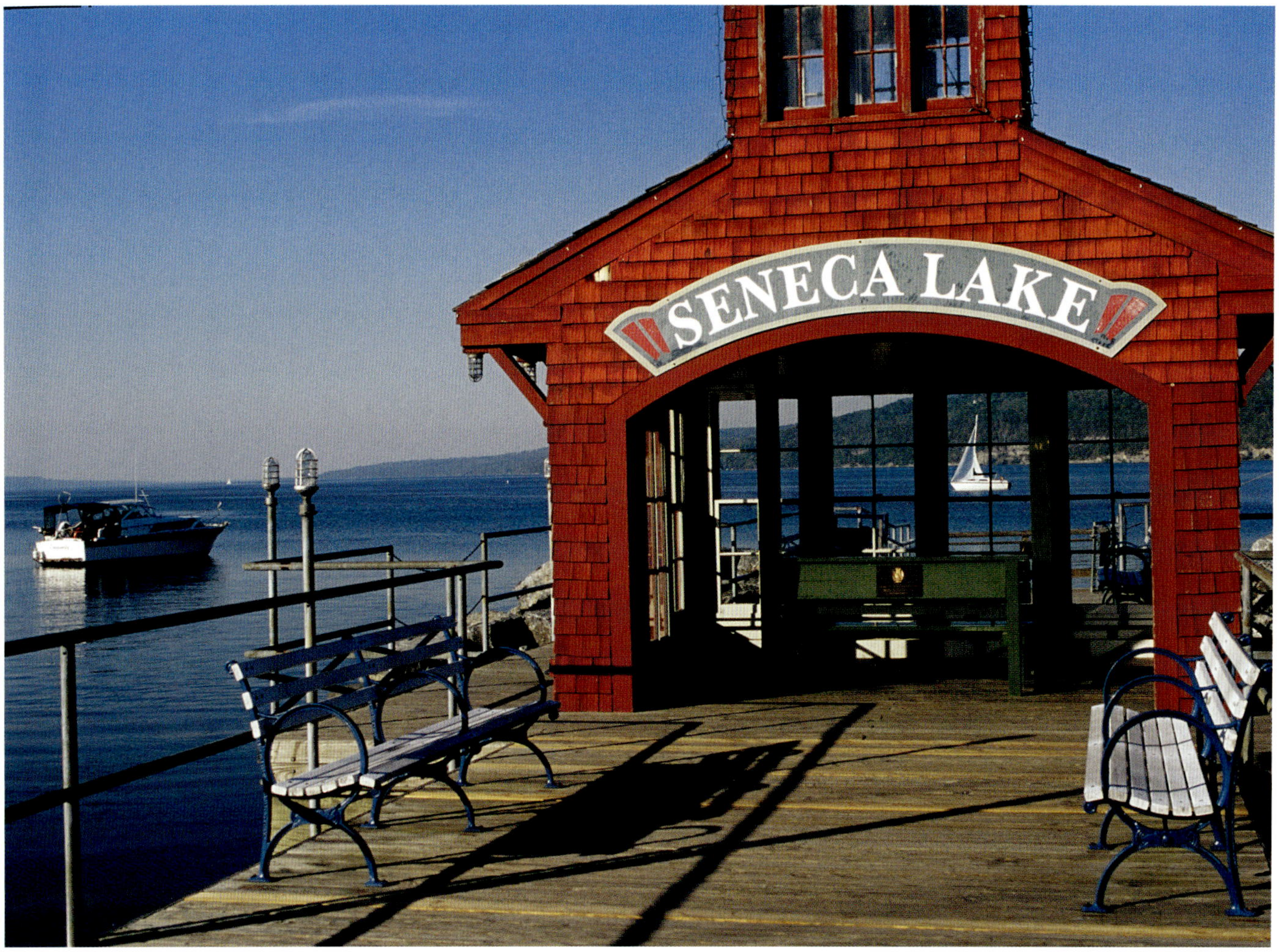

ABOVE

Watkins Glen, at the southern end of Seneca Lake, is perhaps best known for the Watkins Glen International Speedway, but the beauty of the region is apparent when viewing the length of the lake from the town harbor.

BELOW

A Finger Lakes sunset is a spectacular sight. This lakeside view is from the Onondaga Lake Marina, north of Syracuse.

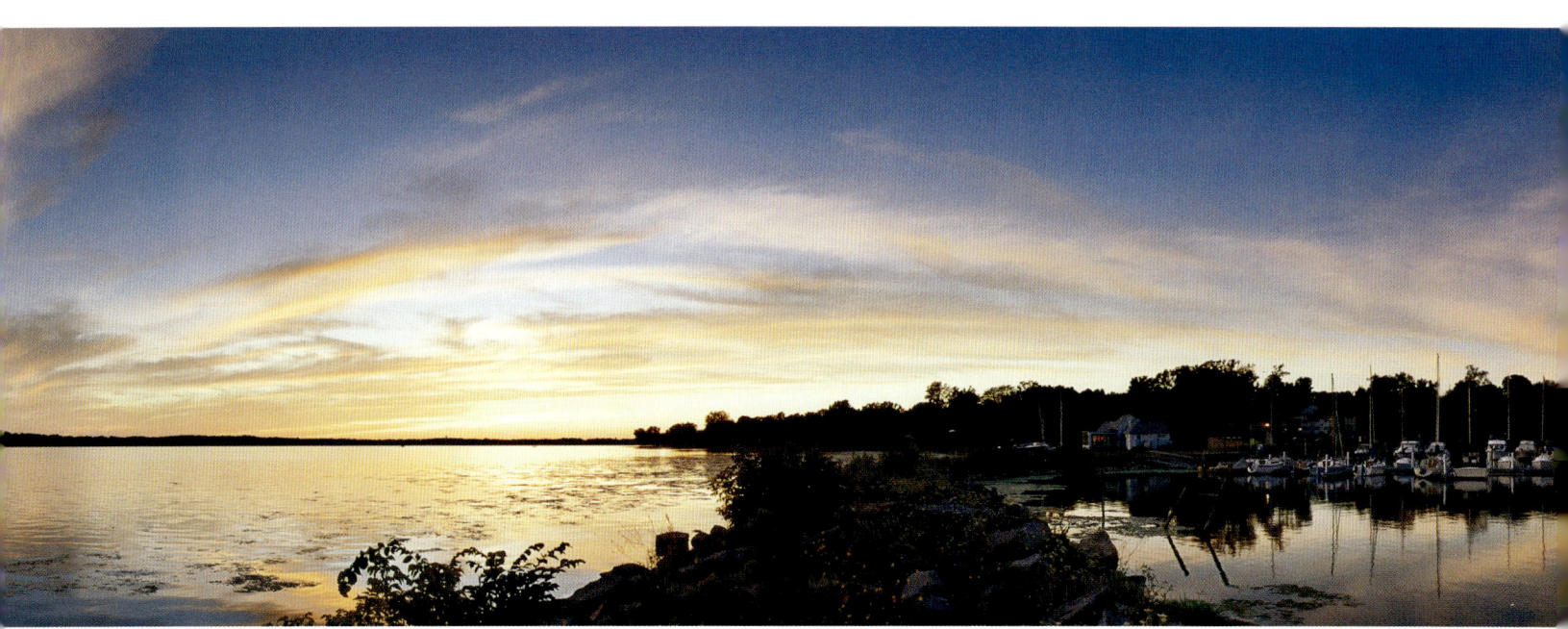

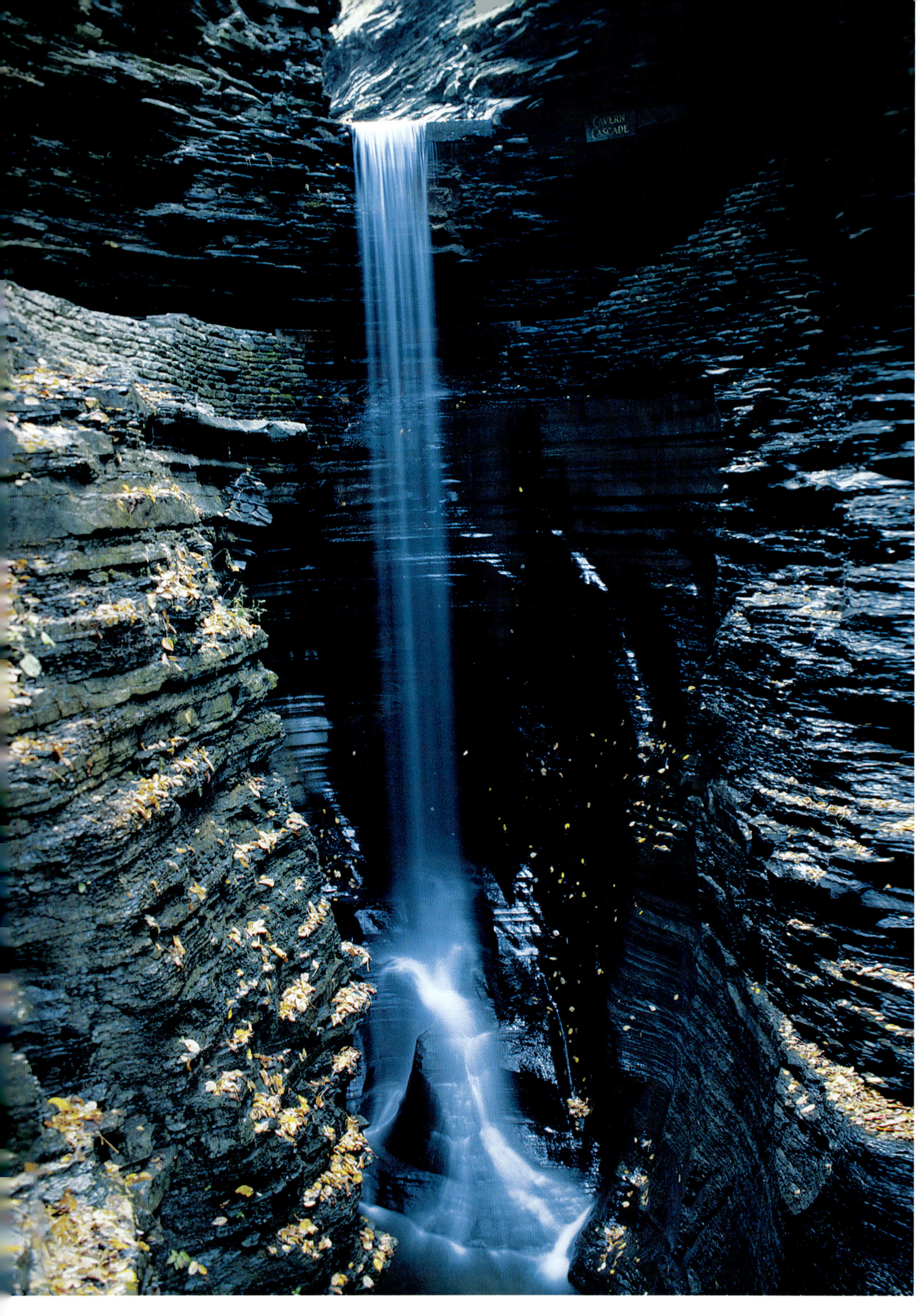

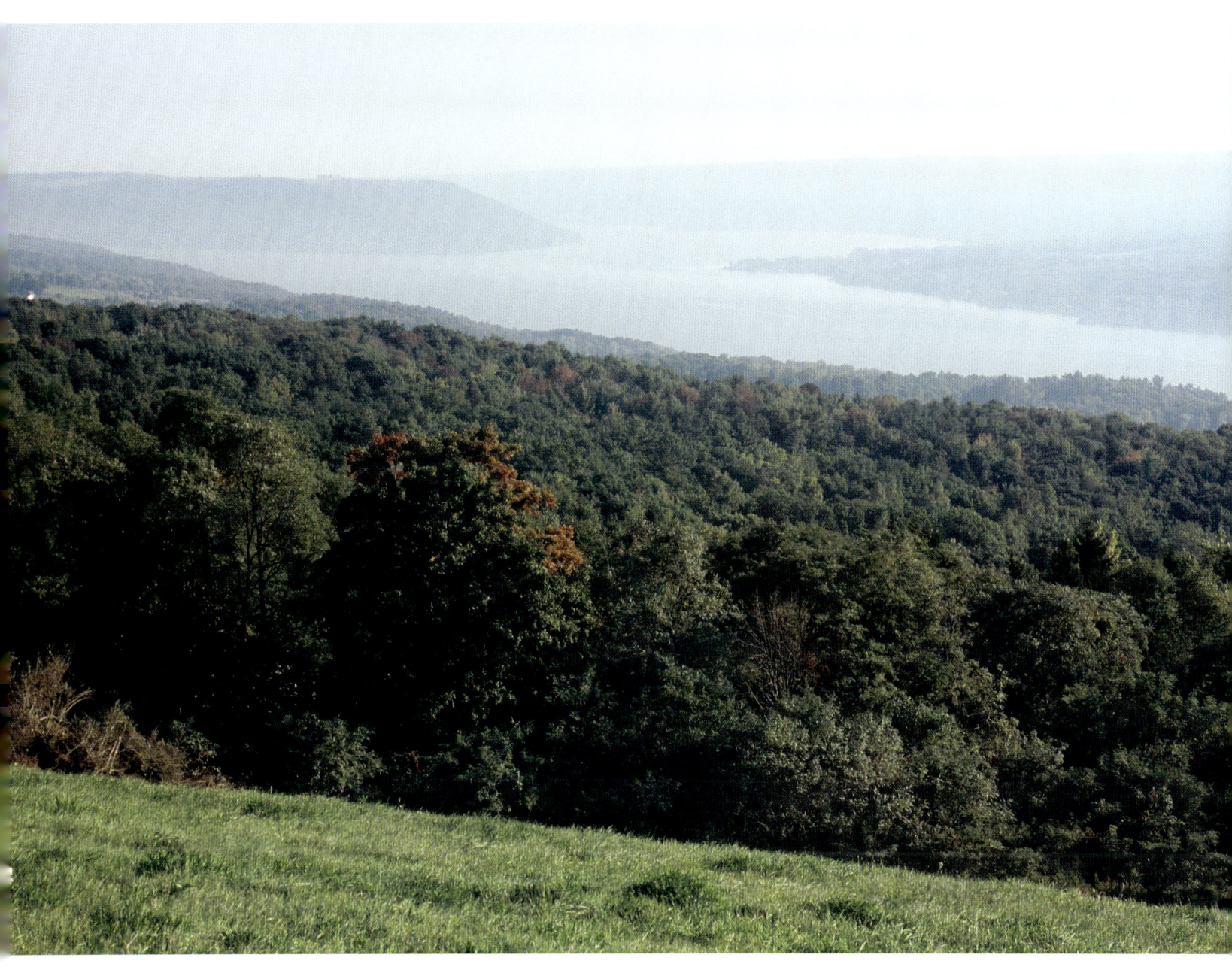

ABOVE

Lakeside roadways offer wonderful views from above beautiful Keuka Lake, known as the "Lady of the Lakes." The Finger Lakes were formed over millions of years during the Ice Age, when advancing glaciers dug deep gouges in the sandstone and shale layers of old stream valleys.

LEFT

The winding pathway at Watkins Glen State Park traverses two-hundred-foot-high cliffs and passes nineteen waterfalls along the two-mile route to the head of the gorge. This is one of many rugged gorges in the southern Finger Lakes.

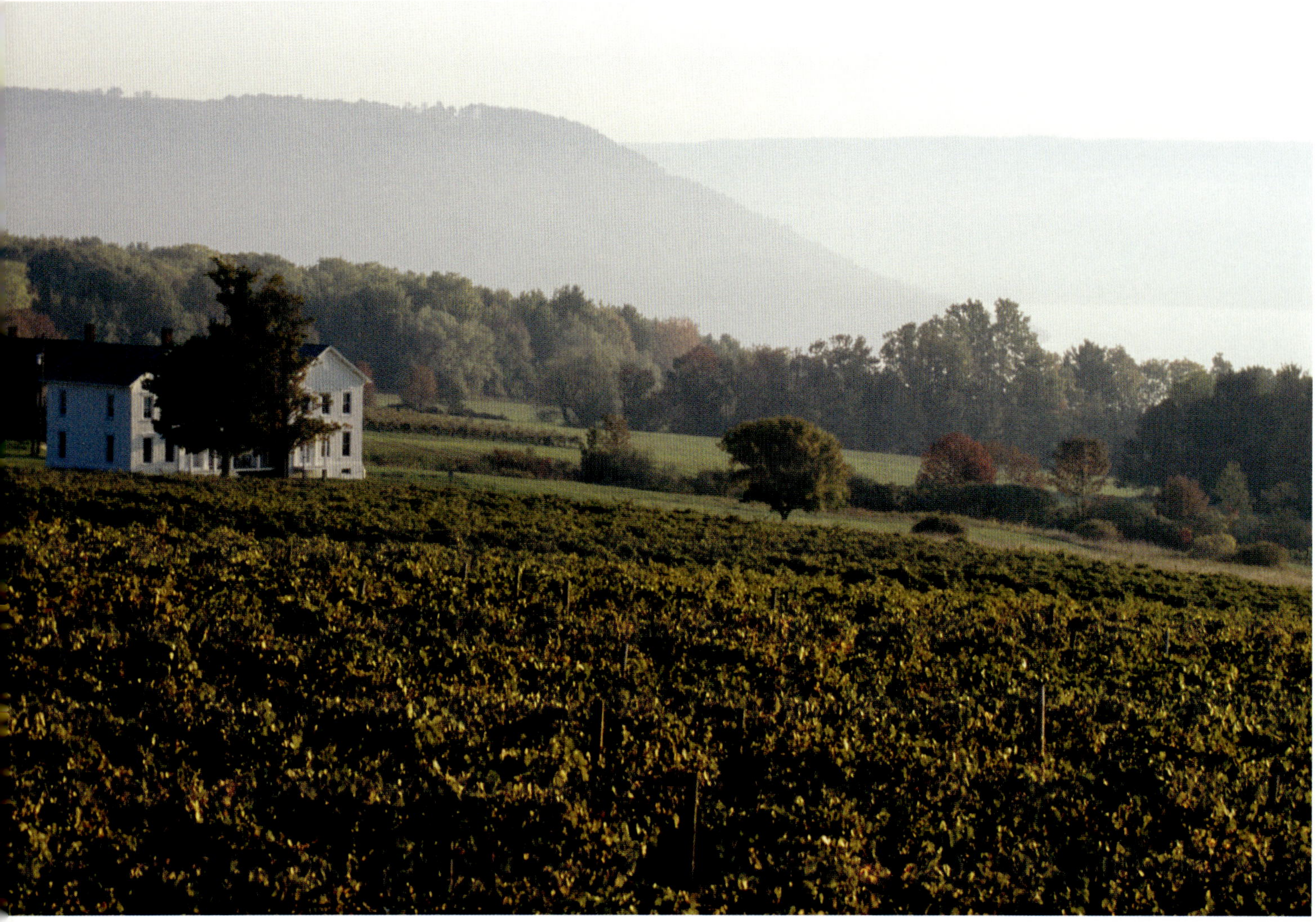

ABOVE

With more than two hundred wineries, New York ranks second in the nation in wine production. The moderating effect of the Finger Lakes on the weather makes this one of New York's best wine-producing regions, and it is home to nearly half of the state's wineries.

RIGHT

Although the Hudson Valley's Brotherhood Winery (founded 1839) is the oldest winery in the country, Bully Hill Vineyards, on Keuka Lake, has the oldest association with the same family, having been owned by the Taylors since 1878.

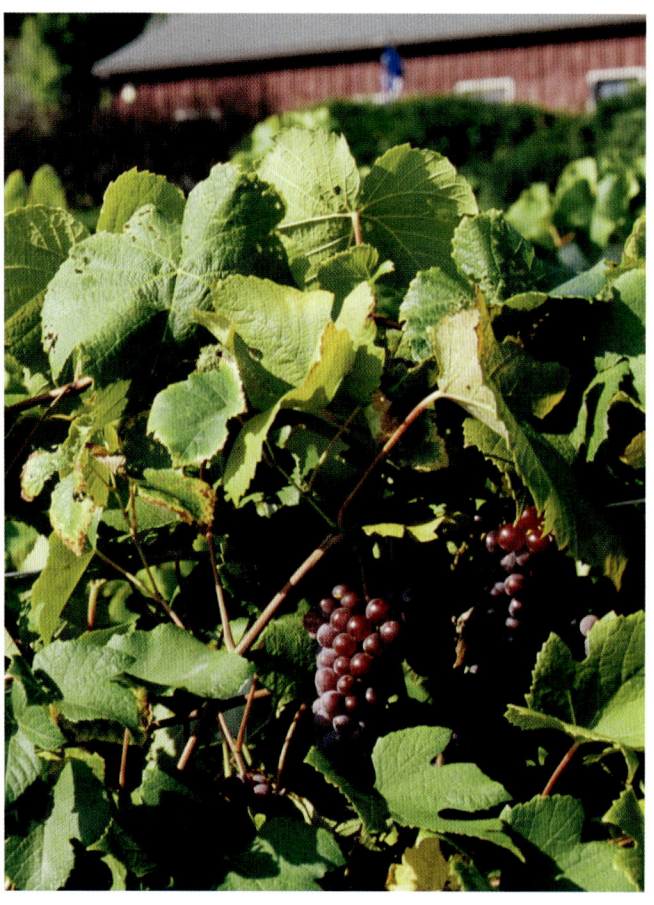

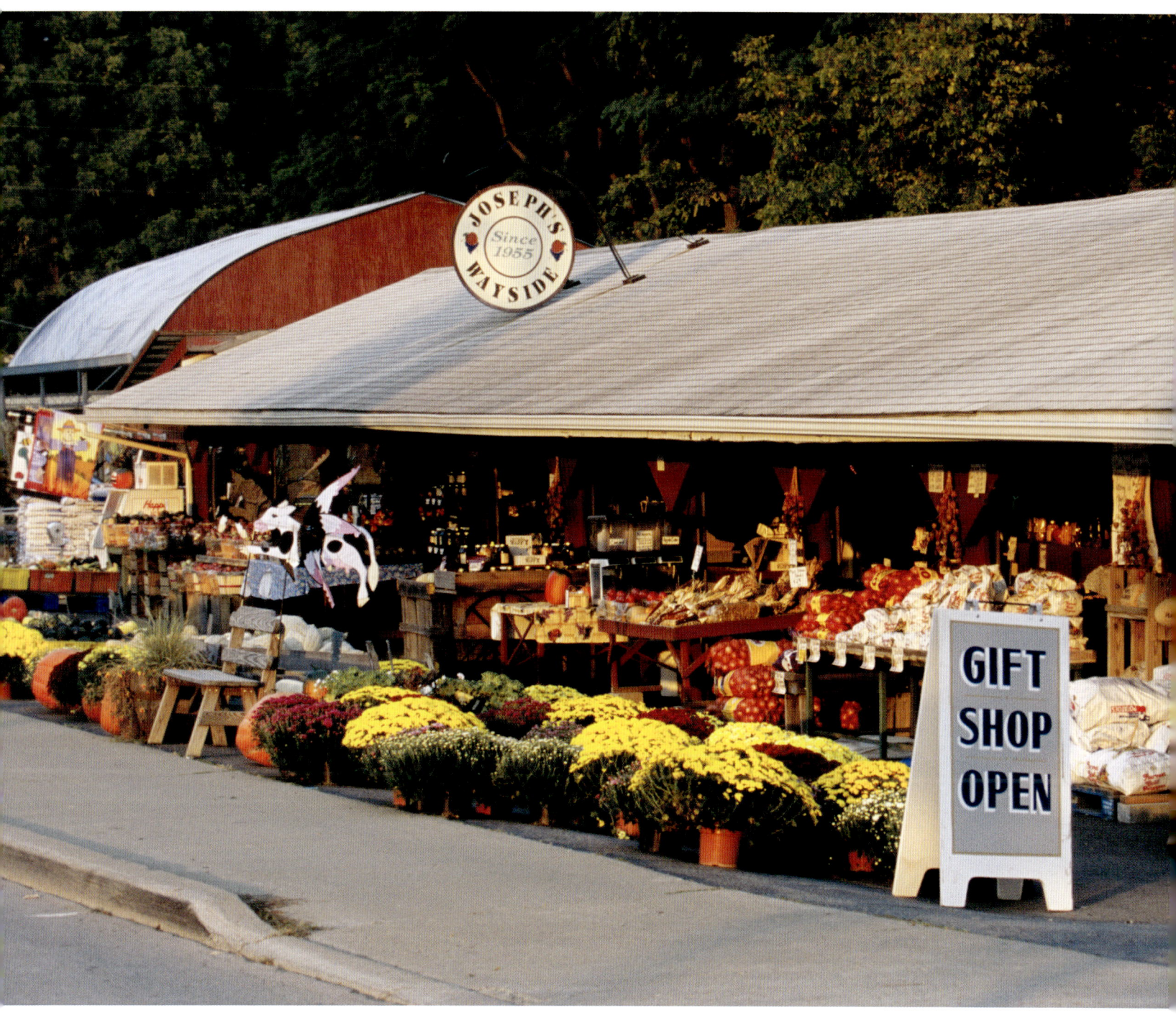

ABOVE

The farmers market in Naples offers typical farm market items, as well as grape pies and bars. Naples is known as the "grape pie capital of the world," and it celebrates with a huge grape festival each fall.

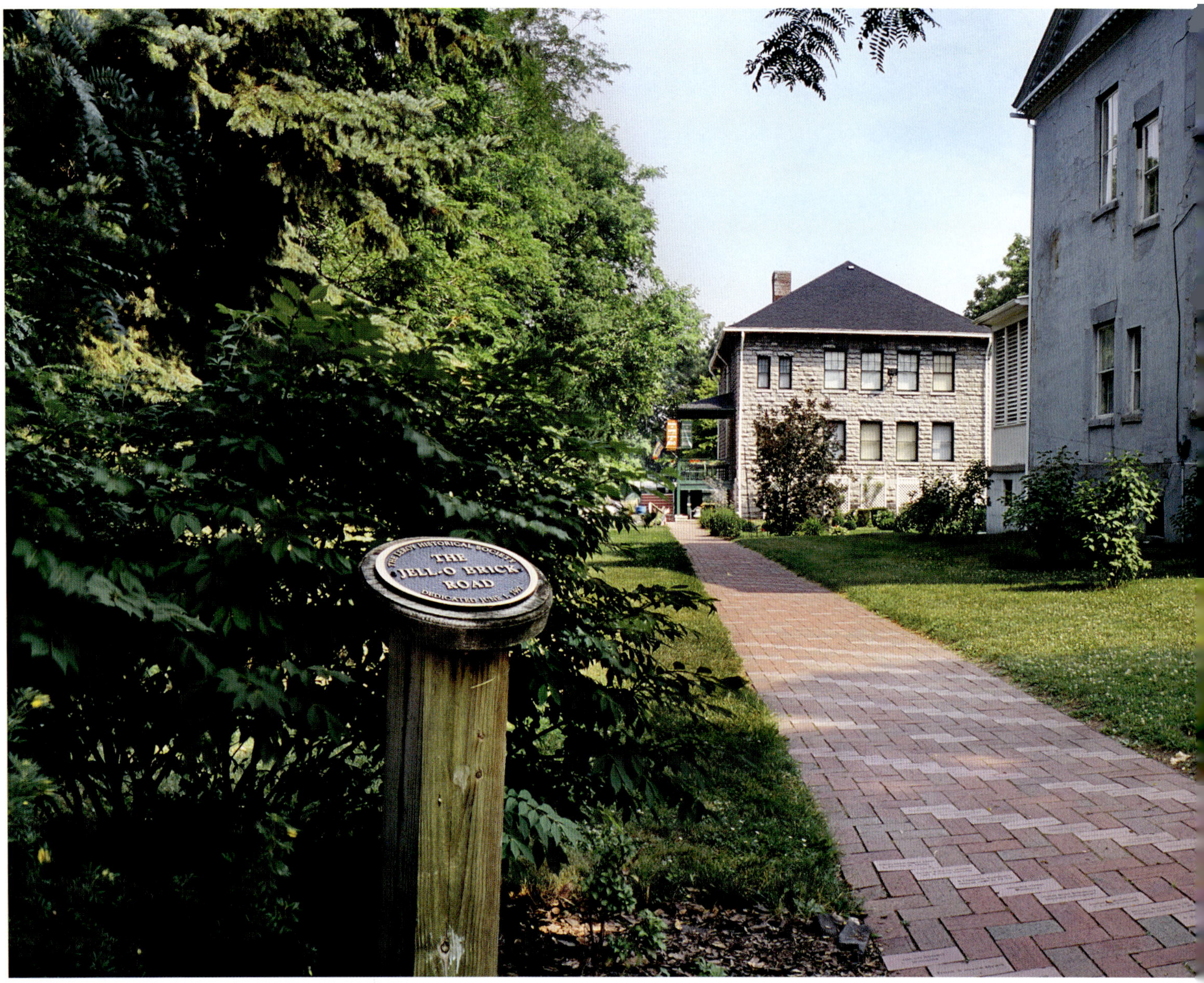

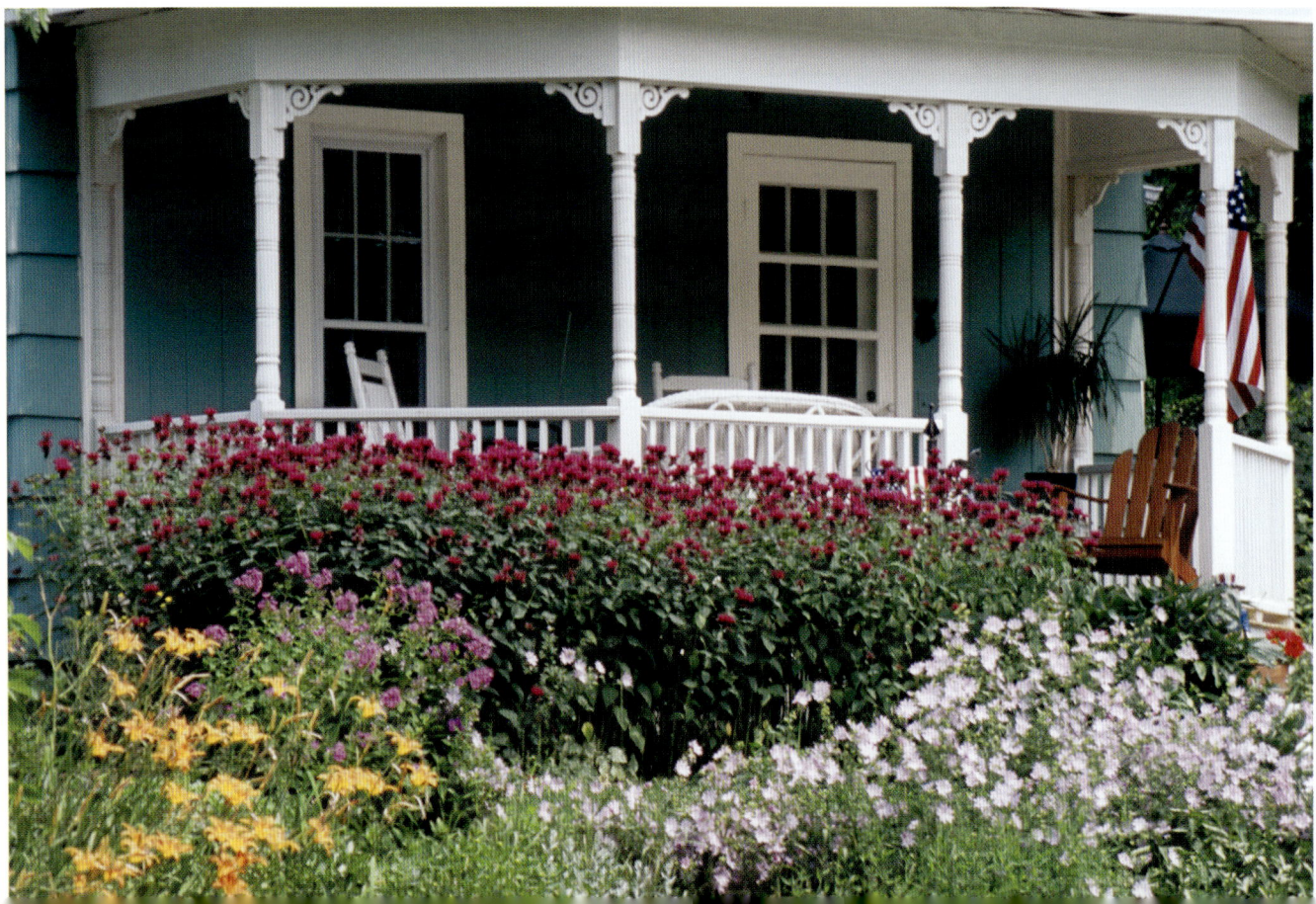

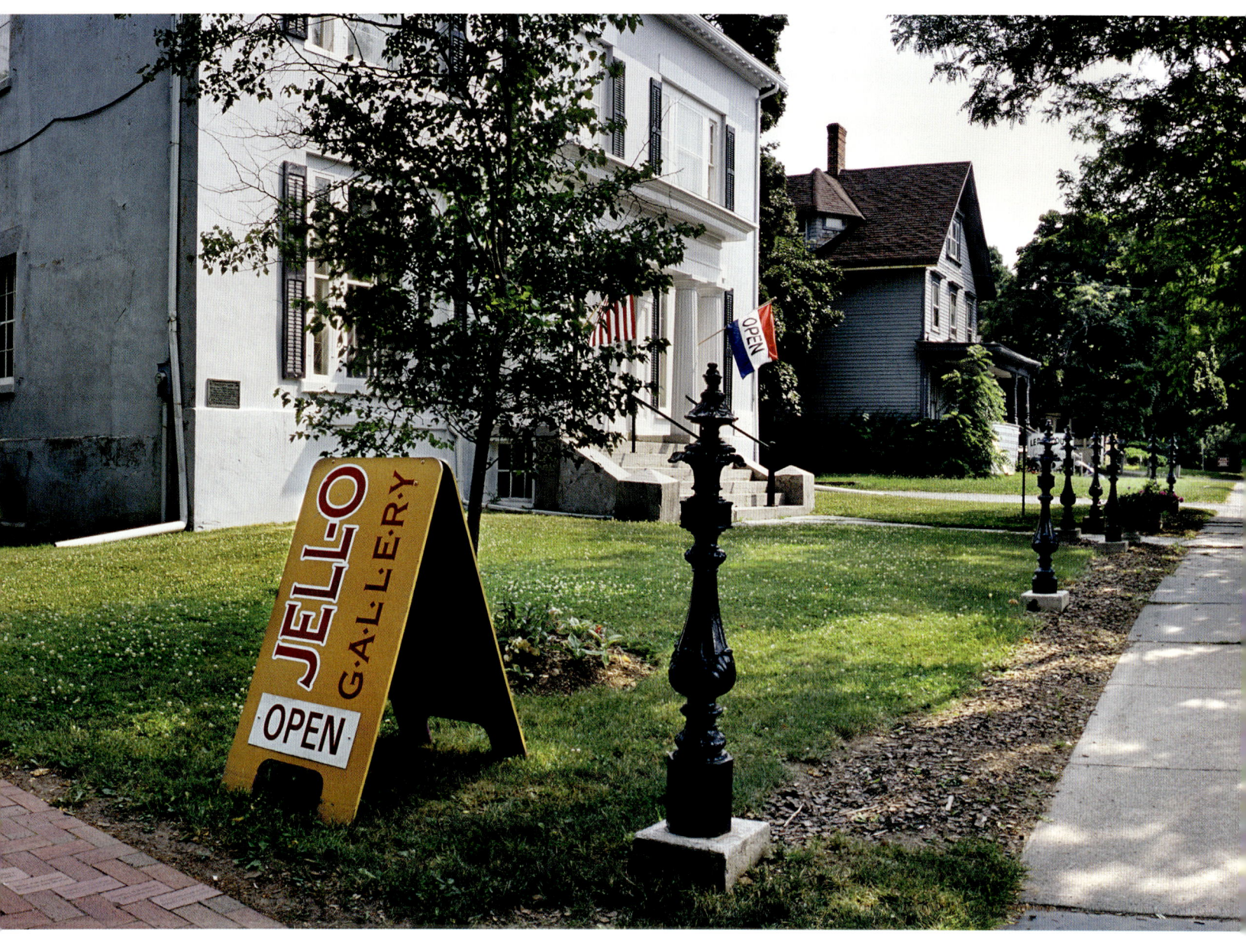

ABOVE

The "Jell-O Brick Road" leads to the Jell-O Museum in LeRoy, where the fruit-flavored dessert was invented in 1897. The museum is located in the building that was originally used to produce Jell-O.

LEFT

At this home in Honeoye Falls, south of Rochester, the front porch is still a relaxing place to sit and watch the world go by.

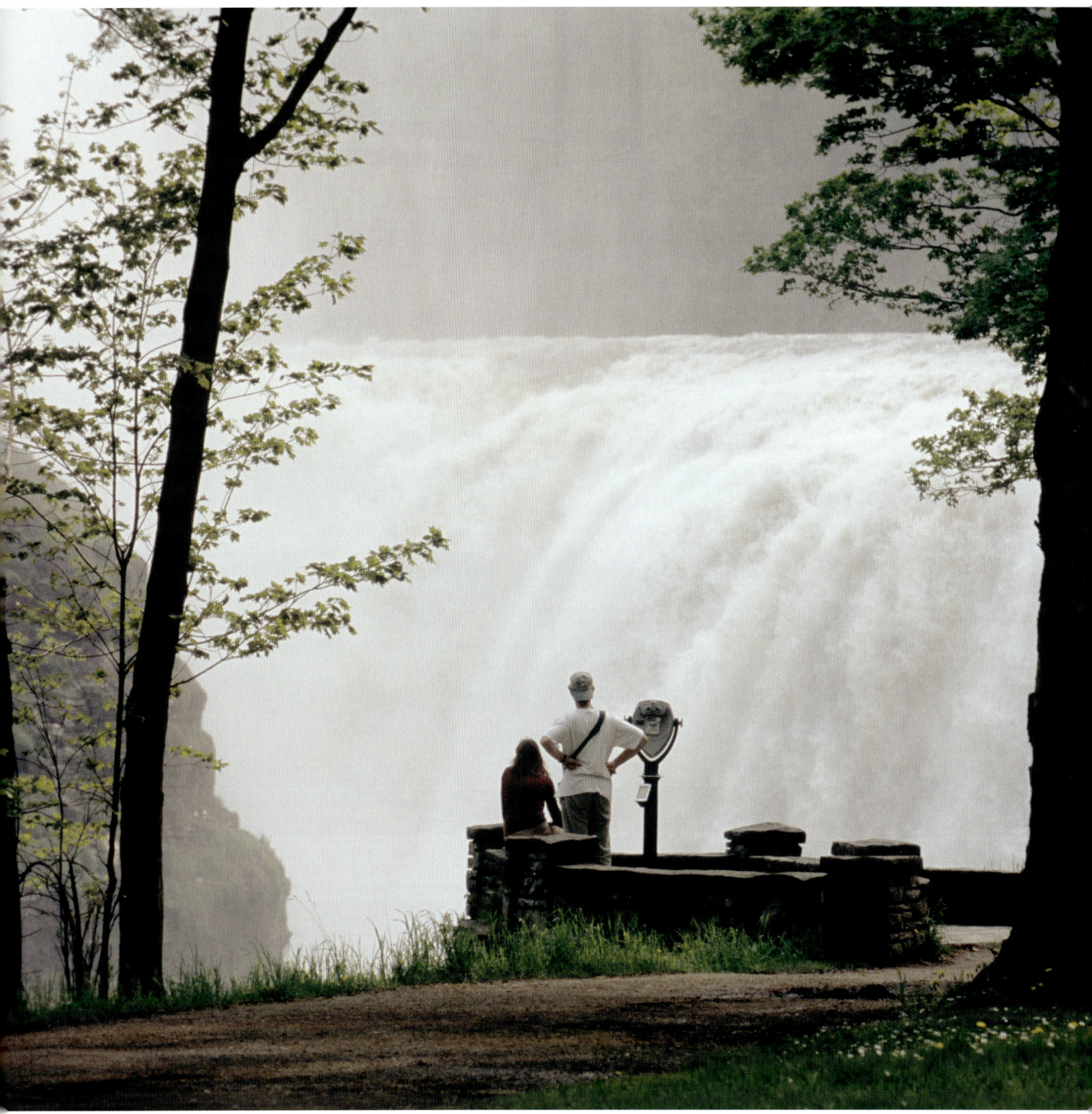

ABOUT

The Western New York Waterfall Survey has tallied 933 waterfalls in the region as of October 2005. Letchworth State Park features some of the most impressive waterfalls and gorges in the entire state.

RIGHT

The Zoar Valley in western New York is replete with old-growth forests, rushing rivers, and dramatic scenery all year round. You can explore the region on one of the many foot trails, or tube down Cattaraugus Creek on a hot summer day.

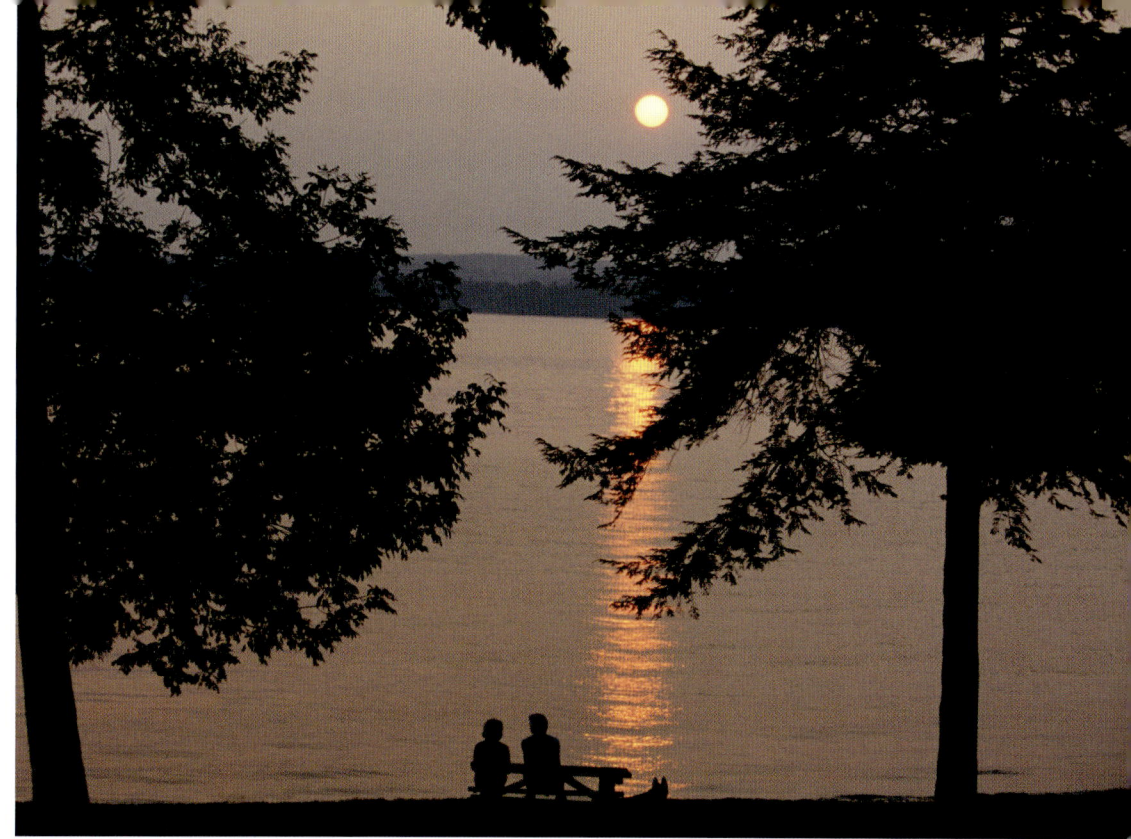

RIGHT
Long Point State Park on Chautauqua Lake is an idyllic location to catch a sunset.

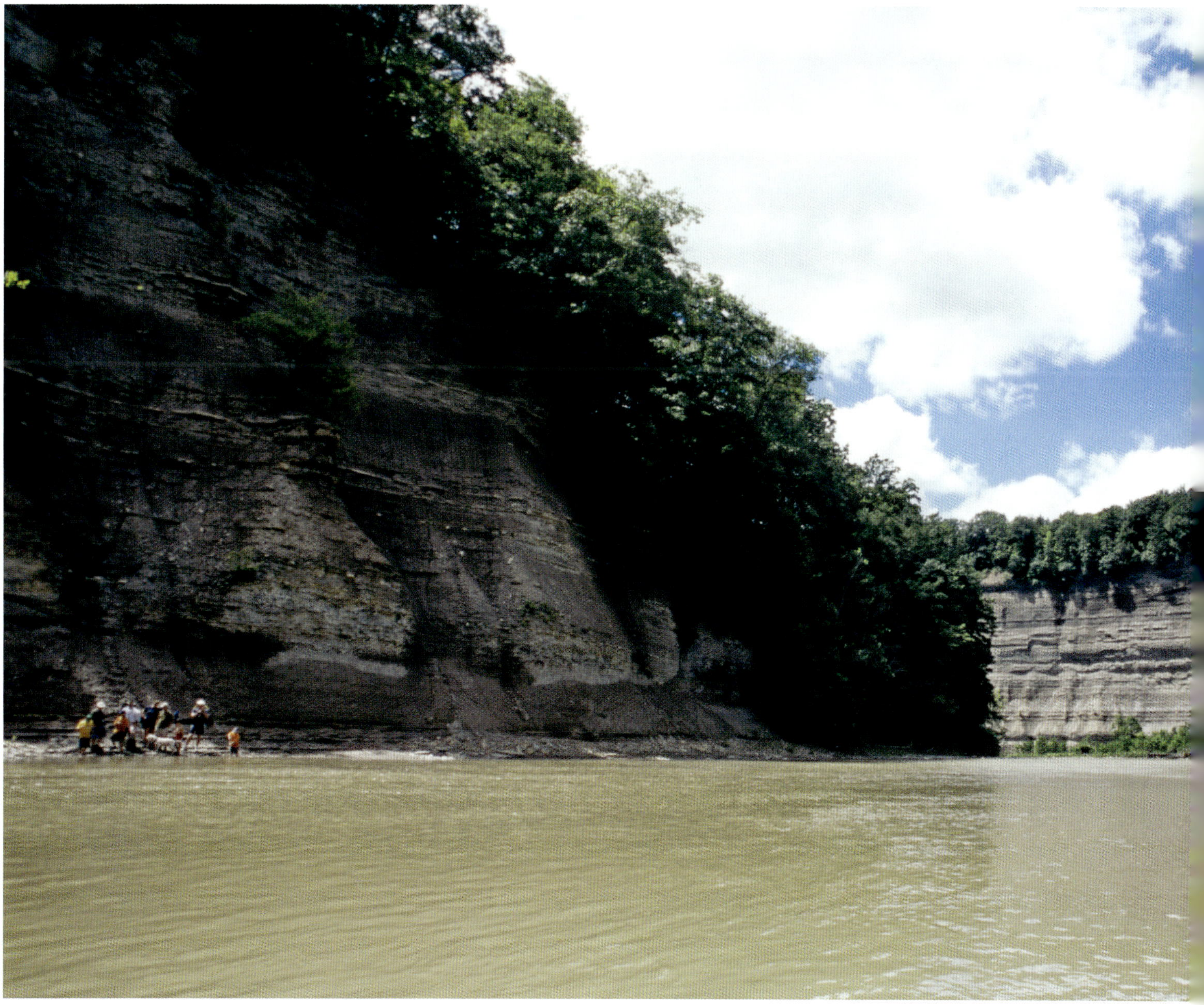

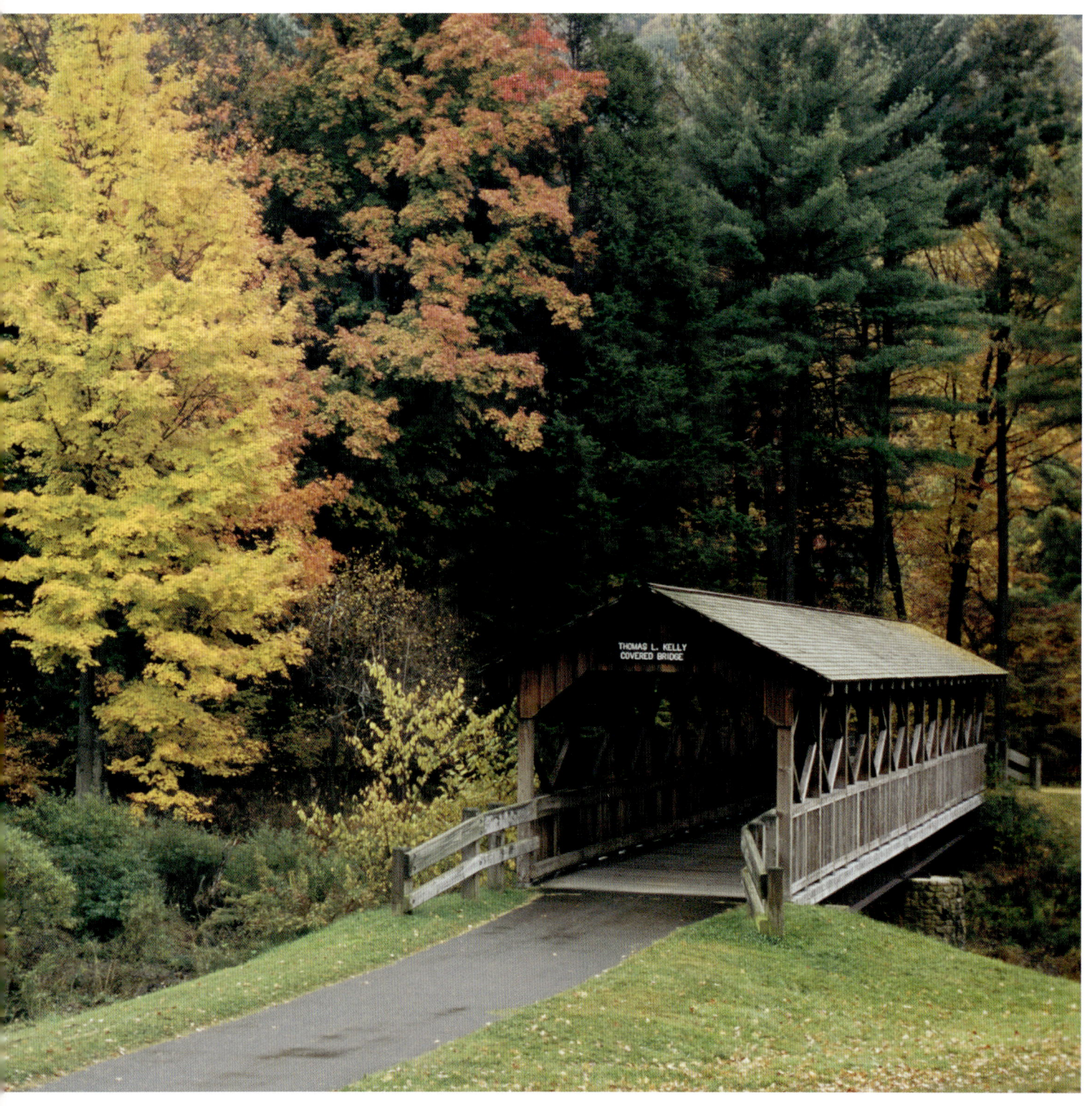

ABOVE

Every fall, vibrant colors cover the rolling mountains of Allegany State Park. The Thomas L. Kelly covered bridge spans Red House Creek in the park.

RIGHT

The Jamestown Audubon Nature Center features exhibits and trails around the sanctuary's wetlands. One of the stars of the preserve is Liberty, a handicapped bald eagle.

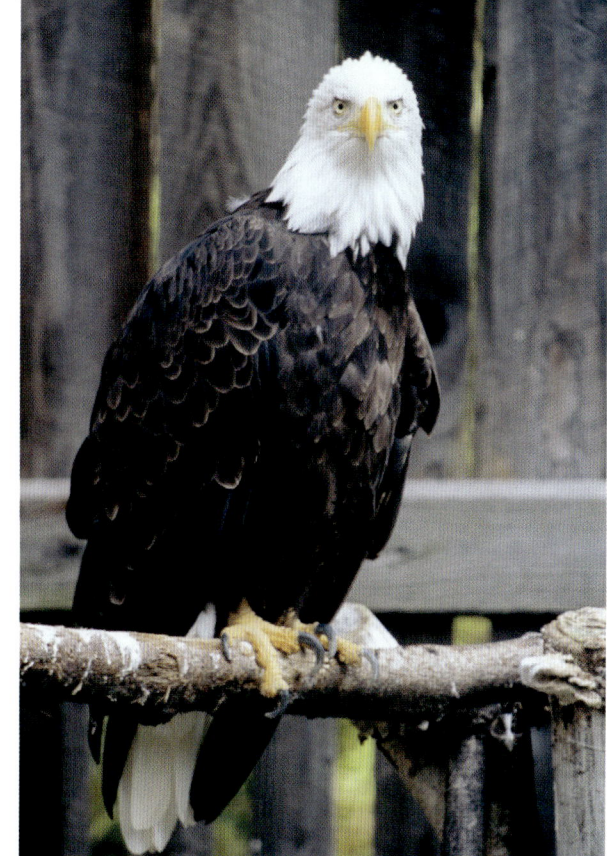

BELOW

The *Chautauqua Belle*, one of only six stern-wheel steamers east of the Mississippi, awaits warmer weather—while the ice fishermen enjoy the colder weather on the lake.

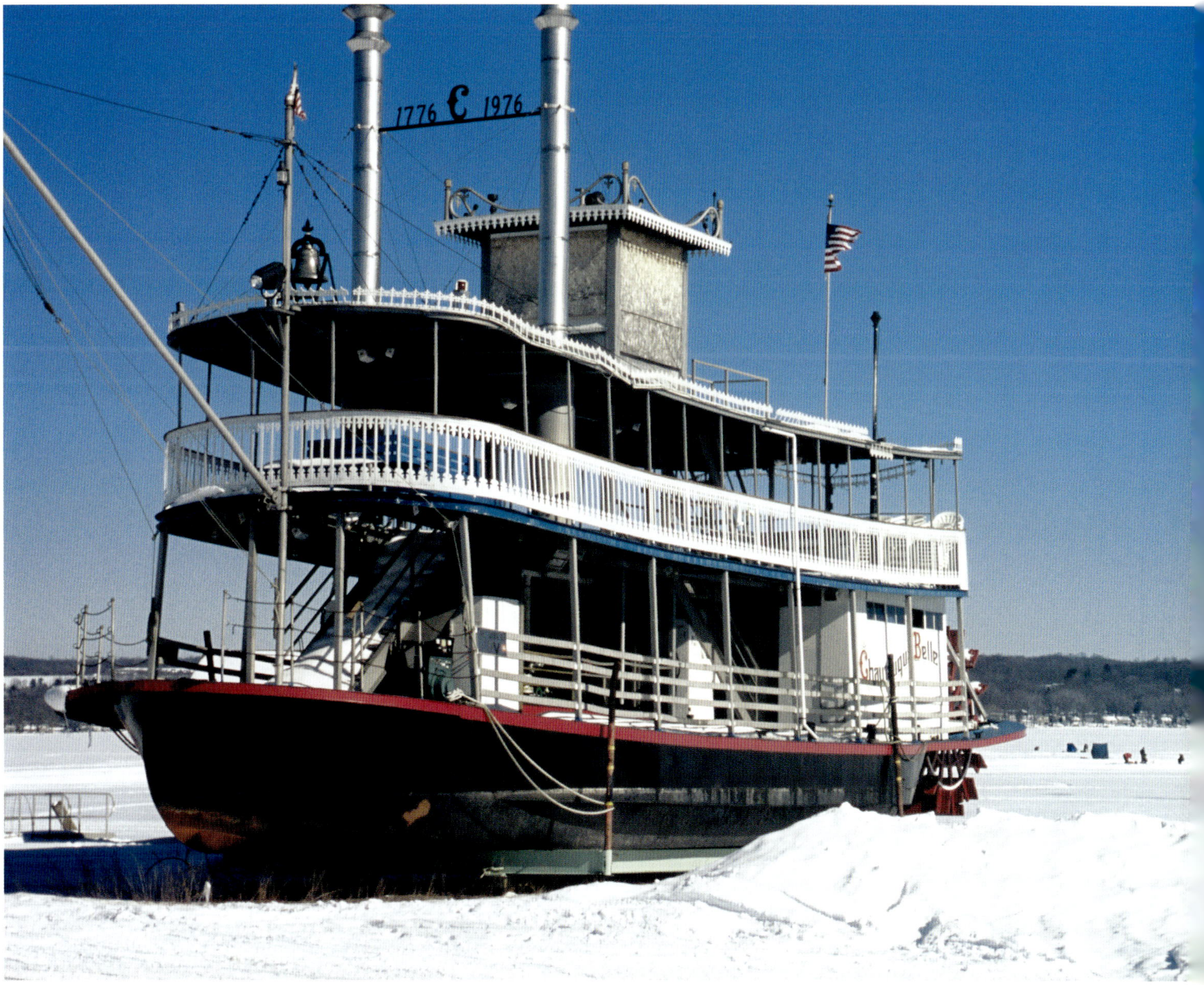

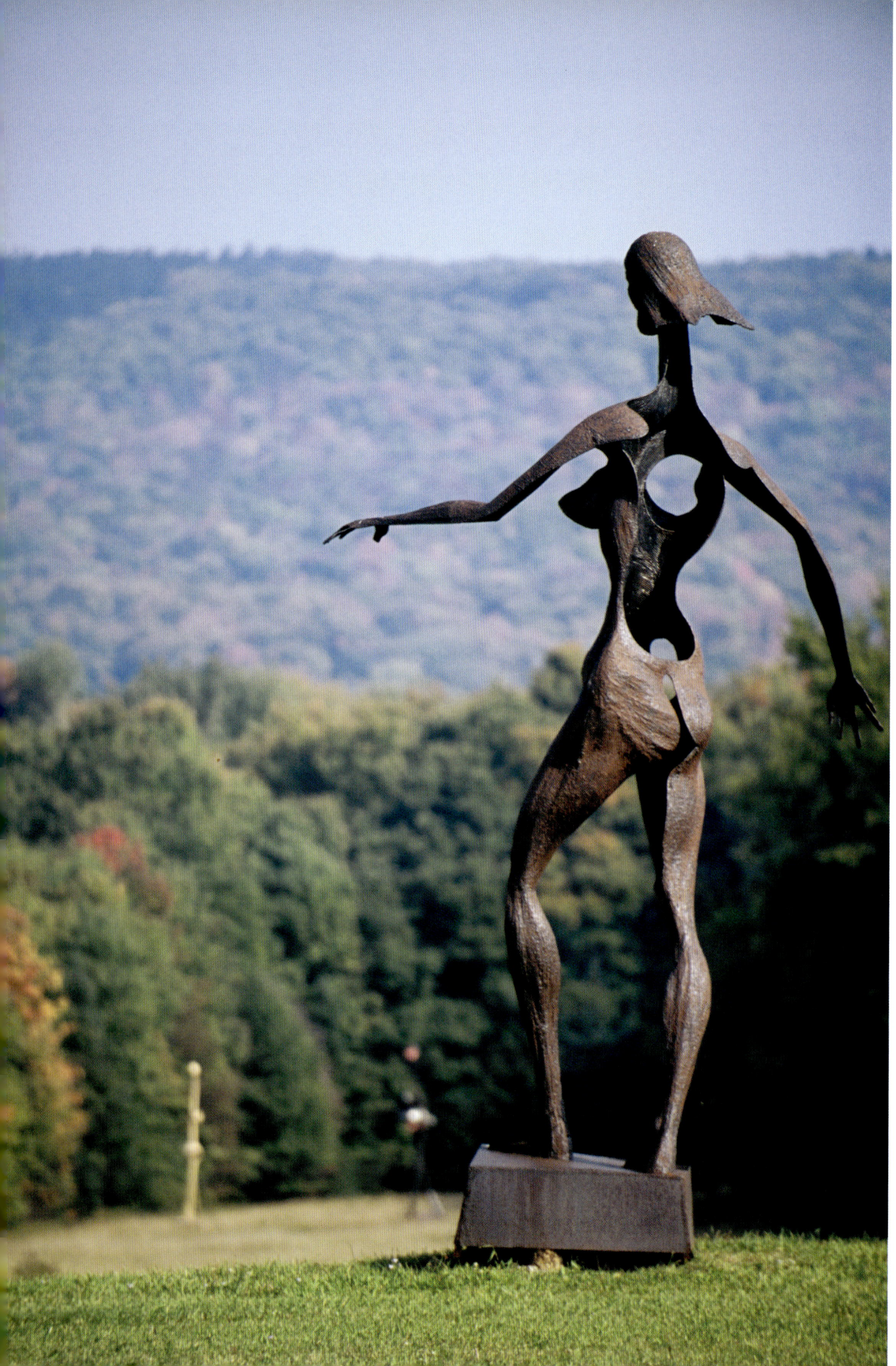

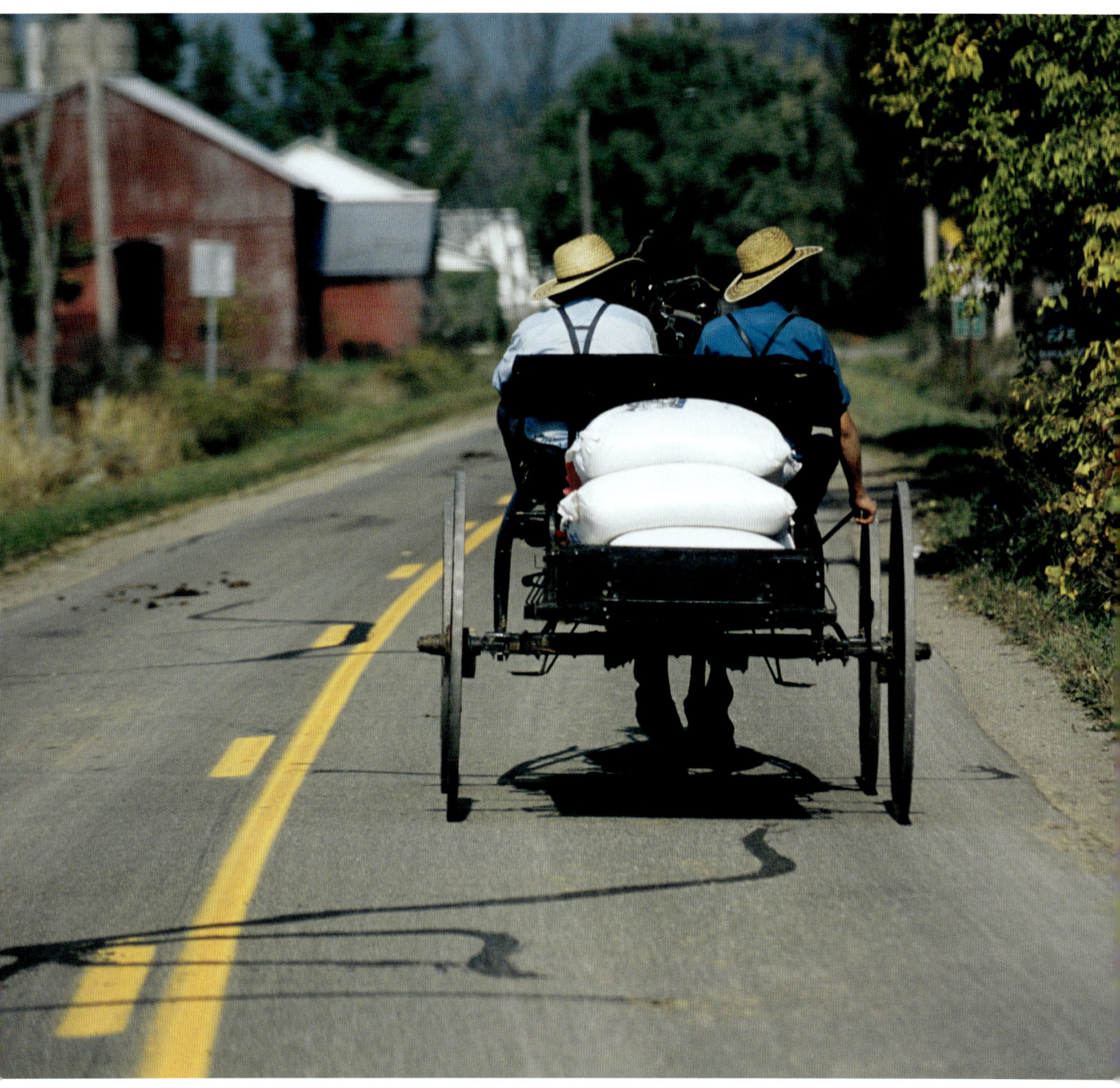

LEFT
Griffis Sculpture Park in Ashford Hollow blends art and nature in an interactive experience. Ten miles of trails lead visitors through a unique blend of sculptures in a natural setting.

ABOVE
Amish communities throughout western and central New York still live life the old-fashioned way, traveling by horse-drawn carriage and employing non-mechanized farming techniques.

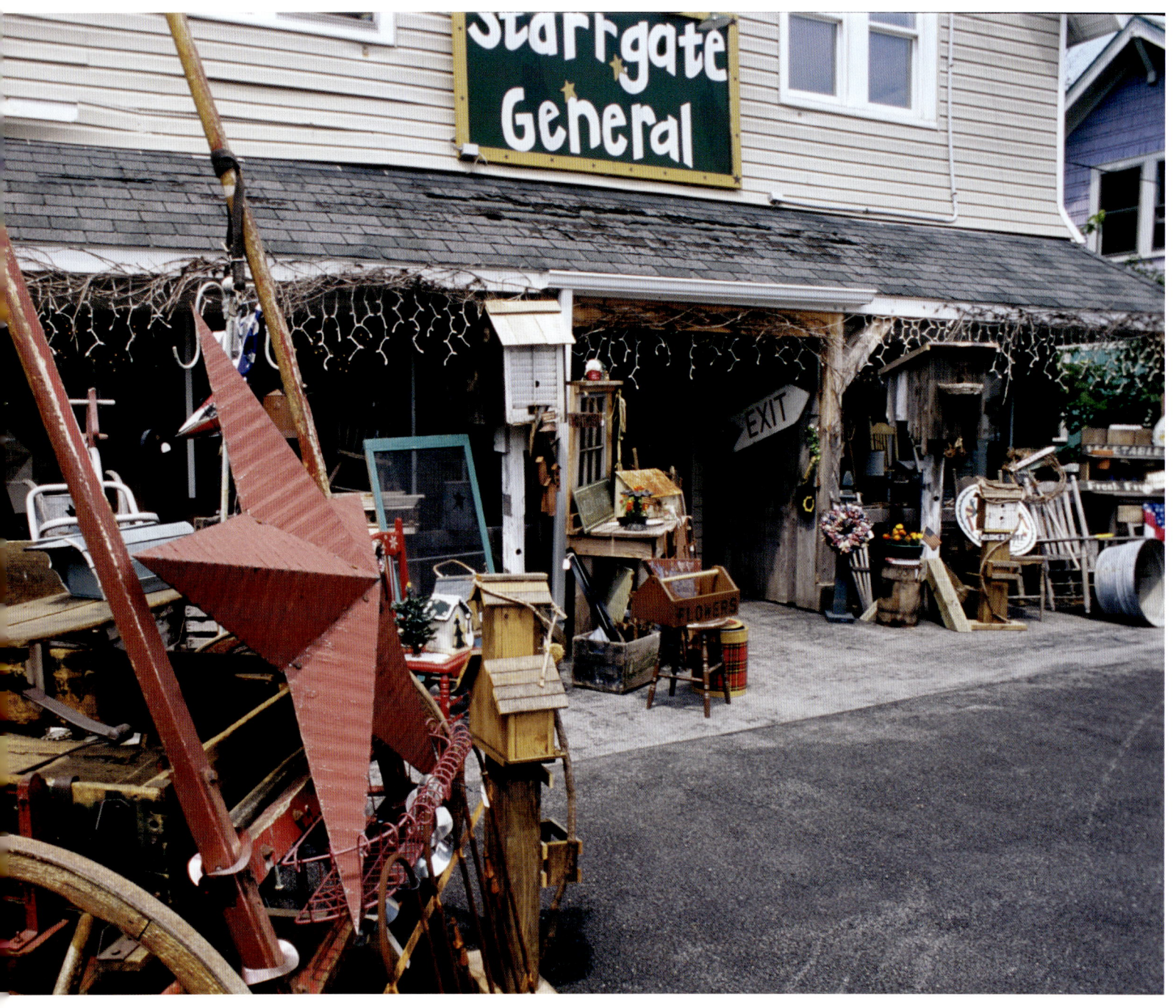

ABOVE

The Starrgate General Store is an eclectic antiques store in the town of Clarence. Founded in 1808, Clarence is the oldest town in Erie County.

RIGHT

A stop at the Twistee Treat in Batavia is always hard to resist on a hot summer day.

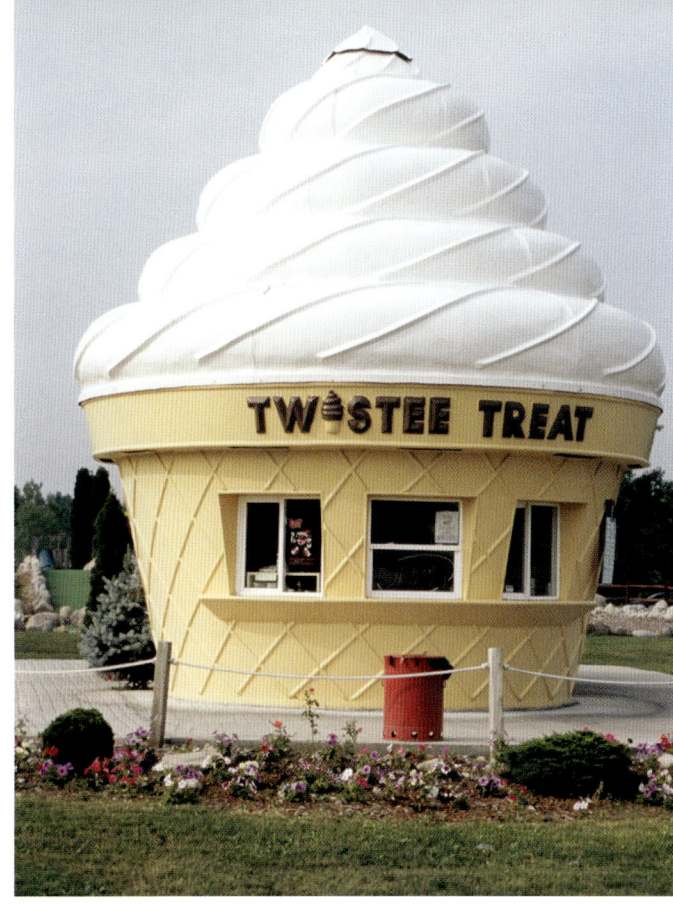

BELOW

In the town of Alabama, a lonely pooch waits in a corner of the barn for the family to come home.

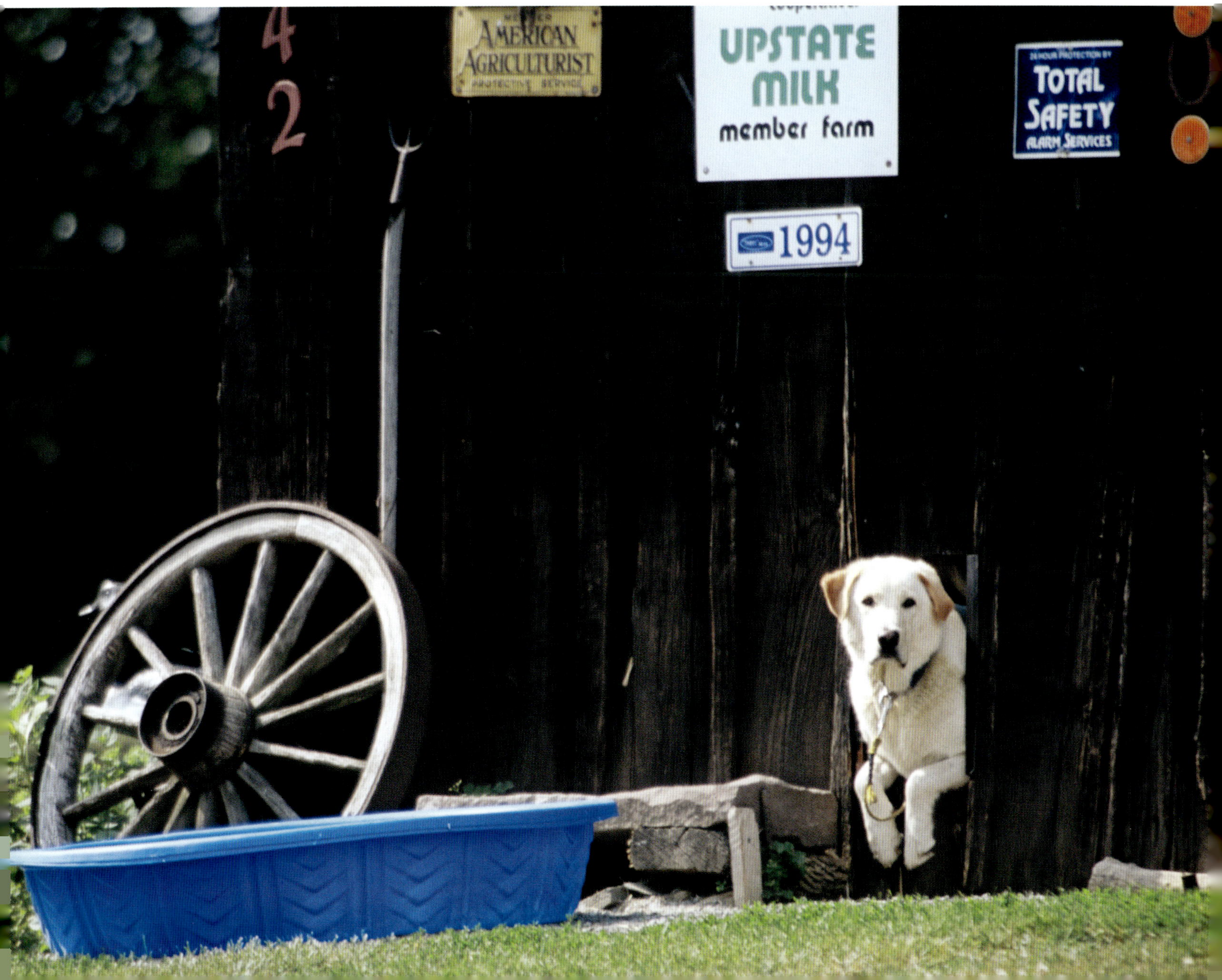

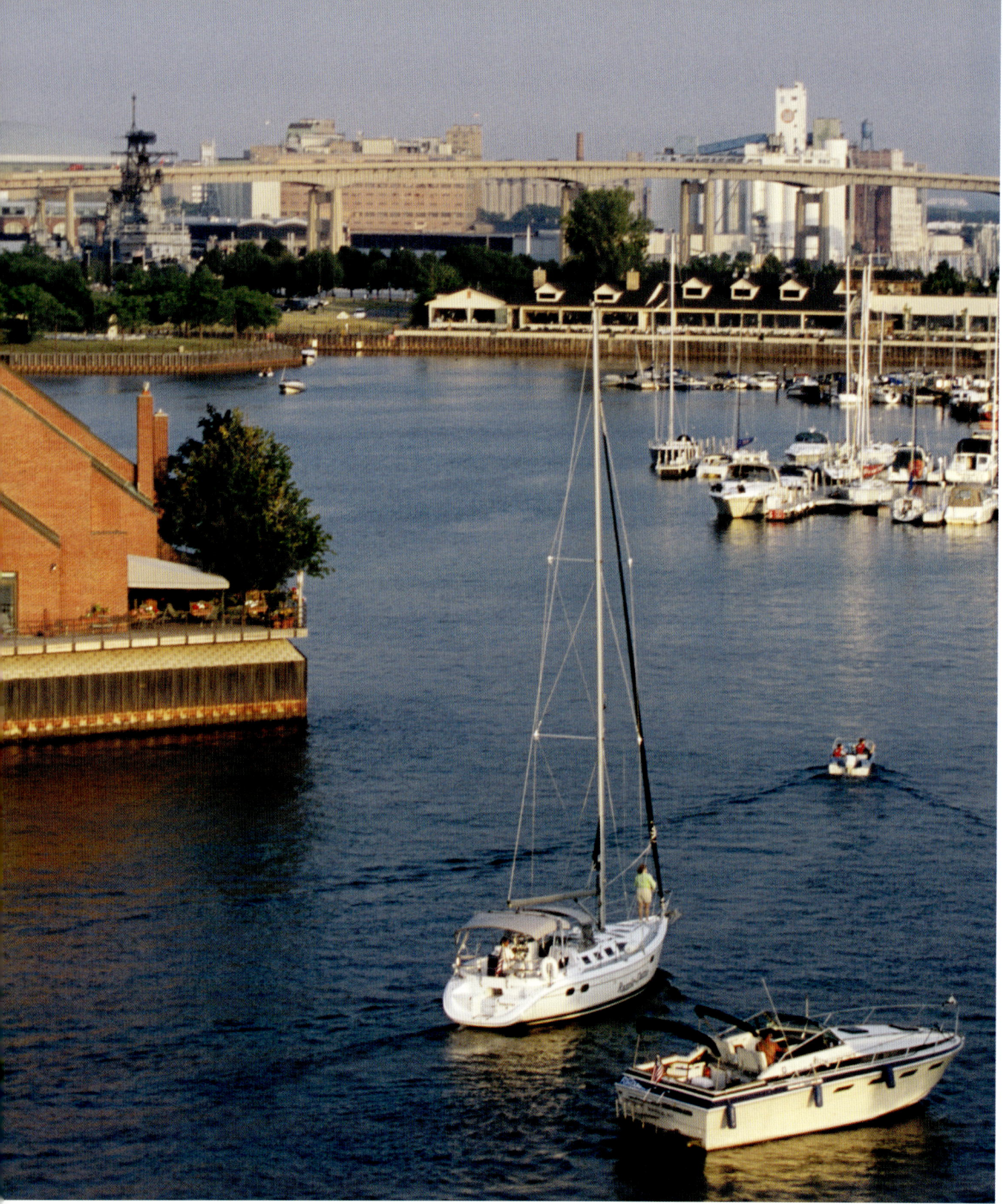

ABOVE

The observation tower at the Erie Basin Marina in Buffalo offers great views of the Skyway, the Buffalo and Erie County Naval and Military Park, and some of the city's old granaries—as well as Lake Erie, the harbor, and downtown Buffalo.

RIGHT

The Buffalo skyline is an interesting mix of contemporary and historic skyscrapers.

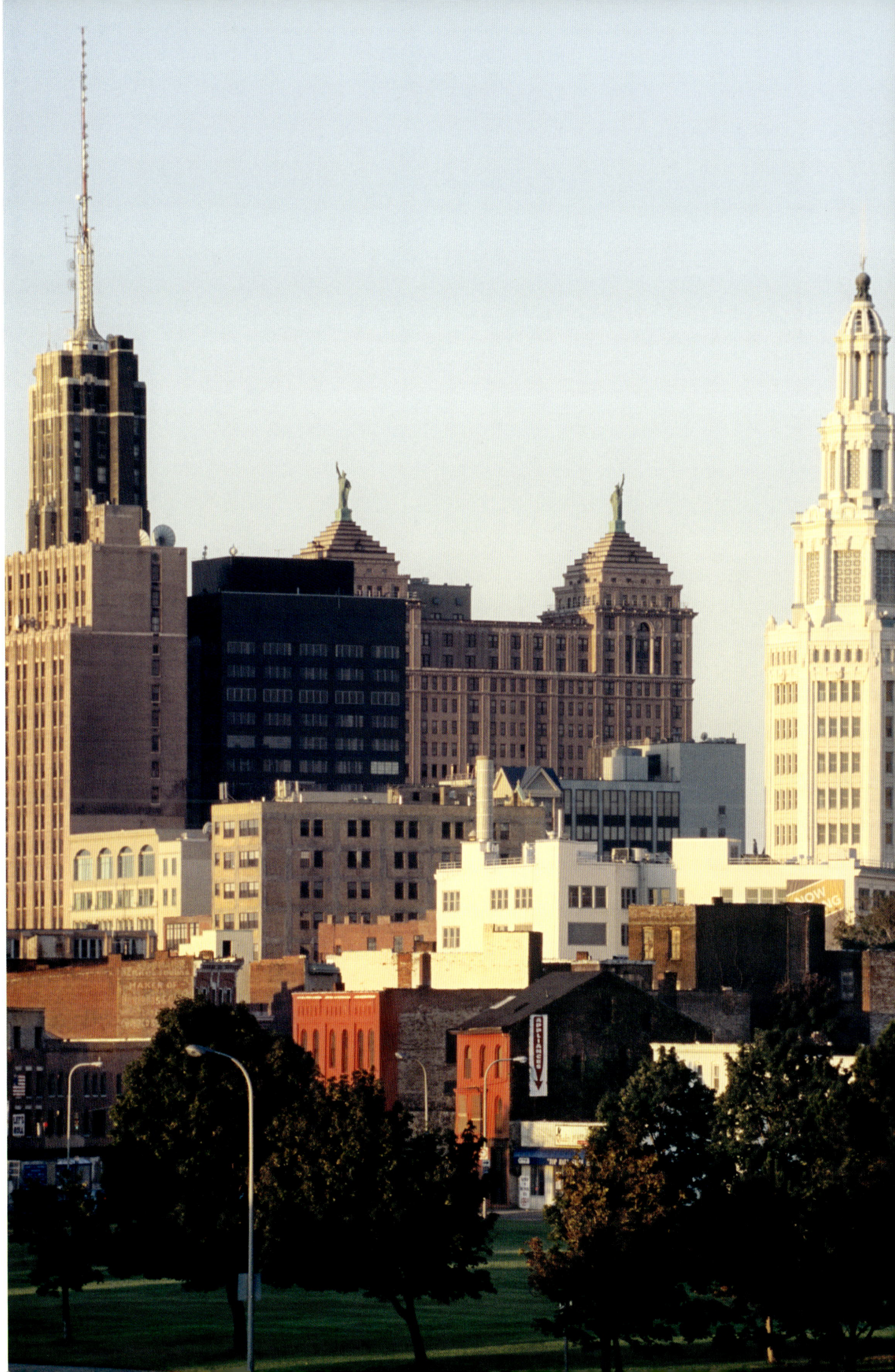

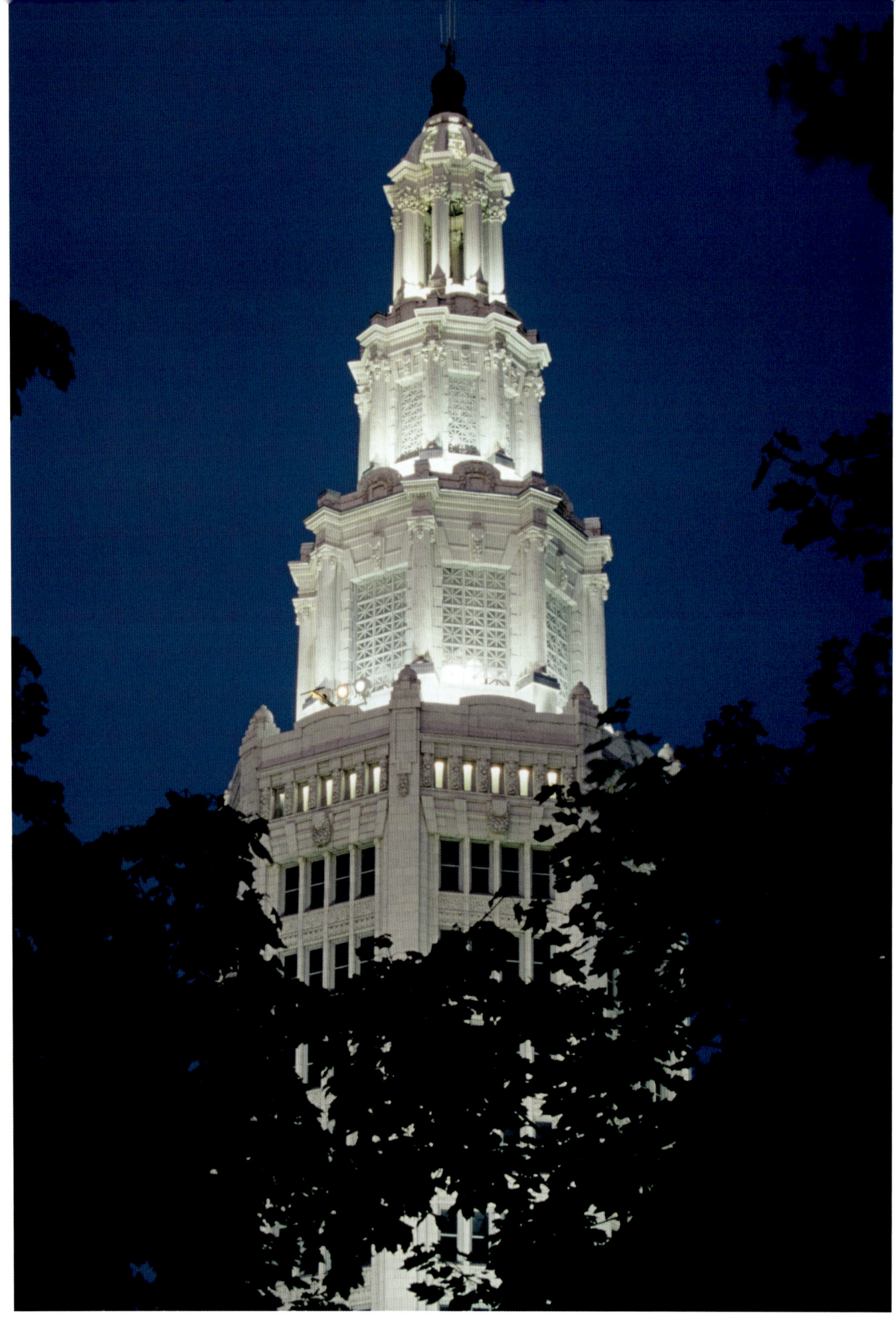

ABOVE

The lighted tower of Buffalo's Niagara Mohawk Building, built in 1912, was inspired by the Electric Tower that was displayed at the 1901 Pan-American Exposition, held in the city.

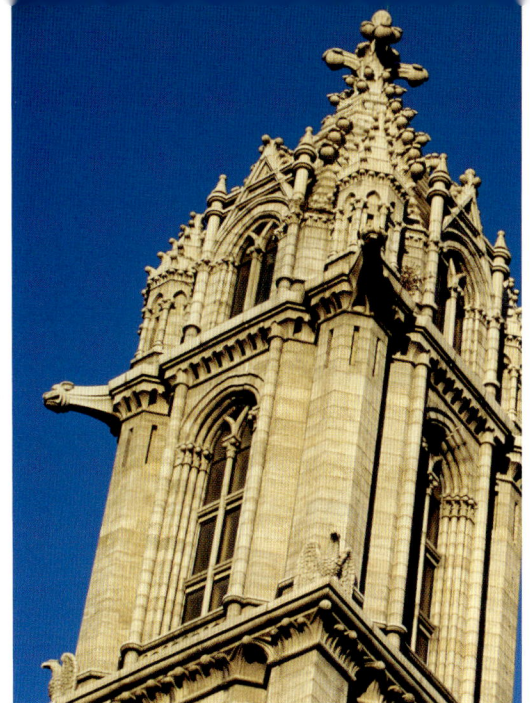 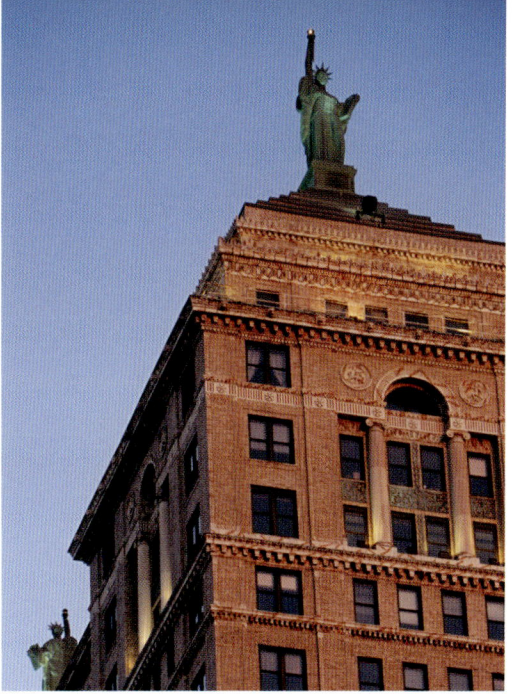

ABOVE LEFT

The old Post Office Building was built from pink granite around the turn of the twentieth century and dedicated in 1901. Today it is the City Campus of the Erie Community College.

ABOVE RIGHT

The 352-foot-tall Liberty Bank Building, built in 1925, features two scaled-down replicas of the Statue of Liberty. They are lit each night and are quite prominent on the Buffalo skyline.

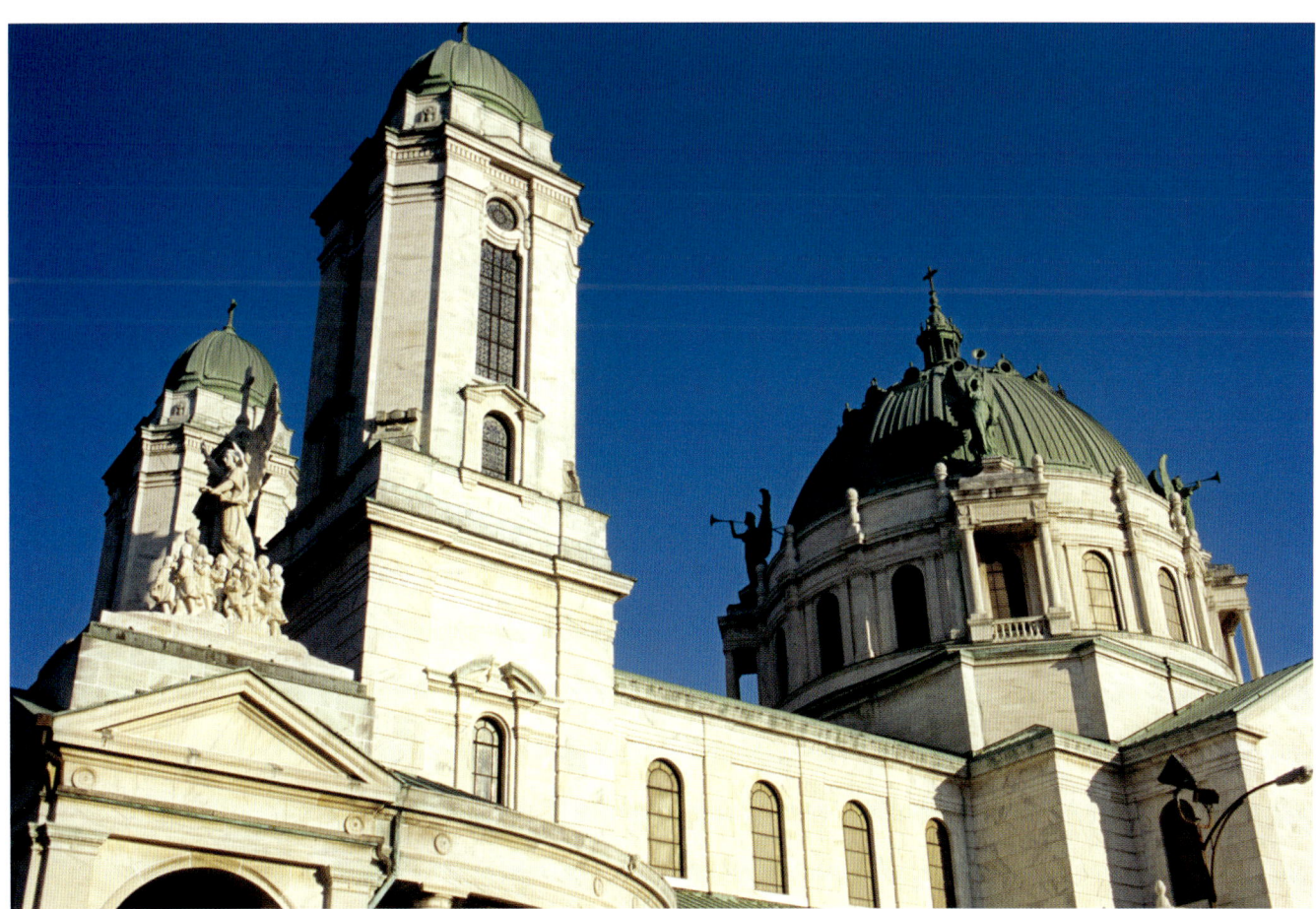

ABOVE

Completed in 1925 in Lackawanna, Our Lady of Victory Basilica was built to be a magnificent shrine to rival any cathedral in the United States. Within a few months of completion, it was designated a Minor Basilica by Pope Pius XI.

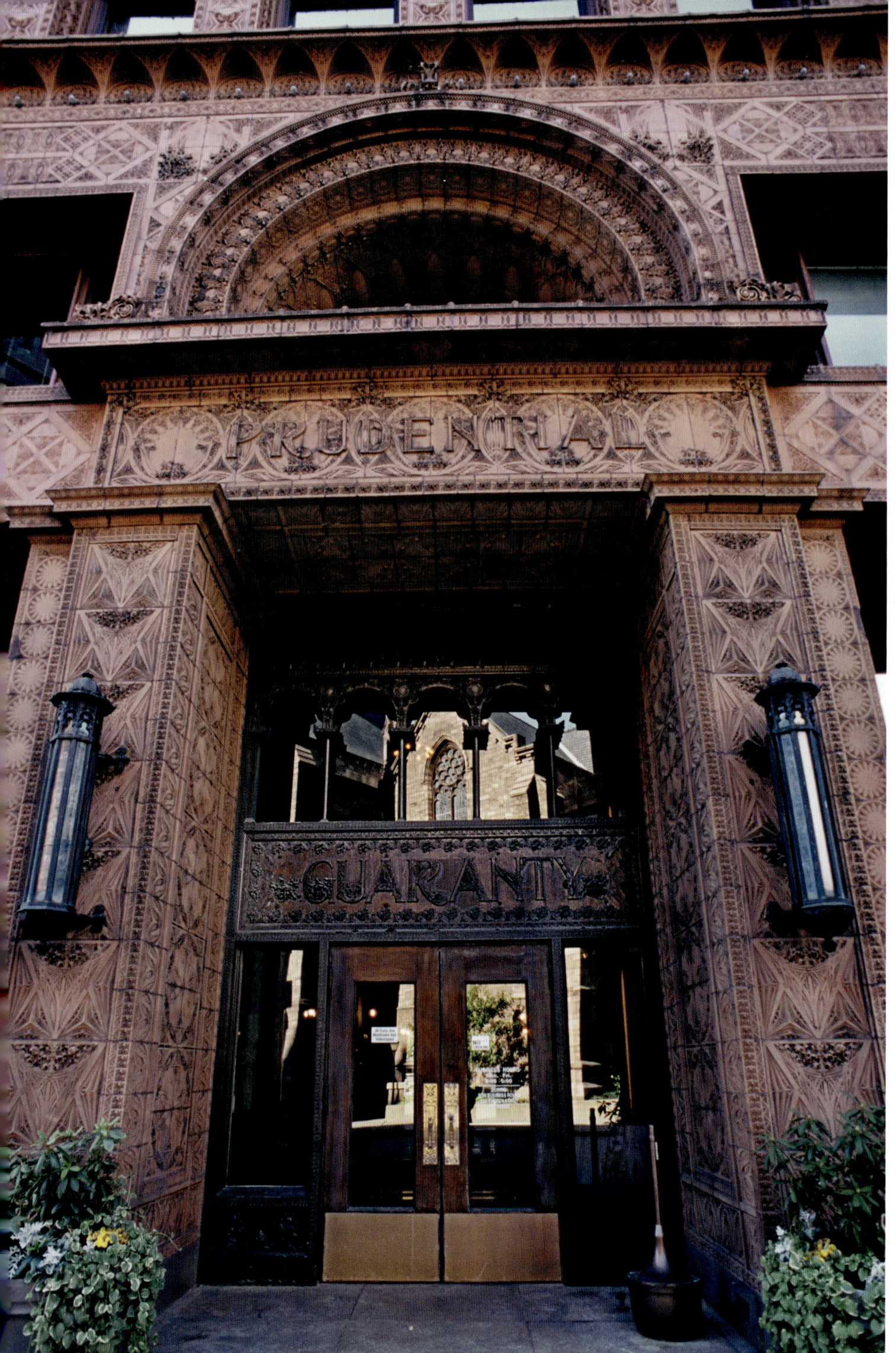

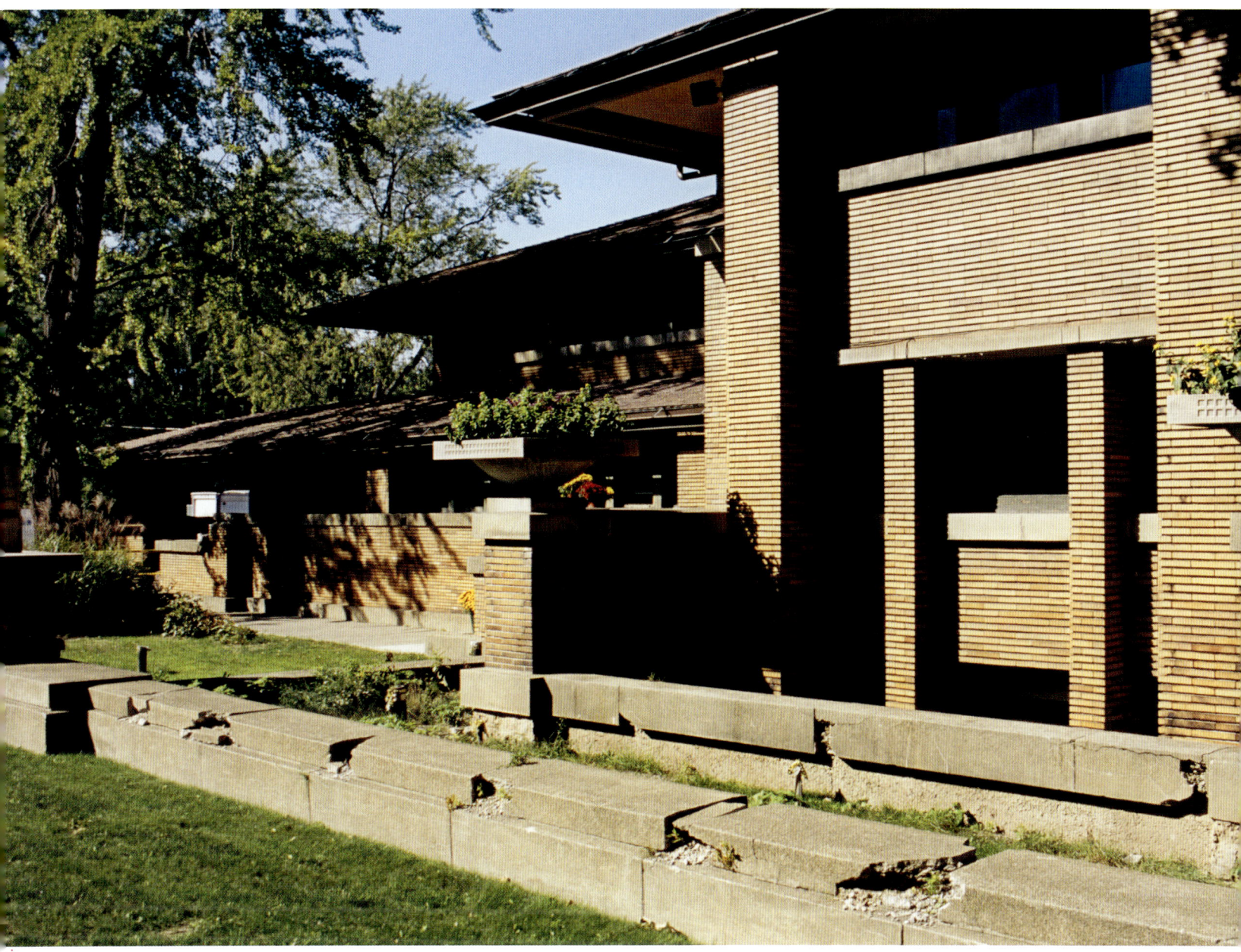

ABOVE

The Darwin D. Martin House Complex was designed by America's leading Prairie-style architect, Frank Lloyd Wright. The five-building, ten-thousand-square-foot complex is undergoing a complete restoration. It is a National Historic Landmark.

LEFT

The work of many of the nation's finest architects can be found in and around Buffalo. Built in 1895, the Guaranty Building was designed by Louis Sullivan and was one of the earliest skyscrapers to have a steel structure supporting a facade. The building's terra-cotta facade is quite ornate.

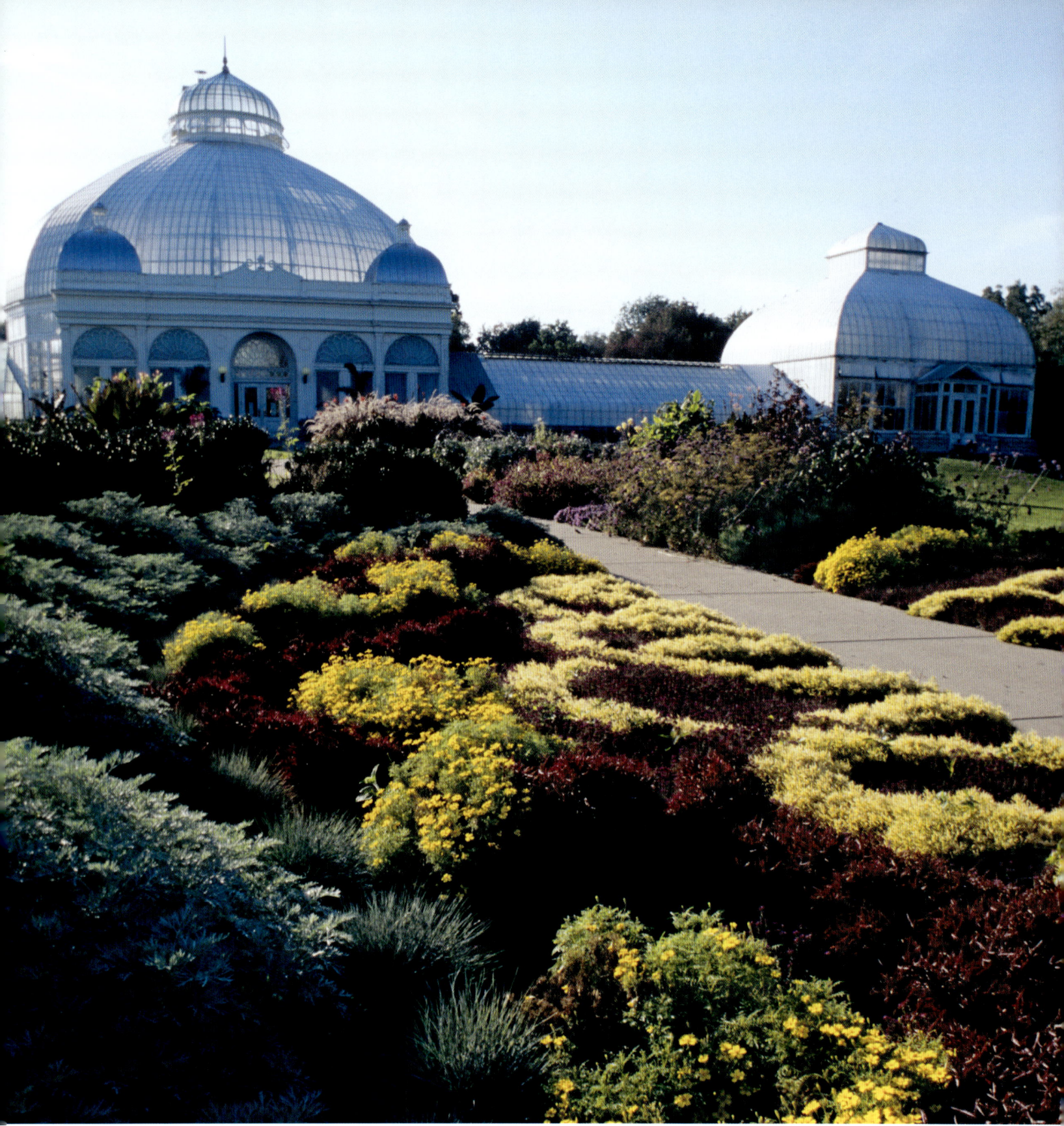

ABOVE

The centerpiece of the Buffalo and Erie County Botanical Gardens is the wonderful Victorian-era conservatory building, highlighted by its displays of tropical and rainforest plants. Located in the 160-acre South Park, designed by Frederick Law Olmstead, the grounds also include formal gardens as well as an arboretum.

RIGHT

The world-renowned Albright-Knox Art Gallery is governed by the Buffalo Fine Arts Academy, one of the oldest public arts organizations in the country.

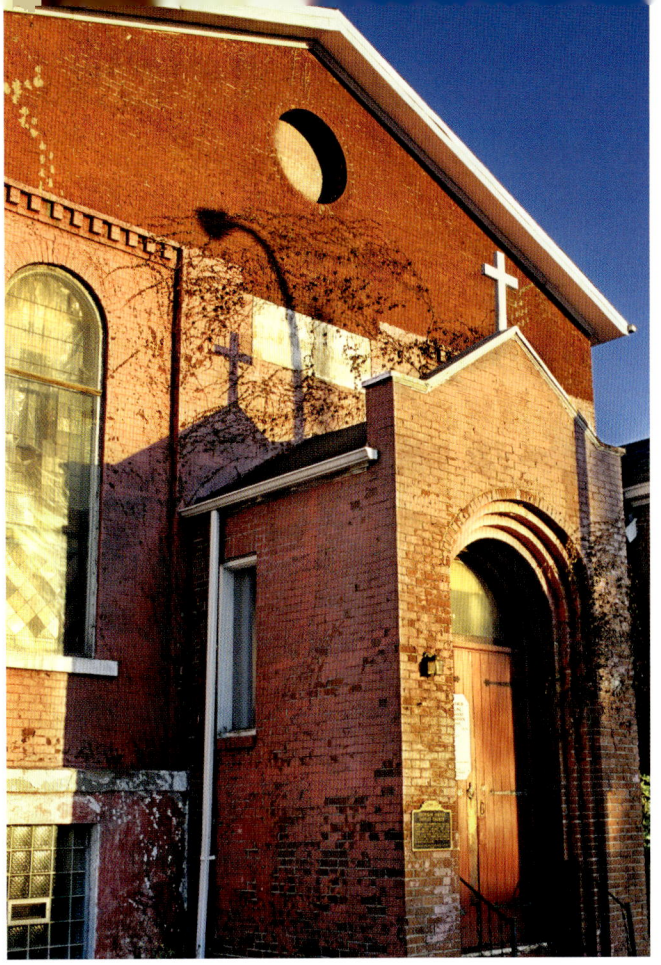

ABOVE

Built as a Baptist Church for free blacks in the 1840s, the Michigan Street Baptist Church in Buffalo was an important stop on the Underground Railroad before the Civil War.

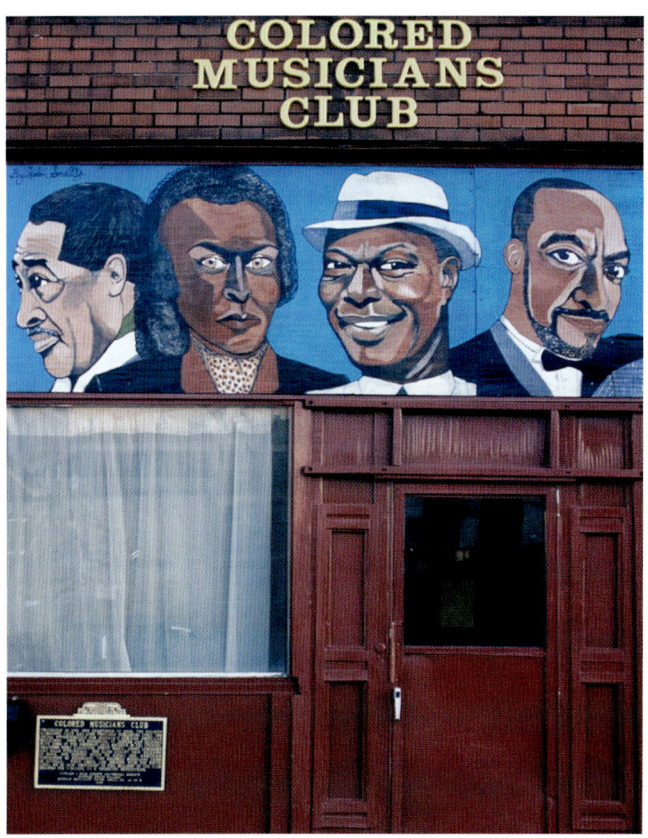

ABOVE

The Colored Musicians Club was established in 1918 as a social club by members of the city's first union of African-American musicians. Among the many jazz luminaries who have performed at this historic building are Duke Ellington, Miles Davis, Ella Fitzgerald, Dizzy Gillespie, and Billie Holiday.

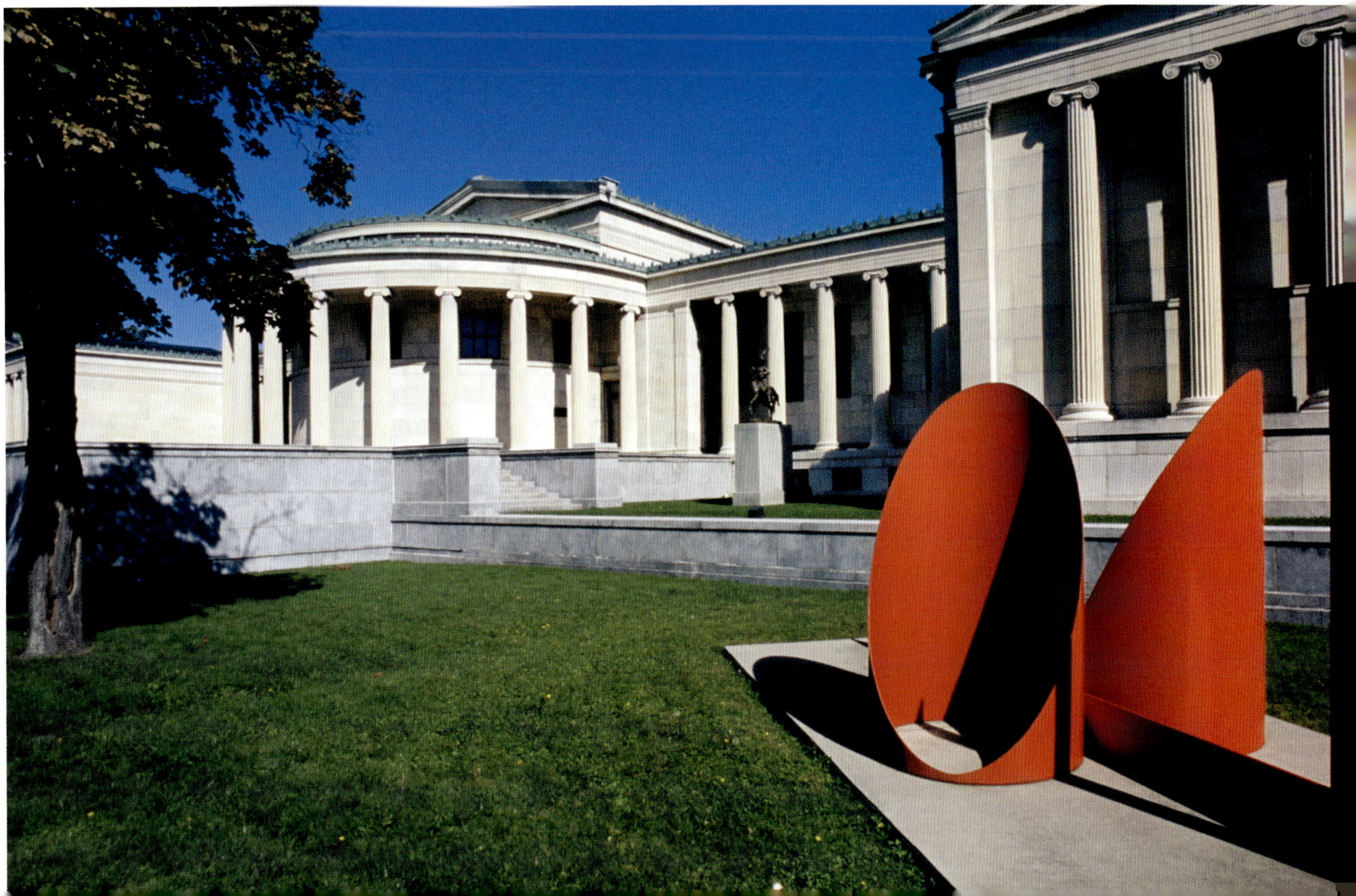

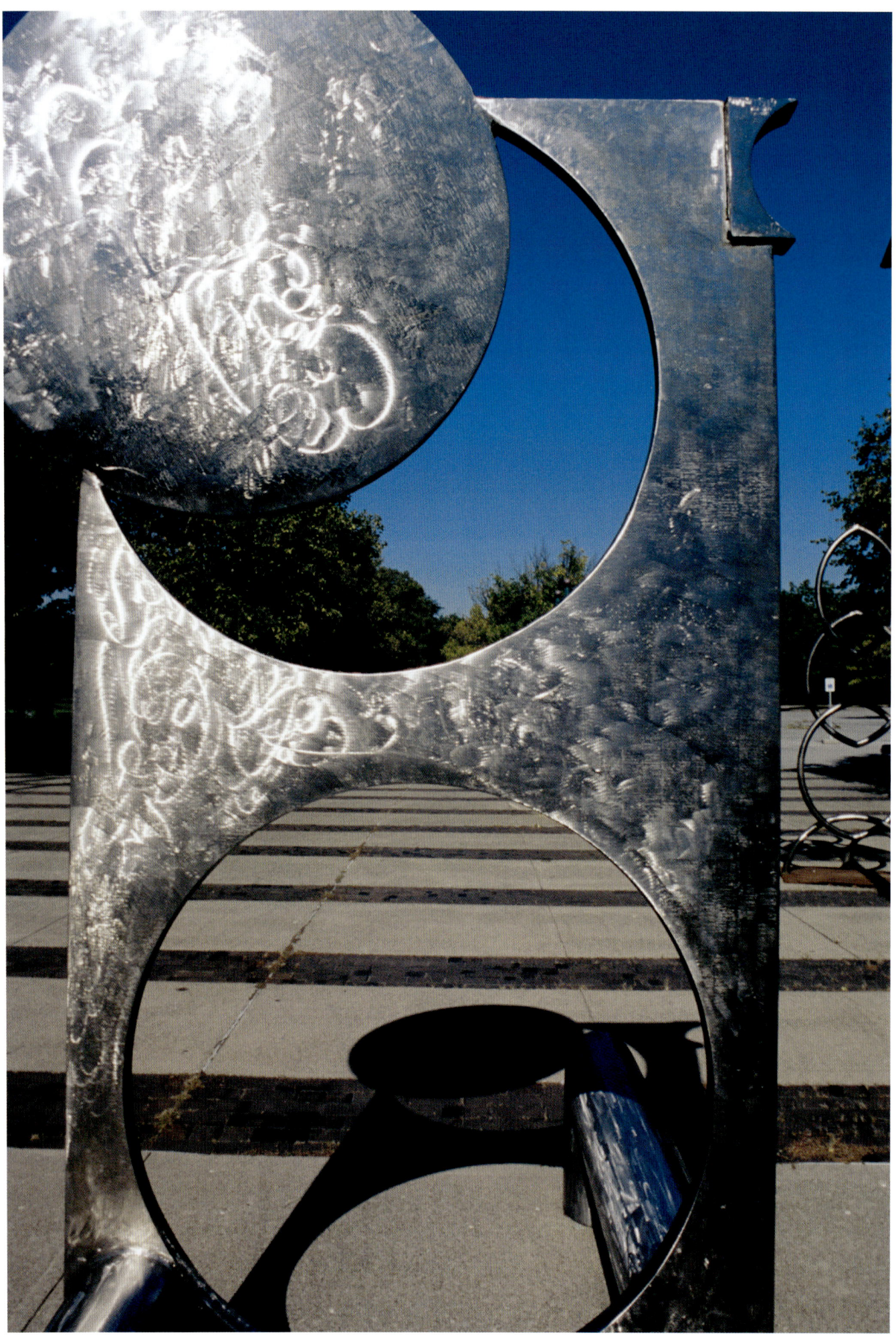

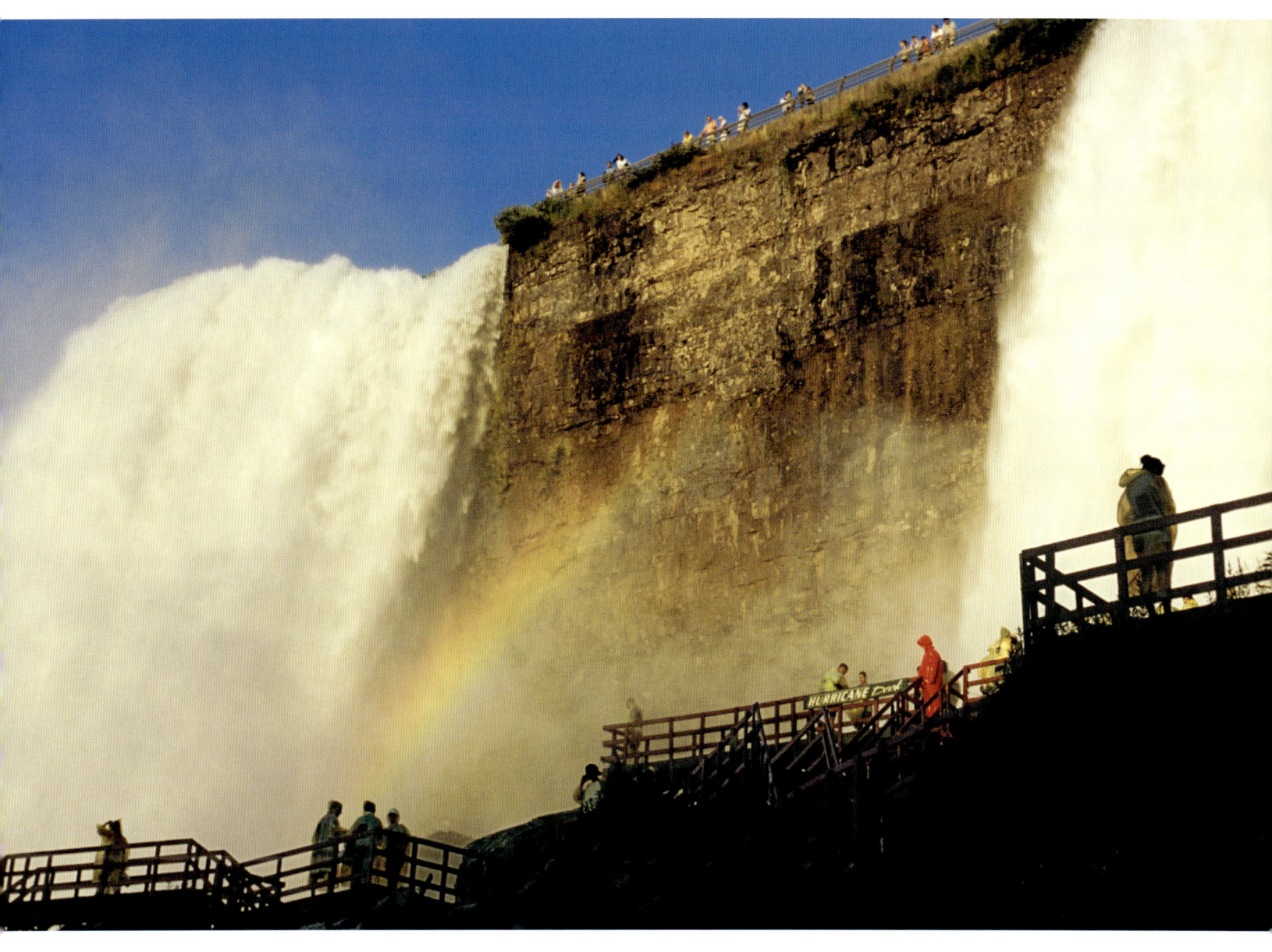

ABOVE

The Cave of the Winds walkway at Niagara Reservation State Park offers the most dramatic viewing of the American Falls and Bridal Veil Falls.

LEFT

Situated on the edge of the escarpment high above the Niagara River Gorge at Lewiston, the two-hundred-acre Artpark is the premier performing arts center in the region.

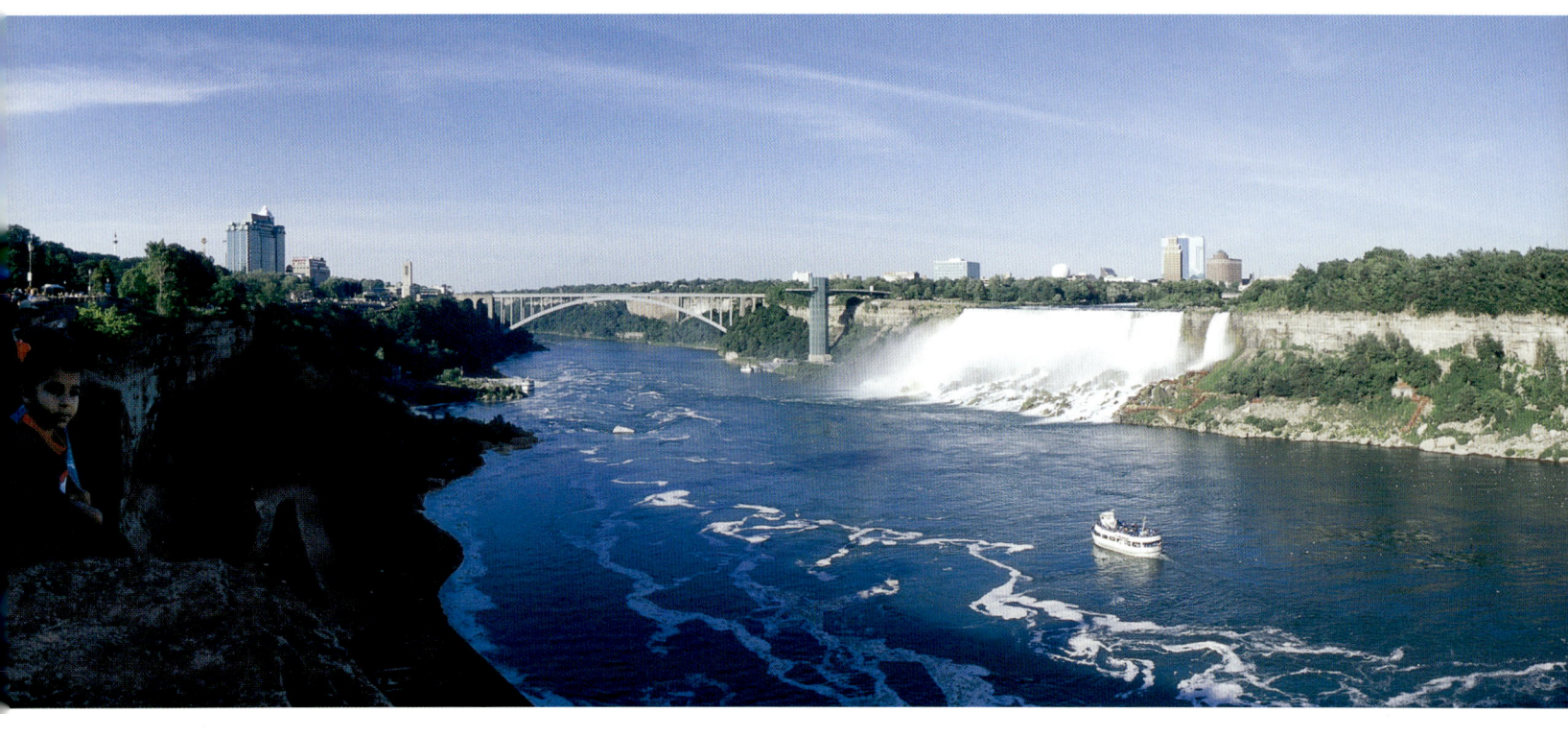

ABOVE

This panorama at Niagara Falls shows the Rainbow Bridge, Maid of the Mist tour boats, the Niagara River, the American Falls, the cliffs of Goat Island, and Horseshoe Falls.

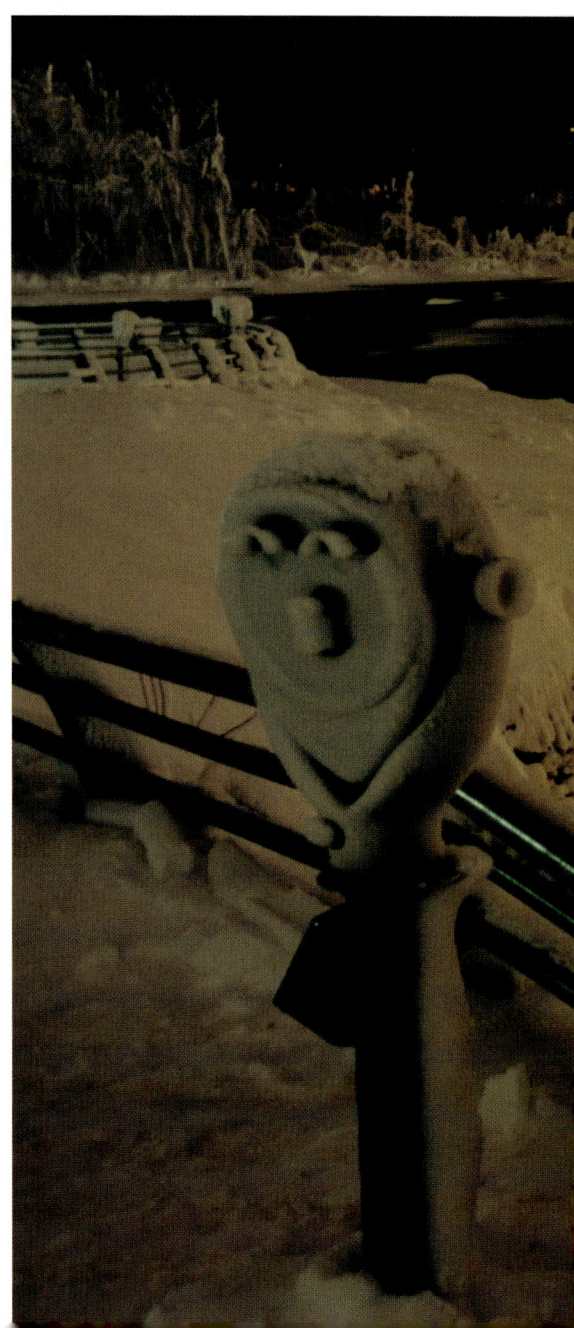

RIGHT

Stunning in all seasons, Niagara Falls became part of the country's first state park with the establishment of Niagara Reservation State Park in 1885. Europeans discovered the falls in 1678, and it became a popular tourist destination for Americans beginning in the 1820s, when the Erie Canal opened up travel to western New York.

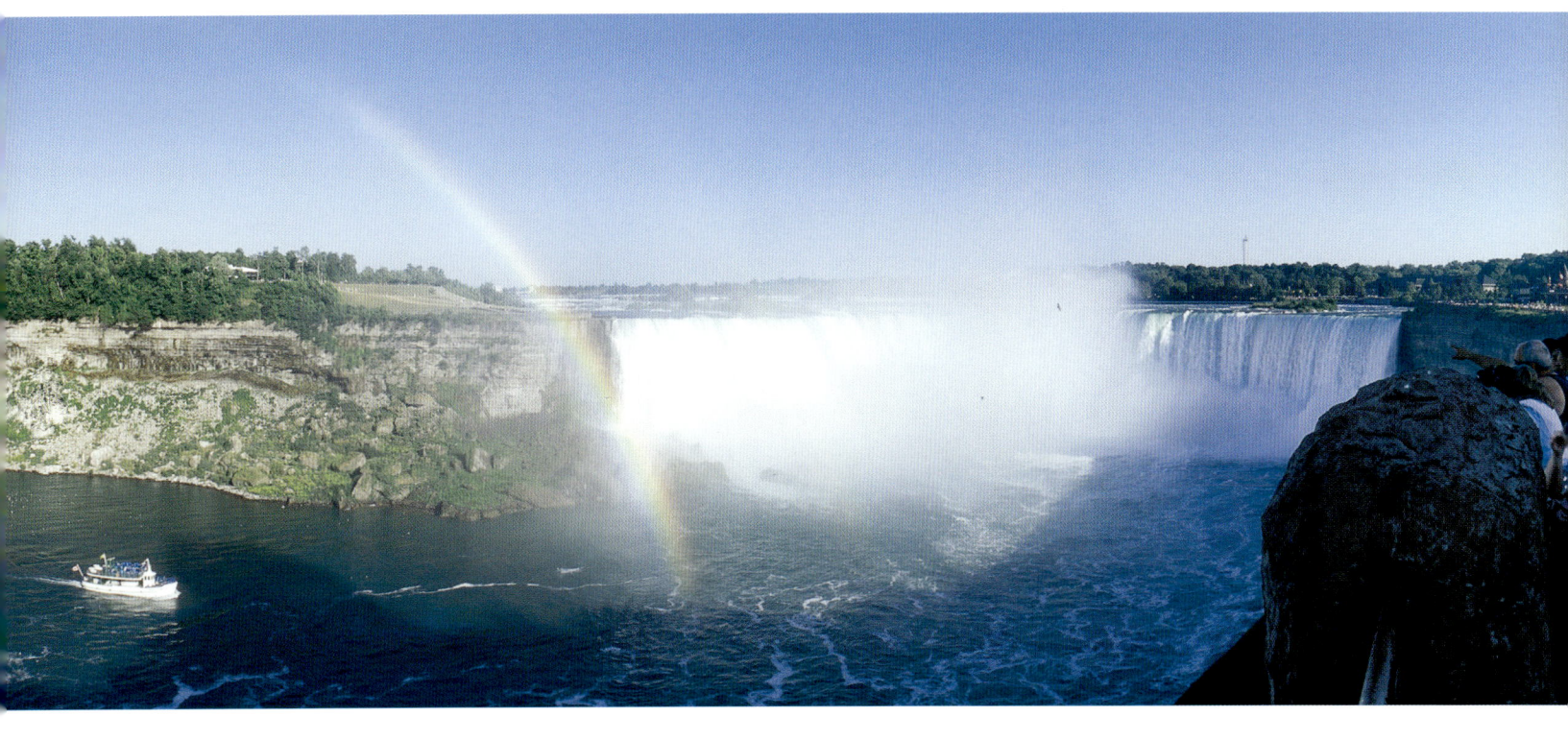

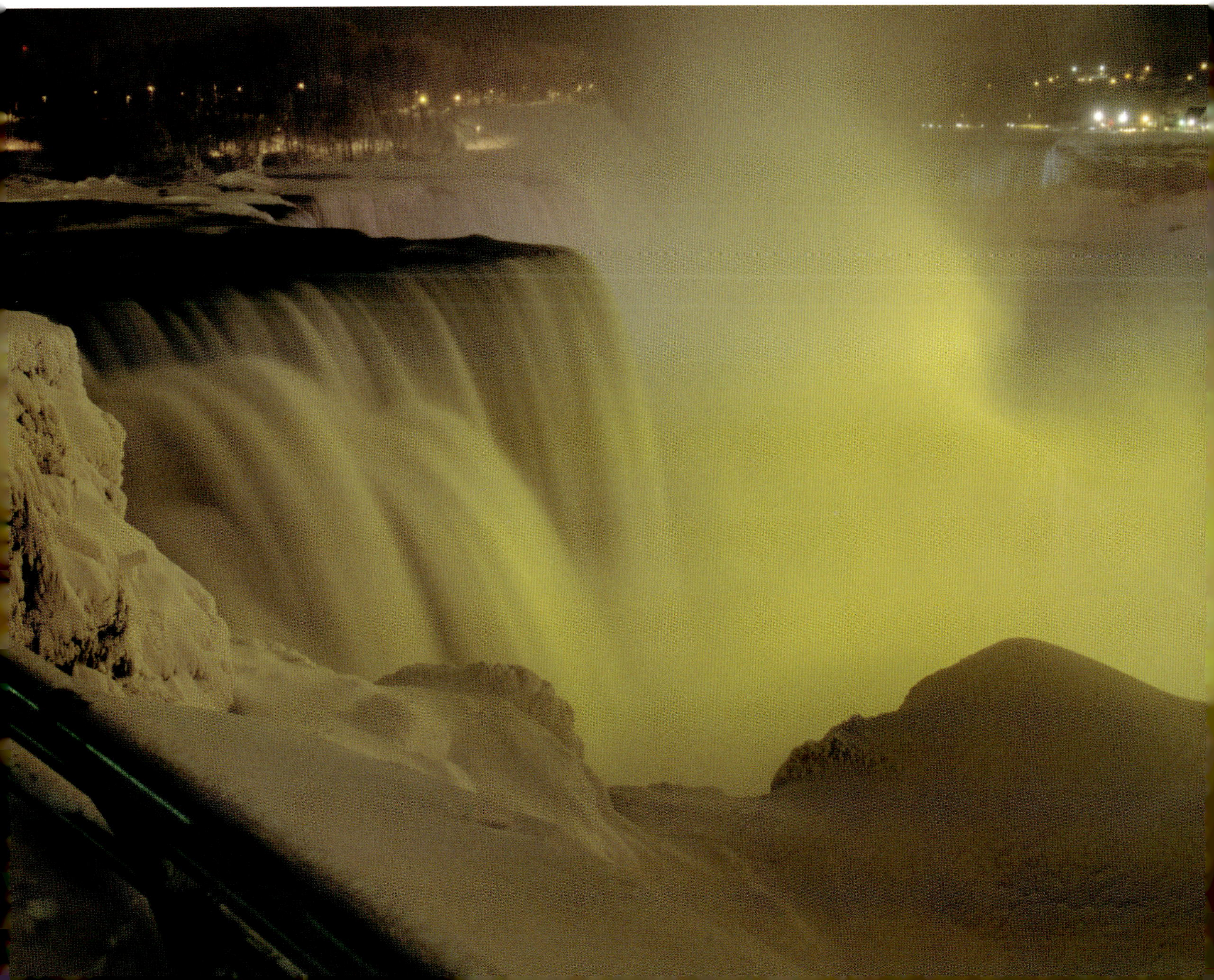

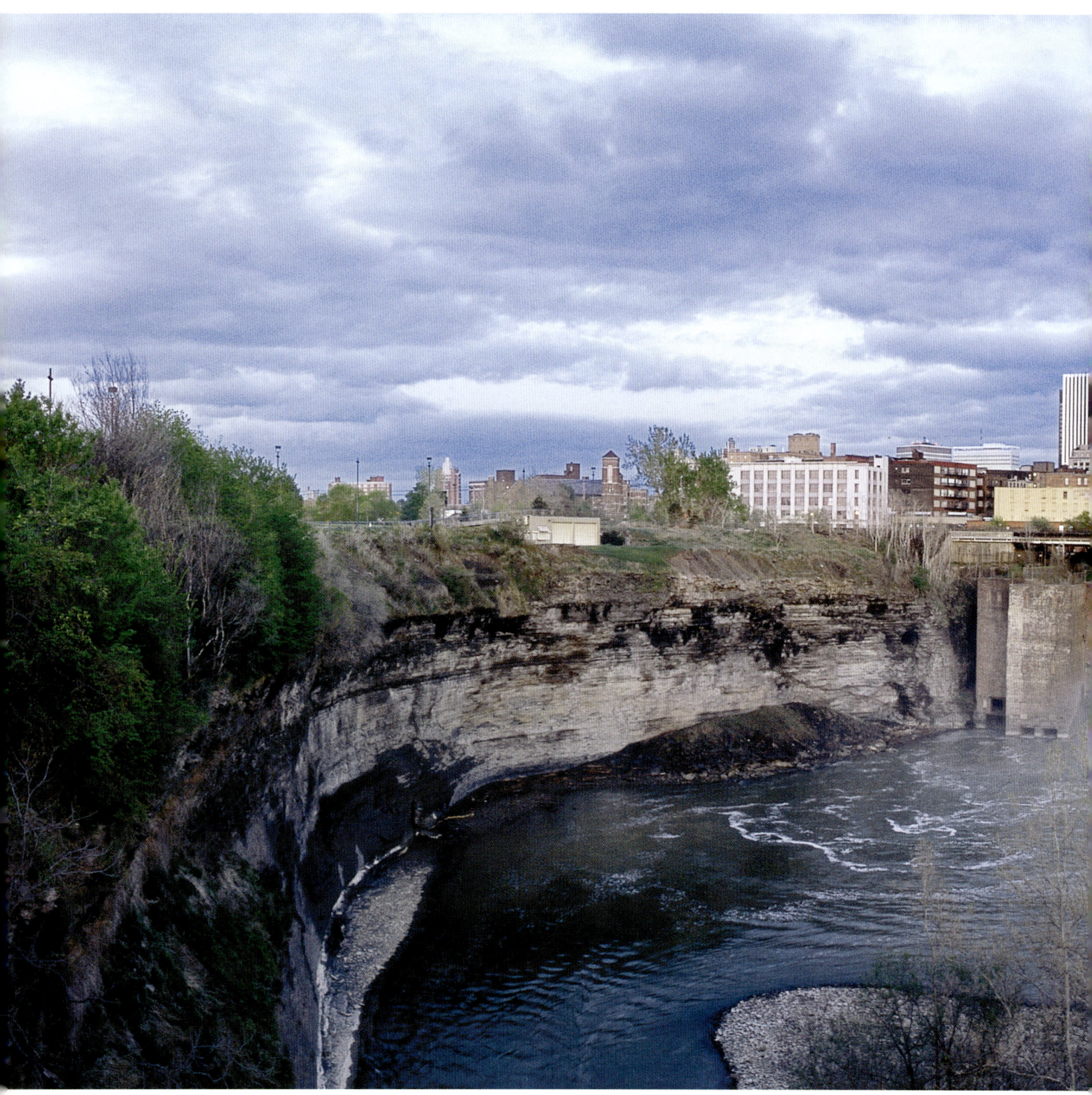

ABOVE

Rochester was the original boomtown after the Erie Canal opened in 1825, growing faster than any other American city. This view of downtown is taken from the pedestrian bridge at the High Falls Heritage Area.

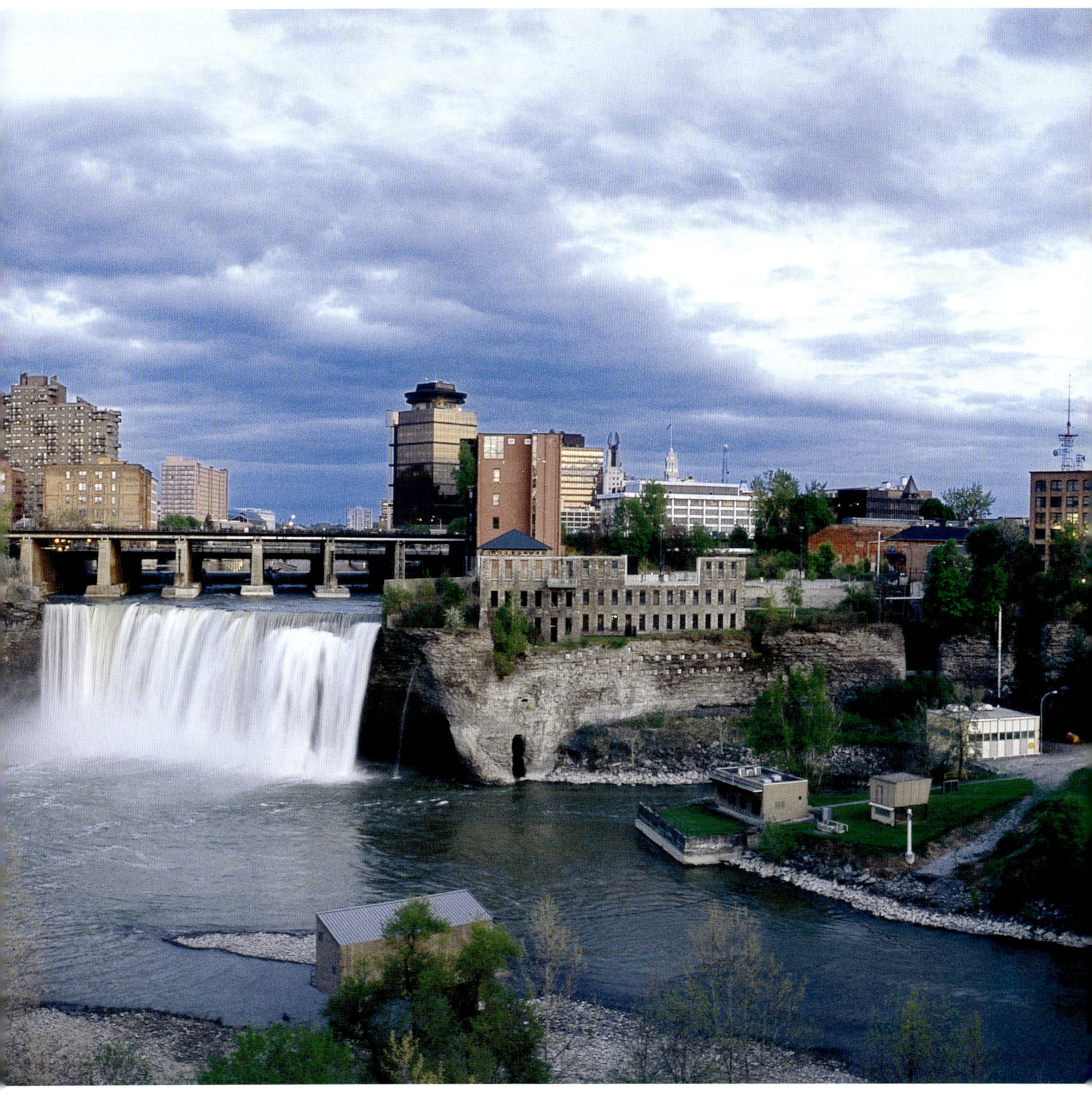

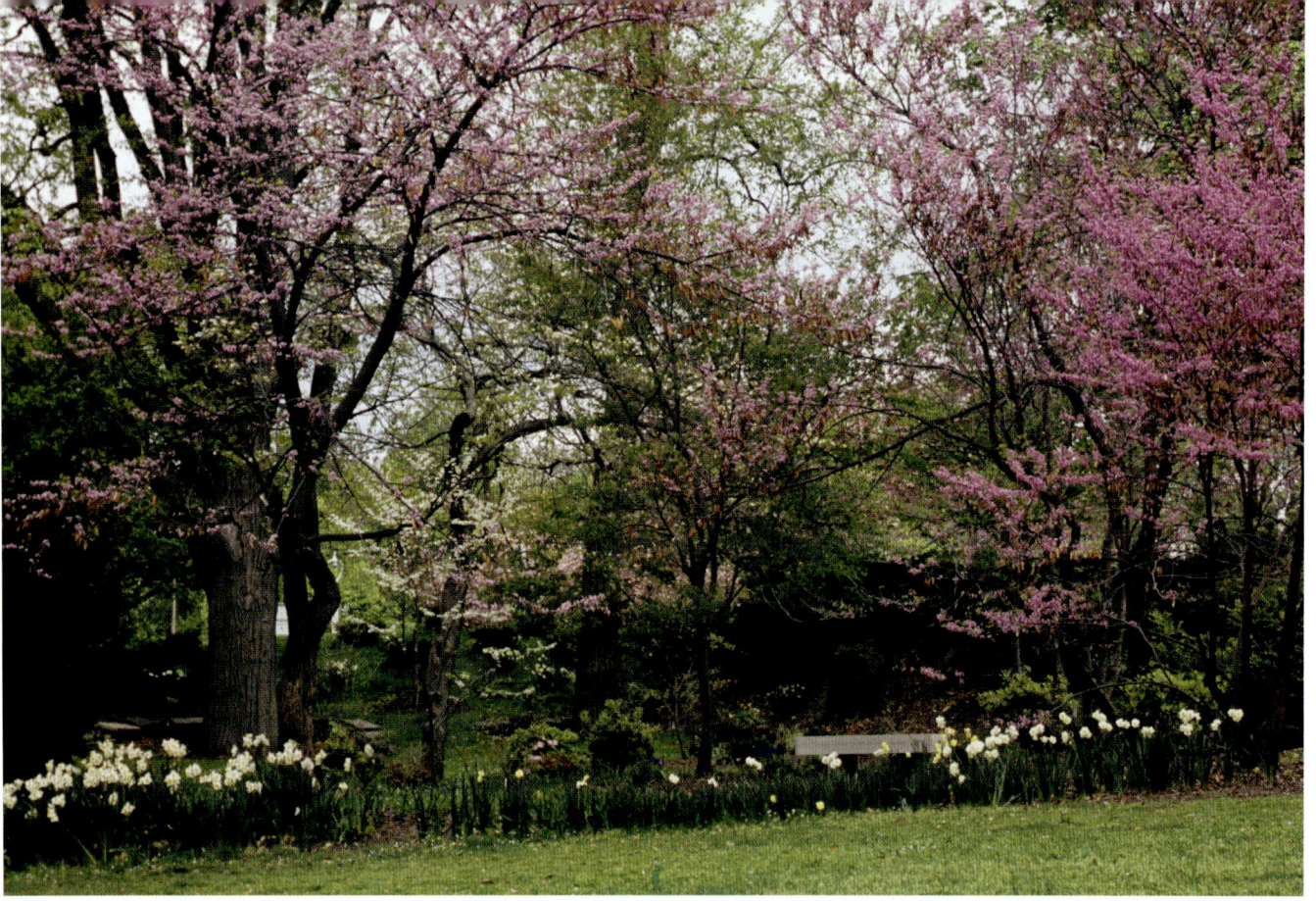

ABOVE

Highland Botanical Park, one of the first municipal arboretums in the nation, hosts Rochester's annual Lilac Festival, which coincides with the blooming of the park's 1,200 lilac bushes.

RIGHT

Some nine hundred cobblestone buildings are located within seventy-five miles of Rochester. This construction style from the mid-1800s relied on local materials and advances in mortar quality.

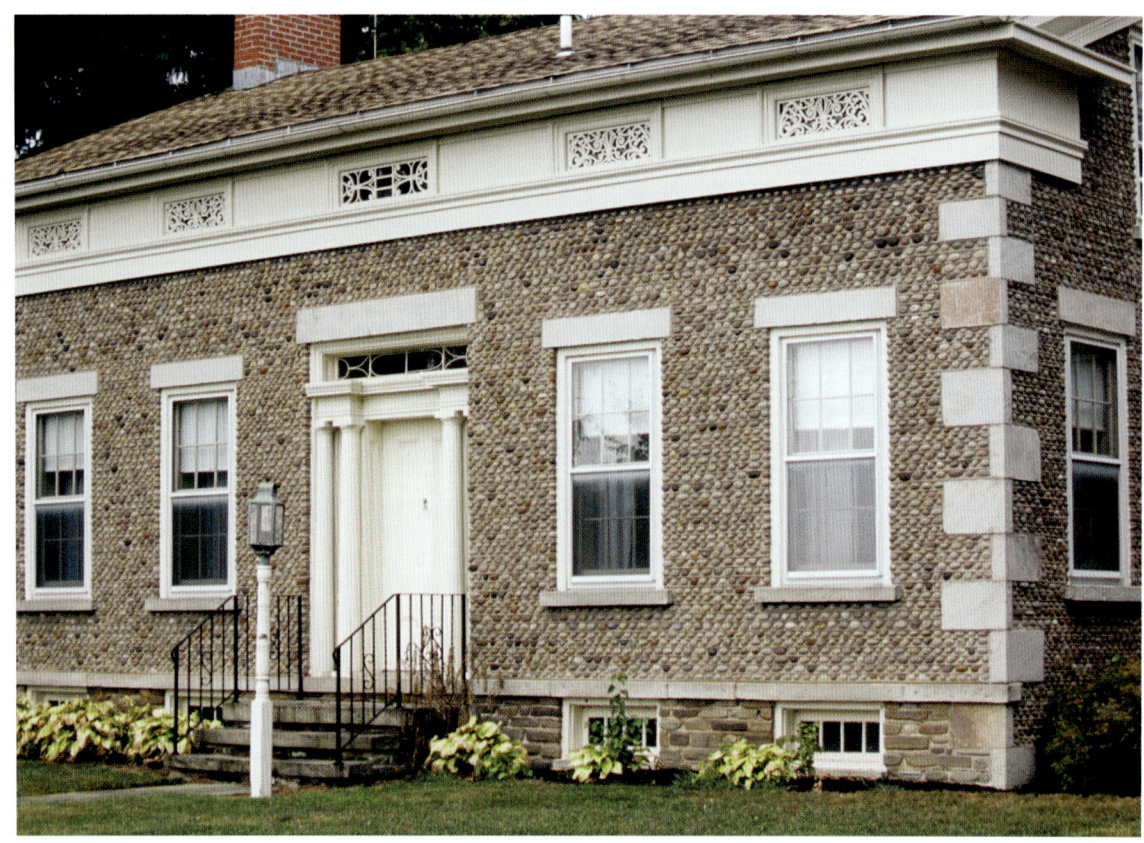

OPPOSITE

The 1822 Charlotte-Genesee Light, at the mouth of the Genesee River near Irondequoit Bay Marine Park, is the second oldest lighthouse on the Great Lakes.

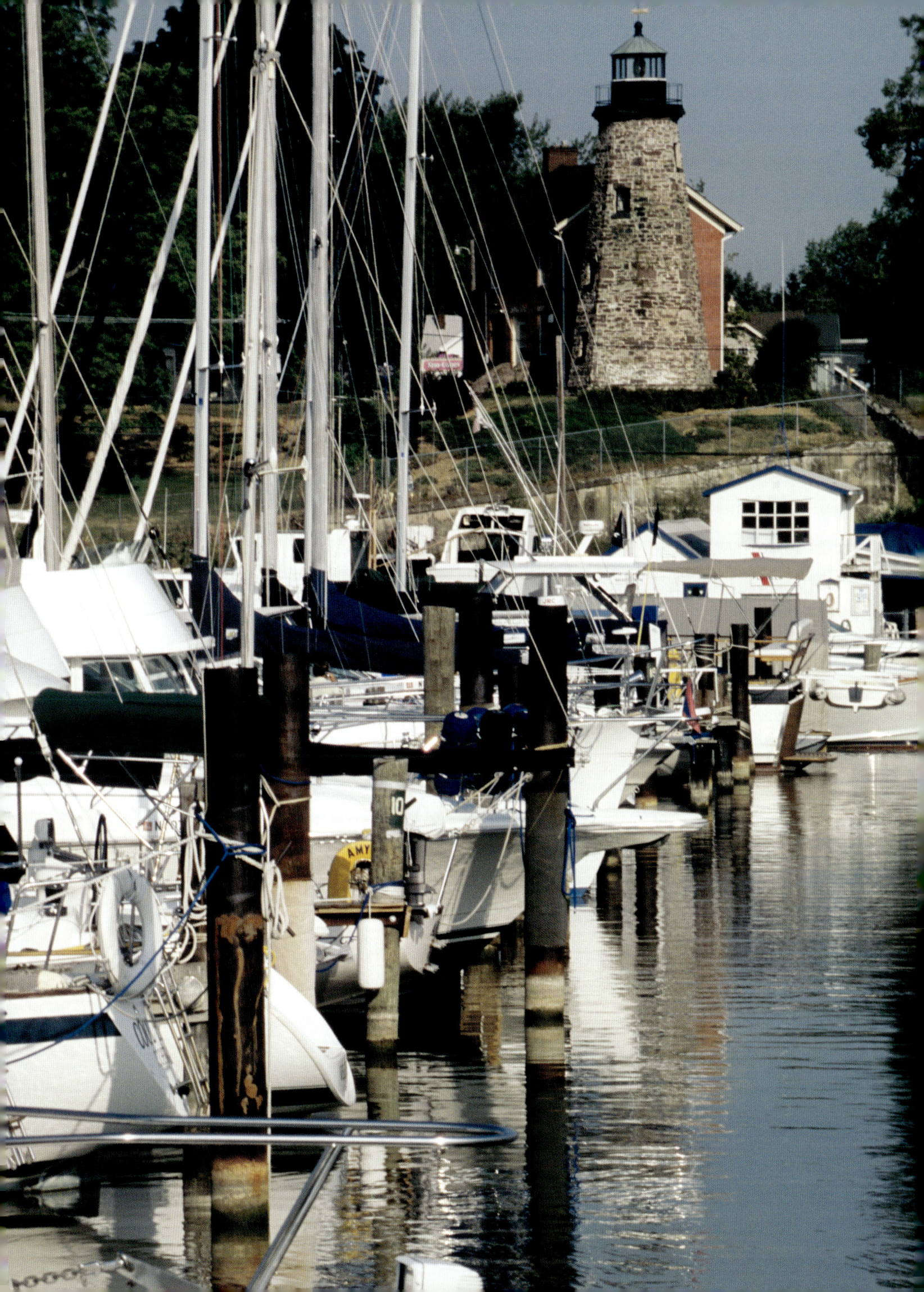

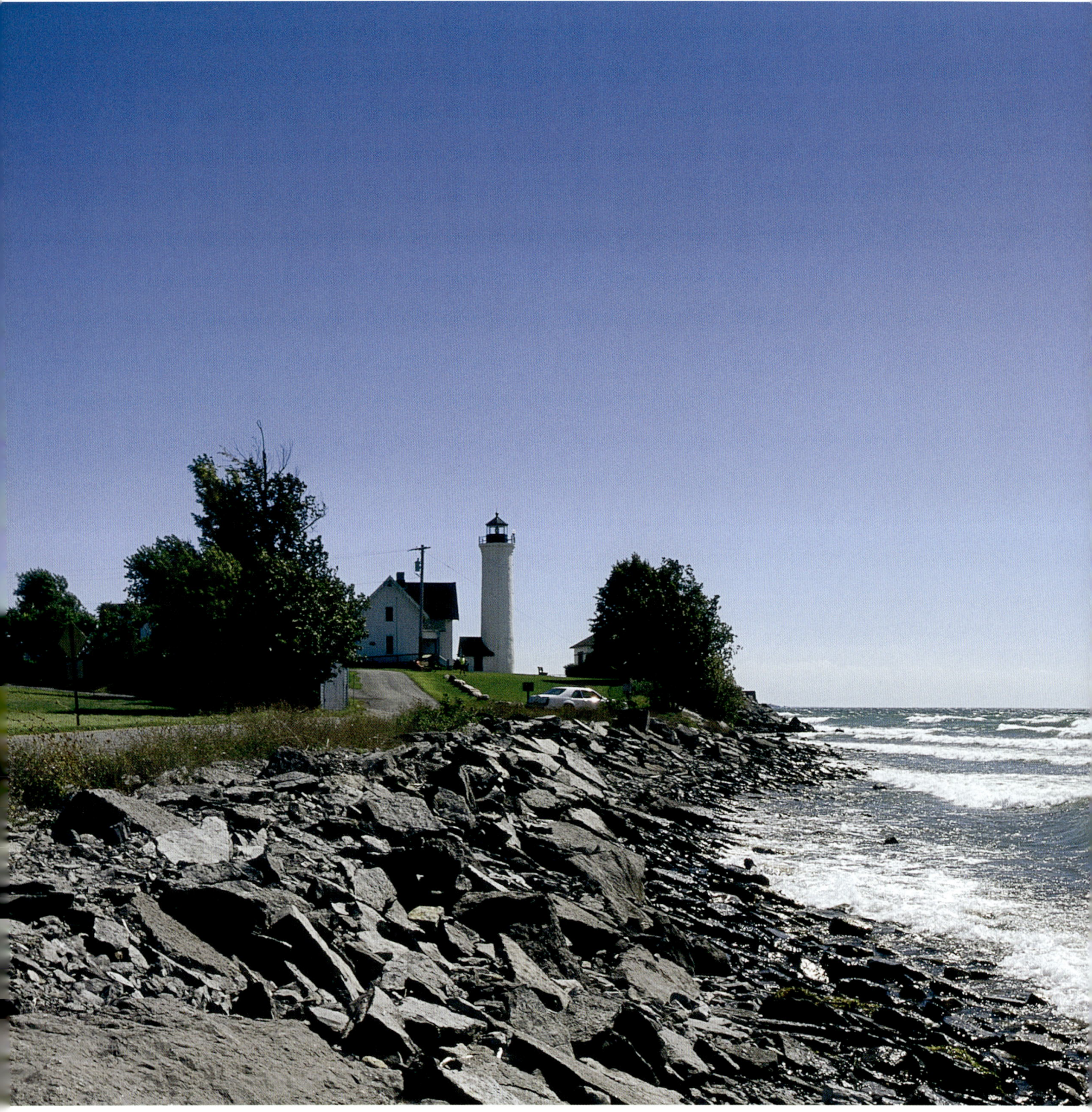

ABOVE

The Tibbetts Point Light has been an active beacon at the mouth of the St. Lawrence River on Lake Ontario since 1895.

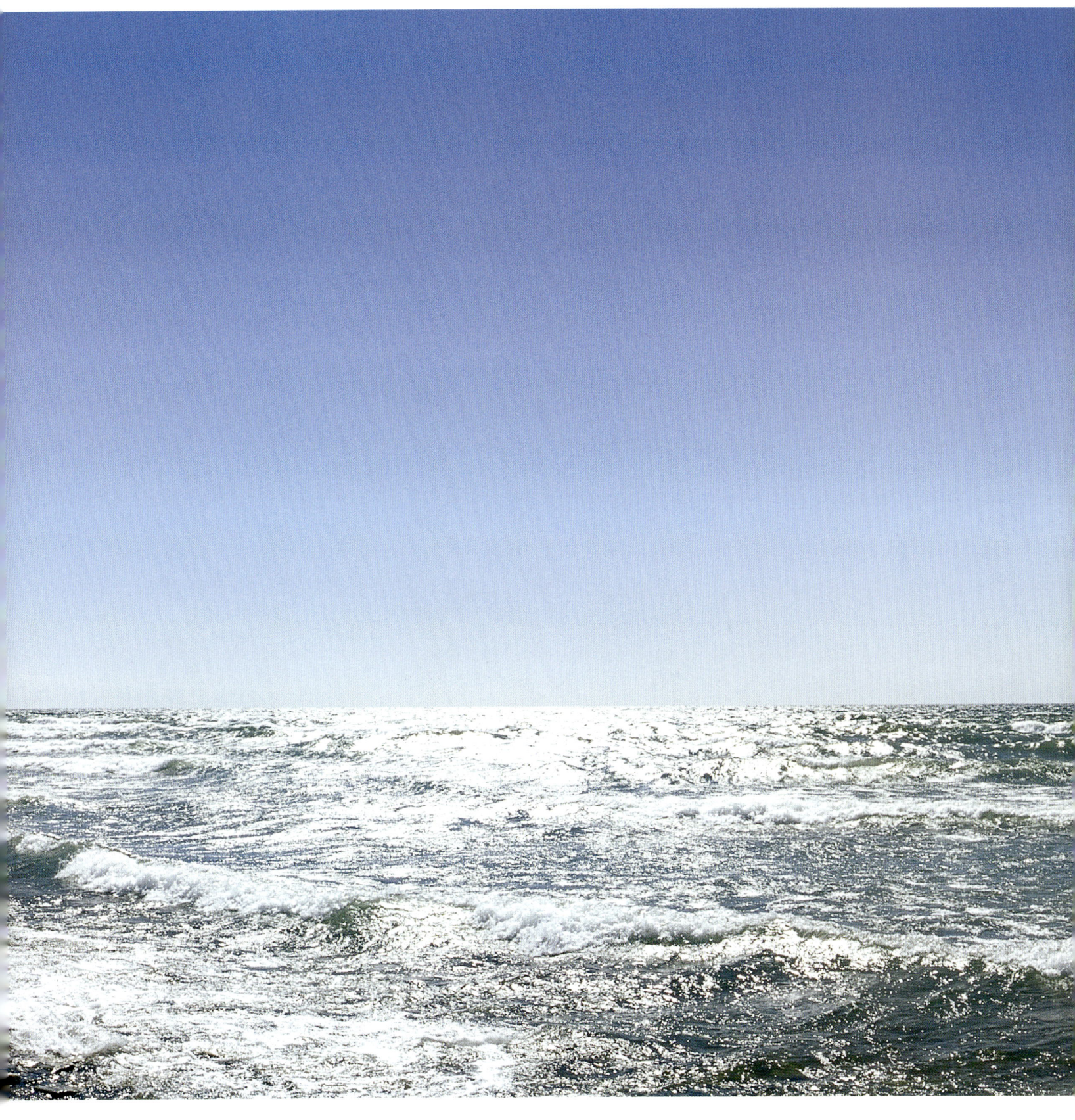

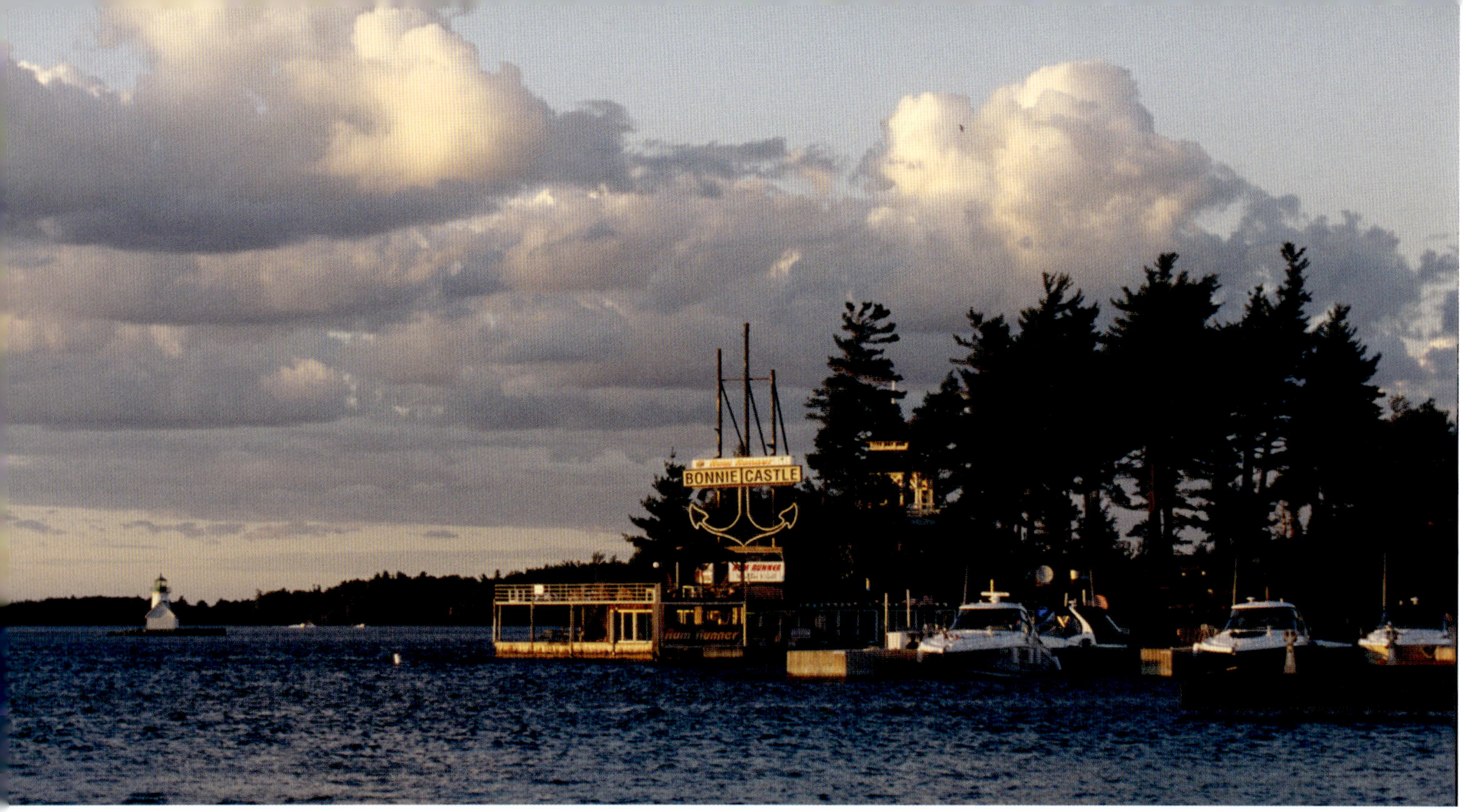

ABOVE

Alexandria Bay in the heart of the Thousand Islands region is a popular destination for fishing, sightseeing, and relaxing. Sunken Rock Lighthouse (in the distance to the left) marks a submerged rock in the St. Lawrence River.

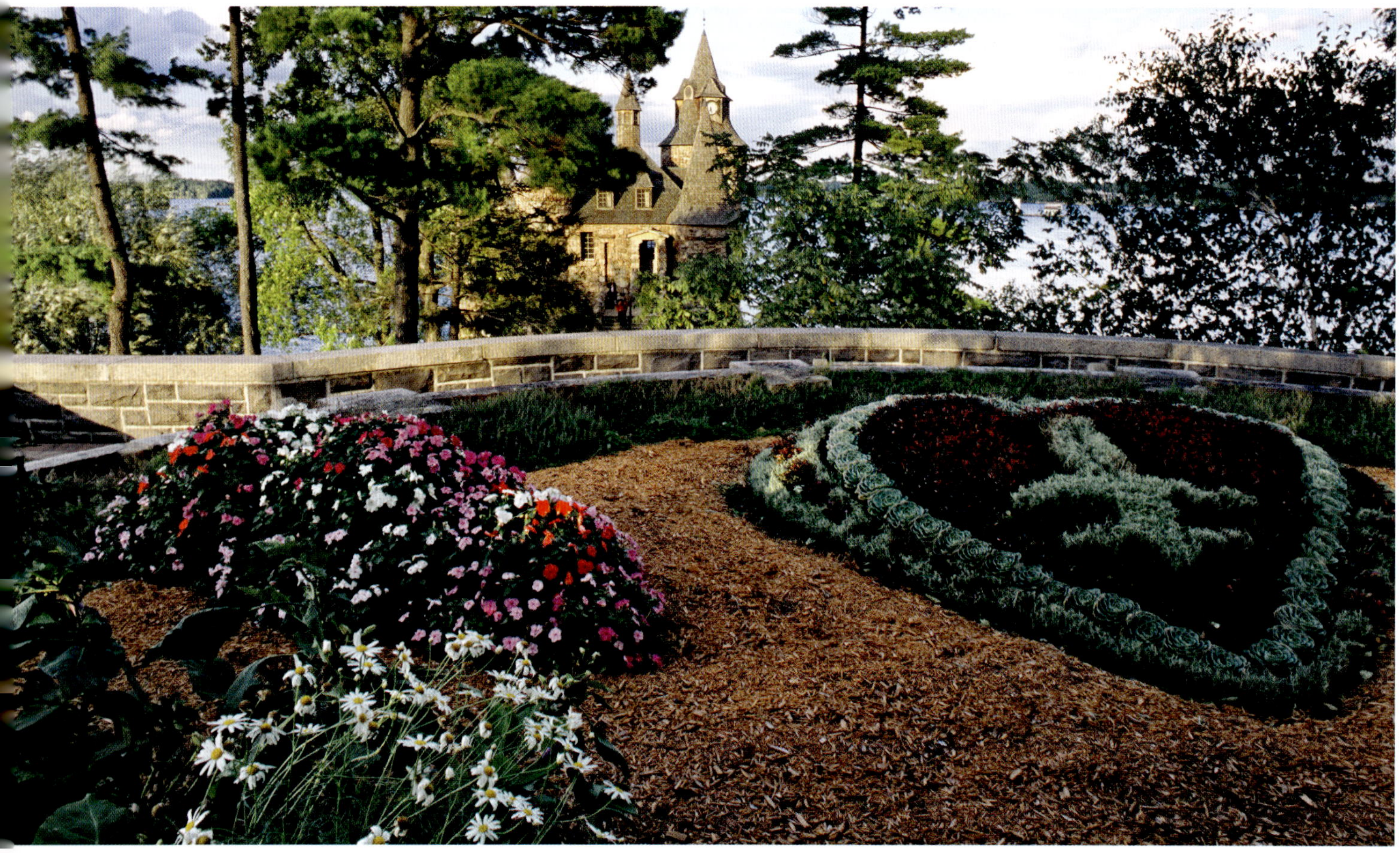

ABOVE

George Boldt, proprietor of Manhattan's landmark Waldorf-Astoria Hotel, began construction of an elaborate castle on Heart Island in Alexandria Bay for his wife, Louise, in 1900, but halted the project when Louise died suddenly four years later. The complex has been undergoing restoration since 1977.

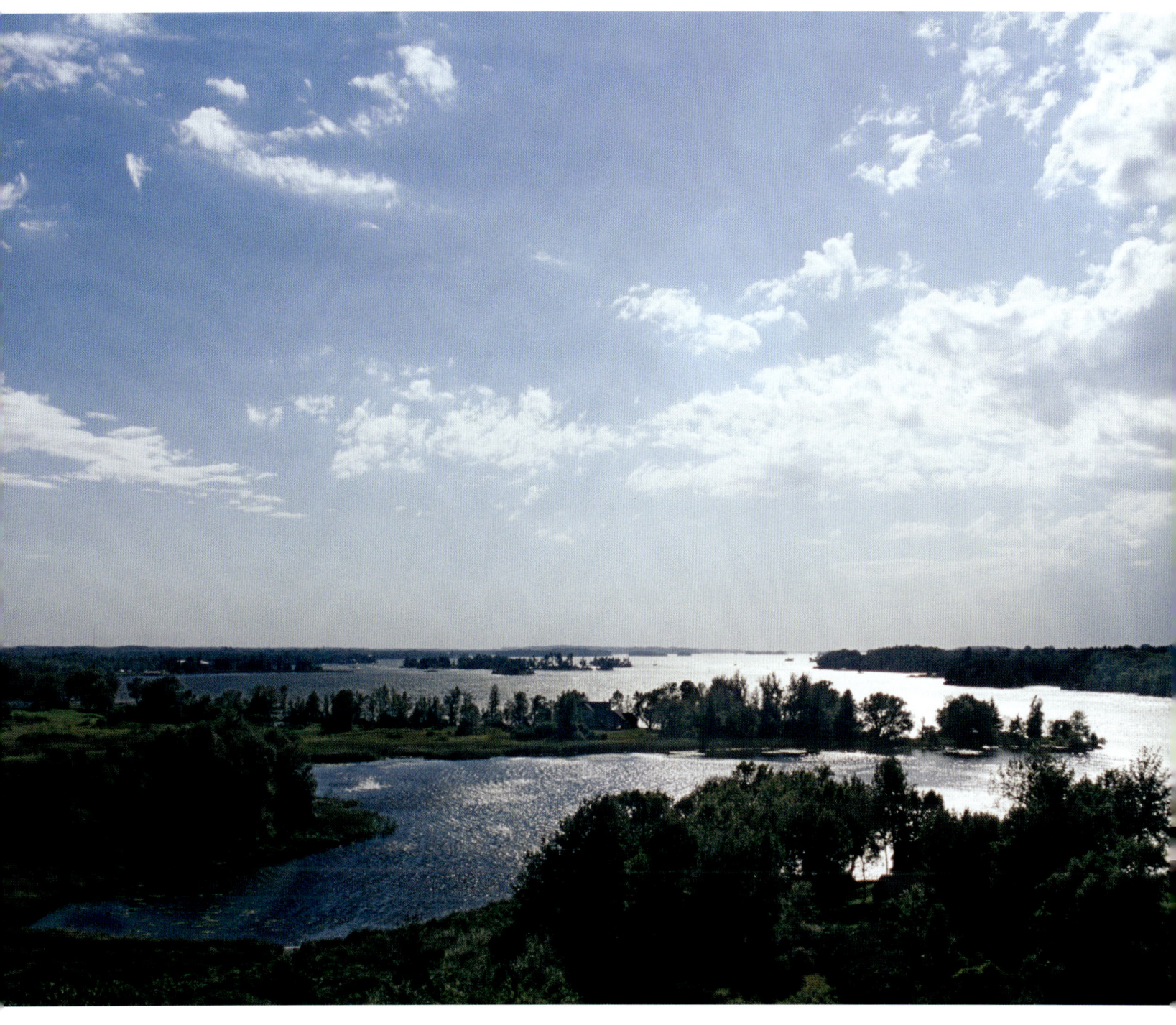

ABOVE

The Thousand Islands region is actually home to about 1,865 islands on a fifty-mile stretch of the St. Lawrence River. This view from the Thousand Islands Bridge overlooks the river's American channel and Wellesley Island.

RIGHT

It's a brisk ride to deliver milk by horse and cart in below-zero winter temperatures. This Amish farm is near the Tug Hill area on the eastern shores of Lake Ontario.

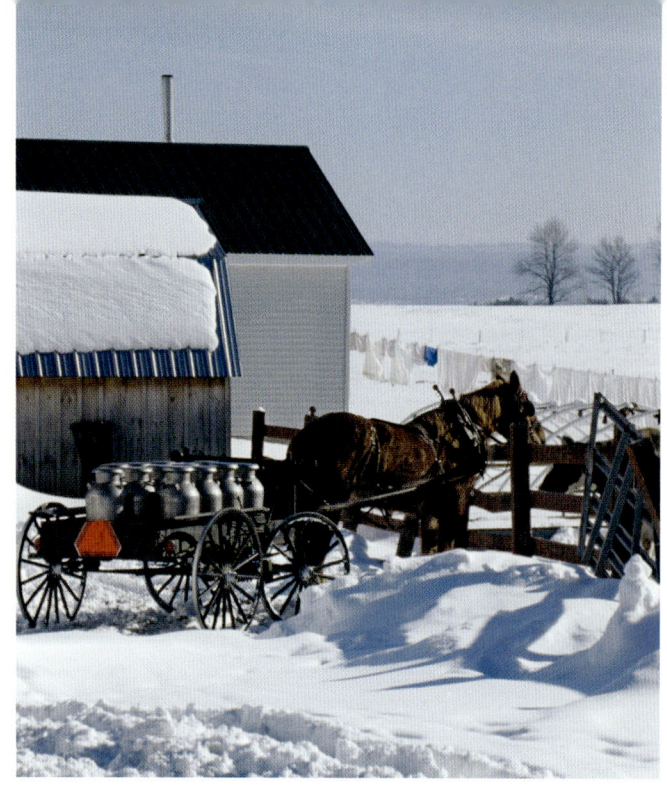

BELOW

Farms are prevalent throughout the plains of the St. Lawrence Valley. This dairy farm is near Cape Vincent in Jefferson County.

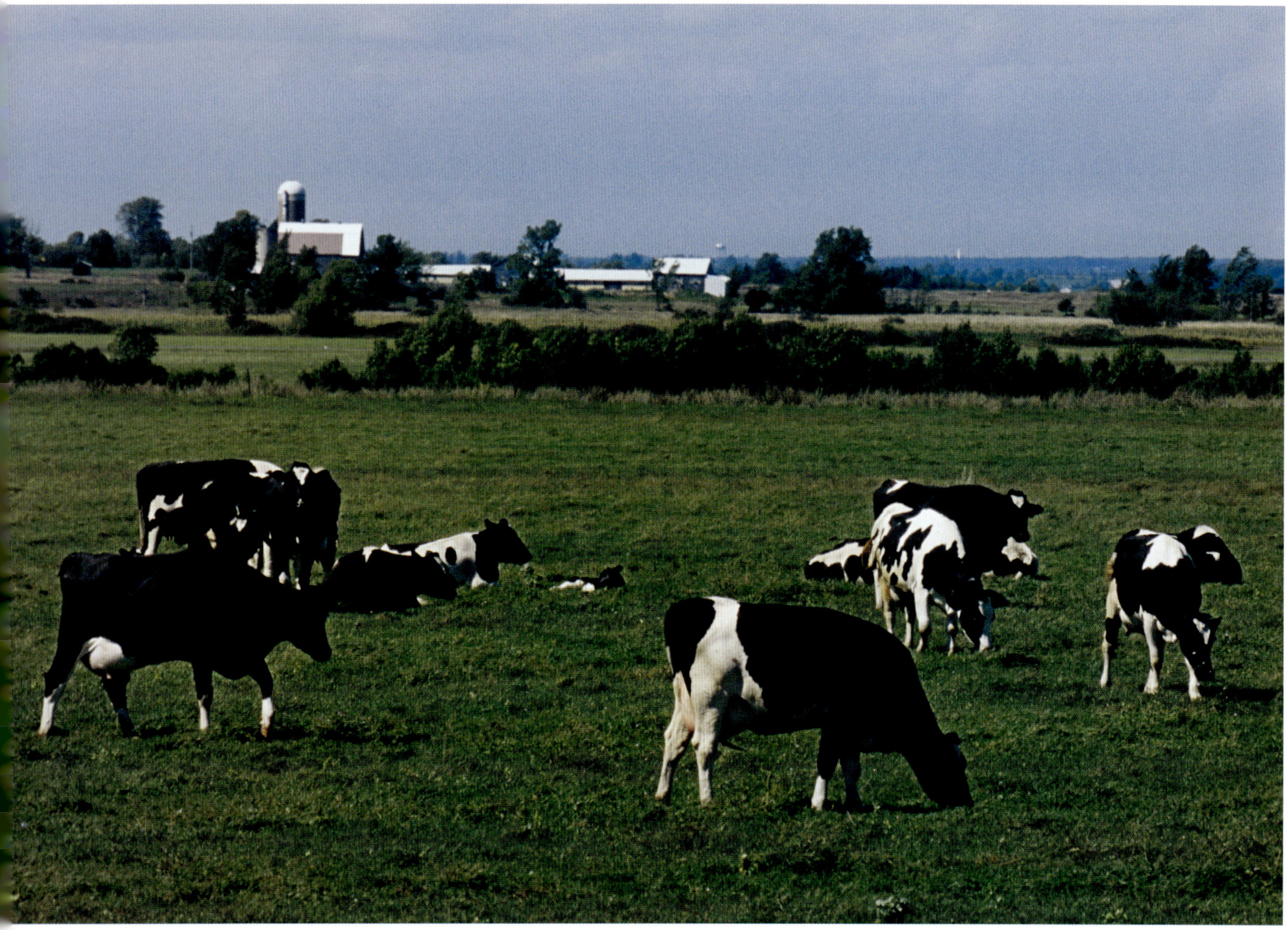

OPPOSITE

The highest annual snowfall east of the Mississippi helps to feed the many streams and waterfalls in the Tug Hill Plateau of northern New York. Pixley Falls State Park has a number of nice hiking trails as well as views of the falls.

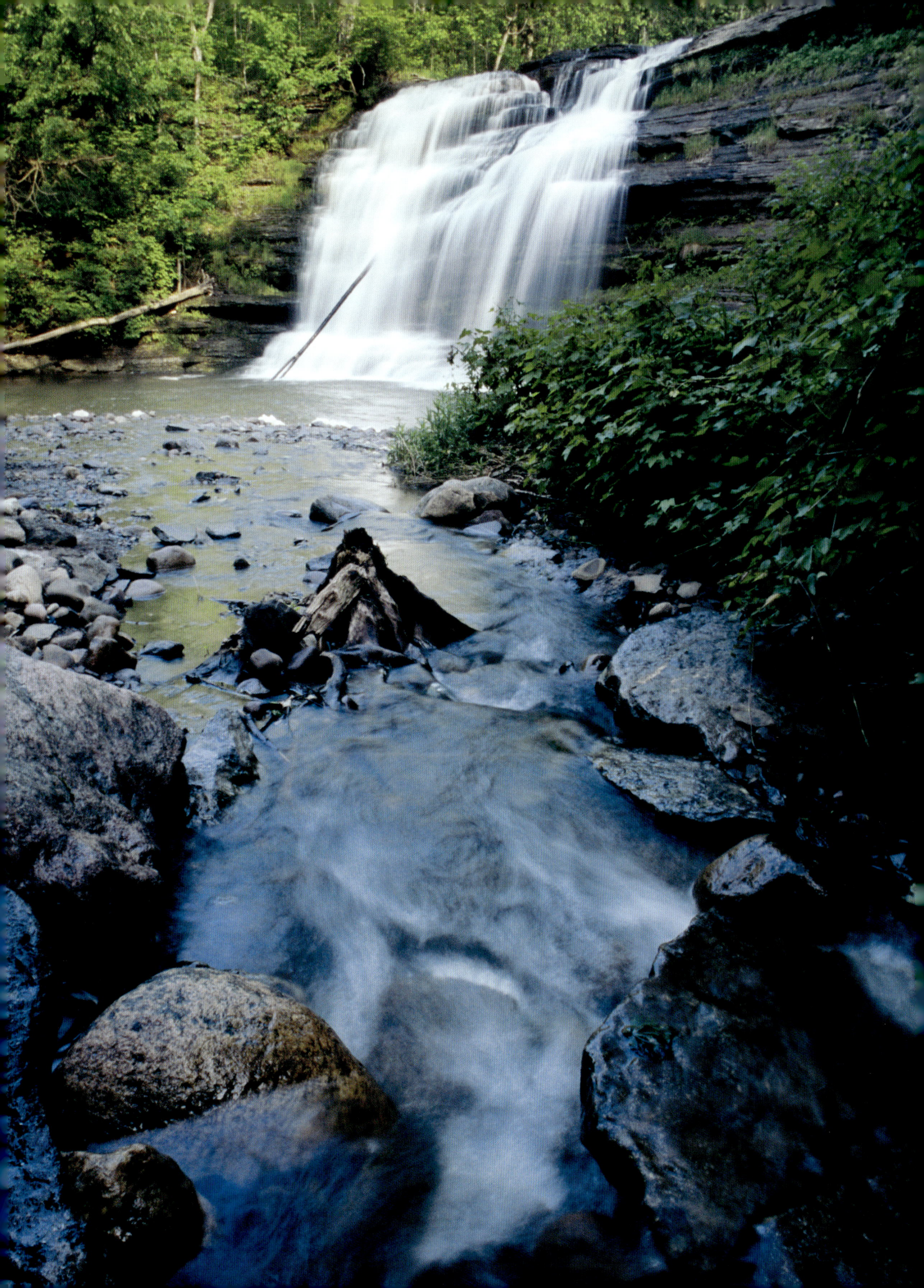

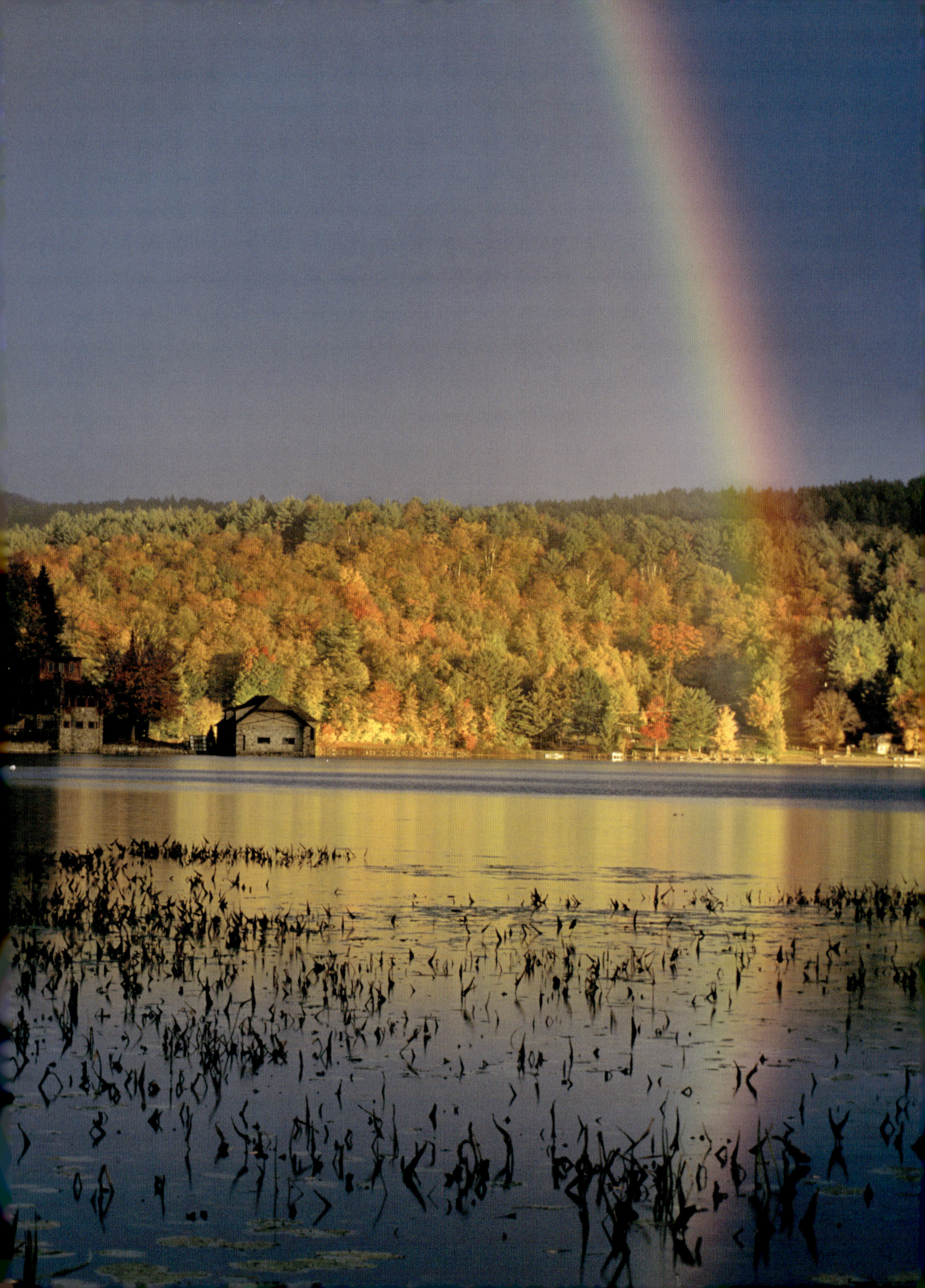

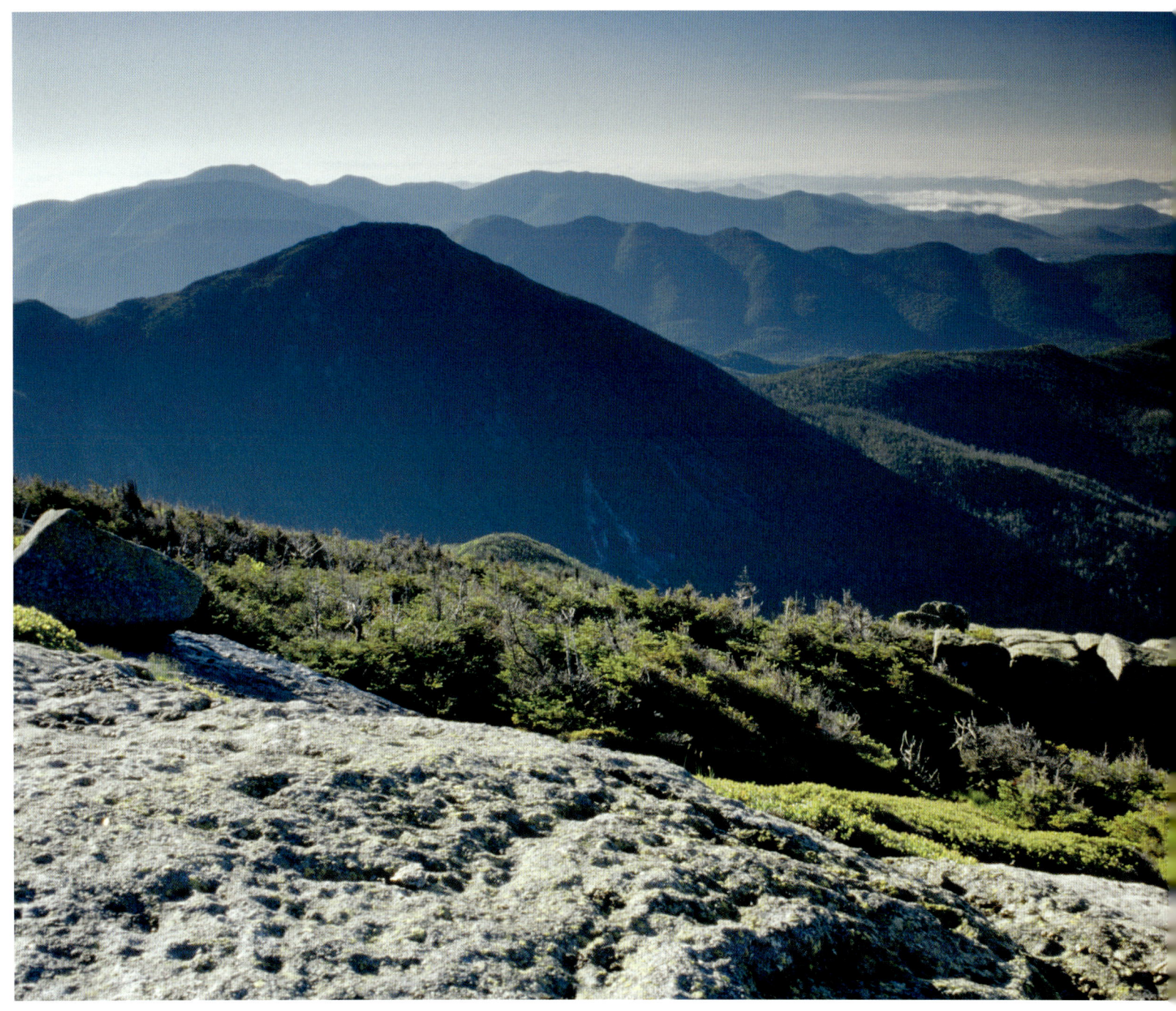

ABOVE

Mount Marcy, at 5,344 feet, is the highest mountain in New York. From Marcy's summit,
the mountains in the six-million-acre Adirondack Park roll off to the horizon in every direction.

LEFT

A rainbow arches high above Brant Lake on a golden fall morning, as showers move in from the west at sunrise.

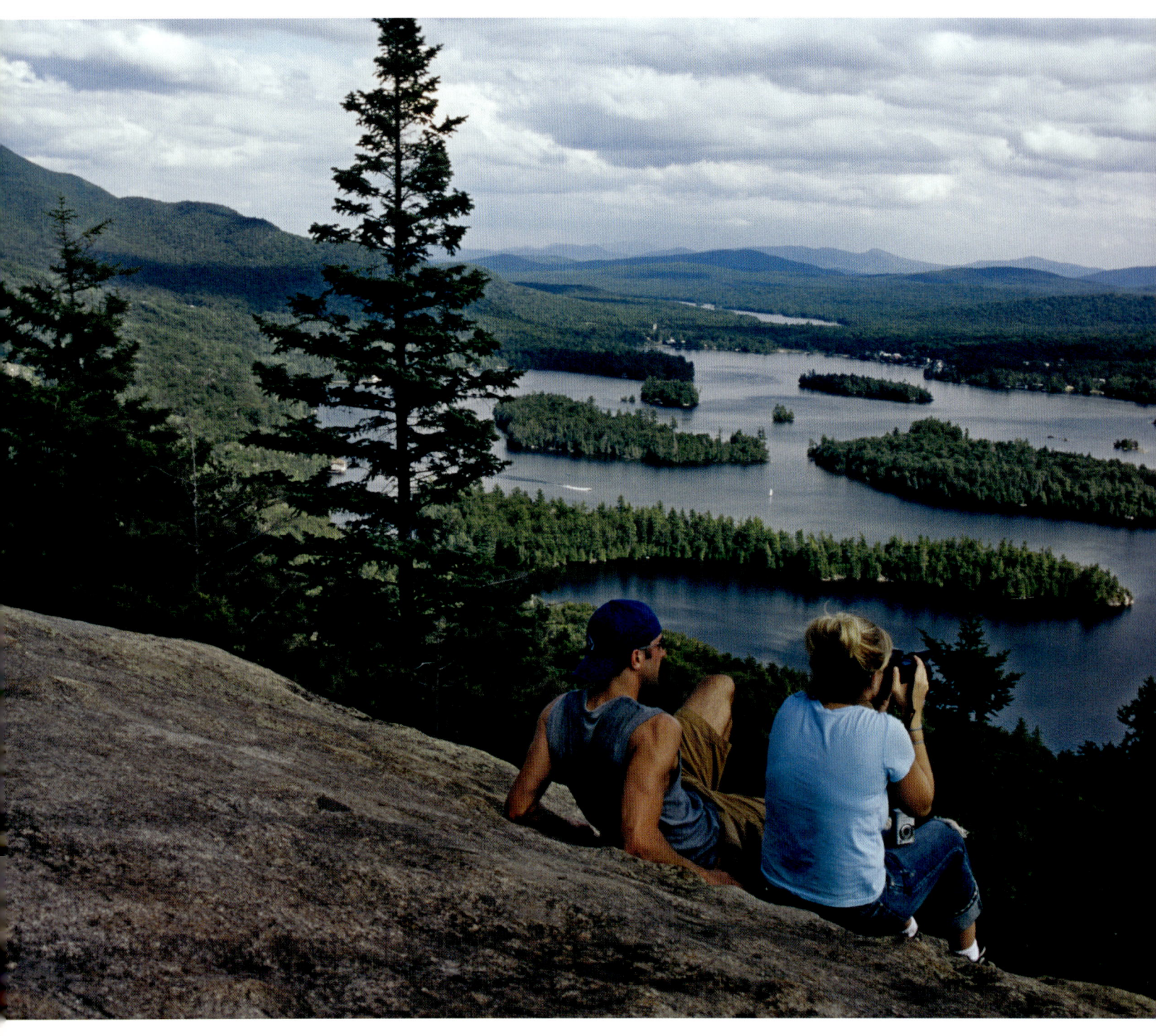

ABOVE

Hiking trails throughout Adirondack Park lead to spectacular vistas such as this spot on Cathedral Rocks, overlooking Blue Mountain Lake in the central Adirondacks.

RIGHT

Over two miles of pathways and stairs lead through the rugged gorge of Ausable Chasm. First discovered by Europeans in 1765, the gorge has been a popular tourist attraction since 1870.

BELOW

Brilliant colors paint the trees, hillsides, and vistas along the Adirondack roadways each fall.

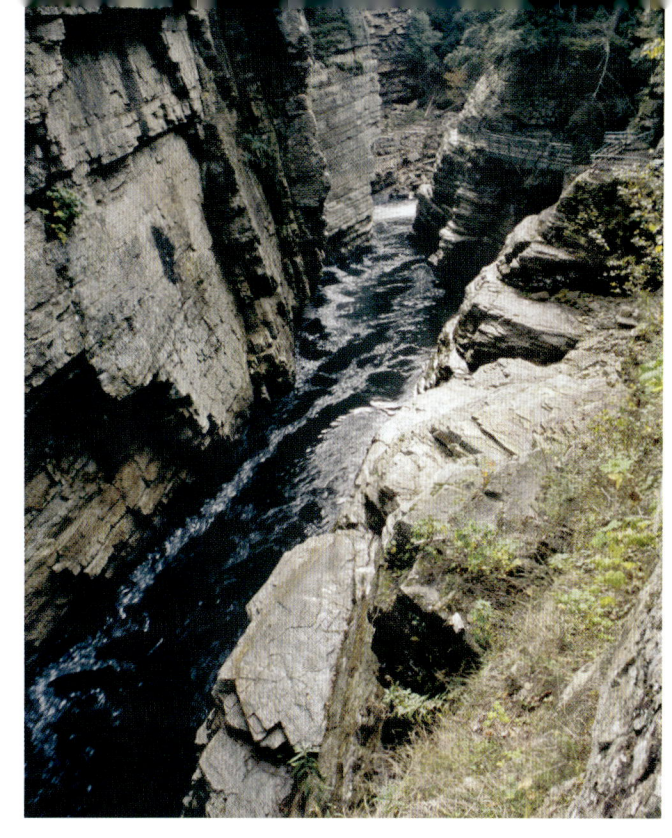

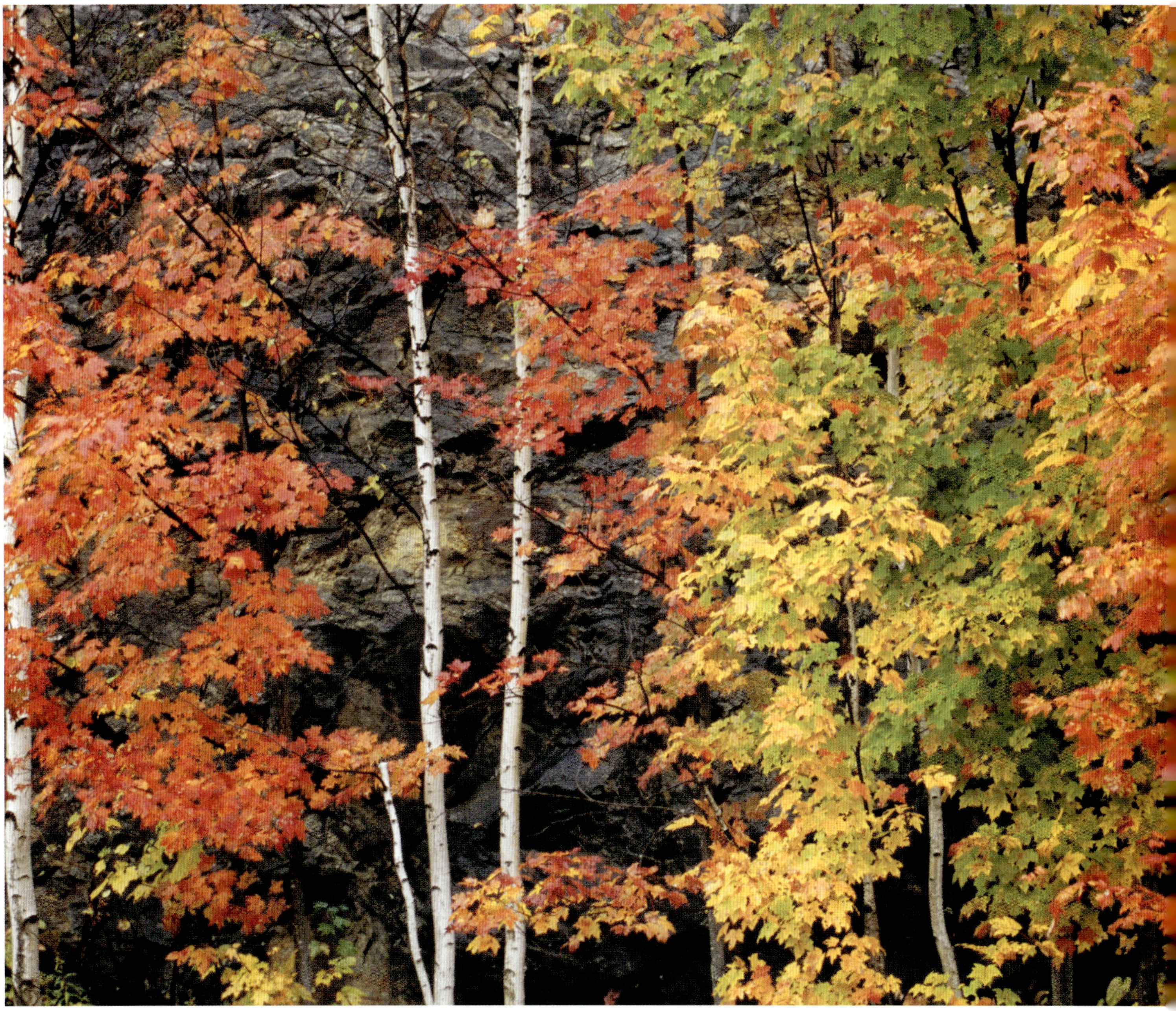

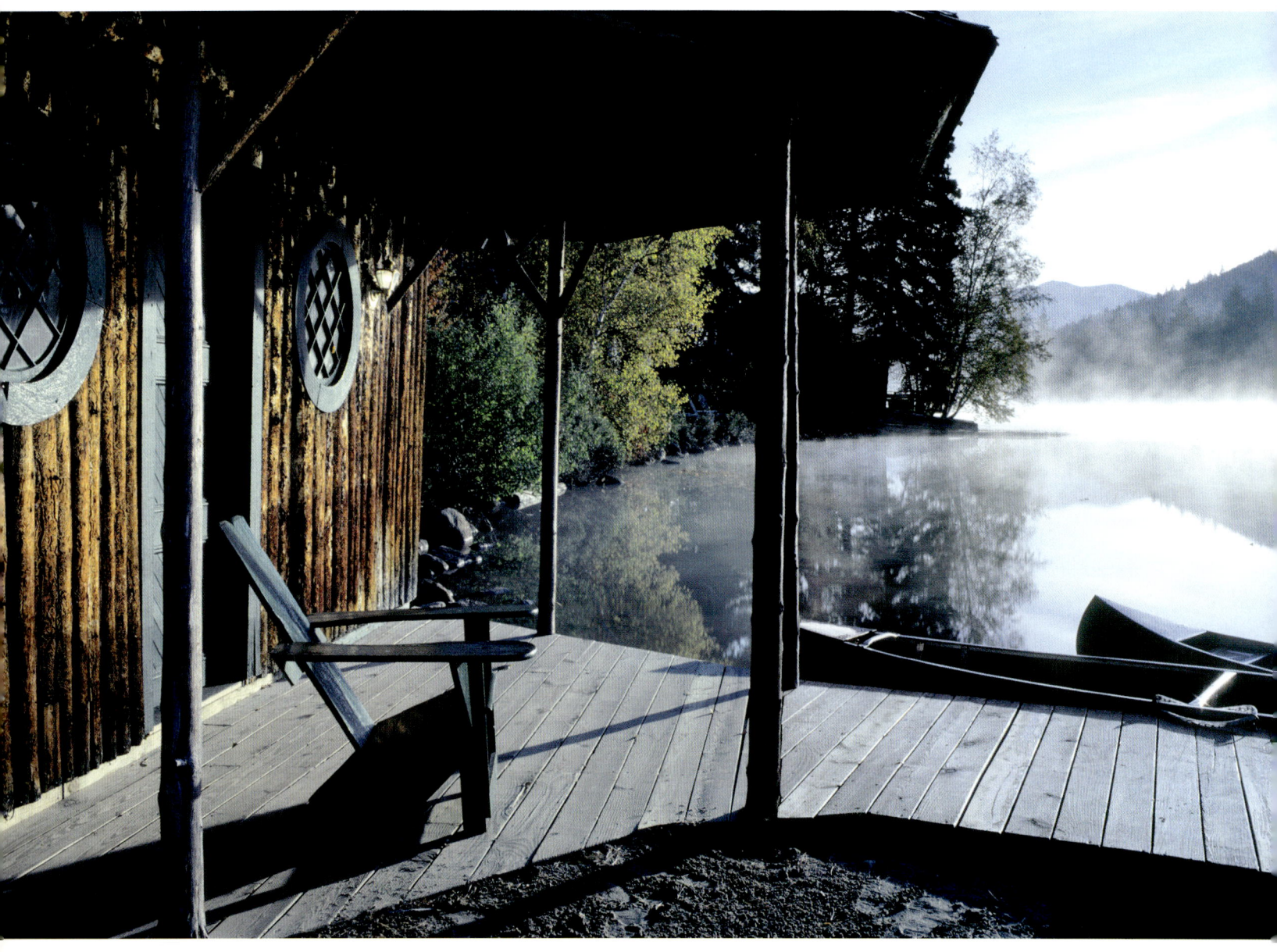

ABOVE

A classic Adirondack morning scene, at the Mirror Lake Inn boathouse—mist on the water, canoes ready for a paddle, and a traditional Adirondack chair for relaxing.

RIGHT
The beautiful Adirondack mountain landscape is an inspiration for many kinds of artists. This trio is playing traditional folk music with the High Peaks as a backdrop.

BELOW
Bill Smith, a well-known storyteller and traditional pack-basket maker in the Adirondacks, learned his craft from Mohawk Indians.

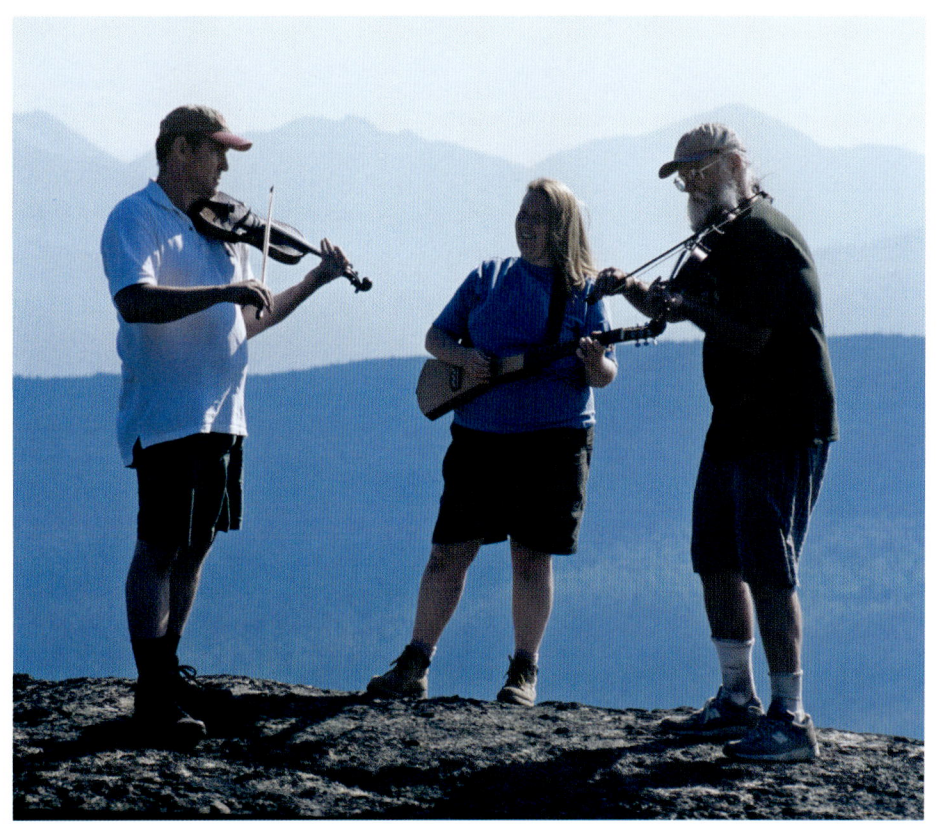

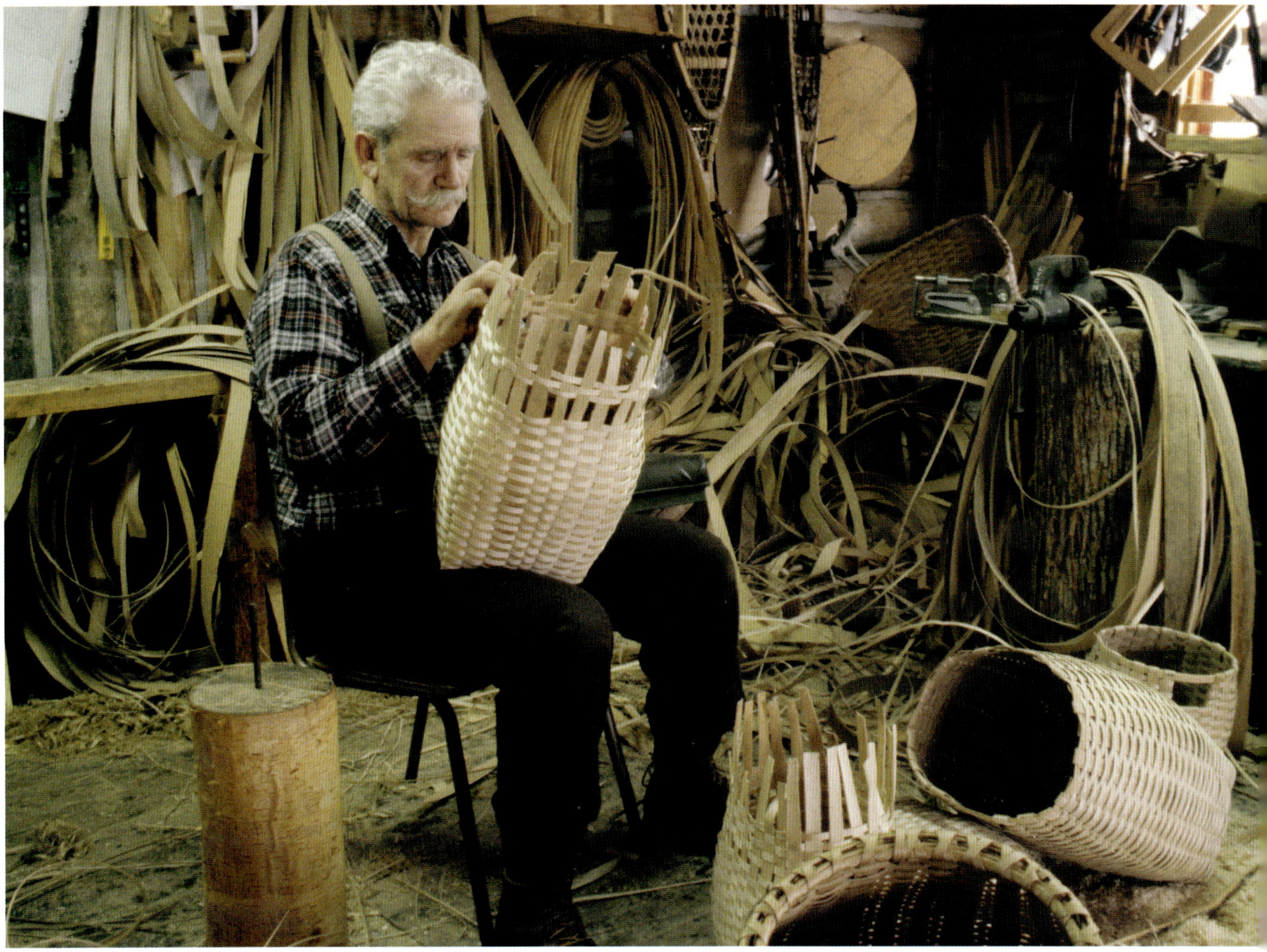

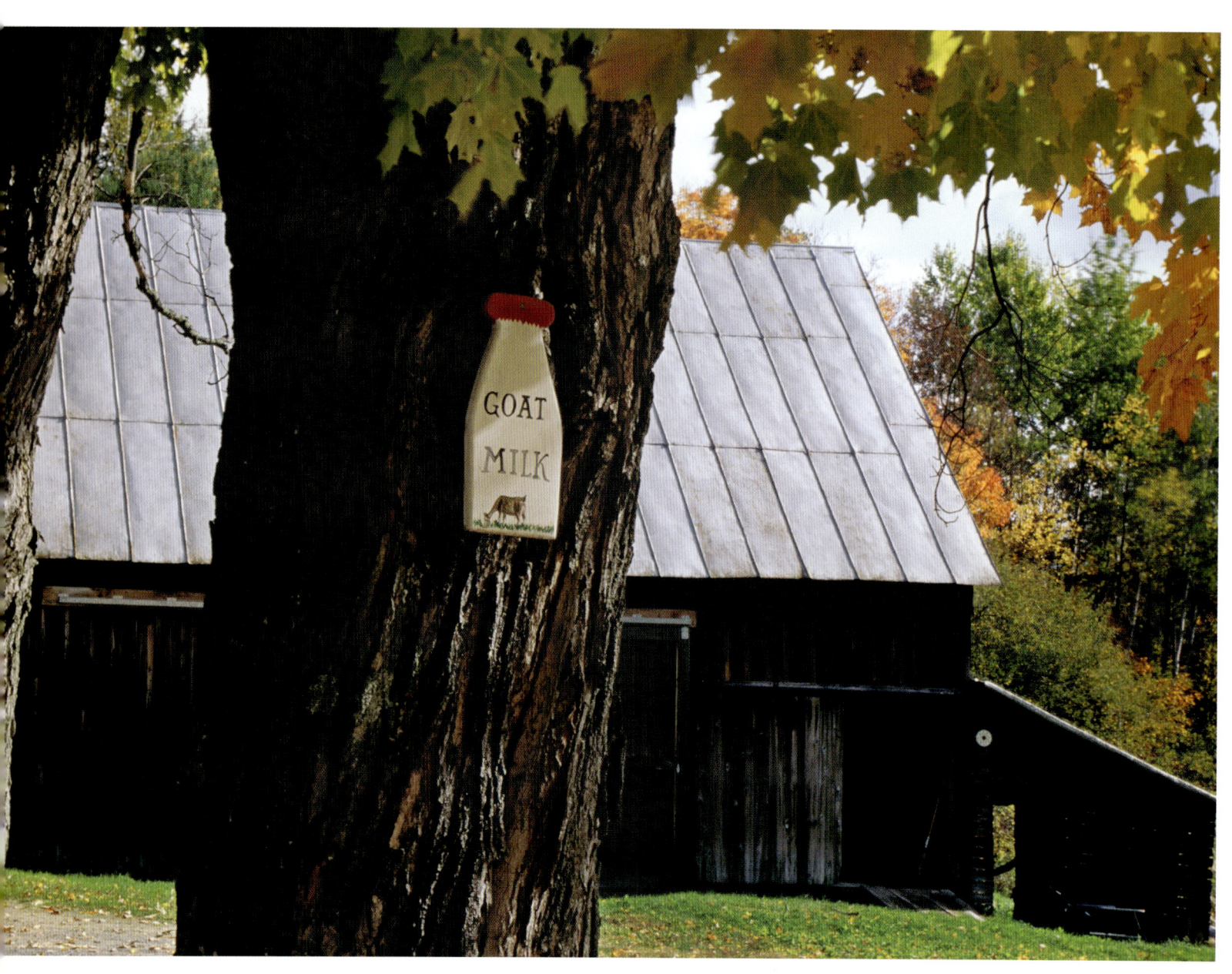

ABOVE

Due to the ruggedness of the landscape, most farms in the Adirondacks are small family operations.

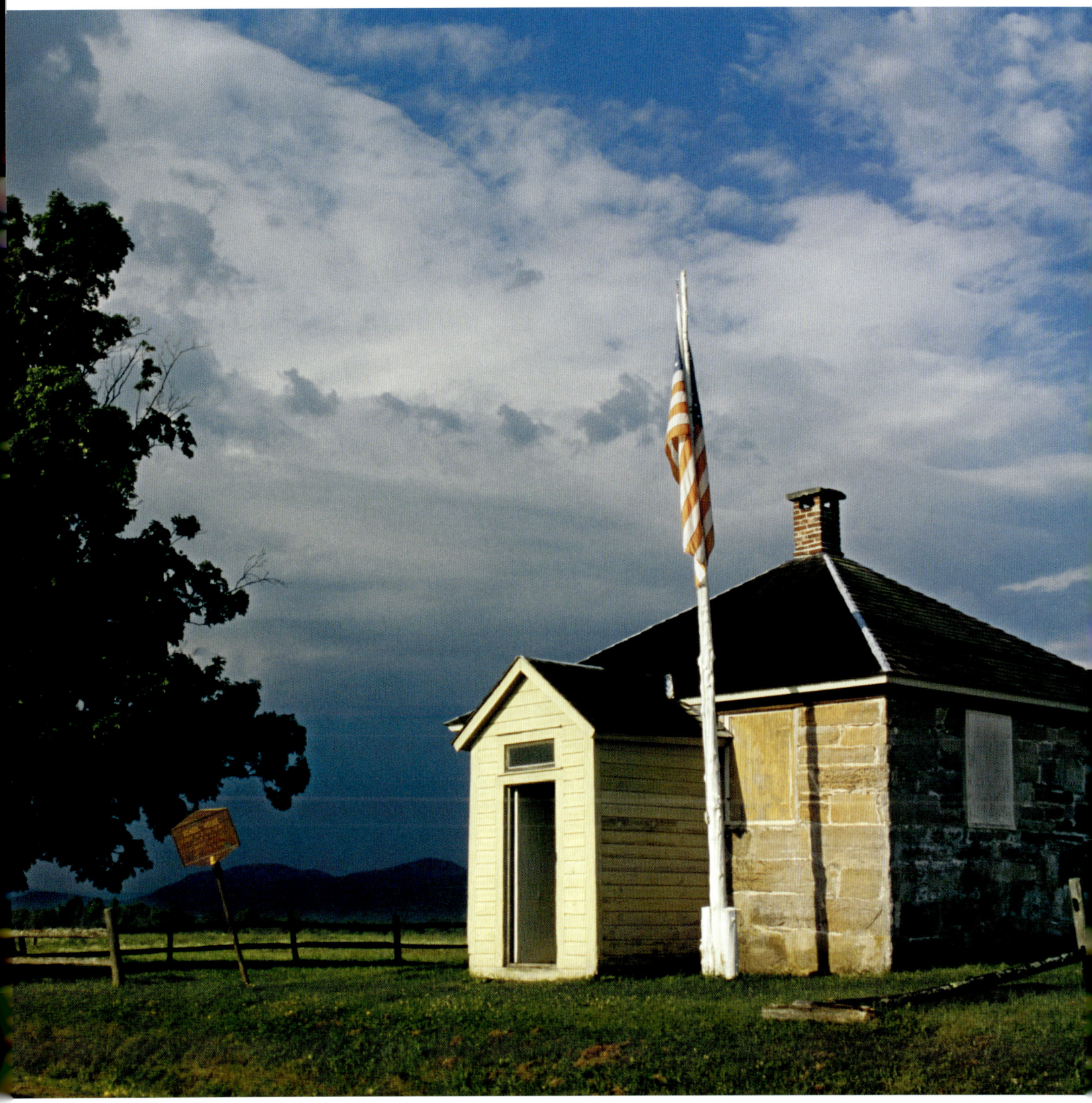

ABOVE

This stone structure, built in 1815 in the Champlain Valley, is the oldest surviving schoolhouse in Essex County. It was in use for over a hundred years.

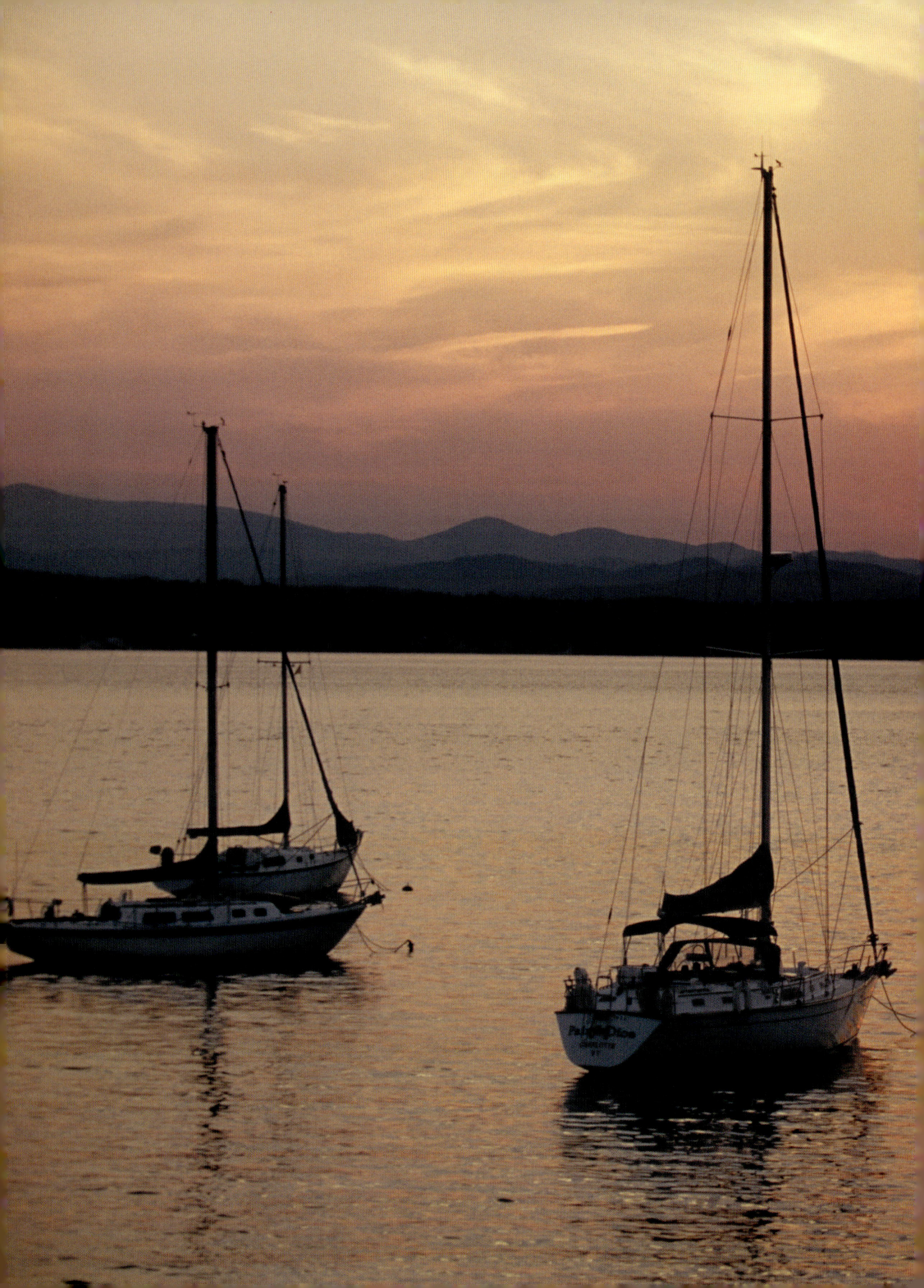

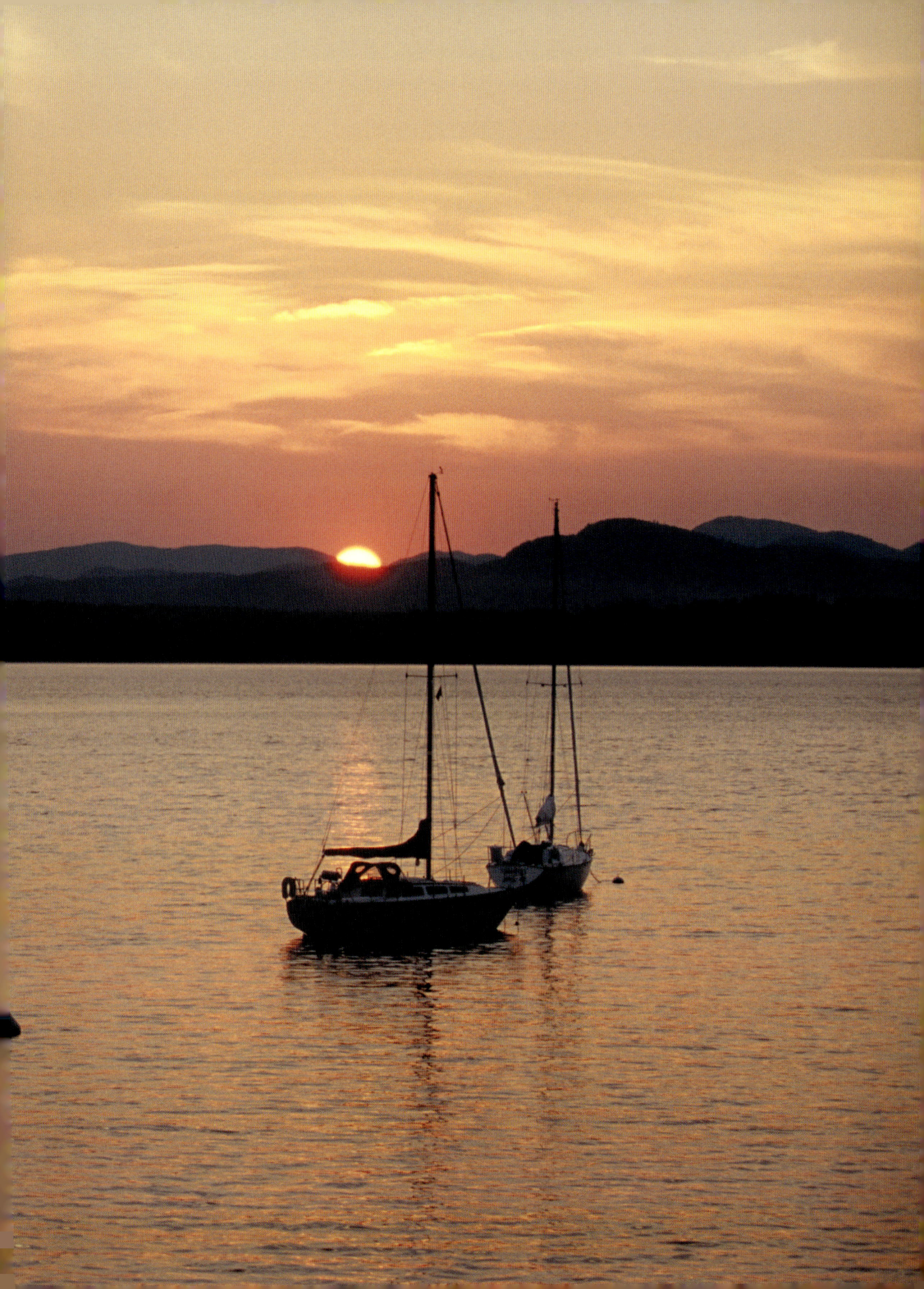

PREVIOUS PAGE

The 120-mile-long Lake Champlain forms the eastern border of the Adirondacks. The ferries that cross the lake between New York and Vermont provide another wonderful way to experience the entrancing mountain views.

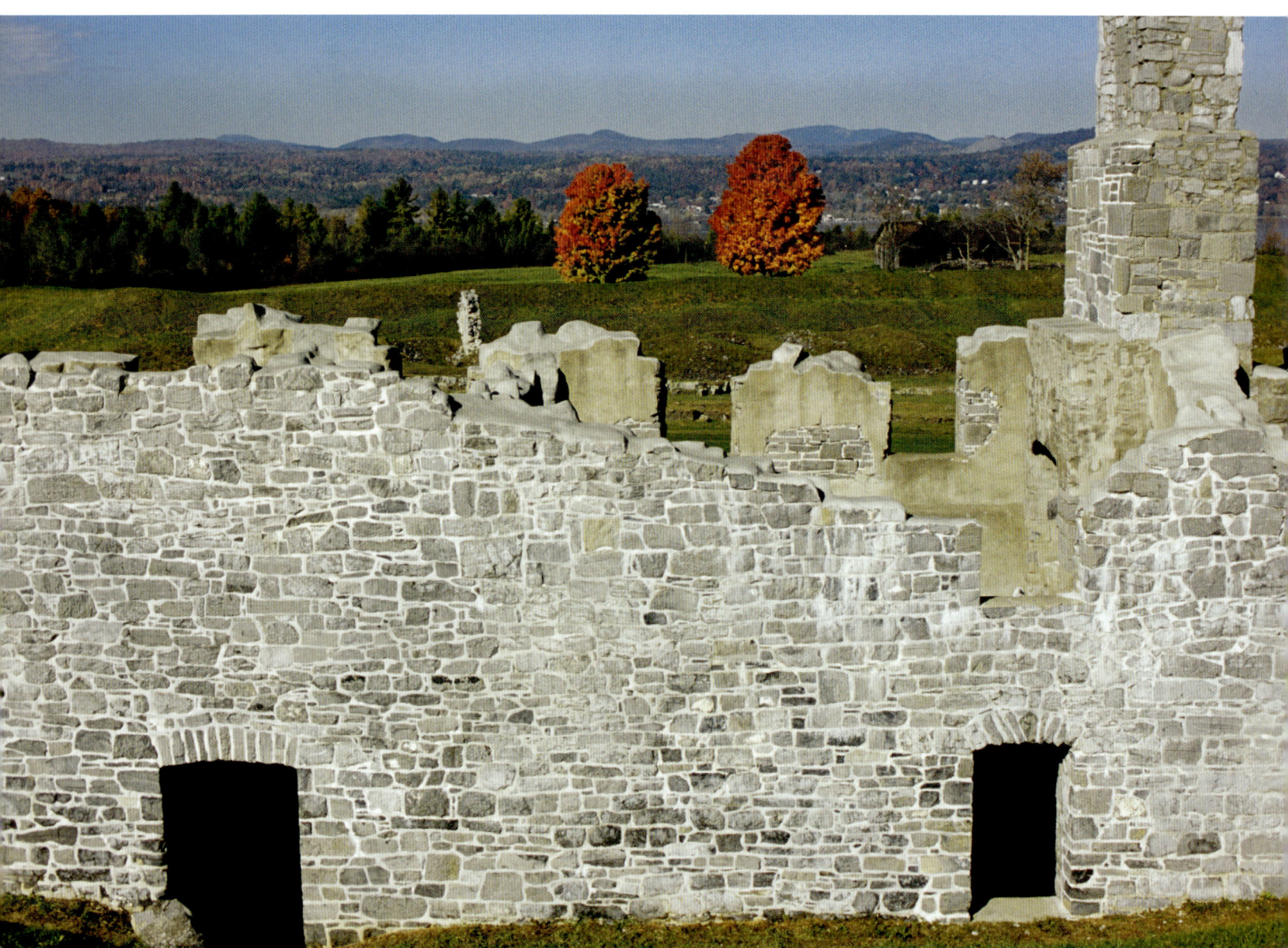

ABOVE

Standing near the shores of the lake, Crown Point was a key position for French and British forces hoping to control the Lake Champlain corridor in the eighteenth century, and the fort played important roles in the French and Indian War and the Revolutionary War. The corridor has been an important transportation and travel route for as long as people have been in the region.

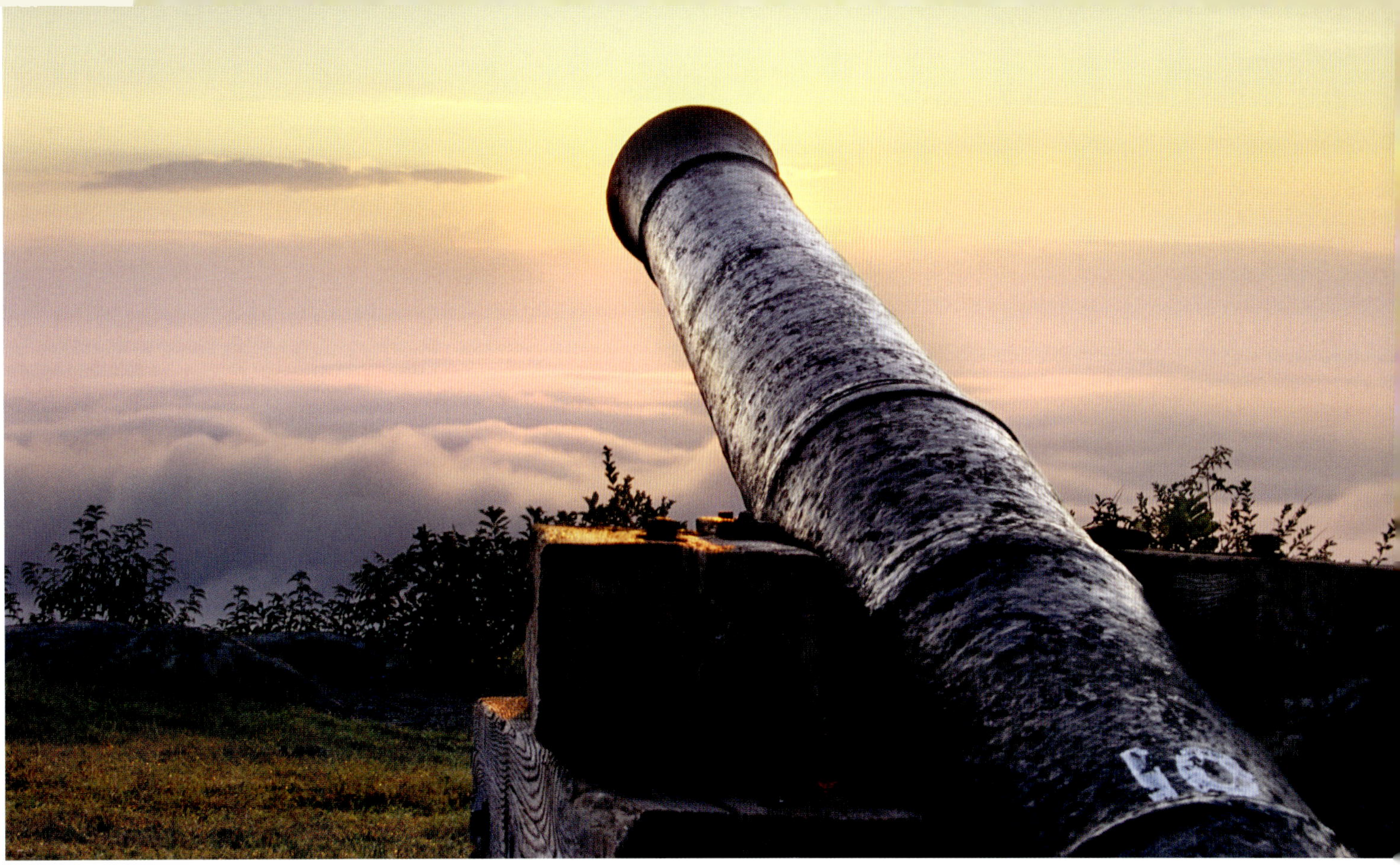

ABOVE

Fort Ticonderoga was located at a strategic point between Lake Champlain and Lake George. During the American Revolution, the British hauled cannons up to this vantage point on Mount Defiance, forcing the Continental Army to evacuate the fort.

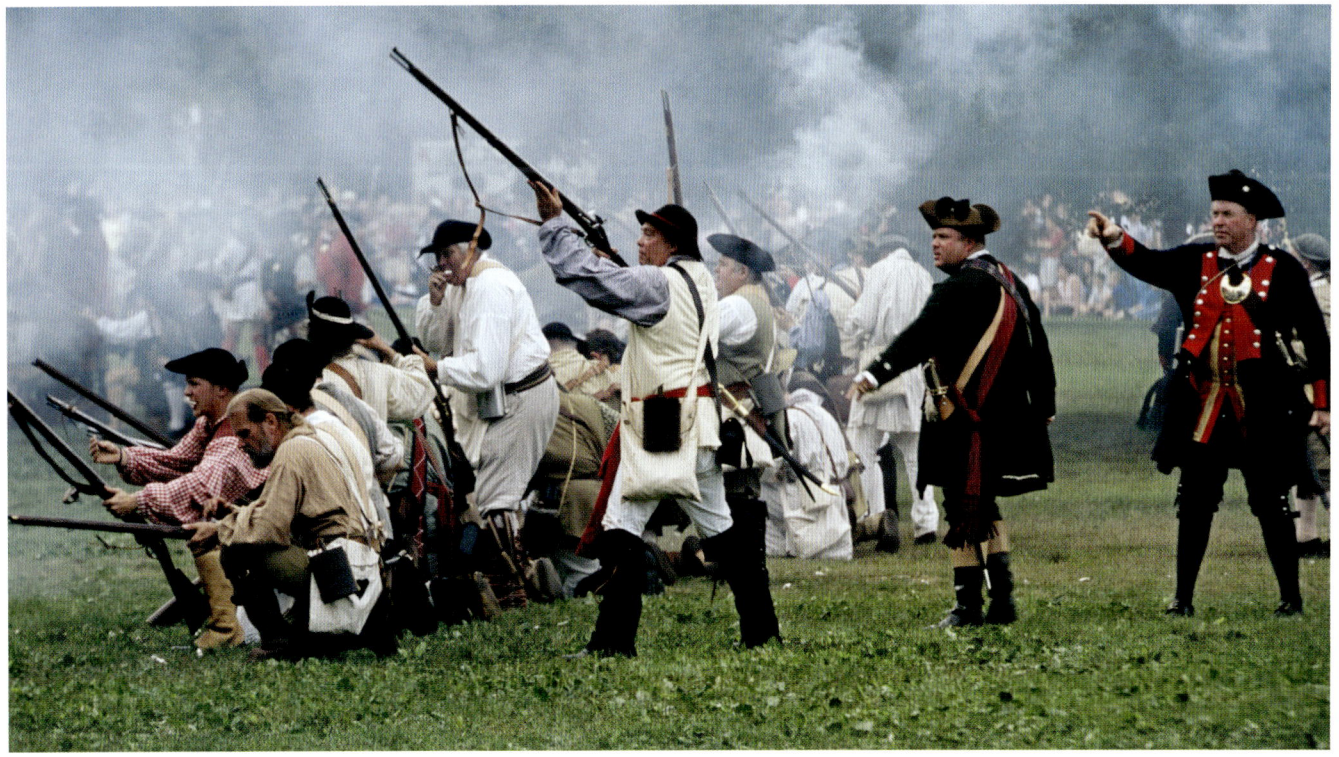

ABOVE

The Battle of Lake George was fought on September 8, 1755, near the beginning of the French and Indian War—and is being re-enacted here at Lake George Battlefield Park. The war, which lasted until 1763, helped to consolidate British control of North America.

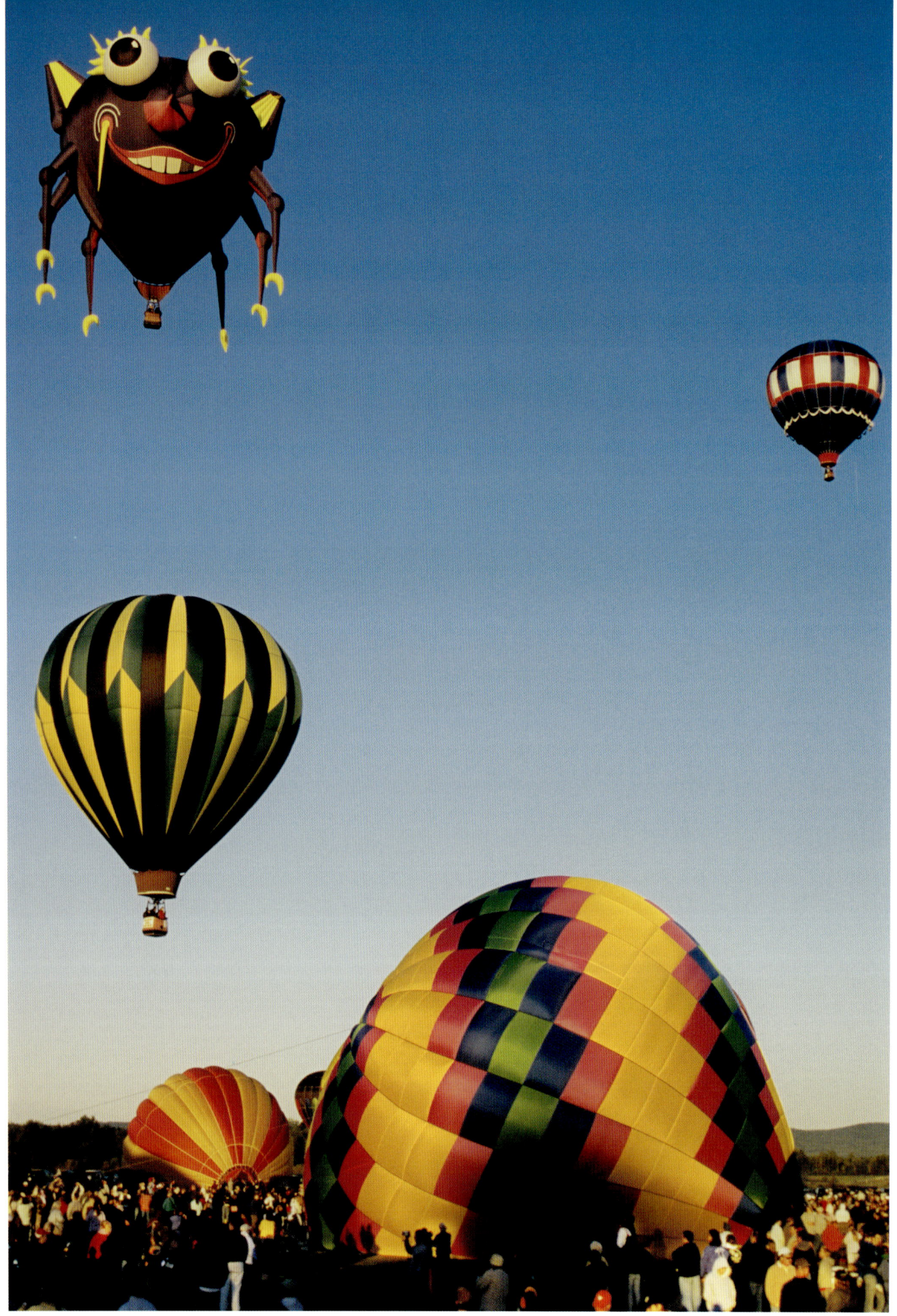

ABOVE

The Adirondack Balloon Festival has been drawing crowds since 1972. Tens of thousands fill the Glens Falls airport each September to witness the more than one hundred balloons lifting off together.

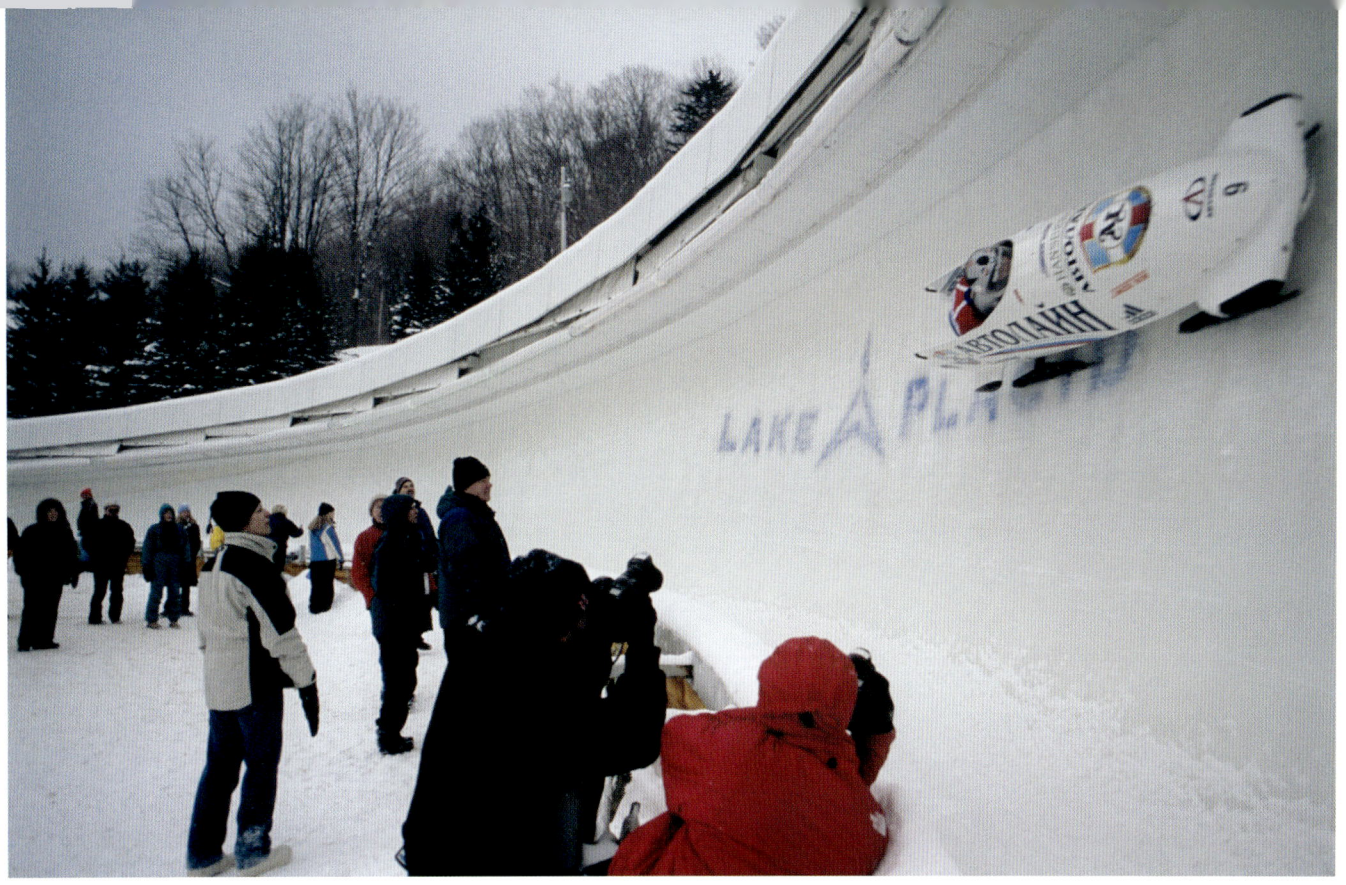

ABOVE

The Verizon Sports Complex, at Mount Van Hoevenberg near Lake Placid, hosts world-class events in biathlon, cross-country skiing, luge, skeleton, and bobsledding.

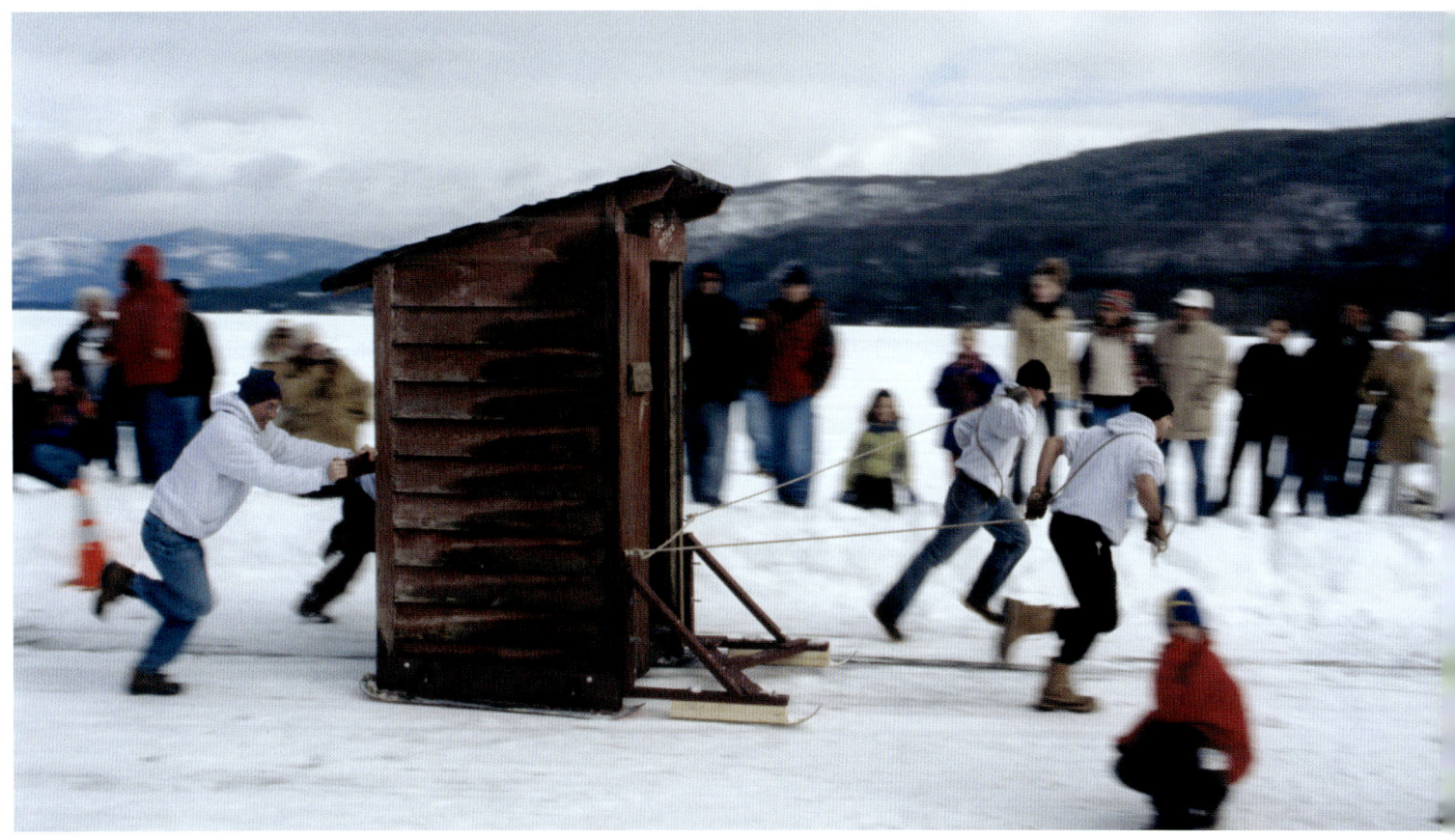

ABOVE

Winters can be long in the north country, and winter carnivals are a fun way to enjoy the season. Outhouse racing is just one typical winter carnival event, along with snowmobile water jumps and races, polar plunge swims, and ice fishing competitions.

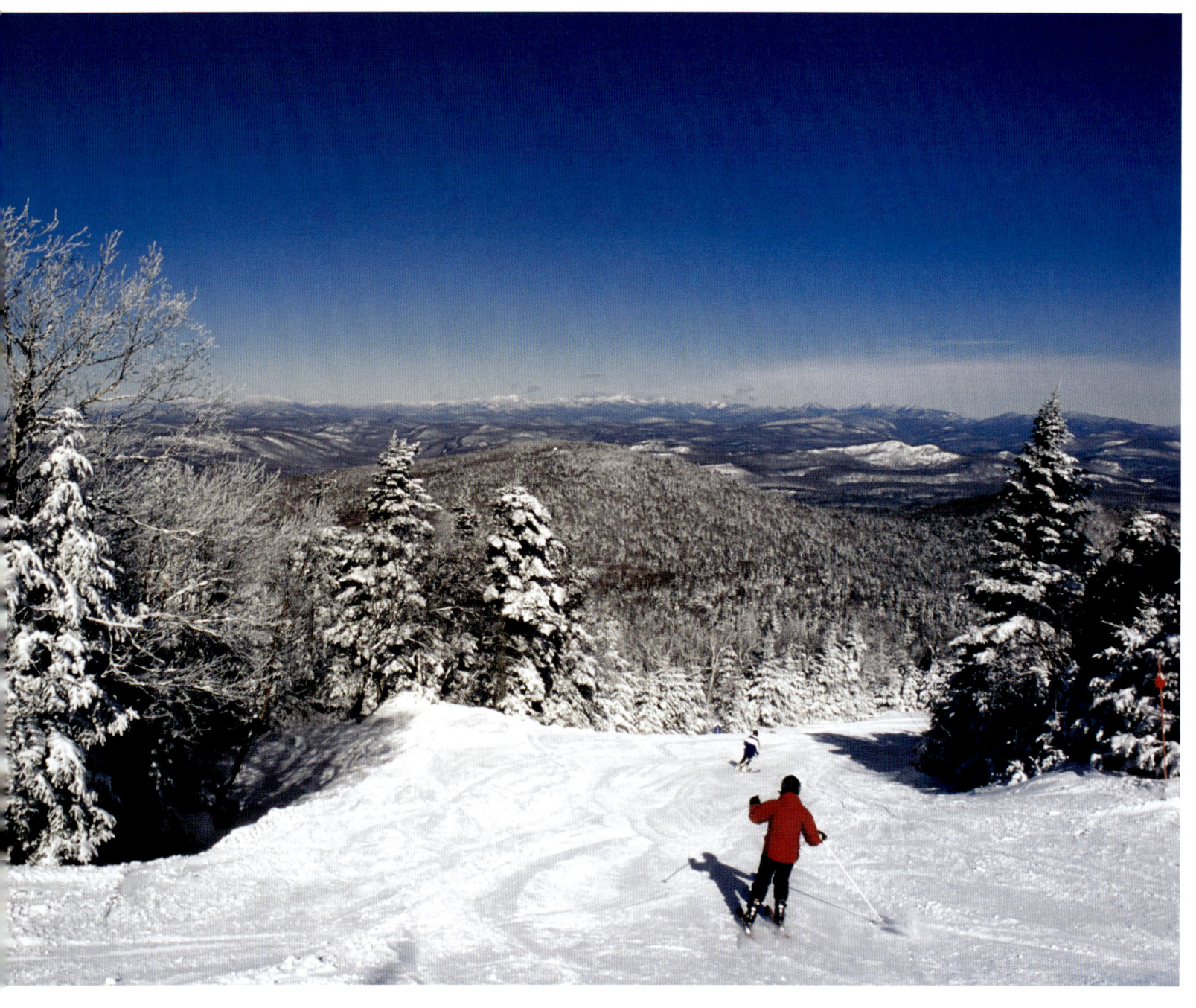

ABOVE

Gore Mountain, in the south central Adirondacks, offers premier downhill skiing with spectacular views of the surrounding area. Whiteface, in Wilmington near Lake Placid, is the Olympic mountain.

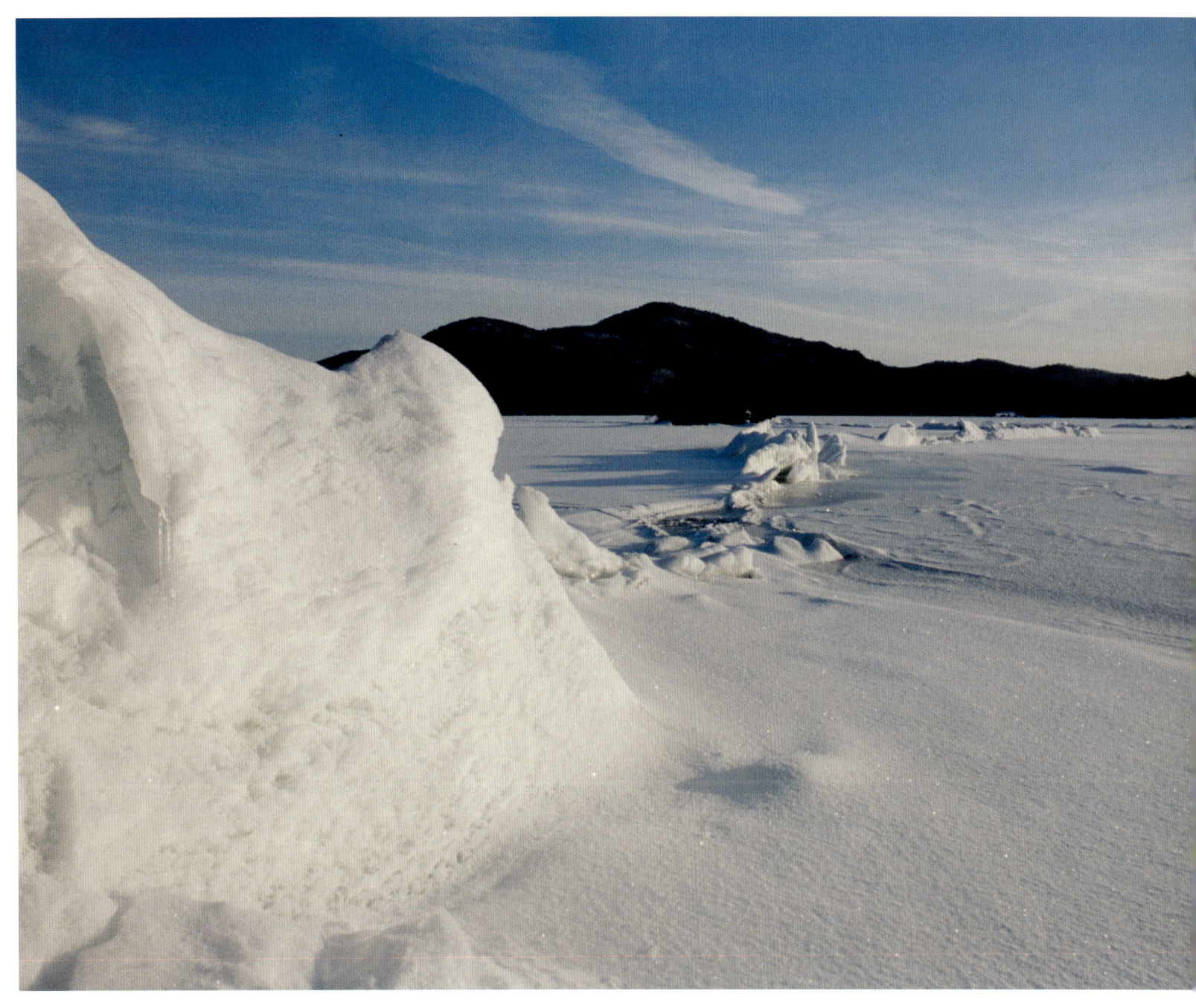

ABOVE

An ice pressure ridge winds its way across frozen Lake George.

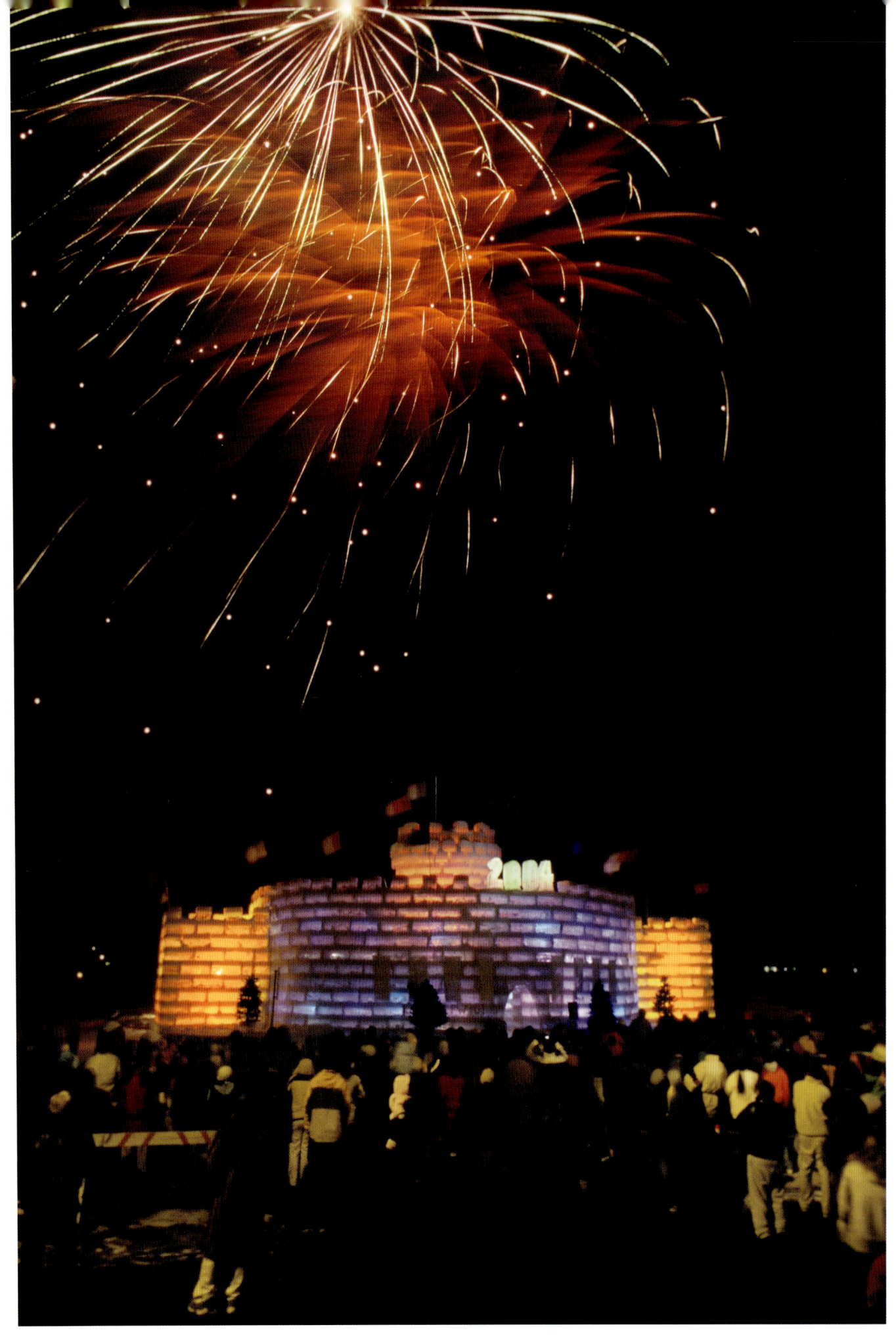

ABOVE

Fireworks fill the night sky above the ice palace at the Saranac Lake Winter Carnival.